ADVANCES IN MOTIVATION AND ACHIEVEMENT

Volume 5 • 1987

ENHANCING MOTIVATION

ADVANCES IN MOTIVATION AND ACHIEVEMENT

A Research Annual

ENHANCING MOTIVATION

Editors: MARTIN L. MAEHR
DOUGLAS A. KLEIBER
University of Illinois
Urbana-Champaign

VOLUME 5 • 1987

 JAI PRESS INC.

Greenwich, Connecticut   *London, England*

SB 39932 /48·50 11·88

CONTENTS

LIST OF CONTRIBUTORS

Carole Ames

Institute for Research on
Human Development
University of Illinois
at Urbana-Champaign

Jere Brophy

Institute for Research on Teaching
Michigan State University

John Condry

Department of Human Development
and Family Studies
Cornell University

Steven J. Danish

Psychology Department
Virginia Commonwealth University

Richard deCharms

Washington University
St. Louis

Helen S. Farmer

Department of Educational Psychology
University of Illinois
at Urbana-Champaign

Howard K. Hall

Department of Leisure Studies
University of Illinois
at Urbana-Champaign

Veronica Ichikawa

Center for Human Growth
and Development
University of Michigan

Douglas A. Kleiber

Department of Leisure Studies
University of Illinois
at Urbana-Champaign

Shin-ying Lee   Center for Human Growth
                                             and Development
                                         University of Michigan

Martin L. Maehr   Institute for Research on
                                             Human Development
                                         University of Illinois
                                             at Urbana-Champaign

Richard A. Monty   U.S. Army Laboratory Command
                                         Human Engineering Laboratory
                                         Aberdeen Proving Ground
                                         Maryland

Lawrence C. Perlmuter   Memory and Learning Clinic
                                         Veteran's Administration
                                             Outpatient Clinic
                                         Boston

Harold W. Stevenson   Center for Human Growth
                                             and Development
                                         University of Michigan

Leonard M. Wankel   Faculty of Physical Education
                                             and Recreation
                                         The University of Alberta
                                         Edmonton

PREFACE

Whenever either of us is asked to give a talk relating to the topic of motivation, there is always someone in the audience who will ask—but what can I *do* to motivate people? Sometimes the one who asks the question is a teacher and he or she is concerned with presenting difficult learning material in an attractive fashion, dealing with certain "problem children," or creating a classroom atmosphere that makes students "want to learn." Sometimes, the questioner is a manager or job supervisor and the questions focus initially on the lack of motivation of today's workers. After some discussion and clarification, the conversation revolves around job design, performance appraisal, pay and reward—or possibly organizational climate and culture. Increasingly, there are those who have a special interest in the motivation of those in care institutions—not just the staff, but the patients as well. A special concern here is the elderly and how one can keep them motivated to do and experience that which helps to provide a degree of quality in their lives. There is something related to all these concerns—and more—in Volume V.

In an important sense, Volume V follows nicely the topics covered in the previous volumes of this series. It builds on the kind of research and theory discussed in these volumes and focuses this theory and research on the kinds of questions that motivation theory and research must ultimately confront: But what can be *done* to motivate someone? Volume V presents a series of papers which not only reflect important advances in theory and research but which additionally spell out in considerable detail the implications for practice. The varied chapters portray how one can use motivation theory to affect human behavior in a variety of important ways.

Of course, this is not a motivation "cookbook." The papers contained in this volume discuss theory and report research which provide a basis for action. The papers dwell more on conceptualizations than on action per se. Thus the chapter by Richard deCharms and the one by John Condry, in particular, focus on broad conceptual issues in motivation intervention. The majority of the chapters consider primarily one specific area of intervention such as school, work, or sport. One chapter (Monty & Perlmuter) considers the special problem of motivating older persons with implications for individuals who establish policy for the care of the aged—or for care generally. Thus, the focus on application is diverse. And, so is the theory from which the applications are derived.

While the guiding theme of this volume is "motivation enhancement," it seems to us that theorist, researcher—and practitioner—will all find something of interest here. The volume is reflective of a number of important theoretical themes in the recent literature. Much of the research reported has not been reported, at least in such an extended fashion, elsewhere. The focus on *enhancement* serves the purpose of specifying the logical implications of research and the theory on which it is based. But collectively, these papers reflect a veritable armamentarium of possibilities in considering what to do about motivating people in a wide variety of situations. While the reader will not find one best way for enhancing motivation across all situations, he/she will be presented with a variety of options worth testing. It is our fond hope—and that of our authors, we surmise—that these chapters will stimulate further work leading directly to practical "know how" and perhaps to motivation enhancement programs. But even at this point we are confident that there is much on these pages that the practitioner will find useful.

Martin L. Maehr
Douglas A. Kleiber
Editors

THE BURDEN OF MOTIVATION

Richard deCharms

"Motivation" carries a heavy burden in psychology. The dictionary defines a motive as, "Some inner drive, impulse, intention, etc., that causes a person to do something or act in a certain way; incentive; goal." Psychologists say that motives activate, guide, and maintain behavior—motivation describes "how behavior gets started, is energized, is sustained, is directed, is stopped" (Jones, 1955, p. vii). Physiological psychologists look for biological bases for motives such as hormonal patterns or electrical stimulation in the brain. Ethologists look for releasing stimuli. Learning theorists speak of reinforcers and search for drive mechanisms. For some, motives are unlearned and pertain to individuals; for others motives are learned in interaction with others. Cognitive theorists speak of conscious intents, goals, and purposes; some artificial intelligence proponents (Dennett, 1978) see intentionality in machines. Social psychologists talk of agency, and see agency as unique to humans (Harre, 1979) because of the human ability to choose actions (autonomy) according to principles (reflexivity). "Motivation" is clearly an overused term but it is not clear to what it uniquely applies. The burden of meaning is too heavy for the beast.

How can we clarify the burden of motivation when even the burden of psy-

Advances in Motivation and Achievement: Enhancing Motivation,
Volume 5, pages 1-21.
Copyright © 1987 by JAI Press Inc.
All rights of reproduction in any form reserved.
ISBN: 0-89232-621-2

1

chology is in question? According to Daniel Dennett (1978), the burden of psychology is to explain intelligence. Other disciplines such as economics, political science, sociology, anthropology *assume* that human beings are rational, intelligent, self-interested agents. It is the burden of psychology to vindicate these assumptions. It is the burden of psychology to explain

> . . . *how there come to be* entities—organisms, human beings—that can be so usefully assumed to be self-interested, knowledgeable and rational. A fundamental task of psychology then is to explain intelligence. . . . The account of intelligence required of psychology must not of course be question-begging. It must not explain intelligence in terms of intelligence (pp. 72–73).

In the fallacy of begging the question, according to Hall (1982),

> "The arguer assumes the truth of a premise that readers may question. The arguer could try to prove the assumption, but does not. He merely repeats it—it is so because it is so" (p. 263).

The burden of psychology, according to Peter Ossorio (1981), is to describe persons adequately in their own terms, to systematize all that we conceive of as uniquely applicable to persons as a whole; not to reduce persons to something else. To argue that persons are like something else is to argue from analogy.

The fallacy of analogy as fact is, according to Hall (1982), a common form of illogic.

> Analogies in argument are most useful. They illustrate the sense in which we mean a statement that might otherwise be too tenuous to be understood . . . But we can fall into another common form of illogic by arguing from analogy as if it were fact . . . take the common analogy that compares the human body to a machine. The analogy can be useful when we study the principles of bodily function, but there is the danger that we will take the analogy as fact, identify the human being and the machine, and treat a person as we would a thing. The analogy is not the thing itself (pp. 265–66).

Dennett's and Ossorio's positions seem to be maximally opposed and mutually exclusive. Dennett proposes that we look at artificial intelligence in nonhuman, physical systems (computers) that he characterizes as "intentional systems." In such a way, according to Dennett, we can avoid the heresy of question-begging. Ossorio proposes that we avoid arguments by analogy, viz., persons are intentional systems, so is a computer, so in order to understand persons let us study computers. To Ossorio this is another kind of question-begging, argument by analogy. The question-begging assumption is made that computers are like persons.

Dennett's attempt to avoid question-begging is the more familiar of the two. He would say—intelligence (persons) must be explained in terms other than those in the intelligence (person) lexicon or level of discourse, preferably in a physical lexicon. Ossorio's attempt to avoid a kind of question-begging is less familiar—persons (intelligence) can only be explained in the person (intelligence) lexicon or level of discourse. If you are asked what a person is, an answer such as persons are like machines, computers, animals, . . . Xs, begs the question. Unique person characteristics are not like anything but persons. Persons are persons. The question is what is it to be a person?

If the burden of psychology is one of the above, the burden of the psychology of motivation is either (a) to explain how human beings (or organisms) come to be motivated without begging the question, i.e., explaining without reference to motivational states, or (b) to explain motivation as a unique phenomenon understandable completely only within its own lexicon. Motivation seems to beg for an analogical, mechanistic explanation because the term motive derives from motion—what moves the organism. Motion is a physical phenomenon controlled, in physical objects, by external forces. So analogies to things like external energy forces are appealing—analogies to things like needs, and drives. The energy that drives a billiard ball comes from an external source; the energy that drives a computer also comes from an external source. The energy that motivates a person comes at least partially from an internal source. This is where the analogy to physical energy seems to break down. Are we left with the question-begging—''motives are motives are motives''?

Since the term motivation is such a multiply-defined, imperspicuous, overused word, we will discuss not motivation but rather *personal causation*. Personal causation is a concept that blatantly trades on both a physical concept—causation—and a human modifier—personal. The argument will be that personal causation is primary and fundamental to explanations of human behavior; intelligence is only inferred from behavior and is, therefore, secondary. The burden of either psychology or motivation is to give us an adequate description and a pragmatic understanding of personal causation.

The argument from personal causation is not an argument by analogy. There is no implication that we can understand personal causation by analogy to physical causation. Quite the contrary; we understand physical causation, insofar as we do, because we experience personal causation. To use the concept of personal causation to help us to understand and to enhance motivation in human beings, we must go beyond analogies and simple non-question-begging explanations of personal causation. To use the concept we must see its place in the whole and adequate concept of a person.

To detail the argument above, a brief description and critique of Dennett's position will be presented followed by a brief description of Ossorio's Paradigm Case methodology. The development of personal causation in the baby through a sequence of neglect and nurturance by the mother is one kind of paradigm case. We will also look at cases described in great literature. A paradigm case from literature suggested by Harre (1984) and exemplified by Dostoyevsky's Raskolnikov (*Crime and Punishment*) and Camus' Mersault (*The Stranger*) will be compared with another using Mark Twain's *Huckleberry Finn*. Finally, the applicability of these cases to the problem of enhancing motivation will be discussed with evidence primarily from elementary schools.

DENNETT'S NON-QUESTION-BEGGING ANSWER FOR INTELLIGENCE

To make our argument clear we must outline briefly the steps in Dennett's (1978) argument in his chapter entitled "Why the Law of Effect Will Not Go Away."

1.   There is a need for a non-question-begging answer to the question—how come intelligent beings exist? The answer is the burden of psychology.

2.   Evolution and the principle of natural selection is an example (if not *the prime* example) of a non-question-begging solution to the question of the existence and origin of species of living organisms.

3.   The Law of Effect is analogous to natural selection. Evolution selects species, effects select responses for survival or extinction.

4.   A distinction is made between "hardwiring" of tropistic and/or instinctual behavior patterns (nest building, web weaving) and learned patterns. Intelligence is learned.

5.   But the simple Law of Effect is inadequate because although behavioral psychologists avoid begging the big question (number one above) they end up begging many little ones in dealing with things like latent learning, curiosity drives, intrinsic motivation (Deci, 1975), and self-reinforcement (Bandura, 1975).

6.   Behavioral psychologists have dealt only with the external environment. By postulating *two environments*, one external and one internal, the problem can be solved.

7.   Just as the outer environment is nothing but a source for input-output of physical events, so the inner environment is nothing more than "an input-output box for providing feedback for events in the brain . . . an inner something that selects." (pp. 77–78).

8.   The inner environment is not entirely genetically hardwired. "A more versatile capacity would be one in which the inner environment *itself* could evolve in the individual as a result of—for starters—operant conditioning. We not only learn; we learn better how to learn, and learn better how to learn better how to learn" (pp. 78–79).

9.   Selection by reinforcers in the outer environment occurs when there is a correlation between response classes and their consequences (eating-drive reduction). By analogy,

> Selection by inner environment is ultimately a mechanical sorting, . . . at the very least there would have to be a *normal* or *systematic* correlation between the physical event types selected and what we may call a *functional role* in some control program. Functional roles will be *discriminated*, and thereby control programs will become well designed (p. 79).

10. Putting this in the less sterilized vocabulary than that of the behaviorists—*adaptive potential behavior control elements* are things like "true beliefs, warranted expectations, clear concepts, well-ordered preferences, sound plans of action, in short all the favorite tools of the cognitive psychologists" (p. 80).

11. Cognitive psychology and the explanation of intelligence is, then, bound ultimately to versions of the Law of Effect.

By starting with the Law of Effect, Dennett has brought back into focus many of the long standing problems of the older area of the psychology of motivation and argued that the psychology of cognition is bound ultimately to it. In this sense the burden of psychology can only be born by resolving the burden of motivation.

The Flaw in Dennett's Argument

The thing that could save Dennett's argument from begging the question would be an adequate characterization of the domain of behavioral control elements that was entirely independent of reference to intelligence. When faced with this problem Dennett shifts from materialistic, behavioristic language. Having given us terms like "physical event tokens" and "discriminated functional roles," he says,

> "It is hard to keep track of these purported functions and effects while speaking in the sterilized vocabulary of the behaviorist, but there is an easier way of talking: we can say that physical event tokens of a selected type have—in virtue of their normally playing a certain role in a well-established functional organization—a *meaning* or *content*. We have many familiar examples of *adaptive potential behavior control elements*: accurate *maps* are adaptive potential behavior control elements, and so are true *beliefs*, warranted *expectations*, clear *concepts*, well-ordered *preferences*, sound *plans of action* (p. 80).

Apparently, we can name a class in behavioristic terms but to name exemplars we must resort to another lexicon, another level of discourse, one which smacks of intelligence. Is there any criterion for "true" beliefs that is independent of intelligence? If we must use terms like true beliefs rather than real materialistic referents, then are we not right back in the middle of a question-begging explanation? This brings us to Ossorio.

OSSORIO'S ADEQUATE DESCRIPTION OF PERSONS

To ask, as Dennett (1978) does, for a materialistic explanation or a physical analog of intelligence or personal causation is like asking for a materialistic explanation of the baseball term "a foul ball." It might be interesting to study the physical forces that result in a foul ball. In principle, all the possible combinations of ball position and speed and bat angle and speed could be divided into those that resulted in foul vs. fair balls. A machine could be built in the laboratory to do this just as a machine, a computer, can be built to simulate intelligence. The concept "foul ball" could thus be reduced to its physical determinants—it could be operationally defined. But in order to do any of this empirical research, one would have to know in advance what a foul ball is. To understand what a foul ball is you have to understand it in its primary context—baseball. Similarly, it might be interesting to look at how the concepts of personal causation or intelligence evolved in our language. It might be interesting to look at vestigial examples by analogy to computers or apes. But to understand such concepts as intention, agency, intelligence, personal causation, language, you have to understand their primary context, persons. This is Ossorio's most fundamental point.

Ossorio's position does not lend itself nicely to a linear step by step set of points. The position is not an argument. Ossorio would say, it is the way things are, or *What Actually Happens* (Ossorio, 1975). What follows are some of Ossorio's major points but they constitute at best an inadequate account of his attempt to present an adequate description of persons.

1.   Persons are unique entities that cannot be understood in terms of some other entities.

2.   The unique aspects of persons (and their actions) constitute the unique subject matter of psychology.

3.   There is a need for understanding persons in their own realm. What do we mean when we use the concept of a person? What difference does it make to conceive of X as a person rather than, for instance, as an acute angle, an ax, an antelope, or an aggregate? What difference does it make in our behavior to treat X as a person rather than as something else?

4.   Language describes what persons are. Contained within language is what we can say about persons. Science is communicated by language. A science cannot be more than we can say. A science of persons cannot be more than what we can say about persons.

5.   Language (description) constitutes the formal boundaries (constraints) within which a science of persons can exist.

6.   The first step in a science of persons is to attempt to get an adequate description of what persons mean when persons talk about persons.

7.   An adequate description must, first and foremost, contain the distinctive aspects, the aspects that distinguish persons from all other entities.

8.   Arguments by analogy, no matter how non-question-begging, cannot, by definition, give a distinctive account of anything.

9.   The way to get an adequate, distinctive description of persons is to start with a paradigm case of personhood.

10.   A paradigm case is an indubitable case. No one would question it as a case of personhood.

11.   A paradigm case should be a complex case, not a simple one. This is because we do not want to miss important elements of personhood. A paradigm case should be an archetypal case.

In essence, Ossorio's position is that if there is to be a science of psychology that is unique, that is distinct from all other sciences, then the science must start by describing what is distinctive in the science, not by showing how, in principle, it could be reduced to other sciences. Persons are talked about as if they were different from animals and other things. If they are really distinctive entities, then the science of psychology should carve its niche by identifying the distinctiveness, not by showing by analogy how persons are like animals or things. Psychology should be able to provide distinctive principles uniquely applicable to persons. Psychology should go for the heart of the matter not the superficial similarities with other sciences.

WHAT IS UNIQUE ABOUT PERSONS?

This is a dangerous and misleading question. In our post-Darwinian age it often leads to arguments about emergent and/or transcendental "essences." To avoid such classic metaphysical conundrums, a simple rewording of the question is necessary. What is unique about persons studying other persons? The answer to _that_ question brings us closer to what is unique in the science of psychology, if we mean by human psychology the study _by_ persons _of_ persons. The answer to the question is now simple. Human psychology is unique in that it is the only science where the scientist and his or her subject are the same—persons. So the "uniqueness" question can be rephrased to read—What characteristics do we (as persons or scientists) attribute to other persons that we do not attribute to other things like rocks or pigeons?

Some writers (like cognitive and information-processing theorists) would argue that intelligence distinguishes human beings from other animals, although they might not contend that intelligence is totally unique to humans. But how do we gauge intelligence in persons? Surely, by their actions. Intelligence cannot be judged without action nor can it have any pragmatic value without action. Intelligence is nothing without action. A person must combine intelligence with intention and skill to produce effective, intelligent actions. Actions that make a difference are the result not of _passive having_ intelligence but of _actively using_ intelligence to engage in actions that cause changes in the world.

Again, some would argue for language as the unique attribute of persons. But language is nothing until it is used. Effective use of language is what makes a difference. Unlike intelligence, however, language in use is itself a type of action. A person must use language to be an effective cause of change in the world.

The uniqueness that we attribute to persons cannot be reduced to intelligence, language, or any single inherent characteristic. Persons are unique as a whole.

Ossorio's paradigm case of personhood combines several aspects to form a gestalt of an intentionally acting person. The aspects include: (1) the identity of the person, (2) wanting, (3) knowledge, (4) skills, (5) performance, (6) achievement (Ossorio, 1981a, p. 15).

The unique difference between what we attribute to persons and to other animals, then, is the intelligent and responsible use of language and action to make a difference in the world. The burden of psychology, therefore, is not the quest for a non-question-begging answer to the thoroughly metaphysical question—"How do there come to be intelligent entities?" The burden is, rather, to give a description of the use of intelligence, language, and skills in personally caused action, a description that is adequate for the understanding of personal action and for the pragmatic goal of enhancing personal causation. Such a description should be contained in a paradigm case.

THE PRIMACY OF PERSONAL CAUSATION

If a grizzly bear enters a camper's tent and mauls the occupants, we attribute to the bear the cause of injury. The bear may be shot but it may not be judged guilty of murder by a jury of its peers. We do not attribute responsibility for morality to any subhuman animal. We do attribute such responsibility to normal human beings. We attribute *personal causation* only to persons. Personal causation entails intelligence (knowing), action (skill, performance, achievement) and moral responsibility. *Personal causation means deliberate action to produce intended change.* Knowledge is acquired so that it can guide action; skills are learned in order to make actions successful; intelligent, skilled action leads to successful achievement. Successful achievement is the result of deliberate responsible action. Personal causation is *not* a single inherent characteristic. It *is* attributed to others and experienced in self as a whole. It is the intelligent use of skilled performance to produce a difference in the world. It is unique to persons (personal) and involves a transitive (Bhaskar, 1979) relationship between the person and the world (causation).

PARADIGM CASE METHOD AND THE BURDEN OF MOTIVATION

Paradigm cases may be used to demonstrate how the parameters of the case (wants, knowledge, etc.) form a unique set of interrelations that clarify persons and their actions. The burden of the psychology of human motivation and action, then, is the demonstration of how we use these concepts that are part of personal causation in understanding persons. The logical job of showing how such concepts fit into a paradigm case of persons is one thing; the demonstration of what difference it makes that we do, in fact, use such concepts is another. The first constitutes the formal aspect of personhood; the second is the content. What difference it makes is the justification of the enterprise. The first embodies an analysis of language as a rule-following structure. The second is the empirical aspect of the burden of motivation. In order to confront the question of the relevance of all this for the enhancement of motivation, let us compare three paradigm cases: first, the very general one of mother-child interaction; second, one suggested by Harre's (1979, 1984) writings on agency; third, one that embodies the concept of personal causation.

The Sequence of Neglect and Nurturance

In order for a paradigm case to be archetypal it must be general and fundamental, encompassing the major formal aspects of the phenomenon. Specific cases, such as Mersault, Raskolnikov, and Huck Finn must exemplify the formal aspects of personhood but may also give some content. We will start with a general, fundamental case—mother and child interaction.

The formal aspect of human action must encompass all actions and reactions. Human beings are social beings; most, if not all, of their actions are accomplished in the context of, and in relation to, other human beings. Actions communicate between human beings. Therefore, two fundamental properties of the form of human action are: (a) interaction and (b) communication. Action in the stream of life is always, in fact, *inter*-action and always attempts to communicate something.

The form of human action should be observable in any human interaction if it is to be general and fundamental. But it might be well to look for it first in a simple case, one that involves only two persons where one of the persons is less complex. The paradigm case could be the interaction between a baby and the mothering or parenting one.[1]

An interdependent relationship that is generalizable over all babies (sexes, cultures, etc.) and over all cases of parenting techniques or customs delineates the formal aspects and gives the clue to the form of human interaction. Relationships that differ from child to child, mother to mother, culture to culture, constitute the content, are problematic, and are the subject of empirical investigations.

At the outset the newborn baby is helpless and completely dependent on the ministrations of the mother. The life of the child depends on the mother satisfying the child's organic needs until the child can learn to "do it himself." The rudimentary form of human action is a sequence of neglect and nurturance. When the child has a biological need, all he can do at first is cry (communicate), although at first crying probably is not intentional. Through the early days of life the child learns to distinguish the mother and to communicate intentionally. The sequence is—need-communication (on the part of the child) and intentional nurturance (on the part of the mother). During the period between need-communication and nurturance, the child suffers neglect. As the child grows older the mother uses the sequence of neglect-nurturance to teach the child to do some things for himself. Details of the process in individual cases result in the variable content of what an individual may learn, but the formal aspects are of more concern to us right now. Formally, the child must learn to cope with neglect. The first glimmering of value arises for the child right at this point. Neglect is bad and nurturance is good. When the mother nurtures, she is good; when she neglects, she is bad.

The child experiences neglect as frustration and may react passively, aggressively, or constructively. Repeated reactions to the sequence of neglect and nurturance may teach the child: (a) the passivity of learned helplessness (Seligman, 1975), (b) the aggressive negativity of stubborn reactance when first the mother tries to use the sequence to "shape" behavior, and/or (c) the constructive cooperative aspect of learning new behaviors to change the situation.

The three possible reactions to neglect result in three *a priori* or archetypal motivational schemata that are the formal aspects of human action in which individual actions (content) are contained. The first two of the three motivational schemata are negative and similar to Maslow's deficiency motivation. They pit the child against the wicked mother. The third schemata is positive, like Maslow's (1968) growth motivation, and puts the child into a learning-to-do-for-himself, cooperative relationship with the mother. The positive *a priori* motivational schema is *personal causation*. When the child learns to do for himself, he learns how to initiate his own activities, he originates his own actions, he acts as an Origin. When the child *re*-acts negatively, either passively or aggressively, he reacts as a Pawn.

In developing the Origin-Pawn concept out of personal causation, deCharms (1968) first defined it in terms of perceived locus of causality following Heider (1958). It appears now that this was superficial, for the child who reacts negatively but with aggression may perceive an internal locus of causality but is still reacting as a Pawn. Several years of research (see deCharms, 1984) have demonstrated the importance of reality perception and personal responsibility in the definition of Origin actions. The person (child) can only really originate successful actions when he realistically assesses the reactions of others (mother) and assumes responsibility for the effects of his actions on others.

It is important to note that the form of this interaction obtains in the earliest mother-child interactions and that the child experiences all three reactions to the sequence of neglect and nurturance and develops all three motivational schemata. Which schema predominates and whether one predominates under certain conditions takes us beyond the formal aspects and into the problematic content that is matter for empirical investigation. Based on the reasoning above, it is clear why we have found empirically that people are not always Origins or always Pawns (deCharms, 1984). The most that can be said is that some persons react more often as Origins than others.

The three motivational schemata thus derived are termed *a priori* because: (a) they determine the form of less fundamental motives, (b) they meet the criteria of generality over the human species, (c) they are exhaustive of the possible outcomes to the paradigm case, (d) they are unique to humans. If they constitute the form of human action, they have two advantages. First, the form (complete with the sequence of neglect and nurturance and the *a priori* motivational schemata) should apply to *any* human interaction. Second, since the content not the form is problematic and based on learning, the content can change within an individual or group. Yet the formal aspects set limits on techniques for changing motives, techniques for enhancing motivation.

Agency

"Being" Primary

In his analysis of agency, Harre (1979, 1984) first distinguishes between an agent and a patient. A patient is a being that must receive an external stimulus to get it moving. The schema for patient is:

$$Being \ plus \ Stimulus \ = \ Action$$

This is recognizable as the typical stimulus-response formulation. The agent, supposed to be the complement of the patient, is a being who by being released from restraint is, as a consequence, capable of action and hence agency. The schema for agent is:

$$Being \ minus \ Restraint \ = \ Action$$

Harre goes on to analyze agency primarily as this release from restraint, and his concern is with how acts of agency can show endeavor, striving, self-restraint, or self-control and self-command (will).

In trying to show that agency is somehow over and above the call of duty, so to speak, Harre takes a cue from Sartre. In order to show the characteristics of agency, actions must be out of the ordinary; they must either (1) demonstrate will power by choosing the right action over the desired action (a moral decision), or (2) demonstrate autonomy by stepping out of a conforming mold or principle of practicality to produce action that is expressive of a higher principle of political or moral rectitude. Harre's example of the latter is Camus' hero in *The Stranger* (1942) who shows autonomous agency with the thoroughly non-practical action of shooting the Arab.

> . . . If we see [Mersault] as engaged in a proof of autonomy, then what seemed unprincipled on the practical plane, since Mersault had no instrumental reason for shooting the Arab, nor was he driven by uncontrollable feelings, becomes principled action on the expressive plane.

It is just the kind of action one would choose in the reflexively-rational mode of action-genesis
to demonstrate autonomy (Harre, 1979, p. 257).

For Harre agency is somehow over and above desired or practical action. One
gets the flavor of breaking out of the conforming mold to do something extraordi-
nary. The conditions for this to happen are the release from restraint. For exam-
ple, one could have hypothesized about 1980 when the Chinese government re-
duced restraint on its people with regard to many things, that a reduction in
restraint in styles of art and music could lead to an outpouring of creativity from
the people. This would be nicely explained by Harre's schema—Being minus
restraint = Action. But the fact is that agency, in this system, takes on an aspect
of the extraordinary. Human beings are not normally, or essentially, agents by
this analysis. Their normal state is one of restraint in which apparently only ex-
ternal stimuli can goad them into action.

If the normal state of persons is restraint, this raises several questions. What
are the restraints? Where did they come from? Does not a schema for agency
presuppose the conditions that restrained the person? As a further illustration one
might consider the imagery in Paul Scott's novels *The Raj Quartet* (1966). The
novels are all about the complicated problems of the British and Indians just be-
fore India was granted her independence (1947). Scott develops a powerful sym-
bol of how all the major characters were caught up in a net of restraints that
forced them into principled actions that take on the character of butterflies
struggling unsuccessfully to escape from a net. The symbol is, in fact, a lace
shawl showing butterflies. Its appearance is accompanied several times with the
comment that the butterflies are trapped in the net. The net, especially in the case
of the British, is their culture, imposed by themselves on themselves to live up to
their principles. The butterfly metaphor seems to capture Harre's agency
schema. Just as Scott's novels graphically describe the butterflies in the net, so
Harre's schema describes a situation where persons are forced to act
autonomously to react against restraints. This would be an example of our sec-
ond schemata listed above.

But in the natural state butterflies are free. How did they get into the net? Do
persons start out in a net and work and mature toward autonomy, toward what
might be called self-actualization (Maslow, 1968)? Is it not possible that per-
sons, like butterflies, are originally free and get caught in the web of culture?

Perhaps agency is not an extraordinary state of persons, but a natural state.
Agency implies more than being, it entails action. Yet restraints to action are
inherent in the interaction and interdependencies of persons with their physical,
interpersonal, and cultural environment. Perhaps, rather than starting with a
"being" as patient (Pawn) struggling to be agent (Origin), or with a "being" as
agent becoming enmeshed in the net, we should start, in a schema like Harre's,
with action rather than with "being."

"Action" Primary

Harre's formula for agency starts with Being as primary. Macmurray (1957) would insist that Being is secondary to Action and would stress that persons in action are persons in relation to other persons as well as the physical environment. The person is not only reactive to environmental stimuli, but must be active in relation to other actors who impose their resistance to actions of the person. Resistance is constitutive of action. Without it, action is impossible. Here is a piece in Macmurray's own words.

> Notice first that I might, for instance, have chosen as example a man's effort to stand still and upright in the teeth of a gale. In that case the resistance would be his resistance to an active force compelling him to move against his will. He is then aware of himself as that which resists the Other. The fact that we can exemplify the experience of resistance either way shows us that in practical experience Self and Other are correlatives discriminated together by their opposition; and this opposition constitutes the unity of experience.
>
> We must notice, in the second place, another aspect of the experience of resistance. The resistance of the Other is not merely a negation of the act of the Self, it is necessary to the possibility of the act, and so constitutive of it. For without a resistance no action is possible. To act at all is to act *upon something*. Consequently, the Other is discovered in tactual perception both as the resistance to, and the support of action. If I lean with all my weight against a door that has jammed, and it suddenly flies open, I find that the resistance which I was trying to overcome was the support of my effort to overcome it. Without it I lose control of my action and fall headlong (1957, pp. 109–10).

What, then, does our new form of Harre's formula give? Harre gave us Being plus or minus Restraint. With this analysis Harre's case looks like this:

$$Action\ minus\ Resistance\ =\ Loss\ of\ control$$

Hardly a case of agency.

Macmurray would start the formula with Action (short for person in action) and substitute Resistance (short for resistance from others) for restraint. Only action (which entails resistance) can produce the experience of "being an agent," the experience of personal causation.

With Action plus Resistance we can have three possible outcomes.

$$Action\ plus\ Resistance\ =\ (a)\ Inaction$$
$$=\ (b)\ Reaction\ against\ resistance$$
$$=\ (c)\ Goal\text{-}Directed\ Action$$

In case "a" the acting person ceases to act in the face of resistance, probably withdrawing from the situation entirely. This is a purely negative reaction and not very productive. Case "a" is reminiscent of the phenomenon of "learned helplessness" (Seligman, 1975).

Case "b" is more active but is still a negative response to resistance because it is a *re*-action to resistance. The resisting agent is calling the shots so to speak. The Other is in control and the person is responding like a puppet. Case "b" is reminiscent of Brehm's (1966) concept of "psychological reactance." In a sense the person is still a pawn to the demands of the resistance and sees the resistance as a threat to his or her intentions.

Only in case "c" is there a positive response to the resistance. For the person who sees the resistance as the path through which he or she can pursue his or her own goals, the resistance is a challenge rather than a threat. The resistance is the condition within which he or she can demonstrate personal causation. Case "c" is the only really positive agency response. (Note that these cases are the same as the motivational schemata that we saw above exemplified in mother-child inter-action.)

It is hard to tell exactly where Harre's cases of agency fit in this scheme. Camus' Mersault engages in an apparently non-goal-directed act—killing the Arab—an attempt, on Harre's interpretation, to show that he is autonomous. As such, it appears to be case "b," Psychological Reactance. Or take Dostoyevsky's Raskolnikov. He killed the "old pawnbroker woman" to prove, against the resistance of evidence, that he was not ordinary but was extraordinary—above the dictates of mundane law. On the other hand if Mersault and Raskolnikov are seen, as Harre implies elsewhere (Harre, 1979), as pursuing a higher principle, then we could make a case for a principled goal and apply case "c."

Be this as it may, our tripartite concept of a person's action (or inaction) in response to resistance apparently has both *general* application and strikes at *fundamental* aspects of persons in action. A type of paradigm case where it seems to apply is in the interaction between mother and child, as we saw above.

Huck Finn—A Case of Personal Causation

To move from some of the most revered (and depressing) literature of Europe to a classic yet light-hearted example from the United States may seem like stepping from an opera to a rock concert, yet it cannot be denied that in a sense personal causation is a uniquely, almost naively, optimistic American idea. Huckleberry Finn escaped from the imprisonment of his father's house and set off in freedom down the Mississippi River. The "resistance" of his father was a challenge, a problem to be solved, not a threat to be feared and railed against. Chapters 5 and 7 describe how Huck decided to escape from the house without being followed by making it appear that he had been murdered. Huck's father was not portrayed as a threat. There is no negative reaction against his father.

> I used to be scared of him all the time, he tanned me so much. I reckon I was scared now, too;
> . . . but right away after I see I warn't scared of him worth bothering about (Twain, 1959, p.
> 27).

To escape was the challenge, the goal toward which he planned and executed his actions.

> He got to going away so much, too, and locking me in. Once he locked me in and was gone
> for three days . . . I made up my mind I would fix up some way to leave there. I had tried to
> get out of the cabin many a time, but I couldn't find no way.

Huck secretly sawed a hole in the floor and dug a passage out.

> I got to thinking that if I could fix up some way to keep pap and the widow from trying to
> follow me, it would be a certainer thing than trusting to luck . . . I says to myself, I can fix it
> now so nobody won't think of following me (pp. 38–39).

The description that follows is not his dreams, or even his plans but *action*.

> I took the sack of corn . . . I took all the coffee and sugar there was, and all the ammunition
> . . . [etc.] I took the ax and smashed in the door.

Having killed a wild pig:

> I fetched the pig in . . . hacked into his throat with the ax, and laid him down on the ground to
> bleed. "Well, last I pulled out some of my hair, and blooded the ax good . . .

He took the sack of meal and made a trail away from the house. After escaping to a canoe:

> I says to my self, they'll follow the track . . . and then drag the river for me. And they'll
> follow that meal track to the lake, and go browsing down the creek that leads out of it to find
> the robbers that killed me and took the things. They won't ever hunt the river for anything but
> my dead carcass (p. 42).

These passages are full of references that could be scored using Plimpton's Origin scoring manual (deCharms, 1976, Appendix A). The manual was developed for coding personal documents for elements of personal causation; specifically, six categories that comprise an Origin Scale. The scale reveals thoughts by persons about originating (hence the term Origin) actions to make a desirable change. The six coding categories are:

1. *Goal Setting*—Self-initiated decisions to pursue a definite goal.
2. *Instrumental Activity*—A self-initiated activity or plan that is instrumental to attainment of a goal.

3. *Reality Perception*—The individual's ability to perceive correctly his or her (a) position vis-a-vis other persons or the environment, (b) possibilities, (c) strengths and weaknesses.

4. *Personal Responsibility*—The individual's willingness to take responsibility for the consequences of personal actions.

5. *Self-confidence*—The individual's confidence in his or her ability to effect changes in the environment (personal or physical).

6. *Internal Causality*—The individual reacts to problems as a challenge to be overcome by positive personal action rather than as a threat to be reacted to by submission.

Each of these categories jump out of the Huck Finn text above. For instance, "I made up my mind I would fix up some way to leave there" (goal setting); "But right away after I see I warn't scared of him worth bothering about" (reality perception); "I got to thinking that if I could fix up some way to keep pap and the widow from trying to follow me," (instrumental activity) "it would be a certainer thing than trusting to luck" (personal responsibility). Huck certainly saw the situation as a challenge rather than a threat (internal causality) and, "They won't ever hunt for anything but my dead carcass" shows considerable self-confidence.

By comparison with Mersault's and Raskolnikov's egregious acts, Huck Finn's actions are more positive, more exemplary of agency and personal causation.

SOME PRACTICAL IMPLICATIONS

If the three motivational schemata or 3 outcomes of personal action plus resistance are, in fact, general and fundamental aspects of persons in action, then the concept of the primacy of personal causation and the paradigm case of persons in intentional action should have broad practical implications. Any relationship between a superior-subordinate should exemplify the paradigm case. Any leader-follower, superior-(manager)-worker, administrator-teacher, or teacher-pupil relationship should qualify. In any such relationship understanding how to enhance examples of case "c," personal causation, and to reduce examples of case "a," learned helplessness, or case "b," negative reactance, should be useful.

The study of leadership as exemplified in Burns' (1978) studies provides a case in point as does Argyris' (1970, 1976, 1982) discussions of leadership and intervention in commercial organizations. The specific application of the ideas presented above has been only directly applied to teacher-pupil interaction (deCharms, 1976) and less intensively to administrator-teacher interaction (deCharms & Natriello, 1981; discussed also in deCharms, 1984).

Teacher-pupil interaction has much in common with mother-child interaction. Ideally, the teacher will strive for the most positive outcome of interaction— enhanced personal causation. Psychological reactance may promote some learning but clearly the teacher should avoid producing learned helplessness in the pupils. Teachers should strive for Huck Finns at best and settle for Mersaults and Raskolnikovs only as a less desirable alternative.

How is the teacher to instill desired behaviors in children? How can a teacher assure that the students will learn? Is this a question of learning only or is the enhancement of personal causation involved? Reducing concepts to materialistic analogs by computer simulation of intelligence or even of learning will hardly help us to answer these practical questions. An adequate description of action starts with personal causation up front and leads to practical suggestions for teachers.

Actions that give the pupil the experience of personal causation, of doing something to change their own situation, will *ipso facto* help the pupils to adapt to their world. At the same time such actions have all the advantages of the principle of survival. Teachers can enhance motivation and assure that learning will occur by helping pupils to experience personal causation.

This reasoning was first used by deCharms (1976) in conducting a long-term study in inner-city schools. Since the above reference reports the study in detail, its results will only be mentioned briefly here. Teachers were given training in helping their pupils to feel more personal causation (Origin Training) and then attended workshops throughout the school year in which they helped to develop exercises designed to enhance their pupils' feelings of personal causation with regard to school work. Results showed that: (1) the pupils' feelings of personal causation increased as measured by the Origin Scale discussed above, (2) attendance and tardiness were positively affected, (3) academic achievement was higher, all in trained classrooms as compared to untrained classes of sixth and seventh graders. Follow-up studies demonstrated long-term effect of the training in the eleventh grade as well as a significantly higher percentage of trained boys compared to untrained who graduated from high school (deCharms, 1984).

Subsequent research has pursued the idea that the most probable place to look for teacher effects that enhance pupil motivation by promoting personal causation is in teacher-pupil interaction, a type of neglect-nurturance sequence. The behavior of both the teacher and the pupil must be observed since they are clearly interdependent. Most classroom studies isolate either teacher behavior or that of the pupils, but Koenigs, Fiedler, and deCharms (1977) reported a classroom observation technique to capture the teacher-pupil interdependence. The goal of the study was to show that in classrooms where the pupils can influence the teacher's behavior, the pupils feel like Origins because they feel more personal causation. By recording each time the pupils tried to influence the behavior of the teacher and how the teacher responded, as well as recording each time the teacher attempted to influence the pupils and whether they responded, these researchers were able to analyze their data in terms of a Pupil Influence Ratio. The influence ratio was a simple count of the pupils' success in influencing the ongoing activities of the class as compared to the teacher's dominance in imposing all activities. It was hypothesized that where pupils and teachers shared influence, pupils would: (1) feel more personal causation, more like Origins, (2) would report a classroom climate of Originship, (3) would be more motivated to learn, and hence (4) would learn more. Using this observation measure in 43 classrooms Koenigs, Fiedler, and deCharms (1977) showed that in classrooms where pupils were allowed more influence, the pupils also reported an Origin climate in the class. Most important, classrooms where more pupil influence was allowed had higher academic achievement scores. (See deCharms, 1984, for more detail.)

Cohen (1978) noted that the Pupil Influence Ratio as used in the previous study contained several types of student request for influence not all of which would be conducive to learning. Some pupil influence attempts were clearly more like negative reactive behaviors as described in case "b" above. Some pupil requests were motivated by attention getting rather than by personal causation and such requests (for example, "May I leave the room?", or "May I sharpen my pencil again?", etc.) would in the long run be counterproductive to classroom affairs and to the students' feeling of personal causation relevant to academic achievement. Cohen divided pupil influence attempts into what she called "noise" and more constructive attempts. She further divided teacher influence attempts into those that imposed restrictions on the pupil's response and those that invited response but implied freedom of choice. Results demonstrated that constructive pupil influence in the classroom was positively related to the Origin Climate of the classroom while irrelevant pupil influence ("noise") was negatively related to Origin Climate. The evidence concerning the teacher's imposing vs. inviting influence was only tentative but was in the direction that would be expected from the concept of personal causation and from the results of subsequent studies by Deci.

Deci, Nezlek, and Sheinman (1981) and Deci, Schwartz, Sheinman, and Ryan (1981) have studied teachers' orientation toward supporting autonomy in their pupils' vs. teachers' orientation toward controlling their pupils' behavior. They found that teachers who supported autonomy in the class tended to have an Origin Climate in their classrooms, as reported by the pupils, and the pupils also reported more intrinsic motivation as measured by a scale developed by Harter (1981, 1982).

What these results seem to imply is that one way, at least, to enhance motivation in the classroom is to encourage the pupils to influence classroom activities and even to influence the teachers' own behavior. This enhances the Origin Climate of the classroom and the feelings of personal causation in the children. Ultimately, high levels of pupil influence on classroom affairs result in increased academic motivation and academic achievement as measured by standardized tests (deCharms, 1984).

DeCharms and Natriello (1981) studied administrator-teacher relationships with emphasis on the school principal. Six inner-city schools, each with approximately 30 teachers, were studied intensively for a year. A hypothesis derived from the writings of Jurgen Habermas (1973) suggested that demands on teachers from the principal that disrupt teacher motivation would lead to teacher dissatisfaction and a crisis in the form of inadequate teaching. The teachers in these schools had experienced considerable disruption in the form of being assigned that year to: (1) a new grade to teach, (2) a new subject matter to teach (for instance, reading specialists teaching arithmetic), (3) a new school, and/or (4) a new principal. A simple five-point disruption index was devised. A teacher who experienced none of the above disruptions was assigned a score of zero. Scores from one to four were assigned in keeping with the number of disruptions experienced by the teacher that year. Sixty-one percent of the teachers had experienced some disruption and 19% had experienced three or four disruptions. In this respect, two-thirds of the teachers had been treated not as Origins but as Pawns. The result was a detrimental effect on the school's climate. Teachers in schools with high disruption indexes reported very low scores on a measure of Origin Climate of the school, whereas teachers in schools where little disruption occurred reported high Origin Climate scores. Unfortunately, no measure of teacher effectiveness was available. There was evidence that the teachers felt that they were not being effective in that they wanted more supervision from the administrators.

These results from classrooms and schools seem more in line with conceiving of successful pupils and teachers as persons encouraged to see school as a challenge rather than a threat, as persons who survive, even thrive, by actively pursuing personal and even group goals within a supportive climate of resistance from the other persons in the environment. These are not the Mersaults and the Raskolnikovs of the world but more like the Huck Finns.

SUMMARY

The burden of meaning of "motivation" is too great. How can we lessen the load? To attempt to reduce it by analogy to materialistic elements is totally inadequate. The fundamental task of the psychology of human motivation is to provide an adequate understanding of the phenomenon as it applies to persons. The concept of personal causation directs our attention to the unique motivational component of persons in action.

Using Ossorio's paradigm case methodology, an adequate understanding of intentional actions of persons was sought. An examination of mother-child interaction suggested that the results of sequences of neglect of the child followed by nurturance by the mother (a sequence suggested by Macmurray's sequence of withdrawal and return) are threefold: learned helplessness, psychological react- ance, and personal causation.

Harre proposed that agency, a concept much like personal causation, entails breaking out of a conforming mold into unusual autonomous action. Mersault, the hero of Albert Camus' *The Stranger*, was suggested by Harre as an example—a paradigm case. A similar example is Dostoyevsky's Raskolnikov in *Crime and Punishment*. Both of these cases exemplify psychological reactance. Mark Twain's *Huckleberry Finn* presents a case of personal causation replete with restraint leading to challenge and intelligent, skillful action to attain a goal.

The adequacy of a description of personal causation can be tested. Does it have practical implications for the enhancement of motivation in persons? In the educational classroom teachers can enhance the experience of personal causation for their pupils by allowing the pupils to have considerable influence in class- room activities—to cause changes in the course of events. Where pupils do wield their influence responsibly they experience personal causation, are more moti- vated, and learn more. At the management level, where the administration (prin- cipals) disrupt ongoing activities of workers (normal teaching expectations), re- duction of feelings of personal causation (feeling like Pawns) can be drastically debilitating.

NOTES

1. For accuracy, we should always specify the gender of the child and the parent. But for clarity, we will refer to the child as "he" and the parent as "mother" or "she."

REFERENCES

Argyris, C. (1970). *Intervention theory and method.* Reading, MA: Addison-Wesley.

Argyris, C. (1976). *Increasing leadership effectiveness.* New York: Wiley.

Argyris, C. (1982). *Reasoning, learning, and action.* San Francisco: Jossey-Bass.

Bandura, A. (1977). Self-efficacy: Toward a unifying theory of behavioral change. *Psychological Review,* 84, 191-215.

Bhaskar, R. (1979). *The possibility of naturalism.* New Jersey: Humanities Press.

Burns, J. M. (1978). *Leadership.* New York: Harper & Row.

Brehm, J. W. (1966). *A theory of psychological reactance.* New York: Academic Press.

Camus, A. (1942). *The stranger.* New York: Random House edition, 1946.

Cohen, M. W. (1979). Student influence in the classroom. Unpublished Doctoral Dissertation, Washington University, St. Louis, MO.

De Charms, R. (1968). *Personal causation.* New York: Academic Press.

De Charms, R. (1976). *Enhancing motivation.* New York: Irvington Publishers.

De Charms, R. (1984). Motivation enhancement in educational settings. In R. E. Ames & C. Ames (Eds.), *Research on motivation in education* (Vol. 1). New York: Academic Press.

DeCharms, R., & Natriello, G. (1981). Evaluation and Teacher Motivation. Final Report, Spencer Foundation, Washington Univ., St. Louis, MO.

Deci, E. L. (1975). *Intrinsic motivation*. New York: Plenum.

Deci, E. L., Nezlek, J., & Sheinman, L. (1981). Characteristics of the rewarder and intrinsic motivation of the rewardee. *Journal of Personality and Social Psychology, 40*, 1–10.

Deci, E. L., Schwartz, A. J., Sheinman, L., & Ryan, R. M. (1981). An instrument to assess adults' orientations toward control versus autonomy with children: Reflections on intrinsic motivation and perceived competence. *Journal of Educational Psychology, 73*, 642–650.

Dennett, D. C. (1978). *Brainstorms: Philosophical essays on mind and psychology*. Cambridge, MA: Bradford Books, MIT Press.

Dostoyevsky, F. (1866). *Crime and Punishment*. New York: Signet Edition, 1968.

Hall, D. (1982). *Writing well* (Fourth Edition). Boston: Little, Brown and Co.

Harre, R. (1979). *Social being*. Totowa, NJ: Rowman and Littlefield.

Harre, R. (1984). *Personal being*. Cambridge, MA: Harvard Univ. Press.

Harter, S. (1981). A new self-report scale of intrinsic vs. extrinsic orientations in the classroom: Motivational and informational components. *Developmental Psychology, 17*, 399–312.

Harter, S. (1982). The perceived competence scale for children. *Child Development, 53*, 87–97.

Heider, F. (1958). *The psychology of interpersonal relations*. New York: Wiley.

Jones, M. R. (Ed.) (1955). *Nebraska symposium on motivation: 1955*. Lincoln: University of Nebraska Press.

Koenigs, S., Fiedler, M., & deCharms, R. (1977). Teacher beliefs, classroom interaction and personal causation. *Journal of Applied Social Psychology, 7*, 95–114.

Macmurray, J. (1957). *Self as agent*. New York: Harper.

Maslow, A. H. (1968). *Toward a psychology of being* (Second Edition). New York: Van Nostrand Reinhold.

Ossorio, P. G. (1975). *What actually happens: The representation of real-world phenomenon*. Columbia, SC: University of South Carolina Press.

Ossorio, P. G. (1981). Explanation, Falsifiability, and Rule-Following. In K. E. Davis (Ed.), *Advances in descriptive psychology* (Vol. 1). Greenwich, CT: JAI Press.

Scott, P. (1966). *The raj quartet*. New York: Avon.

Seligman, M. E. P. (1975). *Helplessness: On depression, development and death*. San Francisco: W. H. Freeman.

Twain, M. (1959). *Adventures of Huckleberry Finn*. New York: New American Library.

ENHANCING MOTIVATION:
A SOCIAL DEVELOPMENTAL PERSPECTIVE

John Condry

INTRODUCTION

What we know and understand about motivation and what ideas we will entertain about it depends, to a very great extent, on implicit and often unconscious theories we hold about the basic nature of the human being. Whether we are aware of these theories or not, they determine which psychological ideas we find believable and which ones we reject as nonsense. These theories serve as the source of our actions toward other people. Because of this, it is wise to begin any discussion of motivation by being forthright about the underlying assumptions to be made about the nature of the human organism and about motivation in general.

Motivation is so broad a term that it may encompass both very large and very small aspects of human behavior, both very short and very long sequences of action. Motivational explanations are usually answers to "why" questions, in

Advances in Motivation and Achievement: Enhancing Motivation,
Volume 5, pages 23-49.
Copyright © **1987 by JAI Press Inc.**
All rights of reproduction in any form reserved.
ISBN: 0-89232-621-2

terms of the force that energizes, directs, and terminates human activity. Some
part of motivation—the part I shall concern myself with here—is deeply en-
twined with social relationships, with the patterns of authority encountered
throughout development—with what they have encouraged, what they have
denied, and how.

So when I talk of enhancing motivation, I will mean the part of motivation that
may be influenced by the relationships we have with other human beings. The
growth of social relationships is what the study of social development is all
about, so this will be a social developmental perspective on the question of how
motivation may be enhanced.

In general I will be talking about two broad types of motivation: *intrinsic mo-
tivation* to be curious about the world and to explore it, and *extrinsic motivation*,
to act in ways approved by the social world around us, which I will call "social
control." There are social environments, social relationships, in which curiosity
and exploration flourish, and there are social environments that are inimical to
the expression of this kind of motivation. The fundamental premise of this chap-
ter is that we may enhance intrinsic motivation, curiosity, by understanding more
about how it functions, and by providing a social environment which is condu-
cive to its growth. A second fundamental premise is that we may also enhance
motivation by using social control in a manner that does not undermine the role
of the self in the internalization of behavior.

My purpose in this chapter, then, is to consider what may be done with social
relationships during the period of development from birth to about 18 years of
age to enhance motivation in these two senses, by using social control in an intel-
ligent manner, and by creating social relationships in which curiosity and explo-
ration may flourish. Before undertaking this endeavor, the terms intrinsic and
extrinsic motivation need some elaboration.

Intrinsic Motivation: Curiosity and Exploration

The conception of motivation which I am calling "intrinsic motivation" is
traceable in part to Rousseau, writing in the eighteenth century, and more re-
cently to Jean Piaget, R. W. White, and Jerome Bruner. In the last few years,
theorists who have written about this topic are Mihaly Csikszentmihalyi, Edward
Deci, Richard deCharms, Susan Harter, Mark Lepper, and others. This view
holds that the human organism, rather than being a "blank slate" at birth, is
complex and well formed, with adequate motivation to learn about the world. R.
W. White called this "effectance motivation," because he believed that it is
based on an inborn desire to interact effectively with the environment (White,
1959; see also, Harter, 1978; 1981, b). Piaget said children have an inherent
desire to "make interesting sights last," which is to say an inherent desire to
have an "effect" on the world, particularly that part of the world they find "in-
teresting." The desire to exert some personal control over the world, and the

perception of such control, is found in very young infants (Watson, 1971, 1972, 1977; Watson & Ramey, 1972). In short, the notion of intrinsic motivation suggests that we are born curious about the world, and this inherent curiosity provides the motive force for most of what we learn when we are free to explore the world on our own.

In recent years, a variety of researchers, working from different intellectual traditions, have developed models of intrinsic motivation. These different views are not so much incompatible with one another as they offer slightly different perspectives on a complicated topic. One group of theorists, for example, views intrinsic motivation in terms of competence, effectance, or mastery (Csikszentmihalyi, 1975, 1977; Harter, 1978, 1981b; Kagan, 1972; White, 1959). From this point of view, activities are intrinsically motivating if they engage the learner in problem solving and goal seeking, if they result in a sense of mastery. From this point of view, human beings are motivated to achieve competence.

A second group of theorists, in their definition of intrinsic motivation, have focused on "stimulus characteristics" which give rise to curiosity: such as complexity, incongruity, and other "collative" variables (Berlyne, 1960, 1966; Hunt, 1965). From this point of view, activities are intrinsically motivating to the extent that they attract our attention, interest, and curiosity.

A third group of theorists has focused on the role of personal causation, self-efficacy, and self-determination in intrinsically motivated behavior (Bandura, 1977b; Bandura & Cervone, 1983; Bandura & Schunk, 1981; deCharms, 1968, this volume; Deci, 1975, 1981; Deci & Ryan, 1985; Condry, 1977, 1978, 1981; Lepper & Greene, 1978b). From this point of view, an activity is intrinsically interesting when it allows the person some degree of personal control and self-determination, if it leads to a sense of self-efficacy.

Intrinsic motivation may be distinguished from other extrinsic motive forces, such as social control, in terms of what sets it off, what maintains the focus of attention while the motive force is engaged, and what eventually terminates it. Thus, intrinsically motivated activity is typically set off by novelty and incongruity (Berlyne, 1966) or "challenge" from the environment (Deci & Ryan, 1985; Harter, 1978, 1981b, 1982), although it is obvious that what is novel, incongruous, or challenging changes over time for each individual. By contrast, social control is usually initiated by the controller, based on a specific form of behavior which is desired. In most of the research on this topic, the controller either offers a reward or threatens a punishment in order to achieve compliance from the controllee (Lepper, 1981, 1983).

Intrinsic motivation is maintained during the process of learning by exploratory skills, and these may be different than the skills needed to satisfy extrinsic social demands. So the "pattern of learning" could be different for these two types of motivation (Condry and Chambers, 1978). For example, a book read for a class may be read more for what the professor wants the student to learn than for what the student is interested in knowing.

Finally, intrinsically motivated behavior is typically ended when curiosity is satisfied, whereas extrinsically motivated activities are ended when the promised reward or threatened punishment is given (Deci, 1971, 1972a,b; Greene & Lepper, 1974; Lepper, Greene, & Nisbett, 1973). So we may distinguish these two forms of motivation, in part, by looking at the conditions that initiate and later terminate the motivated activity.

It is beyond the scope of this chapter to attempt to weave a theory of intrinsic motivation. The purpose here is only to suggest that there is such a motive force, to describe some of its characteristics, and to wonder about the role of the social environment in facilitating or enhancing it. Even though children are born with intrinsic motivation, the focus of curiosity undergoes many changes throughout the course of childhood, and children become increasingly competent at learning by discovery. In both of these senses, intrinsic motivation may be said to "develop."

The Development of Intrinsic Motivation

If children are born with adequate "intrinsic" motivation to learn, then they don't need to be motivated by the social world so much as they need to have available the *circumstances appropriate for learning*. They need the social conditions that will allow curiosity, inherent in every child, to express itself. Throughout development this involves, among other things, warm and affectionate social relationships with other human beings. These relationships facilitate exploration and curiosity, perhaps through the diminution of fear and anxiety, perhaps through the strengthening of ego, probably both.

In addition to such relationships throughout development, the child also needs a coherent, true, and representative environment in which his or her explorations may be conducted. In short, even though curiosity motivation is "intrinsic," there is much the social world can do to facilitate (or retard) the development of this motive.

Extrinsic Motivation: Social Control

Intrinsic motivation alone will not accomplish all that parents and other social authorities expect or want of children. For one thing, the nature of curiosity is to focus on what the *child* is interested in doing, not necessarily what the parents or any social authority would have the child do. It is inevitable that there will be conflicts between the "intrinsic" desires of the child and the "extrinsic" desires of the parents, and later, other social authorities. Bowel and bladder control, around two years of age, is reputed to be one of the first of these "conflicts" to appear in almost all families, although attempts to influence or control the infant probably begin long before this, and expectations about control relationships may be well established by two years of age.

The way in which control is accomplished, the means, is a consideration as important as the ends, the goals sought. It is the different means of control that are reflected in the different patterns of authority encountered throughout development, not so much the different ends.

Intrinsic vs. Extrinsic Motivation: Curiosity vs. Social Control

In recent years, many studies have demonstrated that there is often a negative relationship between intrinsic and extrinsic motivation, between curiosity and intrinsic interest on the one hand, and social control, exemplified by offers of reward and threats of punishment, on the other (Condry 1977, 1981; Deci 1975, 1981; Deci & Ryan, 1985; Lepper, 1981; Lepper & Greene, 1978a). Tracing the roots of research on this problem back to the "Forbidden Toy" experiments of the 60s and 70s, Lepper (1981) shows that over a large number of studies the magnitude of attitude and behavior change is often inversely related to the size of the incentive offered as an "inducement," in order to motivate change.

Thus, under the right conditions, the stronger incentive produces attitude change in the *opposite* direction to what is desired by the person offering the incentive. For example, in several studies children were introduced into a playroom full of toys and told they could play with all but one (very attractive) toy. Two levels of threat were used: "mild" and "severe." In the mild threat condition, the child was told not to play with the toy and "if you do I will be very disappointed in you." In the severe threat condition, the child was told not to play with the toy and "if you do I will be very disappointed in you and I'll tell your teacher you are acting like a baby."

Over several studies, Lepper and his colleagues (see Lepper, 1981) showed that children changed their attitudes and their behaviors in the desired direction, for example, refused to play with the "forbidden toy," more so in the *mild* as opposed to the *severe* threat condition. This effect was true for some time after the manipulation, even in different circumstances from the original test. So several weeks later, when a different experimenter introduced these same children to these same toys, with *no injunctions* about what may be played with, children who were in the "mild" threat condition of the original study still avoided playing with the "forbidden toy," compared to children in the severe threat condition, who played more with the forbidden toy. And, in fact, the inverse relationship between incentive magnitude and subsequent attitude and behavior change is more widespread than this.

Additional studies since the time of the Forbidden Toy experiments have shown that *positive incentives*, designed to encourage the child to learn or perform, may result in less learning, or performances contrary to the intentions of the controller (Condry, 1977, 1981; Deci, 1971, 1972a,b; Lepper, Greene, & Nisbett, 1973; Greene & Lepper, 1974). The implications of these findings are clear: if we are interested in "enhancing intrinsic motivation," if we want curiosity and exploration to flourish, we would be wise to limit the degree to which we attempt to control the human being, even when we do so with rewards rather than punishments, and even when we do so with the best of intentions.

Piaget put it this way, "Each time one prematurely teaches a child something he could have discovered for himself, that child is kept from inventing it and consequently from understanding it completely" (Hall, 1970, p. 32). This radical thought reveals a final important point about the assumptions underlying this chapter. I will concern myself with the *long term internalization* of behavioral skills and cognitive schemata, and with how the development of these may be facilitated by the social world. More than any other, this issue of long-term vs. short-term interests is central to confusion about the consequences of social control.

Researchers who use techniques of "behavior modification" often cite evidence showing that rewards and other incentives function perfectly well to keep behavior under control and, in general, the stronger the incentive, the greater the degree of compliance. There is no doubt that this is true if one adopts the proper time perspective. Many "behavior modification" studies are concerned only with short-term goals, with immediate compliance (see Rosenthal & Zimmerman, 1978). What happens tomorrow, or in another classroom, is not a focus of most of this research. With this relatively narrow interest, the strength of the incentive used to accomplish "behavior control" may well be directly related to immediate compliance. In fact, the more harsh the threat or strong the reward, usually the faster and more complete the compliance (Ross, 1975), if speed is the only issue. The disadvantage with this approach is that it requires constant surveillance and tends to be the most temporary in its influence (Kelman, 1961).

Once again, the issue of the "relationship" between the controller and the controllee is of importance. For some controllers, there are no "long-term" interests in the child's internalization of a behavior, just the short-term interest in behavior control. For other people in the child's world, long-term change is the most important thing. In this chapter we shall concern ourselves with what kinds of skills and schemata the child develops in the long run as a consequence of social control, not just with overt behavior controlled within a narrow time frame.

The Tools of Learning

If the motivation to learn about the world may be supplied from different sources, internal and external to ourselves, the information existing in the world, the knowledge to be acquired, may be said to exist on different "levels" as well (Gibson, 1979). To extract this information the child needs certain behavioral and conceptual structures, certain behavioral skills and cognitive schemata. These are the tools of learning, the means of satisfying curiosity and of exploring the world so as to acquire information from it. Even though the child inherits the potential for the expression of these skills, they must be refined by virtue of interaction with a specific real world (Bruner, 1974a,b). We consider each of these tools of learning below.

Direct learning. All living organisms are born with some capacity to interact with the world directly: to perceive it, to learn from it, and to act intelligently within it. Although the child is certainly hedonistic at birth, as many have noted, the child is also quite sensitive to contingency, especially the kinds of contingency encountered by virtue of interacting with other human beings (Watson, 1971, 1972, 1977). The laws of classical and operant conditioning operate at this level of direct interaction. The laws of observation and persuasive communications have yet to be specified (but, see Bandura, 1977b, for a beginning).

The direct form of learning is slow and tedious, the organism must respond, suffer the consequences, interpret them properly, etc. If this were the only means human beings had of acquiring knowledge, they would know very little and it would take a great deal of time to learn that. Luckily, our species has the potential for other means of acquiring knowledge, other means of extracting the information available in the world.

Observational learning. Once sufficient development occurs, a second level of learning becomes possible which is more indirect; both in the sense of being more decontextualized (Bruner, 1974a) and in the sense of the organism not having to directly experience the consequences of action. This capacity is sometimes called imitation, modeling, or simply observational learning (Bandura, 1977a,b; Bruner, 1974a).

Not only can we learn by experiencing the world and its outcomes directly, but we can also learn by seeing another creature, like ourselves, doing an act and experiencing the consequences. Even though some imitational behaviors appear very early (Meltzoff & Moore, 1977), it is not until about 18 months of age that children start to become proficient in observing a model and patterning their actions after what was seen (Bruner, 1974a).

Learning by observation requires the development of a certain amount of behavioral control as well as certain cognitive capacities, such as:

1. some rudimentary sense of the self as a separate actor (Bruner, 1974a),
2. the ability to both understand (Bandura, 1977b), and
3. act out the sequence observed in the proper order (Bruner, 1974b).

The important point is that once this level of learning is available to the child it makes possible a wider range of knowledge to be acquired, at a faster pace than is possible with direct interaction. To some degree also, it changes the nature of what is required of the social environment (Bruner, 1974a). The ability to learn by observation is a late evolutionary development, many creatures do not acquire knowledge in this manner.

Symbolic learning. The final level on which information in the human social environment is available so that with the proper "equipment" it can be "picked up," is the symbolic level of representation involving language. In order to learn from symbols, a good deal of conceptual and social development must have occurred. Most children do not even begin to use language until the second year of life, and their communicative abilities are quite limited throughout the period of primary socialization.

These different levels of information acquisition are important for two reasons: first, they emphasize the thing that develops in intrinsically motivated behavior, the skills that underlie exploration and curiosity. Second, these levels are also correspondent with the kinds of pressure the social world can bring to bear in order to get a human being to behave. So these different levels represent the three kinds of social control that are possible: coercion, example, and persuasion.

Overview

The purpose of this chapter, then, will be to describe how motivation may be enhanced throughout the course of early social development, from birth to young adulthood. We will focus on two kinds of motivation: curiosity or intrinsic motivation, and social control or extrinsic motivation. In both of these instances we will focus on the nature and structure of social relationships that are related to the enhancement of both kinds of motivation.

The sections to follow are arranged in developmental sequence, considering only the period from birth to full sexual maturity—that is, from birth to about 18 years of age. It is clear that this is not all of development, since this is only the beginning, but what happens into adulthood is another story. It will have to be told elsewhere.

In this chapter we will divide the period to be discussed into *three stages of development*, because during these different stages the focus of intrinsic motivation is different, the environment, particularly the social environment, is different, and the child's skills and abilities are different. Comparing one stage to another, the child has different interests, different capacities for learning, and different people to learn from.

The three stages of development and the years they cover are: *primary socialization*, from birth to about six; *secondary socialization*, from six to about 12; and *tertiary socialization* from 12 to 18 years of age. For each stage of development, we will consider both how intrinsic motivation may be facilitated by the social environment, and how extrinsic motivation or social control may be used so as not to inhibit the expression of curiosity, and so as to promote internalization and the development of the self.

PRIMARY SOCIALIZATION

We have already noted that at birth the child has strong (if limited) interests and desires, and thus begins life as a highly complex organism capable of, to some degree, satisfying these interests, and capable of rapidly learning the means to satisfy others. The child is born with the capacity and the motivation to learn. Before we consider the nature of this motivation and the role of the social environment in facilitating it's growth, let's consider what the world is like, what is out there to be learned.

The world has a correlational and causal structure, it consists of things that have certain common features and which interact with each other and with us, the human beings, in certain characteristic ways (Neisser, 1976; Rosch, 1974, 1975). The humans of the world also relate to each other in certain specific ways (Kelley, 1971, 1973; Kelley & Thibaut, 1985; Thibaut & Kelley, 1959).

Intrinsic Motivation During Primary Socialization

During the period from birth until six years of age, the focus of the child's *intrinsic motivation* is in learning about the correlational and causal structure of the world, primarily the physical world near at hand, including other people as (animate) physical objects. It is during this period that most of what E. J. Gibson (1969) calls "perceptual development" occurs. The environment of socialization is the home. During this period, the child is also exposed to the first experience of extrinsic social control.

Children thus begin life with intrinsic desires, interests, and some skills for extracting information, for learning about the world and satisfying this curiosity. Children are especially "sensitive" to the information contained in "contingent" interactions, most of which involve another human being (Watson, 1977).

The social environment plays a central role in getting these (discovery learning, exploratory) motivational systems going, in providing the circumstances that allow them to flourish, and in providing the child with interesting environments, including other people, to explore. How do parents accomplish all of this, and what happens if they don't?

Attachment and affection. Exploration proceeds best, it turns out, when the child has formed a close and secure affectionate relationship with another person. This is often called an "attachment" relationship (Ainsworth, 1967; Ainsworth & Bell, 1971; Bowlby, 1969). A central role played by the social environment, beginning at birth, is to allow and encourage the child to develop this attachment relationship so that early curiosity and exploration may begin to flower. Children who are deprived of early affectionate relationships often become passive, morose (Spitz, 1962; Skeels, 1966), and show the depressed syndrome of "help-lessness" (Seligman 1975).

There is compelling recent evidence to suggest that the attachment relation-ship, usually between mother and child, may be characterized as one of three types (Ainsworth, Bell, & Stayton, 1974; Sroufe & Waters, 1977; Maccoby, 1980, p. 84), that persist over time (Matas, Arend, & Sroufe, 1978). While the majority of children are "securely attached," at least some children may be seen as "avoidant," and others as "resistant" (Sroufe & Waters, 1977). It is not clear from this research whether these patterns are the result of parent-child interac-tions or to what extent the child is genetically predisposed to such patterns. What is clear is that most of those children who are securely attached do better in nurs-ery school and are considered "better adjusted." Children falling into the resist-ant and avoidant categories have more difficulty in nursery school and demon-strate less competence compared to children who are coded as securely attached (Matas, Arend, & Sroufe, 1978).

Providing a stimulating environment.   If curiosity is to be stimulated and development progress, if the child is to be able to act "competently" in the world, a second role of the social environment is to provide the child with a co-herent, varied, and interesting social and physical world to explore. The child must be exposed, eventually, to an accurate and representative sample of the world, and this will be true at every stage of development, not just the first.

I take this as a "given," I have no direct proof of it. But it seems obvious that faced with a coherent but false reality, children commonly develop structures which reflect the world to which they have been exposed. Thus a false reality, especially a false social reality, often leads to difficulty later in adapting to the next circle of relationships. For example, nursery school teachers often see chil-dren who, in their first few weeks of school, are likely to push and shove another child when they want something. Often this comes about because this kind of minor aggression is permitted in the home, usually more so from boys than girls. So when the child comes to nursery school, he is not aware that aggression of this sort is not usually permitted outside the home. In a minor way, the child has been exposed to a false view of reality; at least, what is allowed in the home was not correspondent with what is permitted in the school.

So although the motivation to learn about the world is intrinsic, for it to de-velop properly during the period of primary socialization the child should have available a secure and affectionate relationship with another human being, and the child should be exposed to some amount of the variety of what the world has to offer. During the period of primary socialization, the social world must pro-vide both if intrinsic motivation in the form of curiosity and exploration is to develop properly.

Social Control During Primary Socialization

During the period of primary socialization children also encounter their first experience with extrinsic motivation or social control. The means available to adults for the control of children are most limited during this early stage of life. The means of social influence or control correspond to the three levels of information discussed earlier. That is, the social world can control children directly by rewarding or punishing them, or indirectly by serving as models and examples for observational learning, and/or finally by the symbols of language and the use of "persuasion" (Kelman, 1961; Bandura, 1977a,b).

With regard to social control there are three broad questions we can ask:

1.   why is it applied? That is, what purpose do adults have in mind when they try to control the behavior of a child? What ends or goals do they seek?
2.   how is control applied? That is, what techniques are used to assure compliance, and what does the controller expect to accomplish with these techniques? What means do they use?
3.   what is the relationship between the controllee and the controller?

In short, we can ask about both the means and ends of social influence and control and about the nature of the social relationship involved. Generally our interest will be in the means rather than the ends, and with long-term rather than short-term relationships.

The role of different "means" of control is evident in research on the control of crying. Here the goal is consistent across all parents—to get the child to stop crying unnecessarily—but the kinds of techniques used, the means, are quite different in different families. In one study of this (Ainsworth, Bell, & Stayton, 1974), one group of parents attempted to stop the infant from crying by responding as soon as the child cried, while the second group did not respond immediately, but rather waited and postponed their actions. These differences in response came about because the parents held different "theories" about the child. The parents who delayed their response did so because they were afraid that to respond immediately would "spoil" the child. The parents who responded immediately were not worried about "spoiling" the child, rather they wanted the child to realize that they would answer every need. The parents who responded immediately had children who, in the long run, cried less than those who delayed their response.

These findings are important for several reasons: first, because they reveal that attempts to gain some form of control over the child, to apply "extrinsic motivation" to change the child's behavior, may come shortly after birth, a good deal earlier than the onset of bowel and bladder control around the age of two (often cited as one of the first ''conflicts'' between the parent and the child). Second, in attempting control, parents begin to establish what will be their ''style of interaction,'' in this case immediate vs. delayed response (Ainsworth et al., 1974, call these ''sensitive'' vs. ''insensitive'' parents). Third, these differences in treatment probably arise from implicit ''theories'' held by the parents about the nature of the child, about how social control should be accomplished, and about the parent's role in the process. Not ''spoiling'' children is one such ''theory'' which carries with it certain ''proper'' and ''improper'' actions, in accordance with beliefs about what parental actions ''spoil'' children.

In addition to crying, what other kinds of behavior are controlled by parents during the period of primary socialization, and what other theories do these facts reveal? There is a good deal written about bowel and bladder control, toilet training, because Freud considered this one of the important developmental milestones (Hall, 1954). In Freud's theory, toilet training ushers in the ''anal stage'' of development by introducing a conflict between the desires of the child and the desires of the parents. Since this kind of conflict is threatening to the child, a proper resolution of it is needed for the continued growth of the ego. As was true of the control of crying, in the case of toilet training there is widespread agreement about the importance of the child learning some form of control, but there are a variety to techniques used to accomplish the common goal (Sears, Maccoby, & Levin, 1956).

Parents also exert influence over the child during the period of primary socialization to encourage general obedience (''when I say 'no' I mean it . . .'') and to stop various behaviors such as thumb sucking and bed wetting which the parents find objectionable (Maccoby, 1980).

There is evidence for differences in parental treatment of boys and girls, both in terms of aggression control, and in terms of toy, dress, and activity preferences. Most children are discouraged, to some degree, from acting aggressively as a consequence of frustration. Goodenough (1931) reports that the incidence of ''angry outbursts'' increases until about 1½ years of age, decreasing thereafter to stabilize at different levels for boys and girls (boys show more). The meaning of these data is unclear, although they are often used to demonstrate the likelihood of aggression being biologically mandated in boys (Maccoby, 1980, p. 120).

In general, there is evidence that more parental control, in terms of restrictiveness, is exerted over boys during the period of primary socialization than over girls (Maccoby & Jacklin, 1974, p. 319). This may arise from parental beliefs that boys are, by nature, more uncontrollable and so must be brought under control earlier, with greater severity; or because girls, being more mature at birth, are more sensitive to social cues from parents so they learn more quickly. The issue is unresolved.

Given that the ''ends'' sought by parents in controlling their children during the period of primary socialization are widely diverse and society specific (at least some are), is there a best *means* of accomplishing whatever ends or goals are desired? Is there a best way to exert control over another person, and in particular, another person of this young age, during infancy and early childhood? We have already noted that different methods of influence are available to the controller, depending, in part, on the age (and developmental stage) of the controllee. In addition, there is experimental evidence, from several studies, which taken together suggest a rule for the use of "direct" social control of the reward/punishment type. This rule is called the "*minimum sufficiency principle*" (Lepper, 1981).

This principle states that in using direct methods of social control, the controller should offer just enough reward, or threaten just enough punishment, to accomplish compliance, nothing more. A level of incentive, either reward or punishment, which is not quite enough, and a level which is "overly sufficient," may both result in "counterproductive" outcomes, where a person's attitude may strengthen for doing exactly the thing prohibited (Lepper, 1981; Condry, 1981).

So it may be that a rule for early parenting, about the means not the ends of influence, is that the least amount of pressure necessary should be used to bring about change. It is during the first stage of life, during primary socialization, that the issue of direct control is paramount. As the child grows older into the period of secondary socialization, other more subtle means of control become available.

Summary of Primary Socialization

During the period of primary socialization, from birth to about six years of age, the child is intrinsically motivated to acquire knowledge of the world, and the child is exposed to the first experience of social influence, of extrinsic control. What behaviors the adults (usually the parents) seek to control is partly determined by considerations of social living in a particular culture (e.g., toilet training), and partly by idiosyncratic parental desires. The means used to accomplish these ends vary widely across parents, and they are limited during this early stage of life due to the child's limited grasp of the "tools of learning." Research indicates that when using methods of direct control, the minimum necessary to achieve compliance is the best strategy, since either too little or too much is likely to result in "undesired" or "counterproductive" outcomes. This result, in turn, seems to be related to the importance of the self, and to personal commitment, in resisting or acquiescing to social control attempts. It is the person's degree of compliance with the influence attempt, in addition to the magnitude of the incentive which, jointly, determines the attitudinal/behavioral outcome (Condry, 1981; Lepper, 1981).

When parents exert control, what they try to control usually arises from "theories" about what children should or should not be doing. The means used, that is, how the parents try to accomplish their goals, also comes from certain theo-

ries about how to make children behave, and about the role of parents in develop-
ment. Theories of both ends and means are undoubtedly culturally bound, at
least to some degree.

An important aspect of these early attempts at social control is not just what is
controlled, but also that they establish a "style of interaction" regarding control
. . . how it is exercised, under what circumstances, what to expect if one does or
does not obey, and so forth. This style of interaction will come to be what the
child expects and knows of social influence as he or she enters the next stage of
socialization.

SECONDARY SOCIALIZATION

During the years from 6–12, the environment which the child has available to
explore expands greatly, and there is extensive "cognitive" development as
well, so the child is able to understand more complex facts about the world.
Where the first six years was spent largely in the environment of the home, the
next six years is almost equally divided, in terms of time, between the home, the
school, the peer group, and the television set. These are often called "agents of
socialization."

Television is a source of information but not, except in a limited way, control.
However they are influenced by it, children do not have a social relationship with
the television set. In this chapter our focus is on the social world, so we will look
closely at the home, the peer group, and the school as the socializing agents who
attempt to "motivate" the child, who try to change the child's behavior by
exercising social control. During this stage, like the first, the child is both intrin-
sically and extrinsically motivated. The basic structure of motivation remains
much the same, but the focus of it changes, and the child becomes more
proficient at learning by discovery. Up to this time, the child has been "social"
only in terms of the home and the near-to-home social environment. During the
next period, the child becomes social in the sense of becoming part of the society
in which she lives.

Intrinsic Motivation During Secondary Socialization

During the years from about six to 12, the focus of the child's attention
changes from an interest in the near physical and social world of the home to the
broader world of society. The child begins to learn about social roles and a much
wider range of "proper" or socially appropriate behavior is learned, from many
different "teachers." The child goes from a period of learning the basic facts
about the world and the fundamental skills of exploration, to one of using this
knowledge and skill for exploring the world of society. During this time the child
begins to establish a social identity.

Not only is the focus of curiosity different during the second period of socialization, but "explorations" are conducted in different social environments as well: not only in the home, but also with peers, and in institutions such as schools, churches, and organized groups (Condry & Siman, 1974). As a result of this experience, the child begins to develop concepts about social roles, values, needs, and sources of social influence. The child learns the proper behavior in a number of social circumstances.

A reflection of this learning is to be found in the "schemas," especially the social schemas, the child is able to understand (Neisser, 1976). These schemas may be found in conceptions about sex roles and moral values, where the child's understanding of the world goes from being narrow, concrete, and egocentric, to a broader, more mature understanding of social causality (Condry, 1984). A consequence of this new focus of intrinsic interest is that the child comes to a greater understanding of the structure of social causality (Kelley & Thibaut, 1985).

Thus during the period of secondary socialization, the major focus of the child's curiosity is about the structure of the social world, and where he or she *fits* into that structure. The child satisfies this curiosity by establishing a social identity, by developing a social self.

Social Control During Secondary Socialization

Even though they are still of central importance, parents are no longer the sole sources of information and control as they were during the stage of primary socialization. Peers and teachers play an increasingly important role, both as sources of warmth and affection, as sources of information about the world, and as people who, because they have a relationship with the child, may use techniques of social control in order to "motivate" the child to act in certain ways.

During the period of secondary socialization, the child is capable of being influenced by information at all three levels (direct, observational, symbolic), although the child becomes more proficient at learning by both observation and persuasion (Bandura, 1977b). Thus while the tools of learning remain the same, they become more precise, refined, and sophisticated during the period of secondary socialization. In the use of observational learning, for example, there is evidence that in the years 6–12 the child is now able to focus on such variables as the social appropriateness of the model (Perry & Bussy, 1979), and the degree to which the model is "similar" to the self (Brown & Inouye, 1978), in deciding who and what to imitate. In the sections to follow, we will consider the kinds of social control exerted in the three different social environments of secondary socialization: the home, the school, and the peer group.

Social control in the home. As the child gets older, direct methods of exerting power are generally replaced by persuasion and by reasoning rather than using rewards and threats of punishment to "motivate" behavior (Baumrind,

1970; Maccoby, 1980). This development should provide for greater internalization of behaviors, following the principle of minimum sufficiency. Teaching by example and persuasion is the less "intrusive" and "salient" method of control. Are there differences in how parents try to control their children? Are there differences in parental style? If so, what are these differences, and what are the consequences for development?

For the last 20 years or so, Diana Baumrind has been researching this question with parents and children in Berkeley, California (Baumrind, 1966, 1967, 1970; Baumrind & Black 1967). Baumrind has found that parental "style" (of influence) can be categorized as falling into "three types": Authoritarian, Authoritative, and Permissive. The parents who display the *authoritarian* style prefer more direct and intrusive forms of control, and they are concerned most about obedience. The *permissive* families prefer little or no control (but they show more warmth to their children than authoritarians). When contrasted with the other two groups, *authoritative* parents have children who are more socially competent, more mature, and more able to withstand frustration. The authoritative types of parents are most likely to use reason with their children, to explain and legitimize their actions.

Other than Baumrind's work, not much is known about this topic, the types of control exerted in the home during the years from 6–12 (because few recent surveys are available), and even less is known about control exerted outside the home, by peers and school authorities, because this topic has not been the focus of extensive research.

Social control in the peer group.   The kinds of influence available to peers is by social acceptance (which could be classed as a form of reward, and its withdrawal, a form of punishment), modeling, and persuasion. To the extent that the child identifies with the group and desires to be a part of it, the more effective should be the use of social acceptance and modeling as forms of social influence (Condry & Siman, 1974). Since the research is scarce, we know relatively little of the kind of "ends" or goals sought by peer groups in their use of social influence, or of how and when such control is exercised. What do peers pressure other kids to do, and how? We do know that the different sexes have different types of relationships with their peers (boys have more friends, partly because they play more organized sports; whereas, girls have fewer friends but more intimate interactions with them (Maccoby & Jacklin, 1974, p. 205), and that the influence of peers (relative to parents) tends to increase during this period of life (Condry & Siman, 1974).

Peers not only serve as sources of affection and support, they also teach us about the world, even though, once again, relatively little is known about the process of learning via social interaction. One recent study demonstrated that the process underlying cognitive social development, learning from peers, may be shown to depend on the relative cognitive stage of the participants and the amount and kind of communication in the group (Tudge, 1986). Children exposed to a more "advanced" stage of thinking from peers often show advances in their own thinking at a later date, depending on the amount and type of communication within the group. By the same token, however, children exposed to peers at a lower stage of intellectual development, often dropped down a stage in thinking, if only temporarily.

In general then, peers may be said to pressure youngsters because they provide either sources of affection or information the child finds to be useful. The powers of peers increases steadily throughout childhood, relative to other socializing agents.

Social control in the school.   Two kinds of control are exerted by authorities in the school, the direct control of rewards and punishments, not unlike parents (and justified by the school's position *in loco parentis*), and the more symbolic control exemplified by grades (Harter, 1981a). This pattern of using punishment to stop unwanted behavior (which the child is, presumably, interested in doing) and rewards to encourage behavior the child is (presumably) not intrinsically interested in, is a common one in both home and school (Condry, 1978, 1981). But the "means" of controlling behavior may be very different in these two environments. An interesting problem for research concerns the fit between the different uses of social influence in the home and the school, and the effect of this potential conflict upon the child. For example, if it is possible to designate parents as authoritarian, authoritative, or permissive, then perhaps it is possible to describe schools in this manner as well. To the extent that children become adapted to one kind of control during the period of primary socialization, they may experience difficulty with different types of control in the different social institutions of middle childhood. Children going to a school designated as "authoritative" (using a balance of warmth and control) if they are from either authoritarian or permissive homes should have some trouble, at least early on. An authoritative school should be too "up tight" for the permissive children and "too loose" for the children from authoritarian homes. In a study done many years ago, Lewin, Lippitt, and White (1939) demonstrated that movement from a group characterized by one type of control (e.g., democratic) to another type (e.g., laissez faire) could be problematic for the child, in the sense of requiring a period of adaptation to the new social atmosphere (see also Patterson, 1986, regarding antisocial behavior).

The use of grades, by the schools, involves both control and information, as Deci has noted (Deci, 1975; Deci et al., 1982). Grades can be rewarding (or punishing), but they can also be informative of learning, and especially of learning relative to others in the class. There is evidence to show that to the extent that the informational aspects dominate, the use of grades for social control has less of an "undermining" affect on motivation, compared to use of grades that stress the control aspects (Lepper, 1983; Ross, 1975).

There may be sex differences in how the school dispenses rewards and punishments for performance in math classes, depending on "theories" held by the teachers about differential mathematical ability in boys and girls (Dweck, 1975; Dweck & Elliot, 1983; Dweck & Goetz, 1978). More research is needed about this topic: the expectations held by teachers about students and the role of these beliefs in subsequent performance in the school.

Summary of Secondary Socialization

During the years from 6–12, motivation has the same character or "nature" as it has had from the beginning in the sense that affectionate and accepting relations encourage exploration to proceed, and a realistic sample is required. But during this period those relationships are had with peers and teachers as well as parents.

It is obvious that each of these social agents has different types of power available for use. Parents may still use reward and punishment power (although it is probably getting more difficult to do so). By this time children should have strong and clear expectations about parental control. Peers may use social acceptance or rejection, a form of direct—reward/punishment—power, although more commonly peers use modeling and persuasion as the underpinnings of their influence.

The child should come out of this period, for better or worse, with a social identity, that is, with some sense of where he or she fits in the world of other people, and what to expect of them, and the self, in a variety of social situations. Things might just stay this way if it were not for the fact that puberty intrudes and changes the focus of curiosity one more time. This ushers in the final stage of socialization discussed in this chapter, the period of tertiary socialization.

TERTIARY SOCIALIZATION

The period of tertiary socialization, the years approximately from 12–18, begins with puberty and with the coming of adolescence. This stage is characterized by a final changing of the body to the adult form, and a concomitant set of social demands to begin assuming an adult role. The same socializing agents are available, the parents, the peers, the school, and television, although the influence of some increase and others decrease during this last period. Television is thought to be less of an influence, partly because during this period television watching declines steadily (only to increase as a more "adult" life is established). The amount of television watched during adolescence is less than at any other period of life, either earlier or later (Nielsen, 1985).

Other "agents of socialization" change their valence as well during the third period of socialization. Peers become more important, and perhaps parents and teachers a little less so, and all of this can be understood if we focus on intrinsic motivation and ask ourselves where the main focus of curiosity is directed next.

Intrinsic Motivation During Tertiary Socialization

During the final period of development the focus of intrinsic motivation turns inward to the self, in an attempt to establish an "individuated identity." By adolescence youngsters should have a firm grasp of knowledge about the physical world, and a fair understanding of society, of the social world. A "social identity" should be well on the way to being established. But now, as the child reaches puberty, new demands for "adult" behavior and decision making (such as the necessity of making plans for the future) force the youngster to search for a deeper knowledge and understanding of the self. During this stage, the child's attention and intrinsic interest turns to developing an "individuated," unique identity (Condry, 1978, 1981, 1985; Zimbardo, 1969). One way to contrast this stage with the last is to say that during the period of secondary socialization the child asked "Where do I fit in the world of other people? Where do I belong?" Whereas during the period of tertiary socialization, the child is now wondering, "How am I different from the other (similar) people in the world? How am I unique?"

Social Control During Tertiary Socialization

In attempting to establish an "individuated" identity, freedom from intrusive control is more important than ever, because the youngster now needs to separate the demands (and abilities) of the self from the demands and abilities of the social world *near at hand*. Peers, because they are less intrusive and provide important comparative information, continue to be popular; but parents and school authorities are seen, by many adolescents, as inimical to their strivings for self determination. Nowhere in development is the clash between intrinsic and extrinsic control more prominent than during adolescence.

If children are difficult to control during the period of secondary socialization, by all reports the difficulties increase during adolescence. Why is this the case? Partly it is due to the fact that direct power is less and less viable as a form of influence. It becomes harder and harder to reward and or threaten them with material things, leaving as techniques of control, "example" (which is based on attraction) and persuasion (which requires a shared understanding). But youngsters are less attracted to their parents during this period, partly because they are trying to separate themselves, conceptually, from these same people. To some adolescents, this often means doing the "opposite" of what they see the parents wanting and doing. Thus, the type of influence remaining to parents during this (tertiary) stage of development is persuasion. This form of influence is hard to use because it is based, to a large degree, on a shared understanding of the world and a shared value system (Kelman, 1961). It is, however, the longest lasting form of influence.

A parent of a teenager trying to stop his/her daughter from going out with the leader of a motorcycle gang has limited options. The girl can be "ordered" not to go, but the parent must be able to back up non-compliance with some threatened sanction (or compliance with reward) sufficiently strong to compel the behavior. Parents can also influence by "example," (they can say, "I would not have done that as a youngster, and so you should not"), but this form of influence is based on attraction, and, as noted, the child may be wanting to separate herself from the parental image, not to be like it. Persuasion is thus the only means left. But the parents may reject the gang leader for just the qualities the daughter finds attractive in him, and if so, it is more difficult to be persuasive.

School authorities have the same sorts of difficulties when attempting to control youngsters at this stage of development. The teenager's intrinsic interest in establishing an individuated identity makes youngsters of this age quite sensitive to most attempts at control. At the very least, it makes them ask of every request, "is this what *I* really want to do?"

Reform schools.   The fundamental conflict between the needs of the controller and the needs of the controllee, the struggle between control and freedom, is most starkly reflected in the behavior control exerted in so called "reform schools." These social institutions have much greater control over the behavior of their charges than in the public schools, and they allow considerably less freedom. Reform schools are like a surrogate family for children whose real families have failed, in one way or another, the task of socialization. Reform schools lean more heavily on control than on encouraging freedom and self-determination in development, even though their rhetoric calls for both (S. Condry, 1985). It is easier and safer to exert control over someone than to relax some controls and take the chance of encountering misbehavior. But this form of social constraint which is intrusive and salient, as we saw from Lepper's research, leads to less internalization of the very attitudes and behaviors that are desired. Reform schools are an issue for the period of tertiary socialization, because it is particularly during this period that the child must be accorded freedom, in order to establish an individuated identity.

Given all of this, how does one enhance intrinsic motivation during the tertiary stage of development? The same rules apply as before: be warm and accepting, use minimally intrusive methods of control such as persuasion, and continue to encourage exploration in a variety of different environments. One of the major challenges for socializing agents at every stage of development is to allow the amount of freedom and responsibility the child can reasonably be expected to handle, without putting the child in jeopardy. This problem is especially acute during adolescence, because the limits being pushed by the child during this stage are "adult" limits of behavior, particularly in terms of sexual behavior, and poorly thought-out actions can have life-long consequences.

THEMES AND CONCLUSIONS

The child begins life with a certain "personality," expressed mostly as potential, including quite powerful motivational structures related to curiosity. The child is also capable of being manipulated by the social world, initially with the use of fundamental motivational structures involving pleasure or pain, and later in more subtle, indirect ways. During the first 18 years of development, the child encounters various "social worlds," consisting of people with whom the child has some relationship. Broadly speaking, these are: first, the world of parents, then, the world of school, and finally, the world of peers.

In this chapter, my purpose has to been to describe this social-development process and to ask the value-laden question: if we are interested in "enhancing motivation," what is to be done? In particular, what can be done with social interactions to assure that curiosity and exploration, what I called "intrinsic motivation," is given a chance for its fullest expression, and that extrinsic motivation, social control, is used in such a way as not to undermine the important role of the self in the internalization of attitude and behavior patterns? What themes emerge from this description?

Freedom and Responsibility

The first theme is of the importance of progressively increasing freedom and responsibility. In part, this developmental sequence is a consequence of the child's acquisition of the tools of learning, of the ability to "extract information" from the world to which he or she is exposed. The child is not born with each of these "tools" in place, but rather acquires them slowly, through the course of interacting with a specific real environment. In part, the social world plays a role by providing a social atmosphere conducive to learning, and when using social control, by using techniques appropriate to the child's level of ability and by changing as the child does. To be able to do this, parents and school authorities must be "sensitive" to the children in their charge, and they must have a view of the child, a theory, which is correct. Inaccurate theories can lead to treatment which is not appropriate and which, in the long run, diminishes rather than enhances motivation. It is also true that the child is capable of much learning without the intervention of authorities. Both parents and school authorities need to be reminded that what children learn is a great deal more than they are "taught" by any outside force.

Moreover, as we have seen, teaching a child to "behave" in a specific manner is a difficult endeavor, it involves an understanding of the complex relationship between incentive magnitude and attitude/behavioral outcomes, and an intimate knowledge of the person to be taught. More powerful techniques and incentives are easier to use, and they appear to bring about quick results. But in the long run, the stronger incentives may produce less internalization. We saw how this fact produces a conflict between the person attempting control and the person at whom the control attempt is directed. The needs of the two are often diametrically opposed, especially as we look at social influence beyond the home. Thus, one key to the type of incentive used is the time perspective of the controller. People concerned about what happens to the child in the future are likely to use different techniques than those who have little stake in the child's future.

Enhancing motivation often involves a sacrifice on the part of one member of a social dyad, giving up some measure of control and responsibility in order to allow the other to acquire it. Parents make this sacrifice because they care about the child's future, and because they believe that it is one of the necessary aspects of the parenting role. But school authorities, and later authorities in the world of the workplace, may be more focused on the immediate demands of the situation rather than the long-term character development of the person under their control.

A Representative Environment

Over and above providing an "atmosphere" in which development may flourish, over and above providing freedom to explore, parents and other socializing agents enhance development by providing a sample of the environment which is true and representative. When social control techniques are used, in addition to using them at the appropriate level, it is important that the demands reflect the true correlational and causal structure of the world. Parents not only make demands on the child to behave, they are also part of the world the child is trying to understand. If the parental actions are consistent and coherent, the child learns one thing about social authorities, whereas inconsistent and incoherent actions must result in another view, on the part of the child, about what is to be expected of the world. Children learn both from and about parents, and the nature of the world they meet when first they arrive, the home, must set the style for the next round of expectations, from social authorities outside the home.

The Self and Intrinsic Motivation

Too much control by the social world can stifle curiosity. Why is this the case? Throughout this chapter I have suggested that the self was intimately involved with this process, both in terms of determining the focus of curiosity, and in terms of determining the outcome of social control attempts. To show how this is the case, we contrast two circumstances: one where the child is free to act and one where the social world makes a similar demand for the child to act.

Let us say I want my daughter to learn to jump the creek out in back of our house, so I take her out and ''order'' her to jump it. We want to contrast this circumstance with one where she takes herself out and tries the same thing. In the first case social control is being used to get the child to do something that, in the second case, the child does for reasons of her own. In this example, we have the same behavior—jumping the creek—either motivated intrinsically or extrinsically.

Now, let's say that the child fails to make the jump and lands in the creek, what does the child learn in each of these circumstances? In the first place, in both scenarios, the child learns that she cannot yet jump the creek. But in the instance where she went out on her own, she *also* learns something about herself. In order to decide whether or not she could do it, she had to search her own background before she made the jump, she had to ask herself if she could, and, then, she had to test this ''theory.'' Regardless of the outcome, in the freely chosen situation she learns more about *herself* than in the situation where the motive force came from outside herself, in this case from me.

We return, again, to Piaget's radical statement about teaching. For the self to grow it needs to be able to ''discover'' the world, freely, in the sense of not being too constrained or too directed by the social environment. We have already noted that one characteristic of the various social worlds to which the child is exposed is that they differ in how they treat children, exactly along these lines of control and freedom (Maccoby, 1980, p. 380).

What lies at the heart of these differences in treatment? One suggestion is that they come from ideas about children that parents and other socializing agents have organized into ''theories'' of childrearing, including theories about the nature of the child and the role of socializing agents in ''promoting'' development. Differential treatment seems to arise from these theories about both the means and the ends of childrearing. If the theories changed, then perhaps the treatment would as well. Where we get these ''theories,'' and how they change with time and experience is an important question.

Social Relationships

The final theme to be extracted from the study of social development and motivation is the centrality of a series of social relationships to our motivational well-being. At first these are had with parents, relatives, and siblings in the home, during the period of primary socialization. We have noted how these other people effect the child's ''motivation'' in a variety of ways, both directly by making demands on the child to adopt certain behaviors, and indirectly by what kind of social atmosphere they create, what kinds of exploration they permit and allow.

The family is a constant presence throughout all three stages of development, although its strongest influence is during the early years of primary socialization. The family gives the child the first ''taste'' of social control, and the family may also encourage or discourage exploration. The school has its strongest influence during the period of secondary socialization, and, as we saw, a particularly important issue is the correspondence between the authority structure of the home and the structure of the school. Peers are a powerful influence, especially during both the second and third stages of development outlined here. During the third stage (tertiary socialization) the role of peer expands to include sexual companions. Throughout development these social relationships can play a role of diminishing fear and anxiety, providing affectionate contact, and strengthening egos. They can also, of course, have the opposite effect. To the extent that motivation can be enhanced it can also be diminished, even though we have focused on the "enhancement" part in this chapter.

The view of motivation outlined here represents a departure from earlier theories in that it begins with a view of the child at birth as complex and well formed, with adequate initial motive to learn. This view of motivation sees the child as "active," in that it places trust in the child's intrinsic desire to learn about the world, and it is more cynical about the ease with which social influence is accomplished. As much as it is concerned with learning, the current view of motivation is also concerned with the nature of the world to which the child is exposed.

The one central element to this analysis has been the self. The self is at the heart of the notion of curiosity in the sense that what engages the attention of the self goes through systematic changes throughout childhood. The self was also critical to the role of social control. Not only does the self determine the outcome of a social control attempt, but when we try to "teach" children, we may undermine the role of the self in learning by discovery. If there is any single key to enhancing motivation, then, it involves enhancing the self, strengthening the self, and setting the self free to explore the world.

REFERENCES

Ainsworth, M. D. (1967). *Infancy in Uganda: Infant care and the growth of attachment.* Baltimore, MD: The John Hopkins Press.

Ainsworth, M. D., Bell, S., & Stayton, D. (1974). Infant-mother attachment and social development: Socialization as a product of reciprocal responsiveness to signals. In M. P. M. Richards (Ed.), *The integration of the child into a social world.* London: Cambridge University Press.

Ainsworth, M. D., & Bell, S. M. (1971). Some contemporary patterns of mother-infant interaction in the feeding situation. In A. Ambrose (Ed.), *The origins of human social relations.* London: Academic Press.

Bandura, A. (1977a). *Social learning theory.* Englewood Cliffs, N.J.: Prentice-Hall.

Bandura, A. (1977b). Self-efficacy: Toward a unifying theory of behavioral change. *Psychological Review, 84,* 191–215.

Bandura, A., & Cervone, D. (1983). Self-evaluative and self-efficacy mechanisms governing the motivational effects of goal systems. *Journal of Personality and Social Psychology, 45,* 1017–1028.

Bandura, A., & Schunk, D. H. (1981). Cultivating competence, self-efficacy, and intrinsic interest through proximal self-instruction. *Journal of Personality and Social Psychology, 41,* 586–598.

Baumrind, D. (1966). Effect of authoritative control and child behavior. *Child Development, 37*(4), 887–907.

Baumrind, D. (1967). Child care practices anteceding three patterns of preschool behavior. *Genetic Psychology Monographs, 75,* 43–48.

Baumrind, D. (1970). Socialization and instrumental competence in young children. *Young Children, 26,* 104–119.

Baumrind, D., & Black, A. E. (1967). Socialization practices associated with dimensions of competence in preschool boys and girls. *Child Development, 88,* 291–327.

Berlyne, D. E. (1966). Curiosity and exploration. *Science, 153,* 25–33.

Berlyne, D. E. (1960). *Conflict, arousal, and curiosity.* New York: McGraw-Hill.

Bowlby, J. (1969). *Attachment.* New York: Basic Books.

Brown, I., Jr., & Inouye, D. K. (1978). Learned helplessness through modeling: The role of perceived similarity in competence. *Journal of Personality and Social Psychology, 36,* 900–908.

Bruner, J. S. (1974a). Nature and uses of immaturity. In K. Connally & J. S. Bruner (Eds.), *The growth of competence.* New York: Academic Press.

Bruner, J. S. (1974b). The organization of early skilled action. In M. P. M. Richards (Ed.), *The integration of the child into a social world.* London: Cambridge University Press.

Condry, J. (1977). Enemies of exploration: Self-initiated versus other-initiated learning. *Journal of Personality and Social Psychology, 35*(7), 459–477.

Condry, J. (1981). Experimental approaches to intrinsic motivation: Implications for the use of social control. Paper presented at the American Psychological Association.

Condry, J. C. (1978). The role of incentives in socialization. In M. R. Lepper & D. Greene (Eds.), *The hidden costs of reward.* Hillsdale, N.J.: Lawrence Erlbaum Associates.

Condry, J. C. (1984). Gender identity and social competence. *Sex Roles, 11*(5/6), 485–511.

Condry, J., & Chambers, J. (1978). Intrinsic motivation and the process of learning. In M. R. Lepper and D. Greene (Eds.), *The hidden costs of reward.* Hillsdale, N.J.: Lawrence Erlbaum Associates.

Condry, J. C. & Siman, M. (1974). Characteristics of peer and adult oriented children. *Journal of Marriage and the Family, 36,* 543–554.

Condry, S. (1985). Therapy implementation problems in a residence for delinquents. Paper presented at the annual meeting of the Eastern Psychological Association, Boston, Mass.

Csikszentmihalyi, M. (1975). *Beyond boredom and anxiety.* San Francisco: Jossey-Bass.

Csikszentmihalyi, M. (1978). Intrinsic rewards and emergent motivation. In M. R. Lepper & D. Greene (Eds.), *The hidden costs of reward.* Hillsdale, N.J.: Lawrence Erlbaum Associates.

de Charms, R. (1968). *Personal causation.* New York: Academic Press.

Deci, E. L. (1981). *The psychology of self-determination.* Lexington, Mass: Heath.

Deci, E. L. (1971). Effects of externally mediated rewards on intrinsic motivation. *Journal of Personality and Social Psychology, 18,* 105–115.

Deci, E. L. (1972). The effects of contingent and non-contingent rewards and controls on intrinsic motivation. *Organizational Behavior and Human Performance, 8,* 217–229(a).

Deci, E. L. (1972). Intrinsic motivation, extrinsic reinforcement, and inequity. *Journal of Personality and Social Psychology, 22,* 113–120(b).

Deci, E. L. (1975). *Intrinsic motivation.* New York: Plenum Press.

Deci, E. L., & Ryan, R. M. (1985). *Intrinsic motivation and self-determination in human behavior.* New York: Plenum.

Deci, E. L., Speigel, N. H., Ryan, R. M., Koestner, R., & Kauffman, M. (1982). Effects of performance standards on teaching styles: Behavior of controlling teachers. *Journal of Educational Psychology, 74,* 852–859.

Dweck, C. S. (1975). The role of expectations and attributions in the alleviation of learned helplessness. *Journal of Personality and Social Psychology, 31,* 674–685.

Dweck, C. S., & Elliot, E. S. (1983). Achievement motivation. In E. M. Hetherington (Ed.), *Handbook of Child Psychology* (Vol. 4). New York: Wiley.

Dweck, C. S. & Goetz, J. E. (1978). Attributions and learned helplessness. In J. Harvey, W. Ickes, & R. Kidd (Eds.), *New directions in attribution research* (Vol. 2). Hillsdale, N.J.: Lawrence Erlbaum Associates.

Goodenough, F. L. (1931). *Anger in young children*. Minneapolis: University of Minnesota Press.

Greene, D., & Lepper, M. R. (1974). Effects of extrinsic rewards on children's subsequent intrinsic interest. *Child Development, 45*, 1141–1145.

Gibson, E. J. (1969). *Principles of perceptual learning and development*. New York: Appleton-Century-Crofts.

Gibson, J. J. (1979). *An ecological approach to visual perception*. Boston: Houghton Mifflin.

Hall, C. S. (1954). *A primer of Freudian psychology*. Cleveland: World Publishing Co.

Hall, E. (1970). A conversation with Jean Piaget and Barbel Inhelder. *Psychology Today, 3*, (May), 25–32, 54–56.

Harter, S. (1978). Effectance motivation reconsidered: Toward a developmental model. *Human Development, 1*, 34–64.

Harter, S. (1981a). A new self-report scale of intrinsic versus extrinsic orientation in the classroom: Motivational components. *Developmental Psychology, 3*, 300–312.

Harter, S. (1981, b) A model of mastery motivation in children: Individual differences and developmental change. In W. A. Collins (Ed.) *Minnesota Symposium on Child Psychology* (Vol. 14) Hillsdale, N.J.: Erlbaum.

Harter, S. (1982a). The perceived competence scale for children. *Child Development, 53*, 87–97.

Harlow, H. (1953). Mice, monkeys, men, and motives. *Psychological Review, 60*, 23–32.

Hunt, J. McV. (1965). Intrinsic motivation and its role in psychological development. In D. Levine (Ed.), *Nebraska symposium on motivation* (Vol. 13). Lincoln: University of Nebraska.

Kagan, J. (1972). Motives and development. *Journal of Personality and Social Psychology, 22*, 51–66.

Kelley, H. H. (1971). Attribution in social interaction. In E. Jones et al. (Eds.), *Attribution: Perceiving the causes of behavior*. New York: General Learning Process.

Kelley, H. H. (1973). The process of causal attribution. *American Psychologist, 28*, 107–128.

Kelley, H. H., & Thibaut, J. (1985). *Social Relationships*. New York: Wiley.

Kelman, H. C. (1961). Process of attitude change. *Public Opinion Quarterly, 25*, 57–78.

Lepper, M. R. (1983). Extrinsic reward and intrinsic motivation. Implications for the classroom. In J. M. Levine & M. C. Wang (Eds.), *Teacher and student perceptions: Implications for learning*. Hillsdale, N.J.: Erlbaum.

Lepper, M. R. (1981). Intrinsic and extrinsic motivation in children: Detrimental effects of superfluous controls. In W. A. Collins (Ed.), *Minnesota symposium on child psychology* (Vol. 14). Hillsdale, N.J.: Erlbaum.

Lepper, M. R., & Greene, D. (Eds.) (1978a). *The hidden costs of reward*. Hillsdale, N.J.: Erlbaum.

Lepper, M. R., & Greene, D. (1978b). Overjustification and beyond: Toward a means-end analysis of intrinsic and extrinsic motivation. In M. R. Lepper & D. Greene (Eds.), *The hidden costs of reward*. Hillsdale, N.J.: Erlbaum.

Lepper, M. R., Greene, D., & Nisbett, R. E. (1973). Undermining children intrinsic interest with extrinsic rewards: A test of the overjustification hypothesis. *Journal of Personality and Social Psychology, 28*, 129–137.

Lewin, K., Lippitt, R., & White, R. K. (1939). Patterns of aggressive behavior in experimentally created "social climates." *Journal of Social Psychology, X*, 271–299.

Maccoby, E. E. (1980). *Social development: Psychological growth and the parent-child relationship*. New York: Harcourt Brace Jovanovich, Inc.

Maccoby, E. E., & Jacklin, C. N. (1974). *The psychology of sex differences*. Stanford, CA: Stanford University Press.

Matas, L., Arend, R. A., & Sroufe, L. A. (1978). Continuity of adaptation in the second year: The relationship between quality of attachment and later competence. *Child Development, 49*, 547–556.

Meltzoff, A. D., & Moore, M. K. (1977). Imitation of facial and manual gestures by human neonates. *Science, 198,* 75–78.

Perry, D. G., & Bussey, K. (1979). The social learning theory of sex differences: Imitation is alive and well. *Journal of Personality and Social Psychology, 37,* 1699–1712.

Rosenthal, T. L., & Zimmerman, B. J. (1978). *Social learning and cognition.* New York: Academic Press.

Neisser, U. (1976). *Cognition and reality.* San Francisco: Freeman.

Nielsen, A. C. (1985). *Nielsen report on television usage.* Northbrook, IL: Nielsen Inc.

Patterson, G. R. (1984). Performance models for antisocial boys. *American Psychologist, 41, 4,* 432–444.

Rosch, E. H. (1974). Universals and cultured specifics in human categorization. In R. Breslin, W. Lonner, & S. Bochner (Eds.), *Cross-cultural perspectives on learning.* London: Sage Press.

Rosch, E. H. (1975). Cognitive representations of semantic categories. *Journal of Experimental Psychology: General, 104,* 192–233.

Ross, M. (1975). Salience of reward and intrinsic motivation. *Journal of Personality and Social Psychology, 32,* 245–254.

Sears, R. R., Maccoby, E., & Levin, H. (1975). *Patterns of child rearing.* New York: Harper.

Seligman, M. E. P. (1975). *Helplessness.* San Francisco: Freeman.

Skeels, H. M. (1966). Adult status of children with contrasting early life experiences. *Monograph for Social Research in Child Development, 31,* 3.

Spitz, R. A. (1962). Hospitalism: An inquiry into the genesis of psychiatric conditions in early childhood. In R. S. Eissler (Ed.), *The psychoanalytic study of the child* (3rd ed., Vol. 1). New York: International University Press.

Sroufe, L. A., & Waters, E. (1977). Attachment as an organization construct. *Child Development, 48,* 1184–1199.

Thibaut, J. W., & Kelley, H. H. (1959). *The social psychology of groups.* New York: Wiley.

Tudge, J. (1986). Collaborative problem solving in the U.S. and the U.S.S.R.: The effects of peer social interaction on cognitive development. Unpublished Ph.D. Dissertation, Cornell University.

Waters, E., Wippman, J., & Sroufe, L. A. (1979). Attachment, positive affect and competence in the peer-group: Two studies in construct validation. *Child Development, 50,* 821–829.

Watson, J. S. (1977). Perception of contingency as a determinant of social responsiveness. In E. B. Thomas (Ed.), *The origin of the infant's social responsiveness.* Hillsdale, N.J.: Lawrence Erlbaum Associates.

Watson, J. S. (1972). Smiling, cooing, and "the game." *Merrill-Palmer Quarterly, 18,* 323–339.

Watson, J. S. (1971). Memory and "contingency analysis" in infant learning. *Merrill-Palmer Quarterly, 17,* 139–1, 55–76.

Watson, J. S., & Ramey, C. (1972). Reactions to response-contingent stimulation in early infancy. *Merrill-Palmer Quarterly, 18,* 219–227.

White, R. W. (1959). Motivation reconsidered: The concept of competence. *Psychological Review, 66,* 297–333.

Zimbardo, P. G. (Ed.) (1969). *Cognitive control of motivation.* Glenview, IL: Scott, Foresman.

FEMALE MOTIVATION AND ACHIEVEMENT:
IMPLICATIONS FOR INTERVENTIONS

Helen S. Farmer

Gender differences in achievement motivation and related constructs have been documented repeatedly over the past 30 years (Farmer, 1976; Komarovsky, 1946; Steinkamp & Maehr, 1983). The evidence for gender differences in achievement motivation is fragmentary and often contradictory. Alper (1974) echoed this conclusion when she entitled her article on gender differences in achievement motivation "Now you see it now you don't." For example, in the 1970s there were research findings with negative implications for female achievement in the attribution literature (Dweck, Davidson, Nelson, & Enna 1978; Nicholls, 1980) indicating that females were less intrinsically motivated and that their approach to achievement situations was characterized by learned helplessness. Then Frieze, Hanusa, and McHugh (1982) published a review in which they concluded that gender differences in success/failure attributions were relatively negligible. Other research has focused on gender differences in "need

Advances in Motivation and Achievement: Enhancing Motivation,
Volume 5, pages 51-97.
Copyright © 1987 by JAI Press Inc.
All rights of reproduction in any form reserved.
ISBN: 0-89232-621-2

for achievement'' and ''fear of success'' (Horner, 1978). Here too the findings are inconclusive, and Tresmer's (1976) review dampened enthusiasm for this line of research.

From a somewhat different but related body of research, one which investigates the career development and decision-making process, there is evidence that gender differences in achievement can be traced in part to the narrower range of occupational fields considered by women, compared to men (Farmer & Backer, 1977; Gottfredson, 1981). Social role expectations in our society differ for men and women in important ways affecting their valuing of work and family roles. Some occupations are seen as more suitable for men, others for women, and still others are gender neutral. Some researchers and practitioners interested in enhancing the achievement of women (Hackett & Betz, 1981) have focused on identifying ways to increase the likelihood that women will choose occupations nontraditional for their gender, those that pay better and are higher in status (i.e., lawyer, doctor, engineer, scientist).

Career development theorists such as Donald Super (1980) view the career development and choice process as one in which an individual becomes increasingly aware of his/her values, interests, abilities, and aptitudes and of the training and employment opportunities in the society at large. Enhancing career choices for both genders, in this view, involves facilitating awareness of these factors through experiences which increase the likelihood an individual will choose an occupation based on this knowledge rather than on social role expectations. Some women will choose traditional work roles given this knowledge and experience and some will choose nontraditional roles. Super's theory stresses the importance of both reducing the sex role stereotyping of occupational and homemaking roles through provision of relevant experiences and information, and teaching decision-making skills to enhance informed choices.

Research on achievement motivation and career development and choice can benefit from some form of cross-fertilization. A model introduced in 1976 (Farmer) presents sets of *personal* (self-concepts) and *environment* influences (family, community, the economy, etc.) impacting both career and achievement motivation. This model, extended to include a set of *background* factors (Farmer, 1985), is reproduced in Figure 1.

Figure 1 presents a model that is multidimensional and assumes that a broad range of interacting factors in the environment and in the self, over time, influence the strength of the various achievement and career motivation dimensions. As noted in the Farmer (1985) article, the model is based on social learning theory (Bandura, 1978), which, since it was introduced (Kantor, 1924; Koffka, 1935; Lewin, 1935; Murray, 1938; Rotter, 1954) has evolved into a reciprocal influence theory of self and environment.

Explanations of human behavior have generally favored undirectional causal models emphasizing either environmental or internal determinants of behavior. In social learning theory,

GENDER DIFFERENCES IN CHILDHOOD MOTIVATION AND ACHIEVEMENT

Based on the theoretical perspective represented in the model (Farmer, 1976, 1985) childhood (i.e., birth to adolescence) experiences in the family, school, and community are viewed as important and significant influences on career and achievement motivation as these are experienced in later adulthood. As noted earlier, this theoretical model does not view early experiences as determining, that is, establishing the strength and direction of motivation for the rest of a person's life. Instead the theoretical model assumes a dynamic view of development in which both the *past* and the *present* are viewed as powerful influences on motivation and related behavior.

The research evidence for gender differences in children entering school is well summarized by Greenberg (1985). She reported that boys and girls enter kindergarten with different abilities, experiences, and achievements: girls' opportunities for verbal experiences exceeds that of boys'; boys' opportunities for spatial experiences exceeds that of girls'; girls' opportunities for small muscle experiences exceeds that of boys'; boys' opportunities for large muscle experiences exceeds that of girls'; girls' opportunities with repetitive experiences exceeds that of boys'; boys' opportunities for inventive experiences exceeds that of girls'; girls' opportunities for nurturing experiences exceeds that of boys'; boys' opportunities for managing experiences exceed that of girls'; girls' opportunities for one-to-one (intimate) relationships exceed that of boys'; boys' opportunities for group relationships exceed that of girls'; girls' opportunities for role rehearsal experiences exceed that of boys'; boys' opportunities for experiment with a wide range of future career and life options exceed that of girls'; girls' opportunities to learn from adult models exceed that of boys'; boys' opportunities to learn from direct instruction exceed that of girls'; girls exceed boys in gaining early impulse control; and boys exceed girls in experiences that confirm their self-worth and value. The fact that these gender differences exist when children enter kindergarten suggests that family socialization practices continue to differ for boys and girls in ways that effect their achievement motivation.

This section will attempt to identify the most important early childhood influences affecting motivation, especially gender differences in motivation. Three outcomes are highlighted: first, gender stereotyping of occupational and homemaking roles; second, the differential development of important aspects of the self concept; and third, the differential development of achievement related skills. Following the description of these gender differences, some programs are described which are intended to counter the negative effects of gender differentiated experiences in early childhood.

Early Family Influences on Motivation and Achievement

The early family environment plays a critical role in establishing achievement related self-concepts and behaviors. In this regard, the research of Crandall and Battle (1970) is relevant. Crandall and Battle, of the Fels Research Institute in Ohio, have conducted a longitudinal study of 38 men and 27 women from birth to age 26. The focus of their study was on the childhood determinants of adult achievement behavior. They were also interested in gender differences. The socioeconomic status of Crandall and Battle's subjects ranged from lower middle to upper middle class, based on Hollingshead's (1957) classification system, and did not include the lower class group. Some childrearing antecedents were compared for achieving men and women with less achieving men and women. Mothers of the higher achieving adults were observed to make deliberate efforts to train them in cognitive, motor, language, social, and personal skills during the years three through ten. In the earlier years (i.e., 0–3) these children were observed to choose difficult rather than easy achievement tasks. During the years 3–6 they were observed to provide help to siblings and peers. In the years 6–10 they were more likely to persist on achievement-related tasks.

Some additional information was obtained for the higher achieving adult women. More of these subjects had mothers who were from the lower as compared to the upper middle class and who placed a high value on academic achievement for their daughters. These achieving women were observed to exhibit more achievement-related behaviors during their pre-school and elementary school years. They asked for more help on achievement tasks during the years 3–6, they played more with opposite sex toys during the years 6–10, and by adolescence, they were more internal in their attributions for success. The Crandall and Battle findings are useful because they provide longitudinal data on childhood correlates for gender differences in adult achievement. However, because these data were collected on men and women growing up prior to the 1970s and 1980s, prior to sex equity legislation, findings should be viewed cautiously. For example, the finding with respect to achieving women and lower middle-class mothers may no longer pertain. It may be the case today that upper middle-class mothers support achievement in their daughters as much as the lower socioeconomic class mothers. However, we can place more confidence in Crandall and Battle's findings shared by both achieving men and women. It appears that from the earliest age these men and women were encouraged to achieve by their parents and that both positive values and expectations were engendered in them at home for achievement.

Relating the Crandall and Battle findings to Bandura's (1977, 1982) self-efficacy change model, it is possible to identify three of the four change agents depicted in Figure 2 operative in the childhood environments of achieving adults: vicarious experience (i.e., parents model achievement behaviors); verbal persuasion (i.e., parents encourage achievement behaviors in their children); and performance accomplishments (i.e., parents provide skill training in achievement-related skills).

Hoffman (1986) has summarized research on the effect of the working mother on sons and daughters. In particular, there appears to be an increase in independence for daughters of working mothers. Employed mothers' children are more likely to have responsibilities (i.e., performance accomplishments) related to the home and this has been found to relate positively to self-esteem and ego development in children of both genders. Also, employed mothers tend to have a greater role in family decision making and thus appear as more competent and effective to their daughters and sons (i.e., vicarious experience). More daughters of working mothers name their mothers as adult role models, compared to daughters of nonworking mothers. One conclusion might be that enhancing independence and self-esteem for girls is a by-product of having a mother employed outside the home. Future research might well find a link with enhanced self-efficacy feelings for these children as well.

Relating the Crandall and Battle findings to the Farmer (1985) model (Figure 1) it appears that environment factors (i.e., parent behaviors) influenced personal factors in the child's growing self-concept and their achievement behavior in important ways. For example, achieving adults were found to have, as children, internal attributions for success, they were independent, persisted at achievement tasks, and chose tasks that were challenging rather than ones that were not. The interaction of the personal and environment influences on achievement motivation and behavior can only be inferred from the evidence presented by Crandall and Battle and by Hoffman, but it seems a reasonable inference.

Occupational and Homemaking Stereotypes

Research reviewed by Gottfredson (1981) indicates that sex role occupational and homemaking stereotypes are learned early in life and have become quite stable by age seven. Occupational stereotypes affect achievement motivation in important ways. In particular, stereotypes limit the number and type of occupations considered appropriate for either gender. Pre-school children tend to view occupations as adult roles and they rarely identify with them. However, by age six children are strongly aware of the gender appropriateness of role behaviors (i.e., who cooks and who uses a saw). It is not uncommon for children of this age, raised in homes where both parents work as professionals, to say, "Girls don't become doctors," or "Boys can't be nurses." Between the ages nine and twelve, preadolescence, children become highly sensitive to evaluation by their peers and somewhat later to social group expectations and values. During this period, occupational stereotypes are less fixed than they will be later during adolescence. Developmentally, this period (i.e., age 9–12) is one in which attitudes and values are held more tentatively. The opportunity to effect change through educational interventions that take advantage of the importance of peer group pressure during this age period should be evident.

Reducing Stereotypes

Several hundred programs (American Institute for Research, 1978) have been developed nationally that are aimed at reducing occupational and homemaking stereotypes. The goals for these programs are broad. They are designed to change stereotyped attitudes, values, and behaviors. Consistent with Title IX of the Education Amendments (1972), several schools have encouraged or required boys to take home economics and girls to take industrial arts courses. Wirtenberg (1979), for example, found that seventh grade boys and girls who took coeducational home economics and industrial arts courses emerged from these experiences more tolerant of opposite sex involvement in nontraditional role behaviors. The program had, in fact, changed social norm expectations for participants. However, when asked if they as individuals would choose occupations nontraditional for their gender, the changes observed were much less dramatic. Personal interests had not changed as a result of experience with nontraditional activities (i.e., cooking and sewing for boys; industrial arts for girls). This distinction between changing social norms and changing personal values was noted recently by Johnson and Ettema (1982). A program may effectively change a child's attitude about role behaviors appropriate for men and women but have little impact on their personal behavior. Wirtenberg tried to explain her disappointing findings and concluded that while there are real equity benefits from coeducational home economics and industrial arts courses, these benefits are not sufficient to effect changes in students' occupational choices. The classroom environment, Wirtenberg found, was not uniformly supportive of the integration of boys and girls in these classes. She concluded that teachers need training to teach them how to nurture nascent student interest in nontraditional roles and behaviors.

A program worth mentioning with respect to reducing occupational and homemaking stereotypes is Project Freestyle (Johnson & Ettema, 1982). Materials for this project consist of thirteen half-hour TV video-tapes, each containing two fifteen-minute presentations portraying multiracial groups of teenagers and their families engaging in nonstereotypic activities both at work and at home. Intended for use with children in grades three through six, participating students learn about the changing roles of both women and men at home and work. Each program is accompanied by a teacher's guide, a student comic book/activity book, and a parent diary. This program, originating in Los Angeles but pilot tested nationally (Johnson & Ettema, 1982), was successful in changing attitudes about socially acceptable behaviors for men and women. Girls' attitudes toward boys' behaving in nurturing, helping roles in the family, and engaging in occupations that are traditionally feminine (i.e., nurse, elementary school teacher) became significantly ($p < .05$) more positive. Boys' attitudes toward girls' participation in athletics, in occupations that are traditionally masculine (i.e., engineer, draftsperson), leadership roles, and acting independently also became significantly more positive. In addition, significant positive gains were obtained for girls and boys for their attitudes towards nontraditional role behaviors for their own gender. Freestyle Project evaluators also measured change related to personal interest in behaving in nontraditional ways in the home and in nontraditional occupations at work. More gains were observed for girls than for boys in this regard. Girls obtained significant gains in terms of their interest in choosing occupations requiring mechanical and scientific abilities. Boys obtained similar gains in interest in the helping or service occupations. It is important to point out that this program addressed changing attitudes and behaviors in both work and home roles. Some programs, focusing on one or another of these roles, while ignoring the other, have been less successful in changing stereotyped attitudes and behaviors.

The Freestyle Project may have been more effective than Wirtenberg's intervention because it used both vicarious experience (i.e., role models) and verbal persuasion; a holistic approach, involving teachers and parents, as well as students, as role models. Also, the TV tapes were followed by discussion and an opportunity to try out new behaviors both in the classroom and at home. The age range of the students who participated in Freestyle (i.e., grades 3–6) encompassed students in the pre-adolescent period which, as was noted earlier, is one when attitudes and values are more fluid than in the earlier years. Wirtenberg's students were slightly older and in seventh grade. The evidence for effectiveness of such efforts to reduce stereotypes at earlier ages is not readily available. It may well turn out that pre-school programs are most effective compared to other school related efforts.

Enhancing Skills, Motivation, and Achievement

The influence of parents on achieving behaviors has been found to be mediated through the child's growing self-concept, especially his or her self-concept related to competencies that affect achievement. Bandura's (1977, 1982) research on self-efficacy is relevant here. Gender differences have been found for self-efficacy favoring the male gender, especially self-efficacy related to abilities such as math and science (Hackett & Betz, 1981). These self-efficacy gender differences have been observed in students in high school and college, but less so in grades K–8. However, the foundation for this gender difference is established during the earlier years based on learned values and expectations in the home and school. In self-efficacy theory (Bandura, 1982) an important source of enhancement is mediated through proximal goal setting and self-evaluative reactions. Bandura and Schunk (1981) conducted a study with children who exhibited gross skill deficits and disinterest in math. Through experimental manipulations they were able to enhance both math self-efficacy and math interest for some of these children, those who were provided a self-directed learning situation with unambiguous proximal goals for math achievement. No gains were obtained for children given no math goals, or for those given distal goals for math achievement. The findings from this study illustrate the importance for individuals to understand clearly what kind of behavior is required of them and the nature of the circumstances in which they are required to perform that behavior.

In an interesting study with fourth grade students, Peterson and Fennema (1985) found gender differences in the off-task behaviors of boys and girls in math class which affected their math achievement. Engagement in social activities during math class, either social conversation with the teacher or other students, had a negative effect on math achievement for girls, but not for boys. Other types of off-task behavior had negative effects on boys' math achievement. The off-task behaviors of girls were more acceptable to teachers whereas off-task behaviors of boys were criticized by teachers. Another interesting finding in the Peterson and Fennema study was a gender comparison for the effect of competitive and cooperative math activities. These authors found that competitive math tasks enhanced math achievement for boys but not for girls. The opposite was found for cooperative math exercises in which two or more students worked together to solve math problems. Cooperative exercises benefitted girls but not boys.

Gender differences for internal success attributions found in previous research (Dweck et al., 1978; Nicholls, 1980) favoring the male gender appear to be on the wane on average (Frieze et al., 1982) but some less advantaged subgroups continue to exhibit this gender difference (Anderson, 1983). Anderson's study was with Cherokee Indian children and he found significant gender differences for ability attributions favoring boys. The significance of this gender difference for enhancing achievement motivation lies in the important mediating role internal attributions for success play in future achievement expectations and behaviors. Children who believe they have succeeded because they had the required skill or ability are more likely to tackle similar achievement tasks in the future. Bandura (1982) views internal success attributions as ''performance attainments'' which in turn effect change in self-efficacy cognitions.

Gottfredson's (1981) review of research on career aspiration makes a strong case for the view that students, as early as age nine, set bounds on their occupational aspiration level based on their perception of their abilities. Gottfredson indicated that by grade eight occupational aspiration level is fairly well set. If she is right, it is more difficult to intervene effectively in high school to try and increase student aspiration. Gottfredson's review leads one to encourage both parents and educators to provide support for a positive self-concept with respect to achievement for their children and students from the earliest years.

A third influence on achievement and career motivation is the skill training children are exposed to. In particular, analytical skill, typically found to be higher in boys than girls (Schau, 1985), is related to the decision-making skills used in making realistic and optimizing career choices (Osipow, 1983) and in math achievement. Although career decisions are typically made in high school or later, children in elementary school are faced with challenging problem-solving tasks, and as noted in the Crandall and Battle (1970) study, achieving adults of both genders are ones who choose challenging achievement tasks as children. Analytical skill is important from a very early age for success on most problem-solving tasks. This skill can be taught by parents and teachers. If girls could be provided with such training from childhood, gender difference in analytical skill might well be reduced.

Equity Legislation, Motivation, and Achievement

At least three federal policies have impacted sex equity at the elementary school level (Farmer & Sidney, 1985). One of these, the Career Incentive Education Act (1977) which became part of the Education Consolidation and Improvement Act (1981) has provided funding for the introduction of equity programs into elementary schools. These programs are aimed at enhancing the career motivation of girls and at eliminating sex bias in career education programs. A second federal policy for enhancing equity is the Women's Educational Equity Act (WEEA) of 1974. Under this Act, federal funds have been made available to develop curriculum products for use in the schools. WEEA prepares catalogs annually (Women's Educational Equity Act Publishing Center, 1982) listing the various field tested products available. The third federal policy impacting sex equity related to achievement is Title IX of the Education Amendments (1972). Title IX provides some funding support for training teachers in sex equity approaches in the classroom and mandates equal access to all courses for both genders.

The impact of these federal policies in the schools is limited by the fact that funding for career education has largely dried up, use of WEEA curriculum materials is entirely voluntary, and Title IX requirements rarely impact the elementary school level. Continued funding for WEEA was voted by Congress in late 1984. This source of equity support needs wider publicity to have school systems take advantage of the WEEA materials. More government sanctions behind Title IX guidelines are also needed for these to have impact on the achieving behaviors of girls and of boys.

Summary for Childhood

High achievement men and women were found by Crandall and Battle to have had mothers who encouraged their achievement behaviors in early childhood, and who taught them specific achievement-related skills. In childhood, these achieving adults were observed to choose challenging achievement tasks rather than easy tasks and to persist at these tasks until they were mastered. It appears that when girls are given this kind of early childhood experience they are as likely as boys to become achieving adults. Self-efficacy theory provided a basis for interpreting these findings indicating that vicarious experiences, verbal persuasion, and performance accomplishments played a positive role in enhancing motivation and achievement. The Farmer model also provided a basis for high-lighting the role of environment, contextual determinants of motivation, and achievement.

A positive self-concept with respect to achievement in childhood was found to affect the occupational level chosen by adults (Gottfredson, 1981). The importance of analytical skill for achievement was noted, and gender differences in this skill traced to the differential training of boys and girls. Research reporting programs for enhancing math self-efficacy and math skills were discussed. The positive role of proximal goal setting and self-evaluation was noted. Occupational and homemaking stereotypes, learned at home, at school, and in the community, limit the type and level of occupations boys and girls consider. As a result women are limited to a narrower range of occupations that, on average, pay less and have lower status than those for men. Some educational programs were described that were effective in reducing these stereotypes. It was noted that the more successful programs target changing attitudes and behaviors related to both occupational and homemaking roles. These change programs were found to be consistent with self-efficacy theory and with the Farmer (1985) model. Equity legislation in the 1970s has provided support for educational programs aimed at reducing occupational and homemaking stereotyped behaviors and attitudes, and at enhancing the necessary achievement related self-concepts and skills.

GENDER DIFFERENCES IN ADOLESCENT ACHIEVEMENT AND RELATED MOTIVATION

Research has shown that certain gender differences tend to appear during adolescence that have not been evident at earlier ages (Maccoby & Jacklin, 1974). Such differences include scores on math and science aptitude and achievement tests, especially among more able students (Benbow & Stanley, 1982); and self-concepts such as self-efficacy in relation to math and science. These gender differences tend to lower the achievement aspiration level of young women compared to young men. Surprisingly, however, gender differences in achievement aspiration level do not show up in studies of high school students. On average, young men and women in this age range have similar aspiration levels (Tittle, 1981; Farmer, 1983, 1985; Card, Steel, & Abeles, 1980). The gender gap in achievement level becomes evident a few years later when these young men and women enter the labor market or are dispersed in higher education or homemaking roles (Card, Steel, & Abeles, 1980). Career commitment motivation is also relatively similar for young men and women in high school. In fact, young women score somewhat higher (Farmer, 1985). However, Rooney (1983) found that career commitment scores were significantly lower for young women three years after high school graduation, whereas these scores had not dropped for young men. Programs of intervention during the high school years should take these factors into account.

Other important gender differences seen in high school young people include the stronger influence of competing role priorities for young women compared to young men (Farmer, 1985) and the stronger influence of parent support needed for high career commitment in young women compared to young men (Amiri, 1978; Farmer, 1985). During a period in our history when society as a whole is not strongly supportive of equity in the workplace for women, family role priorities have a dampening effect on women's achievement motivation. Also, the dual pull of home and work roles for women presents greater challenges for decision making related to career choice for women. This need for help with choices, once recognized by school systems, can be an opportunity for educators to enhance the decision-making skills and the choices young men and women make today. Through role models, skill training, decision-making exercises, discussion, and information, some of the dampening effects of the dual pulls of home and work roles may be lessened.

Findings Related to the Theoretical Model

The Farmer (1976, 1985) model has been tested with adolescents by Farmer (1980, 1983, 1985) and Naftchi-Ardabelli (1983). Findings for the relative strength of the influence of the three sets of variables (i.e., background, environment, and personal) on motivation varies depending on the motivation dimension studied. Recall (Figure 1) that three motivation dimensions are included in the model: aspiration, mastery, and career. Findings are reported here for each of the motivation dimensions separately.

Aspiration

Data collected by Farmer and Fyans in 1976 and reported by Farmer in 1980 for 158 high school tenth grade women indicated that aspiration was higher (p <.01) for young women who perceived their environment as supportive of women working (refer to Figure 1 to relate findings from this study to the model depicted there). Another significant predictor of aspiration level in this early study was mastery motivation (p < .01). Findings from this study are important because the support for women working measure, found significant here, was also found to be a significant predictor in later studies (Farmer, 1985). The Farmer model assumes the impact of the present environment (i.e., the opportunity structure) on the motivation of individuals as a key influence, especially for those who may be disadvantaged with respect to work and achievement.

Naftchi-Ardebili (1983) investigated the correlates of aspiration motivation using measures from the Farmer model for tenth, eleventh, and twelfth grade students in an Illinois high school (n = 86 males; 99 females). She found that aspiration motivation was significantly influenced by the environment variables parent support and teacher support. She did not assess support for women working. Naftchi-Ardebili's sample was small, and she did not find significant relationships for background or personal measures with aspiration motivation. One interesting gender difference was observed. Young women felt significantly less encouraged by parents and teachers for their achievement in math and science compared to young men. This gender effect was strongest for the older students in the eleventh and twelfth grades.

Farmer (1983) reported similar levels of aspiration for ninth and twelfth grade young men and women (n = 1234). As noted earlier, other studies have also found no difference in aspiration level by gender for students in high school (Card, Steel, & Abeles, 1980; Tittle, 1981). The fact that after high school the gap between educational and career achievement and aspiration is greater for women than for men is probably due to mediating factors such as marriage, children, and moving when a spouse's job requires it. Rooney's (1983) finding that career commitment had dropped significantly for young women three years after high school graduation lends further support to this view. The Farmer (1983) study did not investigate the relation of self-concept (personal) variables such as success/failure attributions or self-efficacy in math/science to aspiration. It is possible that these two types of influences on gender differences are interactive as depicted in Figure 1 and that their combined impact on achievement is more than the effect of either alone. The Farmer (1983) study compared the homemaking commitment of high school men and women and found, that although for men homemaking commitment was significantly less than for women, it was relatively high (means were 3.36, male; 3.59, female, on a five-point scale). Examination of individual test items on the Homemaking measure indicated that males positively endorsed items indicating that they would never let their career take priority over their family, and indicating that they would be very satisfied, if possible, to devote full time to home and family roles. This positive valuing of homemaking roles by adolescent males in the 1980s has implications for educational interventions. The potential for sharing home and work roles by men and women in the 1980s and future decades appears to be emerging in these young persons' attitudes.

For aspiration motivation in the Farmer (1985) study, the relative strength of the three sets of influences was strongest for background, followed by environment and then personal (Figure 3). This was the only motivation dimension studied by Farmer that was found to be most influenced by background factors (i.e., socioeconomic status, race, verbal ability, school location, and age). The earlier studies (Farmer, 1980, 1983; Naftchi-Ardebili, 1983) with smaller samples had not obtained this effect. Background influences for gender on aspiration were indirect, that is, mediated by other variables in the model (Figure 3). These young women's high aspiration was enhanced by perceived support for women working, verbal ability, and teacher support. For young men, a competitive self-concept, ability attributions, and parent support enhanced aspiration. These gender differences point to the important role of school and other environment

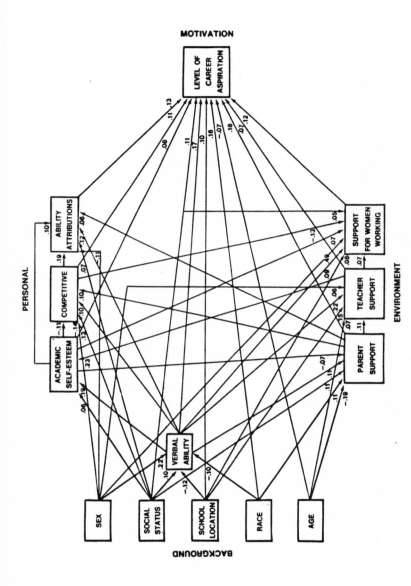

Figure 3. Fitted path model for level of career aspiration; R = .50, chi-square = 25.44(22,1027) *p* < .28 (fit is obtained when chi-square is nonsignificant). Indirect path coefficients, not shown on the figure, were meaningfully large for sex (.12) and social status (.08). *Note.* From "Model of Career and Achievement Motivation for Women and Men." by H. Farmer, 1985. *Journal of Counseling Psychology, 32,* p. 379. Copyright 1985 by the American Psychological Association. Reprinted by permission.

influences on gender differences in aspiration. The findings from this study are consistent with longitudinal studies conducted by sociologists such as Sewell and Hauser (1975). If we accept these findings, it appears that aspiration is influenced by environmental opportunities and support and by the growing, changing self-concept, as well as early perceptions of ability and the constraints of social class and race. Gottfredson (1981) placed the timing for the crystallization of these influences around the sixth grade during the middle school years.

Mastery Motivation

Mastery motivation as defined by Spence and Helmreich (1978) is very similar in meaning to achievement motivation as defined by Atkinson (1978) and McClelland (1985). Mastery represents the motivation to achieve on challenging tasks, including the motivation to persist until mastery is achieved. Spence and Helmreich and Atkinson and McClelland view mastery motivation as open to influences throughout life.

Gender differences observed for mastery (Figure 4; Farmer, 1985) were mostly indirect, that is, mediated by other variables in the model. Young men had significantly higher mastery motivation than young women and it was mediated by an independent and competitive self-concept. For young women, mastery was mediated by math ability, intrinsic values, teacher support, and support for women working.

The evidence related to success attributions for mastery is of interest. As Figure 4 shows, effort attributions for success were significantly related to mastery motivation. Math ability was in turn mediated by effort attributions for success, and each of the three environment variables, parent support, teacher support, and support for women working.

Success/failure attributions are critical self-concepts which mediate self-efficacy perceptions (Bandura, 1977, 1982), and feelings of competence with respect to mastery motivation and achievement. One study (Kessel, 1979) examining gender differences in attributions for math and English courses of sixth and tenth grade students ($n = 362$) found no significant gender differences for the sixth grade students, but for the tenth grade students, boys attributed their math success significantly more to ability than girls, whereas girls attributed their math success significantly more to effort than boys. In addition, Kessel's tenth grade students perceived math as more sex appropriate for boys than for girls (p <.001).

Success attributions assessed for the students in the Farmer (1985) study were investigated further by Farmer, Vispoel, and Maehr (in preparation). Consistent with Kessel's findings, Farmer et al. found that young men had significantly (p < .001) higher ability attributions and young women had higher (p < .05) effort attributions for their successes. The success experiences were not subdivided into math and English courses in the Farmer et al. study, but were classified instead by several contexts (i.e., school, work, sport, aesthetic, social, and fam-

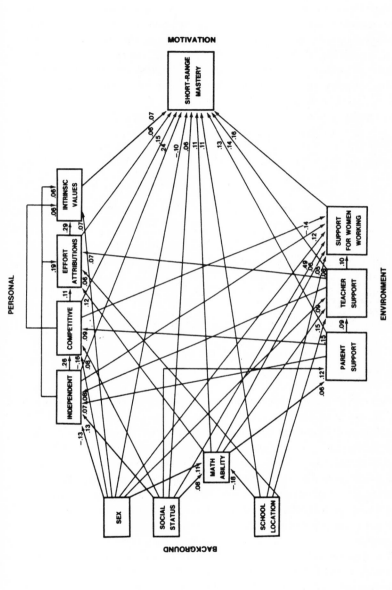

Figure 4. Fitted path model for short-range mastery; R = .53, chi-square = 19.59(19,1030) p < .42. Indirect path coefficients, not shown on the figure, were meaningfully large for sex (female .12; male -.06), social status (.08), and independent (.07). *Note.* From "Model of Career and Achievement Motivation for Women and Men." by H. Farmer, 1985. *Journal of Counseling Psychology, 32,* p. 381. Copyright 1985 by the American Psychological Association. Reprinted by permission.

ily). Ability attributions were not higher for young men compared to young women for school success in this study. Ability attributions were higher only for the sport and social contexts. School successes important to these young people, were not differentiated by gender for ability attributions. This finding appears to conflict with the Kessel finding.

It is controversial in attribution theory whether ability attributions are more important for mastery motivation and achievement than effort attributions. Weiner (1974, 1978) has suggested that effort attributions generate more pride in a person than ability attributions, and thus tend to increase expectancy/value for future achievements in the same achievement area. It may be that self-efficacy represents the feeling, ''I can do it'' (i.e., because I have both the requisite ability and I try hard). Self-efficacy is not strictly based on a sense of ability. The fact that effort attributions mediated math ability (Figure 4) in the Farmer (1985) study suggests that these are at least as important for mastery motivation as ability attributions. A recent review by Forsterling (1985) comparing success/failure attribution theory with self-efficacy theory highlights the positive role of effort attributions for enhancing achievement behavior.

Personal variables contribute most to mastery motivation with about equal and smaller contributions from environment and background variables (Figure 4). The proportions of variance accounted for by each set are 16% (personal) vs. 6% (environment, background). This finding suggests that socialization factors are key influences. It might also be speculated that new socialization experiences influence critical self-concepts in the future and mediate the strength of mastery motivation.

Career Commitment

Long-range career commitment is defined as commitment to the long-range prospects (i.e., advancement, status, money, contribution, etc.) of a career. The relationship found for career commitment with mastery is somewhat stronger than that for aspiration (r = .43 vs. .32) in the Farmer (1985) data. Career commitment has been described by Raynor (1978) as cumulative achievement motivation. An example would be the difference between a grade on a particular test or exam (achievement motivation) and GPA for high school (cumulative achievement motivation). Among the three motivation dimensions studied by Farmer (1985), career commitment alone obtained a significant interaction with gender, and therefore models were tested separately for gender (see Figures 5 and 6). The relative influence of the three sets of factors in terms of variance accounted for females was: personal (29%), environment (6%), and background (3%); for males, personal (14%), environment (5%), and background (1%). Gender differences observed within the personal set were that an expressive and cooperative self-concept, and effort attributions contributed significantly and positively to long-range career commitment for young women but not for young men. Also, homemaking commitment contributed significantly and negatively to this motivation dimension for young women but not for young men. For young men, a personal variable influencing career commitment was personal unconcern (i.e., fear that their successes would impact negatively on their social relationships). This finding was surprising in light of previous work by Horner (1978) on the influence of fear of success. Common personal influences for both young men and women were an independent and competitive self-concept and intrinsic achievement goals. Gender differences were also noted for environment influences. All three influences were significant for young women (i.e., parent support, teacher support, and support for women working). For young men, two were significant and one (parent support) was not. Gender differences were also found for background influences on career commitment. For both young men and women, being a member of a minority race was a significant influence. Both male and female minority students scored higher than white students on career, aspiration, and mastery. Perhaps minority status, similar to femaleness, tends to inflate aspirations in high school (i.e., those who have less try harder) but the gap in earnings as adults for both minorities and women compared to majority white males tends to deflate aspiration later (Card, Steel, & Abeles, 1980). This chapter does not focus on minority differences in aspiration and achievement but the data in the Farmer (1985) study provide support for findings such as those of Card, Steel, and Abeles (1980). An interesting within-female difference was found for minority and majority females on the homemaking commitment measure (Figure 5). Majority, but not minority females with high homemaking commitment have lower career commitment. For young women, but not for young men, math ability was a significant influence. As with mastery motivation, career motivation for young women was influenced by math ability, mediated by parent support, teacher support, and effort attributions for success.

Socialization processes in our society lead to gender differences in role priorities and in self-concepts and work-related skills, reflected in Figures 5 and 6. It was speculated earlier that men are socialized by society to take responsibility as breadwinners and to have high career commitment, whereas women are socialized to take primary responsibility for homemaking. Women with high career commitment must have been influenced in unique ways in the home as well as in the larger society to be committed to a career. Socialization processes lead to a greater valuing of math-related skill and achievement by men, and thus to greater expectations for success in math and math-related careers by men. Women, to be as strongly motivated to achieve in a career, require greater support from parents and teachers for their achievements and achievement strivings.

Some Cross-Cultural Findings for Adolescent Motivation

One controversial aspect of the Farmer (1976, 1985) model appears to be the relative strength of the influence of the various sets of factors (i.e., background, environment, personal) on motivation. Iranian researchers (Amiri, 1978; Tale-

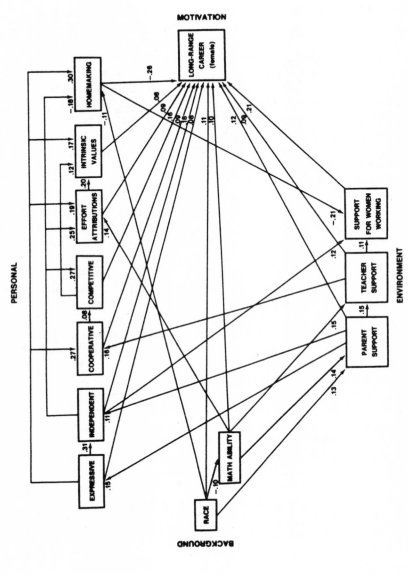

Figure 5. Fitted path model for long-range career: female; R = .63, chi-square = 50.37(42,509) *p* < .18. Indirect path coefficients, not shown on the figure, were meaningfully large for expressive (.09), independent (.13), and parent support/teacher support (.07). *Note.* From "Model of Career and Achievement Motivation for Women and Men," by H. Farmer, 1985. *Journal of Counseling Psychology, 32,* p. 383. Copyright 1985 by the American Psychological Association. Reprinted by permission.

72

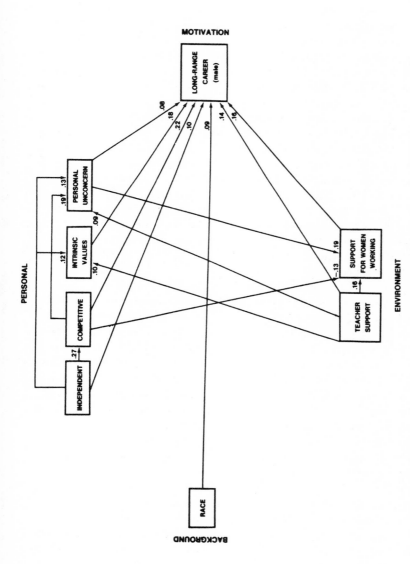

Figure 6. Fitted path model for long-range career:male; R = .44, chi-square = 10.47 (11,540) *p* < .31. Indirect path coefficient, not shown on the figure, was meaningfully large for independent (.08). *Note.* From ''Model of Career and Achievement Motivation for Women and Men.'' by H. Farmer, 1985. *Journal of Counseling Psychology, 32,* p. 384. Copyright 1985 by the American Psychological Association. Reprinted by permission.

ghani, 1978; Tohidi, 1984) who have designed and conducted research using aspects of this model have typically assumed that background and environment factors were more powerful shaping forces, with respect to motivation, than personal attitudes, abilities, or behavior characteristics. This assumption is very likely a result of experiences in Iran where career choice is more frequently proscribed than in the United States. The career a person ends up in, in many countries, is related to government policy and the social class of an individual. In contrast, in the United States a person has considerable freedom to choose an occupation based on personal interests and abilities.

Gender differences in achievement and career motivation in developing countries can be expected to differ from those found in the United States not only because custom and tradition with respect to sex roles differ, but also because government policy with respect to education and employment differ. This section will not attempt to understand the greater complexity represented by motivational differences found in developing countries. However, to the extent that females in the United States are also part of the lower socioeconomic class and of minority race, their occupational choices will be more proscribed than free. Thus, the findings from developing countries may be used to inform our understanding of gender differences in motivation in the United States especially for less advantaged groups.

Nayereh Tohidi (1984) conducted a study in Iran prior to the 1979 revolution. Tohidi studied 200 high school senior women and men (100 each) from upper and lower middle-class residential areas in Tehran. She adapted the Farmer (1976) model as shown in Figure 7. Here we see Tohidi's view that *background* and *environment* factors (i.e., the social structure) have a direct, but not a reciprocal influence on personal behaviors which in turn affect aspiration motivation. Given this assumption, Tohidi used measures to assess the outer and inner ring of Figure 7. The middle ring was not assessed because the influence of these personal factors was assumed to be modest by Tohidi and at best mediating and indirect. Using regression analyses, Tohidi found that aspiration was significantly predicted by both background and environment factors. Gender differences found included a significant difference in support for women working favoring young women ($r = .52$, $p < .01$). Young men scored significantly higher on aspiration ($r = .46$, $p < .01$) and on traditional religious beliefs ($r = .31$, $p < .01$). As predicted, students from the upper middle class compared to those from the lower middle class had higher aspiration, perceived greater support for women working, and perceived more community resources supportive of their careers. It appears that the advantages of upper middle-class persons, which include education, family expectations, and a broader range of experiences, contribute to more positive beliefs about work and the work environment, which in turn enhance their aspiration.

Social class differences for aspiration were less powerful ($r = .21$, $p < .01$) than gender differences ($r = .46$, $p < .01$) for Tohidi's subjects. Gender differences were investigated further by Tohidi using discriminant analyses. The dis-

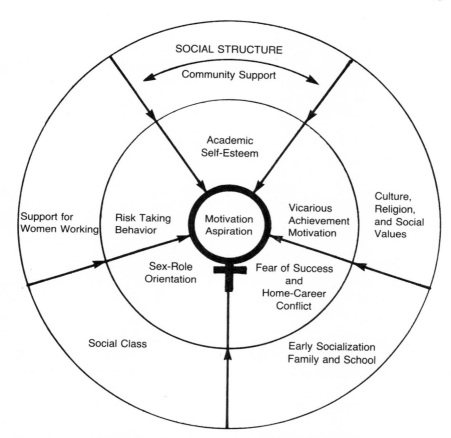

Figure 7. A conceptual model for understanding aspiration motivation in women. *Note.* From ''Sex Differences in Achievement/career Motivation of Iranian Boys and Girls.'' by N. Tohidi, 1984. *Sex Roles, 11* (5/6), p. 469. Copyright 1984 by Plenum Publishing Corporation. Adapted by permission.

criminant profile for lower middle-class young women with low aspiration indicated that these young women also had low scores on the support for women working scale. The lower middle-class young men with high, rather than low, aspiration also had low scores on the support for women working scale. For upper middle-class males, the pattern was more consistent with expectations, those with high aspiration had high support for women working scores. Apparently, upper middle-class young men with high aspiration are more tolerant of an environment supportive of women's career opportunities, whereas lower middle-class young men with similarly high aspiration are not tolerant of an environment supportive of women's career opportunities.

An interaction effect was found for gender $\times$ religion ($p < .05$) in the Tohidi study, and analyzed and reported by Farmer, Tohidi, and Weiss (1982). This

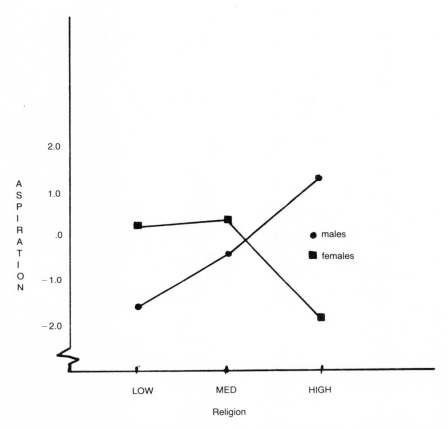

Figure 8. Graphic representation of sex × religion interaction on aspiration.
Note. From "Study of the Factors Influencing Sex Differences in the Career Motivation of Iranian High School Students by H. Farmer, N. Tohidi and E. Weiss, 1982. *International Journal of Interculture Relations, 6,* p. 28. Copyright 1982 by Pergamon Press Ltd. Adapted with permission.

interaction indicated that young men with low scores on religion also had low aspiration scores (Figure 8). The opposite was true for young men with high scores on religion. In contrast, for young women, low to moderate religion scores were associated with moderate aspiration scores, whereas high religion scores were associated with low aspiration. It was inferred that traditional religious beliefs had a dampening effect on the aspiration of these young Iranian women. There was also an interaction for gender × socioeconomic class (p <.01, Figure 9) indicating that lower-class women, compared to lower-class men had less aspiration, but upper middle-class women, compared to upper middle-class men, had higher aspiration. This finding suggests that in Iran upper

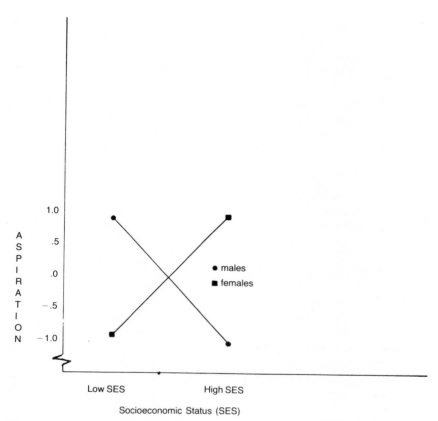

Figure 9. Graphic representation of sex × socioeconomic status interaction on aspiration. *Note.* From ''Study of the Factors Influencing Sex Differences in the Career Motivation of Iranian High School Students by H. Farmer, N. Tohidi and E. Weiss, 1982. *International Journal of Interculture Relations, 6,* p. 30. Copyright 1982 by Pergamon Press Ltd. Adapted with permission.

middle-class status and related experiences enhance aspiration, especially for young women. In summary, Tohidi found aspiration level influenced by gender, social class, and religious beliefs. As noted earlier, she didn't examine the influence of any self-concept variables so we are unable to make comparative statements about the relative influence of psychological vs. environmental/ cultural variables on motivation in Iran based on her findings.

Soudabeh Amiri (1978) took a somewhat different theoretical position from that of Tohidi. Amiri assumed that environmental and cultural factors would be highly influential in shaping Iranian students' career motivation but she also assumed that psychological factors would play some role in their motivation. In particular, Amiri assessed high school students' (300 women, 75 men) valuing of achievement in self (a personal variable), and eight environment variables (early parental socialization, peer influence, counselor influence, teacher influence, parent support, socioeconomic status, religious beliefs, exposure to different life styles, and parent education). To assess motivation she used some scales developed by Super and Cuhla (1976) assessing career commitment, homemaking commitment, and work for support (i.e., economic benefits). The first two of these are the same as measures used by Farmer (1985, Figure 1).

Surprisingly, Amiri did not find young women less committed to the long-range prospects of a career than young men. Young women did score higher on homemaking ($r = .15$, $p < .01$), as expected, and young men scored higher on motivation to work for support ($r = .20$, $p < .01$). Amiri found that the best predictors of the female students' career commitment were parent support ($r = .15$, $p < .01$) for their achievements and valuing of achievement in self ($r = .41$, $p < .01$) reflected in endorsement of such items as, "Getting good grades is important to me personally," and, "Personally, it is satisfying to me to work hard on studies." For young men this relationship was also obtained, but the strength of the relationships were reversed (i.e., parent support $r = .17$; valuing of achievement in self $r = .41$). The counselor and teacher influence measures were not significant predictors in Amiri's study. Peer support influenced significantly and positively only one of the motivation variables, motivation to work for support. Amiri also found that young women from lower socioeconomic backgrounds had higher motivation to work for support. Apparently, their own lack of financial resources motivated them to earn more. As noted above, on average, men obtained higher scores on the work for support measure than women.

In summary, Amiri's findings support the view that young women from the lower middle class are motivated toward work in ways that are different from those for young women from the upper middle class in Iran. Lower middle-class young women are more motivated to work to earn money, and indeed their situation may require that they work. In contrast, upper middle-class young women in Iran are more motivated toward a career for its intrinsic benefits and satisfactions. The fact that support from parents for their achievements, and an internal commitment to achievement were also related to high scores on the career commitment measure for these young Iranian women indicates the importance of family influence and of self-concepts developed in the family for female motivation. For young men, parent support was less important for career commitment than for young women, a finding consistent with some findings in the United States (Farmer, 1985). Peer support, interestingly, was related to work for support, but not to career commitment in Amiri's study, and teacher and counselor influence were not significant predictors for any of the motivation dimensions she studied.

The power of a curriculum intervention to enhance career motivation for students in a developing country was illustrated in a study by Taleghani (1978). In 1978, Taleghani investigated the career motivation of Iranian students, some of whom had been exposed to a career guidance curriculum and others who had not. The students in Taleghani's study who did not experience the career curriculum made their career choices based primarily on prestige factors such as salary potential and did not consider personal fit or as wide a range of occupational possibilities as the students who had experienced the career guidance curriculum. Although this study did not assess gender differences, it points to the power of a career guidance curriculum to increase students' ability to choose careers based on personal as well as environment considerations. Some of the limiting effects due to SES or family sex role socialization might well be reduced through curriculum intervention in the schools.

Anderson (1983) conducted a study comparing the career maturity (Crites, 1978) of Cherokee and white eighth grade students living in rural Oklahoma. He found the expected lower levels of career maturity for the Cherokee sample. Anderson also assessed gender differences and found that both white and Cherokee girls compared to boys scored significantly lower on measures of success attributions to ability and effort. Although recent reviews (Frieze et al., 1982) found only small gender differences on average for success attributions, gender differences appear to persist in disadvantaged females (i.e., Cherokee Indians and whites living in some parts of rural America). Attributions for success to ability and effort are significantly associated with achievement motivation and behavior (Weiner, 1978) and therefore this gender difference should be a continuing concern to educators.

Some Interventions to Reduce Gender Differences

Interventions in high school to enhance sex equity in achievement and related motivation might well aim at decreasing occupational and homemaking stereotypes and at facilitating the development of self-efficacy with respect to critical competencies such as math and science. A society that promoted the sharing of home and work roles equally by men and women would likely promote math achievement equally as well. Interventions aimed at promoting these outcomes seem highly desirable to promote sex equity. Interventions might also teach needed skills such as problem solving and decision making to improve student's career choice process and increase student enrollment in courses nontraditional for their gender. Some examples of programs aimed at some of these goals are described next.

WINC (Northwest Regional Education Laboratory, 1980) is a program for young women conducted in high schools in Portland, Oregon. It is a one-semester-long program which has successfully increased participants' understanding of the ways in which sex role stereotyping limits womens' career planning, preparation, and choices. Participants emerged with more flexible career and life plans compared to a control group.

Harrison (1980) reports findings from a Career Internship Program for girls conducted in West Nyack, New York. This program enhanced adolescents' sense of competence and independence and also taught life planning skills. Participants worked in one of 25 nontraditional worksites and evaluated this experience as enhancing their sense of competence in these work fields.

The Girl Scouts of America have developed a sex equity career education curriculum for Senior Scouts, grades 7 through 12. Their program, "From Dreams to Reality," helps high school students develop life planning skills. Sex equity curriculum materials developed with federal funding through WEEA include *Options: A Curriculum Development Program for Rural High School Students*. This program develops career and life-planning skills and was found effective in increasing nontraditional career choices when outcomes were compared to a control group.

Tittle (1981) designed a set of marriage and parenthood values to parallel the set of work values developed earlier by Katz (1973). Assessment of students' values on these three dimensions permit educators/counselors to discuss traditional and nontraditional values with students and help them separate out values that are based on expectations of others from values that are intrinsically their own. This sorting out process is intended to help students choose careers that are consistent with their own values, as well as their interests and abilities. Farmer et al. (1981) have developed an assessment instrument for high school students which is also intended to increase the likelihood that students consider their home-related values when they engage in career planning.

Some high school programs are aimed at increasing young women's participation in nontraditional occupational fields such as engineering or science. A review of programs selected from a list of more than 300 (Aldrich & Hall, 1980) appeared in 1985 (Stage et al.). The most effective of these programs used a combination of several approaches. For example, such programs provide specific training in spatial relations skill, problem-solving skill, and mechanical skills and encourage young women to enroll in advanced math and science courses. These programs have also tried to change the environment in which math and science courses are taught, by providing more women to teach these classes, and by providing more role models to enhance the relevance of math and science for young women. A third approach used by some programs is sex equity training for parents, teachers, and educational administrators. An example of one of these programs is EQUALS, designed by staff at the Lawrence Hall of Science, Berkeley, California. EQUALS is a 30-hour inservice program for teachers, administrators, and counselors, grades K–12. Its goals are to help these professionals increase the participation and achievement of young women in math and science. Staff from at least 14 other states have attended the inservice training offered by EQUALS at Berkeley. A somewhat similar program in Minneapolis public schools was begun in 1976, called Multiplying Options and Subtracting Bias. These programs emphasize skill training, and increasing the relevance of math and science for the future careers of women. The combining of increased skill with increased perceived relevance is consistent with motivation theory.

Summary for Adolescents

Evidence was presented related to the Farmer (1985, Figure 1) model. For aspiration motivation, gender was found to mediate certain personal and environment factors. For young women, verbal ability, teacher support, and support for women working mediated aspiration. For young men, competitive, ability attributions, and parent support mediated aspiration. Similarly, for mastery motivation gender mediated math ability, intrinsic values, teacher support, and support for women working for young women. For young men, independent and competitive mediated mastery. It was noted that teacher support, and support for women working enhanced both aspiration and mastery motivation more for young women than young men. For career commitment, the effect of gender was strongest. For young women, math ability, expressive, cooperative, and homemaking, the latter negatively, as well as independent, competitive, effort attributions, and intrinsic values influenced career commitment. Also, the three environment measures, parent support, teacher support, and support for women working influenced career commitment for young women. For young men, independent, competitive, intrinsic values, personal unconcern, teacher support, and support for women working influenced career commitment. Contrasts for young women and men included the fact that parent support influenced career commitment for young women, but not for young men. Also, homemaking had a negative influence on career commitment for young women, but not for young men.

Four cross-cultural studies were described, and their findings related to the Farmer model. For Iranian high school students, socioeconomic status, gender, and religious beliefs influenced aspiration. Young women were influenced negatively by high scores on religion, whereas the opposite was true for men. Also, middle-class young women were aspiring to higher level careers than middle-class young men in Iran.

Amiri found for Iranian young women, similar to the findings for American young women, that parent support was a significant influence on their career commitment. Anderson reported that Cherokee Indian young women, compared to Cherokee Indian young men, attributed their successes more to external causes than to internal causes. These cross-cultural findings, it was suggested, may be used to inform understanding of gender differences in motivation in the United States, especially for less advantaged socioeconomic and ethnic groups.

Several programs for adolescents were described. Programs have been found effective in reducing occupational and homemaking stereotypes and in increasing the range of occupations considered appropriate including a number of nontraditional, higher status occupations. Other programs were found effective for enhancing life planning skills, helping young people to plan ahead for home and work roles. Introducing values related to home as well as those related to work into the career decision-making process was also found to be useful in enhancing realistic career plans. Some programs focused on enhancing math and science-related skills and attitudes. These programs were found effective in teaching math-related skills, enhancing math self-efficacy, and enhancing the relevance of math for young women's future careers. At least one program (e.g., EQUALS) was found that aimed at training teachers, administrators, and counselors in sex equity issues and techniques.

GENDER DIFFERENCES IN ADULT MOTIVATION AND ACHIEVEMENT

Evidence from adults with respect to the Farmer (1976, 1985) model is limited. Three studies have been conducted to test aspects of the model (Farmer & Fyans, 1983; Rooney, 1983; Webb, 1983), and seven other studies have examined gender differences in achievement related issues for adults (Farmer, 1984; Farmer & Bohn, 1970; Fowler, 1982; Klein, 1984; Rowan, 1982; Skarjune, 1985; Smith, 1981). First, evidence is presented from the three studies conducted to test aspects of the Farmer model; then findings from the other studies are related to the model. This section concludes with suggestions for enhancing achievement motivation in adult women.

In the Farmer and Fyans (1983) study, 162 married women who had children and had returned to college after an absence were investigated. Two of the three motivation dimensions (Figure 1) were included in this study, aspiration and mastery. Career commitment was not assessed. Two environment variables (community support and support for women working) and five personal variables (fear of success, home-career conflict, self-esteem, sex role orientation, and risk-taking style) were assessed. Given the uneven distribution of measures in the environment and personal sets, it is inappropriate to compare the relative strength of these two sets of influences. The strongest influence on aspiration level for this group of married women was fear of success. This finding was contrary to expectations. Fear of success was expected to interfere with career motivation (Horner, 1978), yet for these married women returning to college after an absence, fear of success was positively associated ($r = .44$, $p < .01$) with high levels of aspiration. Perhaps these women were anxious about their aspirations for success in ways that served them in a positive fashion. It is well known that certain levels of anxiety enhance achievement, while higher levels inhibit achievement. For mastery motivation the strongest relationship was found for low home self-esteem ($r = .36$, $p < .01$). The home self-esteem measure assessed how much people feel supported for their needs by members of their family. Apparently, the less support these women experienced at home the more likely they were to be highly motivated to master achievement tasks.

The women in the Farmer and Fyans study were grouped according to their sex role orientation (Bem, 1981) into androgynous and feminine sex role orientation types. Regression analysis indicated that aspiration was predicted for androgynous women (i.e., those who endorsed masculine self-concepts as highly as feminine self-concepts) by high scores on academic self-esteem ($p < .01$). For feminine sex-typed women aspiration was predicted by high scores on home-career conflict ($r = .41$, $p < .01$). This finding suggests that feminine sex-typed women return to college with high aspiration and high home-career conflict. Although nonsignificant in the regression analysis, the community support measure obtained a significant zero-order correlation with both aspiration ($r = .31$; $p < .01$) and mastery ($r = .31$; $p < .01$) for feminine sex-typed women. It appears that for feminine sex-typed women community support relates importantly to their achievement motivation. This study provided the interesting evidence that for older women returning to college after an absence, high achievement motivation is associated with various kinds of anxieties (i.e., home-career conflict, fear of success, low home self-esteem) as well as some positive factors such as perceived community support for their achievement desires, and high academic self-esteem. The study also provided evidence suggesting that feminine sex-typed women needed more external (i.e., environment) support for their motivation than androgynous sex-typed women.

Rooney (1983) tested an adapted Farmer (1976, 1985) model with 212 adults (112 female, 100 male) who had graduated from high school three years previously. These adults were in various life roles (i.e., employed worker, homemaker, and student). Subjects for the Rooney study were obtained from the high school alumni records of two of the schools used to obtain data in the Farmer (1985) study. Thus some generalizations about the model from adolescents to young adults are possible. Rooney's measures included background (SES, ability), environment (parent support, counselor support, teacher support, and community support) and personal (sex role orientation, attributions for success, success values) variables. Her motivation measures were career commitment, homemaking commitment, work for support (these three from Super and Cuhla, 1976), aspiration, and mastery. Rooney grouped her subjects according to their primary role (i.e., student, worker, or homemaker). There were equal numbers of men and women in the student group (23 each); 75 men and 45 women were workers; and 44 women and no men were homemakers. The student group was distinguished from the other two groups on several variables in the discriminant analyses. They had significantly higher aspiration, higher ability, and perceived greater support from their parents for their achievements and career plans ($p < .01$). Rooney found that for aspiration, background characteristics (ability, socioeconomic status) contributed most, followed by environment (parent support and primary role, i.e., student, worker, and homemaker). The latter factor, primary role, represents the situations people find themselves in. In the regression analyses, the beta weight for primary role was higher than all other beta weights, suggesting the important role the present situation plays in aspiration level. Personal characteristics did not contribute significantly to aspiration for Rooney's sample.

For mastery motivation, Rooney found that one personal characteristic (independent) contributed most, followed by environment (community support), with background (father's education) contributing significantly but least to the regression equation. Primary role did not contribute significantly to this motivation dimension. For career motivation, Rooney found that gender was a significant influence, also environment (primary role, parent support) and one personal factor (independent). She found young women distinguished from young men by their higher educational and career aspiration, a finding similar to that for the adolescents studied by Farmer (1985). However, for Rooney's sample, men had significantly higher career commitment compared to women, whereas in the Farmer study adolescent women had significantly higher career commitment compared to adolescent men. It appears that the transition into adulthood did not diminish women's aspiration level, but it did diminish their long-range career commitment. The fact that aspiration remained high for these young women may be a positive influence for their achievements in later years when the opportunity to return to school or employed work presents itself. Career commitment appears to be less stable, and more influenced by the opportunity structure (see Figure 5).

Webb (1983) was interested in identifying factors that differentiated change-agent nurses (a nontraditional specialization within nursing) from traditional nurses. The nontraditional change agent nurses were considered to be more strongly career and achievement motivated. Discriminant analyses were employed to identify the factors that separated the two groups. Measures used included two environment measures (community support and early family socialization) and seven personal measures (self-esteem, sex role orientation, fear of success, home-career conflict, achievement style, risk-taking style, and attributions for success). Only one variable separated the two groups; self-esteem was significantly higher for the change-agent nurses.

What conclusions, if any, can be drawn from these studies (Farmer & Fyans, 1983; Rooney, 1983; Webb, 1983)? With respect to the Farmer (1976, 1985) model, all three types of variables (i.e., background, environment, and personal) played a significant role in one or another study, but not all three. At best we can conclude that it is important to consider influences from all three sets in trying to understand adult career and achievement motivation. For young adults (Rooney, 1983) the environment and background sets were most influential, whereas for older married women with children (Farmer & Fyans, 1983) the personal and environment sets were most influential, and for the traditional vs. nontraditional nurses (Webb, 1983) the personal were most influential in distinguishing groups.

Two studies (Fowler, 1982; Skarjune, 1985) compared relatively successful professional men and women to determine if there were different influences on their career development. These researchers were interested in knowing if women who were successful professionally, and were more likely to have obtained greater support for their career aspirations and advancement from mentors than similar men. Surprisingly, in both studies significant differences in the support systems of the men and women were not found. Fowler studied assistant professors at a midwestern university. She concluded that women who were successful in obtaining employment as faculty at prestigious universities may not represent typical women. Skarjune studied directors of mental health centers in the state of Illinois. Her sample included all female directors and a matching set of male directors (matched on years as director, educational background, and size and budget of the mental health center). The women Skarjune studied reported similar career experiences to those reported by men in terms of rates of advancement, levels of professional participation, amount of sponsorship, emotional support, and social contact provided by mentors. Some expected differences emerged, however, indicating that the men had more children and more were married than the women directors. This finding is a possible home-career trade-off for successful women. Also, the women directors were involved in support networks that included more higher status colleagues than the networks of the men. It appears that the women who succeed as administrative directors of mental health centers, similar to the women faculty in the Fowler study, experience their career role in ways similar to the men. The fact remains, however, that there are fewer women faculty and fewer women directors of mental health centers (the ratio in Illinois was about one in four) compared to men. Also, women who succeed may be making some home-career trade-offs.

Some researchers have studied dual-career couples in an attempt to better understand their motivation to achieve. Lu Ann Smith (1981) investigated the influence of occupational prestige, career commitment, homemaking commitment, and work for support on the decision-making behavior of dual-worker couples. She was interested in knowing which of these factors predicted egalitarian decision-making behavior and which a more traditional, authoritarian decision-making behavior. She found that for both men and women the higher the prestige level of the occupation the more egalitarian their decision-making. Differences for gender were found for the career commitment and work for support scales. For men, work for support was not significantly related to egalitarian or traditional decision making, nor was it related to level of occupation. For women, work for support was significantly higher in lower level occupation women than higher level occupation women. This difference suggests, that for some of the women Smith studied (i.e., those with high-level careers) work for support (i.e., economic gain) was not as important as it was for men in similar positions. Both men and women in high-level occupations had significantly higher career commitment than men and women in lower level occupations.

Klein (1984, 1986) also studied dual-career couples from a range of socioeconomic levels. She was interested in investigating the factors influencing career satisfaction. She expected background and environment factors to be more potent than personal ones but she included all three types of measures in her study. Contrary to expectation, she found that self-esteem, a personal variable, was the most important influence on career satisfaction, regardless of occupational prestige level. Unlike Smith who found that occupational prestige was an important influence on the decision-making behavior of dual-career couples, Klein did not find occupational prestige important in understanding her question. Other variables assessed by Klein were salary, rate of promotions, and number of vacations each year (environment); marital satisfaction, self-esteem, career commitment (personal); education, age, and number of children (background). Career satisfaction for these dual-career couples was found to be independent of occupational prestige and salary. This finding is consistent with the Skarjune finding suggesting that some women may choose lower level occupations in order to meet their homemaking role demands and at the same time remain "career satisfied," while other women may choose high-level occupations and forego marriage and family, and remain "career satisfied."

Two studies (Farmer & Bohn, 1970; Farmer, 1984) investigated the impact of home-career conflict on career motivation. In the earlier study an experimental treatment was used to reduce home-career conflict for a group of 50 employed women. The treatment began with a prologue describing some attitudes and behaviors of women in relation to achievement. For example, a study by Komarovsky (1946) found that college women were afraid to appear too intelligent because they might scare off potential dates or future husbands. A later study by Mathews and Tiedeman (1964) at Harvard University reported a similar finding. The women in the Farmer and Bohn study were told, "I want you to pretend with me that men have come of age and that: (1) Men like intelligent women; (2) Men and women are promoted equally in business and the professions; and (3) Raising a family well is very possible for a career woman." Following the treatment the women completed the Strong Vocational Interest Inventory, an instrument that relates interests to occupations. These women had taken the same inventory two weeks earlier with standard instructions. A comparison of their scores on the occupational scales pre and post indicated that scores had significantly increased for the following professions: author, psychologist, lawyer, life insurance sales, and physician. In contrast, scores had significantly decreased for business education teacher, steno-secretary, office worker, elementary teacher, home economics teacher, and dietitian. Some of these women were married, others were not. A test for the effect of marital status indicated that there was none. This finding strongly suggests that as long as women believe that: (a) men don't like them to be too successful (i.e., intelligent), (b) that they cannot expect equal treatment at work in terms of promotion and salary, and (c) that they cannot combine raising a family with a highly demanding career, they will choose less demanding occupations. Women's career and achievement motivation is thus modified by their family commitments and the view that their environment discriminates against them in the workplace. This study (Farmer & Bohn, 1970) did not identify which of the three beliefs used in the treatment was contributing most to the effects found. Such an investigation would be important to determine whether role priorities or perceived discrimination were most effective in dampening these women's career motivation. The findings from this study support the conclusions reached by Skarjune and Fowler about the successful women they studied. In a related article (Farmer, 1984) describing the design of a measure to assess home-career conflict, Farmer reported that women in nontraditional demanding occupations such as engineering had less measured conflict than women in elementary teacher education. How the women in the nontraditional careers resolved possible conflict between home and career roles was not investigated.

The finding that self-esteem discriminates adult women in nontraditional careers from those in traditional careers (Webb, 1983) and is predictive of career satisfaction for women (Klein, 1984) may be related to Bandura's (1977) self-efficacy theory. Hackett and Betz (1981) studying college men and women, found significant gender differences favoring men for occupational self-efficacy. These findings were replicated for mathematics self-efficacy in a later study (Betz & Hackett, 1983). Lent, Brown, and Larkin (1984; 1985) have found that career self-efficacy predicts persistence in and level of academic achievement in college science and engineering majors for both men and women. Hackett and Betz hypothesized, based on Bandura's (1977) theory that there are four ways to change self-efficacy feelings: performance accomplishments, vicarious learning (i.e., modeling); emotional arousal (with reduced anxiety); and verbal persuasion. Campbell and Hackett (1985) have found evidence supporting the hypothesis that success experiences in math enhance self-efficacy feelings. Gender differences in achievement motivation found for these adults appear to revolve around feelings of competency for achievement in occupations requiring science, math, and mechanical skills.

Enhancing Achievement Motivation for Adult Women

Enhancement strategies for increasing adult motivation and achievement are somewhat different from those that appear useful for children and adolescents. The focus for children and adolescents was on reducing occupational and home-making stereotypes, enhancing competency self-concepts, and enhancing achievement-related skills including analytical and problem-solving skills. The focus for adults includes these and adds some anxiety-reducing strategies to help overcome the negative effect of some career-related fears (such as math anxiety).

Title IX restricts schools and universities from providing educational opportunities on the basis of gender. Therefore, courses or programs designed to meet women's special needs must exercise caution so as not to lead to further segregation by gender. Many such programs are open to men as well as women. Other programs designed to prepare women to take full advantage of educational opportunities are considered to be within Title IX guidelines.

Women have made some gains in the last 15 years in the fields of math and science. The proportion of women earning Ph.D.'s in science and engineering has risen from 7% in 1965 to 25% in 1980 (National Research Council, 1980). Much of this increase is due to increased proportions of women in the social and life sciences. The percent for women in the physical sciences was about 12% in 1980.

Ekstrom and Marvel (1985) identify three sources of barriers to achievement for adult women returning to college after an absence: institutional, situational, and personal. Institutional barriers include admissions and financial aid practices, regulations, curricula, services, and faculty and staff attitudes that create special problems for adult women. Situational barriers include sociological, financial, family, health, and residential circumstances that may limit the educational participation of adult women. Personal barriers include the psychological and societal factors that affect adult women such as attitudes, expectations, fears, self-concept, sex role conflicts, sex stereotypes, and work values.

Admissions policies for women returning to college after an absence typically require taking a test that may require knowledge or skills that have been lost or never learned. Some campuses now provide tutorial classes to help women prepare for admissions tests requiring math or information that may need updating. Many campuses provide counseling services specifically for women returning to college. Such services frequently provide information, counseling, and a place to meet other returning women. Evaluation of these services indicates that returning women who use these services tend to have higher completion rates (i.e., graduate) compared to those who do not. Some campuses provide childcare; however, surveys indicate that this sorely needed service is inadequate on most campuses (Ekstrom & Marvel, 1985). Personal barriers to achievement for returning women include conflicts between home and career values (Farmer, 1984), lack of information about options for majors, and lack of prerequisite skills and low academic self-esteem.

Klein et al. (1985) offer several recommendations for enhancing sex equity for adult women. They suggest that college level teachers need training in mainstreaming sex equity ideas and practices. Educators should identify demographic and attitudinal changes in the women coming to campus and then modify their teaching and related campus services to meet these changing needs. Educators should encourage the maintenance of women's studies as well as the mainstreaming of sex equity and the new scholarship on women in course content. Educators should improve sex equity in student-faculty interactions, and provide support services such as nonsexist pre-admissions counseling, women's centers, day care facilities, and provisions for student safety. Educators should encourage institutions to conduct self-assessments to identify and then eliminate overt and subtle sex discrimination and stereotyping in admissions, financial aid, and classroom climate. Educators in these institutions should also establish grievance and mediation procedures and criteria and guidelines for students and faculty to use to obtain fair treatment and to avoid sexual harassment and unintentional discrimination.

Programs to Enhance the Participation of Women in
Science and Math-Related Occupations

A variety of programs to enhance the participation of women in occupations related to science and math are reviewed by Stage et al. (1985). One such program at the University of Missouri-Kansas City offers a special section of the introductory math sequence for women only, taught by women. The class is preceded by a one-hour optional tutoring session in which women students work in small groups on math problems and skills. A comparison of the women taking this class with those taking the regular math class indicated the former obtained better grades and a higher completion rate. The women in the special section had been selected because of their weak math grades, thus their better performance takes on added significance. Also, 56% of the special section women went on to enroll in another mathematics course whereas only 17% of the women in traditional math introductory classes did so.

Another program, reported by Stage et al. (1985) at Purdue University combined intensive counseling for women science majors with a course that offered them the opportunity to meet successful women scientists and a special science laboratory class to help enhance prerequisite science skills. These women reported greater satisfaction with their science major than women science majors who did not participate. The number of women involved was small (n = 120) and participants were volunteers thus the results are not directly generalizable.

College students, especially women, often lack the prerequisite math skills to take a course in calculus. When these women choose majors requiring calculus and other quantitative skills, they are frequently "scared" off. To offset this lack of skill and related math anxiety, programs have been introduced on many campuses to teach the prerequisite skills and at the same time address math anxiety. Tobias (1978) pioneered these programs with the establishment of the Math Anxiety Clinic at Wesleyan University. Another approach to reducing math anxiety is to replace reliance on memory (i.e., learning the rules of computation) with greater reliance on problem-solving and analytical strategies. Examples of such programs are those in San Francisco State University, California State University, Long Beach, and Humboldt State University.

As many as 40% of all female scientists drop out of the labor force (Stage et al., 1985) and some programs have been developed to bring some of these women back into school or employment in the sciences. These programs offer updating training, confidence building, and study skills to women who have earned bachelor's degrees in science previously. The programs are typically one academic year in length. One of the most successful of these programs is that at the University of Dayton in Ohio. This program offers a mechanism for career change from general science to chemical or electrical engineering. Of the 71 women participating in the program, 63 completed the program and received an average of three job offers. Several conferences have been held at the University of California at Berkeley for women with undergraduate degrees in science or engineering. At these conferences model women scientists from the community give keynote addresses and lead discussions. Follow-up evaluations indicated that over 75% of the participants had taken some action to advance their science careers and at least one-third had taken a course in math, science, or computer science; also one-third had interviewed for a new job since attending the conference.

Purdue University also conducted a project in the Engineering Department de-

signed to meet the needs of freshmen [sic] women in engineering. They offered
lab experiences with power tools, engines, plumbing and metals, and lectures
from a variety of male and female role models. Pre- and post-test comparisons
showed that women participants had gained in self-confidence related to engi-
neering compared to a control group of women engineering students.

Enhancing Achievement for Employed Women

Catalyst (14 East 60th St., NYC) and Wider Opportunities for Women
(Washington, DC) are two national organizations that provide counseling for
women looking to re-enter the labor market. These agencies have produced sev-
eral publications such as *What To Do With the Rest of Your Life, Your Children
Aren't Old Enough*, and *There's Nothing You Can Do Anyhow*. Current needs
include more programs for employed women, especially programs in coopera-
tion with employers or in the work place.

Summary for Adults

The studies reviewed do not provide conclusive evidence indicating the source
of gender differences in adult achievement motivation and related achievements.
The evidence does provide, however, a basis for implicating both *personal* and
environment factors.

The personal factors associated with achieving women include some factors
common to both genders (i.e., self-esteem) but also include some unique factors
such as home-career conflict and less valuing of work for money. It appears that
self-esteem, whether it is more general self-esteem or task-related self-esteem, is
associated with achievement motivation for adults. For some women, achieve-
ment motivation is associated with fears such as those represented by home-
career conflict measures and fear of success measures. For other women espe-
cially those who have chosen nontraditional occupations (e.g., engineering,
administrative nursing) their assessed home-career conflict is lower than that for
women in traditional occupations (e.g., teaching, nursing). Consistent with these
findings, feminine sex role orientation women were found to have higher meas-
ured home-career conflict than androgynous sex role orientation women. Women
in the Farmer and Bohn study choose significantly more nontraditional careers
when they viewed home and work roles as compatible. Achieving women who
were members of a dual-career couple tended to be less committed to earning a
high salary than comparably achieving spouses.

Environment factors associated with achievement motivation for adults em-
phasize the importance of perceived support for career goals from employers and
important others in their environment. This perceived support was more impor-
tant for feminine sex-typed women than androgynous women in the studies re-
viewed, but no evidence was reported indicating that this type of support was

more important for women compared to men. Farmer and Bohn (1970) found that women choose nontraditional careers significantly more when they perceived support from employers and potential spouses for their career goals. In the Rooney (1983) study of younger adult men and women, the student group was distinguished from the employed and homemaker groups as having higher ability, higher achievement motivation, and greater perceived support from their parents for their achievements. Social role expectations do appear to affect achievement behavior with more achieving women postponing marriage and/or having children compared to achieving men.

Two studies (Fowler, 1982; Skarjune, 1985) compared adult men and women on several factors considered related to career advancement. These studies focused on the contribution of mentors to career advancement and found few gender differences for their samples (assistant professors at an elite university; directors of mental health agencies). They did find, however, that there were home-career trade-offs for women not present for men. Two studies (Klein, 1986; Smith, 1981) compared factors influencing career advancement and career satisfaction for dual-career couples. Smith compared low socioeconomic status (LSES) couples with high socioeconomic status (HSES) couples and found that HSES couples exhibited more egalitarian decision-making behaviors and were more committed to the long-range prospects of a career. Gender differences found by Smith for the more career committed couples (i.e., those with HSES) include less concern to earn a high salary on the part of the women compared to men. Klein found career satisfaction unrelated to socioeconomic level for the dual-career couples she studied. For Klein, the best predictor of career satisfaction was self-esteem. It was suggested that some women may choose lower level occupations in order to meet their other role demands (i.e., home) yet remain career satisfied (Klein, 1986), while other women choose high-level occupations and postpone family responsibilities (Skarjune, 1985).

Rooney (1983) found young women distinguished from young men by their higher educational and career aspiration, a finding similar to that for the adolescents studied by Farmer (1985). However, for Rooney's sample, men had significantly higher career commitment compared to women, whereas in the Farmer study, adolescent women had significantly higher career commitment compared to adolescent men. The fact that aspiration remained high for these young women may be a positive factor in their achievements in later years when the opportunity to return to school or employed work presents itself. Career commitment may be less stable, and more influenced by the opportunity structure, but more research is needed on this point.

Interventions to enhance women's achievement and related achievement motivations are numerous. Such programs were found to exist on most campuses and in many communities. These programs vary in their focus from very specific (i.e., math anxiety programs) to very general. Programs help adult women cope with their multiple roles as wives, mothers, workers, and learners and help women cope with changes such as job loss and retirement. Programs offer support services for childcare, social contacts, role models, information, skill training, employment, and stress reduction. The fact that women's achievements have not paralleled those for men and that a significant gap remains for salaries earned by comparable women suggests that programs aimed at reducing these gaps will continue to be needed for some years to come.

CONCLUSIONS

It is possible to conclude that when the larger picture is in focus, gender differences emerge quite clearly as both issues of learned competence in areas related to achievement and as issues of learned role expectations. What is important in all of this is that early socialization processes are not totally determining for later achievement since socialization processes continue throughout life. The opportunity structure is a powerful influence on the achieving behaviors of adults regardless of their early experiences. As social learning theory suggests, "Psychological function involves a continuous interaction between behavioral, cognitive and environment influences" (Bandura, 1978, p. 344).

The multidimensional model proposed to explain career and achievement motivation appears justified in light of the evidence presented. All three sets of influences, background, personal, and environment were found to significantly influence motivation. The good news was that unchangeable background factors were frequently mediated through environment and personal influences, and, in general, background factors were less powerful than the other two sets of influences. The evidence related to the Farmer (1985) model and evidence from other studies reviewed repeatedly highlighted the significant contribution of environment factors to motivation, especially perceived support for women working. Parent support and teacher support also played an important role affecting motivation. As Astin (1984) noted, the decade of the 1970s has witnessed several changes in the opportunity structure affecting women's achievement opportunities positively. Legislative changes related to training, employment, and advancement are just one example. Thirty-five years ago only about 10% of women with pre-school children worked, today the figure is over 45% (U.S. Bureau of Census, 1981). In addition, technological changes related to health, conception, and childbirth have increased the options open to women. A proliferation of acceptable lifestyles has also increased women's options. *Ms. Magazine* (1983) reported that only 16% of families in the United States conform to the nuclear model (i.e., working father, homemaking mother, and two children). As society changes in the future the impact of these changes will affect women's achievement motivation for good or ill.

Programs aimed at enhancing achievement for women included help with life planning skills which took into account the need to clarify values related to both homemaking and work roles. These programs were also aimed at teaching skills and attitudes enabling women and girls to take advantage of opportunities to enter math and science-related occupations. Effective enhancement programs used a variety of approaches supporting the four influences identified by Bandura (1982) to enhance self-efficacy perceptions. The four influences included role models, new information and experiences, the learning of new skills, and reduction of interfering anxieties and fears. Changing self-efficacy cognitions, enhancing self-statements that attribute success to internal factors and failure to lack of effort appear to be promising ways to enhance achievement motivation for both men and women, boys and girls. Enhancement programs need to be multidimensional, helping girls and women take advantage of new opportunities while at the same time reducing the inhibiting effects of early socialization. Equally important are efforts aimed at changing the environment to enhance the support systems available. Effecting changes in legislation, educational and employment policies, and teacher training are powerful ways to enhance the achievement of women and girls.

REFERENCES

Alper, T. (1974). Achievement motivation in women: Now-you-see-it-now-you-don't. *American Psychologist, 29*, 194–203.

American Institute for Research. (1978). *Career education effectiveness.* Report written for U.S.O.E., Office of Career Education. Palo Alto, CA: American Institute for Research.

Amiri, S. (1978). Career motivation of Iranian high school females with an emphasis on social class, parents, and peers. Unpublished doctoral dissertation, University of Illinois at Urbana-Champaign.

Anderson, G. (1983). A study of Cherokee and White eighth grade student career development: Sex, self-concept and attribution. Unpublished doctoral dissertation, University of Illinois at Urbana-Champaign.

Astin, H. (1984). The meaning of work in women's lives: A sociopsychological model of career choice and work behavior. *The Counseling Psychologist, 12*(4), 117–126.

Atkinson, J. (Ed.) (1958). *Motives in fantasy, action, and society.* Princeton, NJ: Van Nostrand.

Atkinson, J. (1978). The mainsprings of achievement-oriented activity. In J. Atkinson & J. Raynor (Eds.), *Personality, motivation and achievement.* New York: Halsted.

Ayres, A. (1980). Self-efficacy theory: Implications for the career development of women. Unpublished doctoral dissertation, Ohio State University, Columbus.

Bandura, A. (1977). Self-efficacy: Toward a unifying theory of behavioral change. *Psychological Review, 84*, 191–215.

Bandura, A. (1978). The self system in reciprocal determinism. *American Psychologist, 33*, 344–358.

Bandura, A. (1982). Self-efficacy mechanism in human agency. *American Psychologist, 37*(2), 122–147.

Bandura, A., & Schunk, D. (1981). Cultivating competence, self-efficacy, and intrinsic interest through proximal self-motivation. *Journal of Personality and Social Psychology, 41*, 586–598.

Bem, S. (1981). *Bem Sex-Role Inventory: Professional Manual.* Palo Alto, CA: Consulting Psychologists Press.

Benbow, C., & Stanley, J. (1982). Consequences in high school and college of sex differences in mathematical reasoning ability: A longitudinal perspective. *American Educational Research Journal, 19*(4), 598–622.

Betz, N., & Hackett, G. (in press). Applications of self-efficacy theory to understanding career choice behavior. *Journal of Social and Clinical Psychology.*

Betz, N., & Hackett, G. (1983). The relationship of mathematics self-efficacy expectations to the selection of science-based college majors. *Journal of Vocational Behavior, 23,* 329–345.

Blau, P., & Duncan, D. (1967). *The American occupational structure.* New York: Wiley.

Campbell, N., & Hackett, G. (1985). The effects of mathematics task performance on math self-efficacy and task interest. Paper presented at the American Psychological Association Annual Meeting, Los Angeles.

Card, J., Steel, L., & Abeles, R. (1980). Sex differences in realization of individual potential for achievement. *Journal of Vocational Behavior, 17,* 1–21.

Crandall, V., & Battle, E. (1970). The antecedents and adult correlates of academic and intellectual achievement effort. In J. Hill (Ed.), *Minnesota symposium on child psychology* (Vol. 4, pp. 36–93). Minneapolis: University of Minnesota Press.

Crites, J. (1978). *Theory and research handbook for the Career Maturity Inventory* (2nd ed.). Monterey, CA: CTB/McGraw-Hill.

Dweck, D., Davidson, W., Nelson, S., & Enna, B. (1978). Sex differences in learned helplessness, II. The contingencies of evaluative feedback in the classroom, and III. An experimental analysis. *Developmental Psychology, 14,* 268–276.

Elkstrom, R., & Marvel, M. (1985). Educational programs for adult women. In S. Klein (Ed.), *Handbook for achieving sex equity through education* (pp. 431–453). Baltimore, MD: Johns Hopkins Press.

Farmer, H. (1976). What inhibits career and achievement motivation in women? *The Counseling Psychologist, 6*(2), 12–14.

Farmer, H. (1980). Environmental, background, and psychological variables related to optimizing achievement and career motivation for high school girls. *Journal of Vocational Behavior, 17,* 58–70.

Farmer, H. (1983). Career and homemaking plans for high school youth. *Journal of Counseling Psychology, 30,* 40–45.

Farmer, H. (1984). Development of a measure of home-career conflict related to career motivation in college women. *Sex Roles, 10*(9/10), 663–675.

Farmer, H. (1985). Model of career and achievement motivation for women and men. *Journal of Counseling Psychology, 32*(3), 363–390.

Farmer, H., & Backer, T. (1977). *New career options for women: A counselor's sourcebook.* New York: Human Sciences Press.

Farmer, H., & Bohn, M. (1970). Home-career conflict reduction and the level of career interest in women. *Journal of Counseling Psychology, 17,* 228–232.

Farmer, H., Croce, K., Keane, J., Rooney, G., & Smith, L. (1979). *Career motivation project: Report for Mt. Zion High School.* Unpublished report available from the first author at 188 Education, University of Illinois, 1310 S. Sixth St., Champaign, IL 61820.

Farmer, H., & Fyans, L. (1983). Married women's achievement and career motivation: The influence of some environmental and psychological variables. *Psychology of Women Quarterly, 7*(4), 358–372.

Farmer, H., & Keane, J. (1980). *Career motivation project: Gibson City High School.* Unpublished report available from the first author at 188 Education, University of Illinois, 1310 S. Sixth St., Champaign, IL 61820.

Farmer, H., Keane, J., Rooney, G., Vispoel, W., Harmon, L., Lerner, B, Linn, R., & Maehr, M. (1981). *Career motivation achievement planning: C-MAP.* A measure and administrator's manual available from the first author at the University of Illinois, Department of Educational Psychology, Champaign, IL.

Farmer, H., & Sidney, J. (1985). Career education and counseling. In S. Klein (Ed.), *Handbook for achieving sex equity through education* (pp. 338–359). Baltimore, MD: Johns Hopkins University Press.

Farmer, H., Tohidi, N., & Weiss, E. (1982). Study of the factors influencing sex differences in the career motivation of Iranian high school students. *International Journal of Intercultural Relations, 6,* 17–39.

Farmer, H., Vispoel, W., & Maehr, M. (in preparation). *Variation of attribution patterns with achievement contexts.*

Fennema, E., & Sherman, J. (1977). Sex-related differences in mathematics achievement, spatial visualization, and affective factors. *American Educational Research Journal, 14,* 51–71.

Forsterling, F. (1985). Attributional retraining: A review. *Psychological Bulletin, 98*(3), 495–512.

Fowler, D. (1982). Mentoring relationships and the perceived quality of the academic work environment. *Journal of NAWDAC, Spring,* 27–33.

Frieze, I., Whiteley, B., Hanusa, B., & McHugh, M. (1982). Assessing the theoretical models for sex differences in causal attributions for success and failure. *Sex Roles: A Journal of Research, 8,* 333–344.

Gottfredson, L. (1981). Circumscription and compromise: A developmental theory of occupational aspirations. *Journal of Counseling Psychology, 28,* 545–579.

Greenberg, S. (1985). Educational equity in early education environments. In S. Klein (Ed.), *Handbook for achieving sex equity through education* (pp. 457–469). Baltimore, MD: Johns Hopkins Press.

Hackett, G., & Betz, N. (1981). A self-efficacy approach to the career development of women. *Journal of Vocational Behavior, 18,* 326–339.

Harrison, L. (1980). Sex stereotyping programs. In American Institute for Research (Ed.), *Programs to combat stereotyping in career choice.* Washington, DC: U.S.O.E.

Hoffman, L. (1986). Work, family and the child. In M. Pallak & R. Perloff (Eds.) *Psychology and Work: Productivity, Change and Employment* (pp. 169-220). Washington, D.C.: American Psychological Association.

Hollingshead, A. (1957). *The two factor index of social position.* Yale University, New Haven, CT: A. Hollingshead.

Horner, M. (1978). The measurement and behavioral implications of fear of success in women. In J. Atkinson & J. Raynor (Eds.), *Personality, motivation and achievement* (pp. 41–70). New York: Halsted.

Johnson, J., & Ettema, J. (1982). *Positive images: Breaking stereotyping with children's television.* Beverly Hills, CA: Sage.

Kantor, J. (1924). *Principles of psychology,* Vol. 1. Bloomington, IN: Principia Press.

Katz, M. (1973). *Career decision making: A computer-based System of Interactive Guidance and Information (SIGI).* Proceedings of the 1973 ETS Invitational Conference. Princeton, NJ: Educational Testing Service.

Kessel, L. (1979). *Age and sex differences in causal attributions for math and English in adolescents.* Unpublished doctoral dissertation, University of Illinois at Urbana-Champaign.

Klein, H. (1986). *Career satisfaction/dissatisfaction in professional dual career couples: Psychological, socioeconomic and background factors.* Unpublished doctoral dissertation, University of Illinois at Urbana-Champaign.

Klein, S., Russo, L., Tittle, C., Schmuck, P., Campbell, P., Blackwell, P., Murray, S., Dwyer, C., Lockheed, M., Landers, B., & Simonson, J. (1985). Summary and recommendations for the continued achievement of sex equity in and through education. In S. Klein (Ed.), *Handbook for achieving sex equity through education* (pp. 489–519). Baltimore, MD: Johns Hopkins Press.

Koffka, K. (1935). *Principles of gestalt psychology.* New York: Harcourt Brace.

Komarovsky, M. (1946). Cultural contradictions and sex roles. *American Journal of Sociology, 52,* 184–189.

Krumboltz, J. (1976). A social learning theory of career selection. *The Counseling Psychologist, 6*(1), 71–81.

Layton, P. (1984). Self-efficacy, locus of control, career salience, and women's career choice. Unpublished doctoral dissertation, University of Minnesota, Minneapolis.

Lent, R., Brown, S., & Larkin, K. (1984). Relation of self-efficacy expectations to academic achievement and persistence. *Journal of Counseling Psychology, 31*, 356–362.

Lent, R., Brown, S., & Larkin, K. (1985). Relation of self-efficacy to career choice and academic performance. Paper presented at the American Psychological Association Annual Meeting, Los Angeles.

Lent, R., & Hackett, G. (1985). Methodological and conceptual considerations in studying career self-efficacy. Paper presented at the American Psychological Association Annual Meeting, Los Angeles.

Lewin, K. (1935). *A dynamic theory of personality: Selected papers.* New York: McGraw Hill.

Maccoby, E., & Jacklin, C. (1974). *The psychology of sex differences.* Stanford, CA: Stanford University Press.

Maehr, M. (1974). Culture and achievement motivation. *American Psychologist, 29*, 887–896.

Maehr, M. (1984). On doing well in science: Why Johnny no longer excels: Why Sarah never did. In S. Paris, G. Olson, & H. Stephenson (Eds.), *Learning and motivation in the classroom* (pp. 179–210). Hillsdale, NJ: Lawrence Erlbaum.

Mathews, E., & Tiedeman, D. (1964). Attitudes toward career and marriage and the development of life style in young women. *Journal of Counseling Psychology, 11*, 375–384.

McClelland, D. (1985). *Human motivation.* Glenview, IL: Scott Foresman & Co.

Murray, H. (1938). *Explorations in personality.* New York: Oxford University Press.

Naftchi-Ardebili, S. (1983). High school students' perception of their teachers: Relationship to their self-esteem, performance and goals. Unpublished Master's thesis, University of Illinois at Urbana-Champaign.

National Research Council (1980). *Science and engineering doctorates in the United States, 1973 profile and science and engineering doctorates in the United States, 1975 profile: Employment status of doctoral scientists and engineers 1973 and 1975; Science, engineering, and humanities doctorates in the United States, 1979 profile.* Washington, DC: National Academy of Sciences.

Nicholls, J. (1980). A re-examination of boys' and girls' causal attributions for success and failure based on New Zealand data. In L. Fyans (Ed.), *Achievement motivation: Recent trends in theory and research* (pp. 266–288). New York: Plenum Press.

Northwest Regional Educational Laboratory. (1980). *Women in nontraditional careers: (WINC) Final report.* Portland, OR: Northwest Regional Educational Laboratory.

Osipow, S. (1983). *Theories of career development* (3rd ed.). Englewood Cliffs, NJ: Prentice Hall.

Peterson, P., & Fennema, E. (1985). Effective teaching, student engagement in classroom activities, and sex-related differences in learning mathematics. *American Educational Research Journal, 22*(3), 309–335.

Post-Kammer, P., & Smith, P. L. (1985). Sex differences in career self-efficacy, consideration, and interests of eighth and ninth graders. *Journal of Counseling Psychology, 32*(4), 551–559.

Raynor, J. (1978). Motivation and career striving. In J. Atkinson & J. Raynor (Eds.), *Personality, motivation and achievement* (pp. 199–219). New York: Halsted.

Rooney, G. (1982). *A study of career and achievement motivation; three life roles of worker, home-maker, and student; and sex differences.* Unpublished doctoral dissertation, University of Illinois at Urbana-Champaign.

Rooney, G. (1983). Distinguishing characteristics of the life roles of worker, student, and home-maker for young adults. *Journal of Vocational Behavior, 22*, 324–342.

Rotter, J. (1954). *Social learning and clinical psychology.* Englewood Cliffs, NJ: Prentice-Hall.

Rowan, J. (1982). *A study of role overload, nonmarket time use, and coping strategies of middle class, employed women in intact families.* Unpublished doctoral dissertation, University of Illinois at Urbana-Champaign.

Schau, C. Educational equity and sex role development. (1985). In S. Klein (Ed.), *Handbook for achieving sex equity through education* (pp. 78–79). Baltimore, MD: Johns Hopkins University Press.

Sells, L. (1975). *Sex, ethnic, and field differences in doctoral outcomes.* Unpublished doctoral dissertation, University of California, Berkeley.

Sewell, W., & Hauser, R. (1975). *Education, occupation, and earnings: Achievement in the early career.* New York: Academic Press.

Skarjune, J. (1985). Sex differences in career development, professional participation and perceptions of the mentoring and collegial relationships of directors of Illinois community mental health centers. Unpublished doctoral dissertation, University of Illinois at Urbana-Champaign.

Smith, L. (1981). The relationship of interpersonal needs, role-of-work definitions, and occupational prestige to marital structure in dual-earner couples. Unpublished doctoral dissertation, University of Illinois at Urbana-Champaign.

Spence, J., & Helmreich, R. (1978). *Masculinity and femininity: Their psychological dimensions, correlates and antecedents.* Austin, TX: University of Texas Press.

Stage, E., Kreinberg, N., Eccles, J., & Becker, J. (1985). Increasing the participation and achievement of girls and women in mathematics, science, and engineering. In S. Klein (Ed.), *Handbook for achieving sex equity through education.* Baltimore, MD: Johns Hopkins University Press.

Steinkamp, M., & Maehr, M. (1983). Affect, ability, and science achievement: A quantitative synthesis of correlational research. *Review of Educational Research, 53*(3), 369–396.

Steinkamp, M., & Maehr, M. (Eds.) (1984). *Advances in motivation and achievement, Vol. 2: Women and science.* Greenwich, CT: JAI Press.

Super, D. (1980). A life-span, life-space approach to career development. *Journal of Vocational Behavior, 16,* 282–298.

Super, D., & Cuhla, M. (1976). *Work salience inventory.* Available from Donald Super, 23 Mulberry Bluff, Savannah, GA.

Taleghani, N. (1978). The new system of education in Iran: The effect of the guidance cycle on students' career choice. Unpublished doctoral dissertation, University of Illinois at Urbana-Champaign.

Tittle, C. (1981). *Careers and family: Sex roles and adolescent life spans.* Beverly Hills, CA: Sage.

Tohidi, N. (1984). Sex differences in achievement/career motivation of Iranian boys and girls. *Sex Roles, 11*(5/6), 467–484.

Tresemer, D. (1976). The cumulative record of research on "fear of success." *Sex Roles, 2,* 217–236.

U.S. Bureau of the Census. (1981). *Supplementary reports: 1980 census of population.* Washington, DC: U.S. Bureau of the Census.

Webb, M. (1983). The change agent in nursing: A study of achievement in women. Unpublished doctoral dissertation, University of Calgary, Alberta, Canada.

Weinberg, R., Gould, D., & Jackson, A. (1979). Expectations and performance: An empirical test of Bandura's self-efficacy theory. *Journal of Sport Psychology, 1,* 320–331.

Weiner, B. (1974). *Achievement motivation and attribution theory.* Morristown, NJ: General Learning Press.

Weiner, B. (1979). A theory of motivation for some classroom experience. *Journal of Educational Psychology, 71,* 3–25.

Wheeler, K. (1983). Comparisons of self-efficacy and expectancy models of occupational preferences for college males and females. *Journal of Occupational Psychology, 56,* 73–83.

Wirtenberg, T. J. (1979). Expanding girls' occupational potential: A case study of the implementation of Title IX's anti sex-segregation provision in seventh grade practical arts. Unpublished doctoral dissertation, University of California, Los Angeles.

Women's Educational Equity Act Publishing Center. (1982). *Resources for educational equity: 1981–1982 catalog.* Newton, MA: Education Development Center, Inc.

CHOICE, CONTROL, AND MOTIVATION IN THE YOUNG AND AGED

Richard A. Monty and Lawrence C. Perlmuter

AN S-R VIEW OF MOTIVATION

Although many recent treatises on cognition have failed to consider the role of motivation, psychologists nevertheless have long recognized that the proficiency of cognitive performance is determined not only by skill but by motivation. Hull (1943) gave expression to this relationship by use of the terms drive (D) and habit (H). In his theory, additional motivational terms were included such as those referring to incentive factors (K) and stimulus intensity dynamism (V). The way in which these various terms were mathematically interrelated in determining performance is beyond the scope of the present chapter, however a recent discussion of these issues can be found in McClelland (1985).

Advances in Motivation and Achievement: Enhancing Motivation,
Volume 5, pages 99-122.
Copyright © 1987 by JAI Press Inc.
All rights of reproduction in any form reserved.
ISBN: 0-89232-621-2

One version of S-R theory which was influential from the 1940s to the 1960s provided an important role for motivation (e.g., Hull, 1943; Spence, 1956); however, its usage was limited to a homeostatic mechanism. That is, it was assumed that either external stimuli (e.g., electric shocks) or internal needs (e.g., tissue deficits) energized the organism exclusively. Such energy was in a sense a source for the activation of dominant habits which, if appropriate to the homeostatic imbalance, were strengthened by restoring balance to the organism. For example, a food-deprived rat which had acquired a bar-pressing skill may reduce its need for food by pressing a bar which in turn made food pellets available for ingestion. In the process of successfully performing this response, the bar-pressing skill or habit became strengthened as a result of reinforcements which concomitantly reduced the drive (need).

According to this S-R model, the expectation of receiving food was mediated by a classically conditioned response specifically related to the (anticipated) ingestion of food. Such models have been not only heuristic but useful in explaining behavior. One element, however, has been omitted from this early proferred behavioral explanation, namely, a possible role for active or self-initiated mentally driven activities which could *effect* behavior. Such an omission has been the source of vigorous criticism of this and other S-R theories (e.g., Zimbardo, 1969).

A COMPETING FORMULATION OF MOTIVATION

The most direct and one of the earliest assaults on the problem of the homeostatic-based model derived from the work of White (1959) who suggested that organisms are driven by a need for competence. The possibility of behaviors which in themselves do not reduce need states flowed from his theorizing. Indeed, he even suggested that subjects performed responses which might result in drive induction. White's reformulation substantiated the common sense idea that organisms can willfully or voluntarily act upon their environments. Moreover, according to White, organisms may not only learn to control their environments but such control may be motivationally satisfying. Along with this theoretical advance were other formulations which described the individual's need for achievement (Atkinson, 1957) or for power (McClelland, 1975).

The position adopted in the present chapter integrates the passive organism model with a model that argues for a competence need (active organism). In other words, the source of motivation can either be all self-initiated or driven by such variables as tissue deficits and the like, or both.

Furthermore, if it is assumed that individuals can generate internal stimuli to guide their own behavior, the need for an active organism model is substantiated. In addition, if it is recognized that stimuli (e.g., tissue deficits) over which the organism has little control can motivate behavior, then the need for a passive model is likewise vindicated. Moreover, there is evidence that some voluntary or self-initiated behaviors may grow involuntary or reflex-like (Kimble & Perlmuter, 1970). Thus, voluntary behaviors which are the product of an active organism along with involuntary behaviors which are thought to be a product of conditioning argue for the integration of both models in order to adequately explain behavior.

CHOICE AND CONTROL: DEFINITIONAL CONSIDERATIONS

When individuals are provided with an opportunity to select one option from a small number of alternatives (e.g., two to five), they may as a result perceive that they have some control over their environment (Perlmuter & Monty, 1977). However, there are a number of qualifications to this statement. First, the outcome of the choice must have some degree of indeterminancy (Mills, 1970). That is, if one option is associated with a guaranteed outcome while a second option is associated with a probabilistic outcome such a scenario will not increment the chooser's perception of control (Harvey, Harris, & Lightner, 1979). In order for the perception of control to be strengthened, the options must be *similar* in value and in outcome certainty. Further, exclusively non-desirable alternatives do not allow for a meaningful choice (Monty, Geller, Savage, & Perlmuter, 1979), or in Steiner's (1979) terms, autonomous choice. As Shakespeare said in *Hamlet*, "There is no choice in rotten apples." Situations in which value and outcome uncertainty vary independently will not be discussed in this paper but have been treated at length elsewhere (for a more complete discussion see Kahneman, Slovic, & Tversky, 1982). When discussing similarity of options (i.e., a pen vs. a pencil), it is necessary to distinguish this from identity of the options. A choice between two identical options (i.e., two identical pens) does not constitute an autonomous choice, hence does not increment the perception of control.

Both choice and competence need be considered in determining whether the perception of control will be enhanced. For example, an opportunity to choose to solve one of two mathematical equations both of which are similar in difficulty would constitute a choice only if the chooser possessed a level of competence that was appropriate to the challenge. This consideration is of especial relevance when the effects of choice are evaluated in young and aged learners. Indeed, there is evidence that older subjects exhibit lower expectations for success on certain tasks (Prohaska, Parham, & Teitelman, 1984). Moreover, there is evidence that the need for achievement declines with age (e.g., Smith, 1970; see Maehr & Kleiber, 1981 for discussion of this topic). Hence, providing an aged individual with an opportunity to select words to be learned on a paired-associates task may be intrinsically less motivating for the aged than for the proverbial college sophomore whose behaviors frequently include excercises in formal learning and testing. As we will see later in this chapter, some of the conclusions to be drawn from this kind of testing may be somewhat surprising. Indeed, aged individuals do benefit even from the seemingly abstruse opportunity to select words to be learned on a paired-associates task, although the magnitude of the effect may be somewhat diminished with age.

The observation that choice is effective in improving performance is important theoretically as well as practically. The theoretical significance is in suggesting a mechanism by which choice improves performance. When an individual makes an autonomous choice, the feedback provided by that behavior informs the chooser that control is available. In other words, the subjects learn from their behavior. The idea of learning from behavioral feedback (whether veridical or bogus) is central to the effects of choice and has a long history in psychology that is directly traceable to the writings of William James (1890). Other more recent statements can be found in the writings of Kelley (1967) in his principle of covariation, as well as in the works of Shachter and Singer (1962) on the relationship between behavioral feedback and emotionality.

EFFECTS OF CHOICE ON PERFORMANCE

As indicated above, an autonomous choice is possible when the available options are similar. Perlmuter and Smith (1979) conducted an experiment with a group of aged men all of whom were being treated for complaints with memory. Subjects were presented with ten stimulus words each accompanied by two response words of low to moderate meaningfulness (e.g., VICAR, PECAN). The first page of the test booklet contained a series of 10 rectangles and inside of each was a stimulus word, of low to moderate meaningfulness, centered on the left and two potential response words located one under the other on the right. In the Choice condition, subjects selected and circled one response word in each rectangle to be recalled when presented with the stimulus word. In the Force condition, one response word in each rectangle had been circled before being presented to the subject. Subjects were instructed to study the stimulus and circle (or re-circle) the response words. The first test trial presented the stimuli in a rearranged sequence and the subject was to recall and record the respective response words next to the stimulus words. This test was followed by having subjects copy the circled response words onto a designated "study sheet" so that subjects could study their respective S-R pairs. This tactic was also used to insure that both groups had close contact with the learning materials and further served to "personalize" the task for both groups in order to increase the likelihood that the subjects would learn the materials. After the copying task was completed, subjects received another test trial similar to the first. Following the test trial, subjects examined their own study sheets and then received an additional test trial. Study and testing alternated until six test trials were completed.

Figure 1 presents the mean number of correct responses per trial as well as the

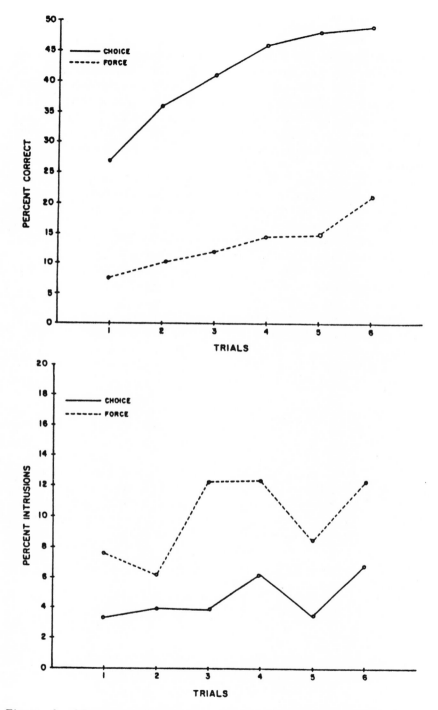

Figure 1. Mean percent correct responses and mean percent intrusions per trial in choice and force (patients) subjects.

mean number of incorrect or misplaced responses (intrusions). As can be seen, subjects in the Choice condition not only learned significantly better than those in the Force condition but the number of intrusions within the Choice condition was relatively low in comparison to the number of correct responses. On the other hand, intrusions in the Force condition were quite high relative to the number of correct responses. Apparently the effects of choice are observable even for subjects who are experiencing problems with memory which they were seeking to remediate.

In a similar experiment, Fleming and Lopez (1981) used paired associate learning with a group of aged subjects, the majority of whom were females. The materials were presented with photographic slides using the anticipation method of paired-associate learning. One group chose response words to be learned to the stimuli while a second group had these assigned. Following the choice/force procedure, each stimulus word was presented on a screen and subjects were to recite the corresponding response term. The next slide to be presented contained both the stimulus and respective response word. Thus, each trial consisted of alternating test and study slides. The results essentially replicated those of Perlmuter and Smith (1979). This replication is important because it was conducted with community dwellers who were not distinguished by problems of memory. Second, the subjects were primarily females in comparison to the males used in Perlmuter and Smith, and finally, the effects of choice were apparent with either the anticipation method or study-test procedures of paired-associate learning.

A similar experiment was conducted by Monty, Rosenberger, and Perlmuter (1973) employing young subjects. During the choice/force procedure, slides were presented containing a stimulus along with five potential response words. In the presence of each slide, subjects either chose or were assigned the response word to be learned. The novel feature of the Monty et al. experiment was that one group chose 100% of their response words while two other groups chose only 25% of the responses, the remainder being assigned by the experimenter. One of these latter two groups (early choice) selected their responses from the initial three slides while the late choice group selected their responses from the final three slides; the other nine response words having been assigned by the experimenter. A fourth group (force) had all of the response words assigned by the experimenter.

Following the choice/force procedure, the anticipation method of S-R learning was used as in Fleming and Lopez (1981). The results showed that the 100% choice group learned significantly better than the force group thus replicating the finding from a previous study with aged subjects. In addition, the early choice group learned as well as the 100% choice group while the late choice group performed similarly to the group offered no choice at all. Thus, the effects of choice were determined by the placement in time of the choice procedure. The identical amount of choice at the conclusion of the task did not benefit performance relative to the force group. Early choice appears to have had an effect which generalized to other sections of the task in which no choice had been permitted.

Using a similar early vs. late procedure, White, as reported by Perlmuter and Monty (1977), showed that performance on a reading comprehension task could be improved significantly by allowing choice at the start of the task. These results were found with grade school children, thus showing that the effects of choice are observable across the age span, a finding which supports, the results of previous investigators (e.g., deCharms, 1979).

LIMITATIONS ON THE PERCEPTION OF CONTROL

The role of similarity of the alternatives from which the choice had been made has been studied by Monty et al. (1979). Subjects were presented with stimulus words each accompanied by two response words. For one group, both response words in each set were of high meaningfulness thus defining the High-High group (HH). For another group, one response word in each set was of high meaningfulness and the other of low meaningfulness, which defines the High-Low meaningfulness group (HL). In the HL group, the high meaningfulness (M) words were identical to the high M words in the HH group.

Only when choice is relatively unconstrained does it enhance the perception of control. For example, a choice between two dissimilar alternatives, only one of which is normatively desirable, constrained the freedom to choose thereby reducing its effectiveness in contributing to the perception of control. The hypothesis tested was that when subjects exclusively chose high M words in the HL condition they would not benefit from choice to the same extent that choice subjects would in the HH condition. A force group was included for whom the alternatives were both of high M. Essentially, the results showed that only when the alternatives were similar did choice enhance performance relative to the force condition. There was one exception to this generality which will be discussed in the next section.

Although both HH and HL groups chose their response words, it could be argued that for the HL group, the rejection component of the choice process had been eliminated a priori. For example, a choice between a gold plated pencil and a wooden pencil is not arrived at by considering first one alternative and then *equally* considering the other alternative. The lowered value alternative is likely to have been easily eliminated from consideration from the beginning. In other words, the alternatives are so dissimilar as to not constitute a choice. Similarly, when an individual is faced with a life and death decision (e.g., to refrain from smoking or to die from smoking) such a set of alternatives are so dissimilar as to constitute a dilemma, not a choice.

Normative Versus Idiosyncratic Influences on Choice

Within the experiment described above, the majority of subjects in the HL condition fulfilled normative expectations and limited their selections to the high M words thus selecting none of the low M words. However, a minority of subjects selected one or more low M alternatives. Although we had no way of predicting *which* subjects would follow the normative pattern exclusively and which would reject it, we predicted that selecting even a single low M alternative should provide subjects with the perception of an autonomous choice, thereby enhancing the perception of control. Subjects in this self-generated (choice) condition learned their high M words significantly better than subjects in the force condition. Apparently they had discovered a choice within the objectively "no-choice" condition and this in turn benefited their performance.

Apparently, the perception of control derives not from the act of choice but rather from the feedback associated with an autonomous choice in which a set of equally attractive alternatives had been presented. Subjects in the HL group who *created* the opportunity for an autonomous choice performed as well as those provided with the opportunity for an autonomous choice (HH group). It is interesting to speculate about the reason for this anomolous selection pattern. One possibility is that for some subjects, certain of the low M words which were chosen were similar in attractiveness to the high M words, which were not chosen. Admittedly, this explanation is tautological. A second possibility, is that the subjects who selected the low M alternatives recognized these as such, but nevertheless desired to create an opportunity for choice. Selecting a limited number of low M alternatives provided these subjects with an opportunity to exercise an "autonomous" choice, thereby augmenting motivation. Presently, we cannot distinguish between these two explanations.

The Role of Rejection in Choice

In an experiment by Monty et al. (1979), some subjects were presented with an HL condition and were instructed to overtly reject the non-desired alternative. The results were in the predicted direction but missed the traditional .05 level of significance. That is, the rejection process resulted in a slightly higher level of performance than the choice condition when the alternatives were dissimilar. However, with a discrimination paradigm, when subjects were required to learn a target word accompanied by one or more similar background words, the rejection process significantly improved performance relative to the choice process (Monty, Perlmuter, Libon, & Bennet, 1982). A recognition test showed that the learning of target words as well as the non-chosen (background) words was significantly elevated by rejection relative to choice.

Choice: An Overview

In summary, the results seem unambiguous in showing that when the requirements for an autonomous choice are satisfied, permitting subjects to learn materials of their own choosing enhances performance relative to a condition in which the identical materials are assigned to be learned. To observe the benefits of choice, subjects must be provided with alternatives which are objectively similar on one or more dimensions (e.g., words similar in meaningfulness). When presented with alternatives which are objectively dissimilar, choice is ineffective so long as the subject predictably selects high M words exclusively. Conversely, selecting even one or two low M words is sufficient to render the entire choice process autonomous and hence effective. Further, it appears as if the more important element in the choice process is rejection. Theoretically, it would be expected that rejection would be relatively more effective in the presence of dissimilar alternatives but such a prediction awaits additional support.

HOW CHOICE AFFECTS PERFORMANCE

Given that performance is enhanced by the opportunity to choose, it becomes necessary to identify mechanisms which may mediate such an outcome. We have seen that the beneficial effects of choice on learning are not simply the result of an opportunity to learn idiosyncratically easier materials. That is, the effects of choice have been shown to generalize to non-chosen portions of the task. Rather, it appears that an autonomous choice increases the subject's perception of control which in turn elevates motivation. Three mediators of motivation have been proposed: arousal, effort, and an increase in resource allocation.

Following Humphreys and Revelle (1984), we will define *arousal* as a change in alertness or attention in response to changes in internal or external stimulation or both. Indications of arousal may be based on physiological measures (heart rate, skin conductance) or on self-reports of alertness and "peppyness." On the other hand, *effort* is included within a motivational rubric as a term which suggests that subjects are trying hard to perform a particular task effectively. Effort may be indexed by the utilization of processing resources in a dual task experiment in which it becomes possible to measure the relative degree of effort devoted to the respective tasks. An increase in *resource allocation* would be indexed by an improvement in performance which was not specific to the chosen task. In one sense, the resource allocation explanation shares some similarity with the arousal explanation but, for example, does not necessarily predict that reaction times (discussed below) would be accelerated as is predicted by an arousal hypothesis.

The results described to this point on the effects of choice on performance do not differentiate between these competing explanations. To test these hypotheses, we will turn to an experiment containing a dual task (Perlmuter, Scharff, Karsh, & Monty, 1980). Subjects in one condition were permitted to select response words to be learned to the stimuli on a paired-associate task while a second group learned the identical materials in the absence of choice. Following the choice/force procedure, subjects learned their paired-associates with the anticipation method. Along with this task, all subjects were required to continuously depress a telegraph key which was to be released quickly in response to presentations of a tone.

As in previous experiments, subjects learned their paired-associates significantly better following choice. Thus, the additional task requirement did not disturb the conventional finding with respect to choice. Since the reaction time task had no explicit element of choice within it, positive effects of choice on reaction time (faster responses) would argue for an arousal explanation of choice whereas slower reaction times following choice would support an effort explanation for choice. The results are contained in Figure 2. As can be seen, reaction time per-

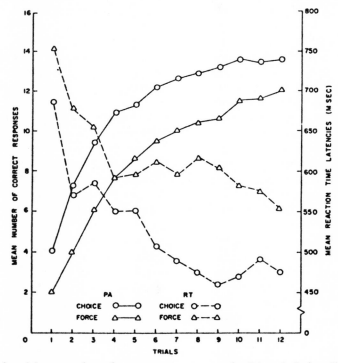

Figure 2.   Mean number of correct responses on the PA task (left ordinate) and mean reaction time latencies (right ordinate) for the choice and force groups (RT condition only).

formance of the choice subjects was consistently faster than that of the force subjects.

The effort explanation did not receive even minimal support. It might have predicted either no difference in performance or an effect favoring the force subjects. Alternatively, it could be argued that the reaction time performance is to some extent confounded by the superior performance of the choice subjects on the paired-associate task. That is, an "easier" task may free resources for the reaction time task. To test this notion, a second experiment (Perlmuter et al., 1980) was conducted similar to the first with a naive group of subjects. One difference in the procedure was instituted. Following the choice/force phase, the reaction time task was unexpectedly introduced and thus delayed the start of the paired-associate task.

Both groups performed the reaction time task and the results (Figure 3) are similar to those seen previously. Apparently, choice increased arousal which in turn benefited performance on the reaction time task over which neither group of

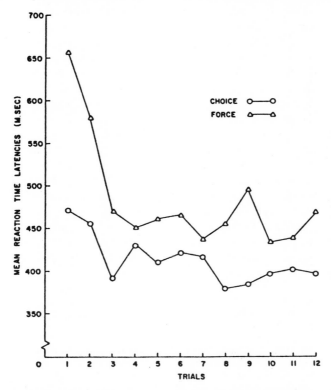

Figure 3. Mean reaction time latencies for the choice and force groups (Experiment 2).

subjects had any explicit choice. Parenthetically, it is interesting to note that re-action time performance was significantly faster when the tasks were performed separately rather than jointly. The extent of the difference provides an index of the amount of resources necessary for the paired-associate task. This cross-experimental comparison should be considered cautiously even though the experiments were run in the same laboratory with subjects drawn from an identical subject pool, they were nevertheless run successively.

A third alternative mediator for motivation may be the increased availability of resources as described by Kahneman (1973). Indeed, there is evidence from our laboratory to support this alternative (Perlmuter & Monty, 1982). Let's describe the task and the manipulations which led us to consider this alternative explanation. Subjects were presented with a page containing two and four word lines and were instructed to learn one word (target) on each line. No explicit mention was made in the instructions about the remaining (background) word or words on each line.

Half of the subjects chose their own target words while the remainder were assigned target words to be learned. An unexpected recognition test was pre-sented in which all of the old words along with an equal number of new words were presented as distractors. On the recognition test, each word had been pre-sented individually. Subjects were instructed to indicate whether the word was old (previously presented) or new as well as how confident they were in their judgments. Only the percentage of correct recognitions was examined.

Results indicated that target words were recognized significantly better than background words, and choice targets were recognized significantly better than force targets. However, the most important outcome was that background words were recognized significantly better by choice subjects than by force subjects. That is, choice subjects learned more about all of the materials (target and back-ground) than force subjects. These results offer strong support for the idea that one mechanism of choice may be mediated by an increase in resources allocated to the task.

In summary, choice appears to produce motivational effects which in turn are mediated by elevations in arousal and in the increased availability of cognitive resources.

CHOICE AND AGING: A CLOSER LOOK

As indicated previously, when aged subjects were permitted to choose response words to be learned to stimuli in a paired-associate task, performance was significantly improved relative to a condition in which the identical materials had been learned in the absence of choice (Fleming & Lopez, 1981; Perlmuter & Smith, 1979). Unfortunately, neither of these studies utilized a young compari-son group which would have provided a measure of the relative effectiveness of choice developmentally. Currently, the only study which has examined the relationship between age and intrinsic motivation is limited by the fact that only the choice condition had been included (McGlinchey, Perlmuter, Sizer, & Nathan, 1985). In their study, young subjects (18–35 years) and aged subjects (55–75 years) were presented with a paired-associate task consisting of a single stimulus word along with two response words. Subjects selected one response word to be learned to the respective stimulus. Following this, a cued-recall test was presented in which the stimulus words were shown and subjects were instructed to recall and record the response words.

Results showed that recall was significantly better for young than for aged subjects, although the level of performance was relatively low for everyone. More interestingly, when subjects were asked to rate on a 1–7 scale how much choice they had in making their selections, aged subjects reported significantly less freedom to choose than young subjects. Overall, these novel results support the notion that age-related changes do attenuate the extent to which subjects perceive choice. These results should be viewed cautiously for a number of reasons. First, it is premature to make a broad statement based only upon a paired-associate task even if the results were found to be replicable. What is needed are a variety of tasks inside and outside of the laboratory which might establish the generalizability of the results, (i.e., to determine whether such an outcome is task independent). Second, it is necessary to replicate the experimental design adding two additional groups, namely, young and aged subjects who are not permitted to choose. This latter manipulation would provide critical information about the extent to which choice augments performance vis-à-vis that seen in aged matched control groups not permitted to choose. Third, McGlinchey et al. inquired about the subject's self-report of freedom to choose *after* the cued-recall test. Therefore, it cannot be determined unambiguously whether performance on the recall test might have influenced the subject's perception of control. To accomplish this objective, some subjects would have to respond to the self-report questionnaire before the recall test and the remainder after the recall test.

Results from another study underway in our laboratory (Perlmuter, Au, & Monty, 1985) bear on the relationship between age and effectiveness of choice in enhancing performance. Subjects were presented with the task of learning 20 (target) words displayed on lines containing either one or three additional words. Although the five-letter words were ostensibly unrelated to one another, they were similar in rated meaningfulness and in form, being constituted of alternating consonants and vowels. On a random half of the lines, subjects chose their target word while on the remainder, target words were assigned. Exposure to each line was time limited depending on line length, i.e., two or four words per line. Subjects ranged in age from 55–75 years.

Basically, the results of a recognition test (Table 1) showed that subject-chosen target words were learned significantly better than those which were assigned. Moreover, background words from choice lines were recognized signifi-

Table 1.   Mean Proportion Correct Recognition (Old Stimuli)

Words Per Line	Choice Condition		Force Condition	
	Target	Background	Target	Background
2	.79	.64	.81	.46
4	.94	.46	.65	.30

cantly better than comparable words from force lines. Thus, using a within-subject choice manipulation, there were benefits of choice with respect to the learning of both target and background words. The importance of this finding is in showing that choice enabled subjects to selectively learn a great deal more about specific materials in the task, namely, those that were present on the choice lines. These results also provide some support for the notion that the variable which mediates choice may be one which increases the availability of cognitive resources since a great deal more was learned on choice than on force lines. Similar results were found with young subjects (Monty et al., 1982) as reported previously. These results are also of theoretical importance because of the possibility that the background words might have interfered with the learning of the target words. That is, in the choice condition, the increased contact with background words might have strengthened their distractive effects relative to the force condition, however, this did not occur. Apparently, choice insulated the subjects against the distractive effects of intrusions. Indeed, there is some evidence, although controversial, that aged subjects are relatively more distracted by the presence of background cues (Kausler, 1982).

This experiment also provided some tentative evidence for an age-related attenuation in the effectiveness of choice on performance. When these subjects were examined in groups aged 55–64 years vs. 65–74 years, results showed a marginally significant effect of age. Analysis of the simple effects indicated that the magnitude of the choice effect was significantly less for older than for younger subjects. The results are consistent with those seen with the learning of paired-associates (McGlinchey et al., 1985), namely that with increasing age there is a diminution in the degree to which choice is effective.

The age-related diminution in the effectiveness of choice, as reflected on laboratory tests, may be a natural sequel to repeated experiences with diminished opportunities for control in the everyday world (Weisz, 1983). For example, the individual in the sixth and seventh decade of life may encounter fewer opportunities for control as well as less effectiveness with respect to efforts at control. During the second and third decades of life, the individual may come to believe that if a certain behavioral regimen is followed, the quality of physical health can be improved. The pandemic practice of physical exercise and attention to diet programs substantiates this idea. With increasing years, certain changes in health status or in physical appearance are inevitable, despite the individual's best efforts at control. Such biologically determined alterations do not gainsay the possibility that the rate of these changes is somewhat dependent upon the appropriateness or effectiveness of the health maintenance program. Rather, it suggests that a program that appeared to be effective at age 20 may not have the identical effects at age 50. In other words, those activities which, in earlier years of life, were effective, may continue to be so, but at a reduced level. To some extent such biologically determined developmental events are likely to diminish the aged individual's beliefs about control, and when provided with an opportunity to choose response words for a paired-associate task, the perception of control is ineluctably diminished as well.

FIELD STUDIES OF CONTROL IN THE AGED

Drew and Waters (1985) provided evidence that routine behaviors affect the perception of control. Specifically, community dwelling aged were provided with an opportunity to learn to play a video game. It may be speculated that the popularity of such games derives in part from the opportunity to exercise control over the environment. They hypothesized that such training would have positive effects not only on change-scores on psychomotor tests but more importantly would enhance self-reports about the quality of life. The authors reported (personal communication) that the participants expressed reluctance in playing video games because they thought these to be more appropriate for young people. However, with encouragement, subjects submitted to a semi-weekly, thirty minute video game exercise for a period of eight weeks. Specifically, the game (*Crystal Castles*) involved a central character in the form of a bear who was enabled to gather an unlimited number of gemstones while seeking to avoid hazards which impeded its objectives and lowered the game score. Of the eleven subjects who received such training, nine showed significant improvements in performance subtests (rotary pursuit, Purdue Pegboard) while, as expected, verbal scores on the Wechsler Adult Intelligence Scale did not change.

Video game experience resulted in higher quality of life scores as measured by a standardized test. Moreover, post-experimental interviews with the participants revealed that experience with the video game resulted in an improvement in the performance of routine behaviors. That is, at the conclusion of the experiment participants indicated that they were more attentive, careful, and purposeful in the performance of daily tasks. Thus, experience with a relatively uncomplicated routine impacted beneficially on the quality of life in the aged. As Langer and Rodin (1976) showed, the responsibility for the care of a plant was of sufficient importance to institutionalized aged to enhance the quality of their behavior and even increased the duration of life itself (Rodin & Langer, 1977).

To account for the above results, it is proposed that individuals draw inferences about their level of competence and control from their performance. Such information is potentially derivable from all activities even those which are labeled routine. This is not to gainsay the likelihood that more major decisions or accomplishments may not contribute as much or more to self-perceptions of competence and control. Rather, for most people, such events occur too infrequently to possess sufficient life sustaining properties.

Paradoxically, routine behaviors, although they contain the seeds for perceived control, lose this feature through the process of repetition. To illustrate this point, let us examine a routine behavior, namely, tying one's shoelaces. Young children learn after much cajoling and some frustration to tie their shoelaces. At the point of accomplishment and shortly thereafter, such a behavior provides a source of competence and control. With repetition of this activity two changes may occur. First, the quality of the performance improves and second the performance grows automatic. The paradox lies in the fact that while increased quality of performance could further nourish the perception of competence, automaticity robs the performer of this possibility. To test these relationships a procedure was designed to make automatic behaviors more conscious (Perlmuter & Langer, 1982). Associated with automaticity is a diminution in the perceived availability of choices. Perceptually, there appears to be only one way to accomplish an automatically performed behavior. Not only does the performer fail to consider alternatives, but more importantly, there is likely to be failure to recall having performed the behavior in the first place.

In a sense, compulsive behaviors share some similarity with automatic behaviors. Let us examine the following scenario. An individual may have a fear of intruders and therefore checks the status of door locks while at home. What begins as a purposeful instrumental response often results in an action which may be performed repeatedly in the course of a relatively short time period until the individual through some fortuitous event is reminded of having performed the act only recently. What does the aging individual learn from this hypothetical experience? The person may come to conclude that the lock-checking action is being performed without the appropriate intentionality and without memory for its performance. Such a series of performances can diminish the perception of control and further reinforce negative stereotypic labels applied to the aged.

Perlmuter & Langer (1982) conducted a study to examine the effects of de-automatizing routine behaviors in order to determine whether this treatment would increase the perception of control. Community dwelling subjects who were participants in a day treatment program were assigned to one of three conditions at random. In the "standard monitoring" condition, subjects reported on *one behavior* each day for two successive weeks. Specifically, subjects were asked to indicate: (1) the first beverage of the day which they chose to consume; (2) how much they drank; (3) how much they enjoyed it. The latter two questions were open-ended. Subjects received a notebook to record their entries each day for one week. At the start of the second week, the notebooks were collected and a new one, identical to the first, was issued.

Subjects in the "varied monitoring" condition were treated similarly except that in the first week they responded to a *different activity* each day, i.e., they were asked to indicate: (1) what color shirt they chose; (2) if it was comfortable; (3) if they enjoyed wearing it. The "beverage question" was also included on one day. In the second week, the identical questions were repeated in the same sequence as that used in the first week.

In the "rejection" condition subjects were treated similarly to those in the second group, except that in addition to indicating what they chose they indicated three alternatives which might have been chosen but were not. They also indicated their enjoyment and satisfaction with the chosen alternative as did the first two groups. These activities were performed for two weeks.

Following the completion of the study, subjects responded to a brief questionnaire dealing with such items as their perception of control over their lives, satisfaction with health, willingness to participate in future research, etc. Questions were answered with a seven-point scale. Although the number of subjects per group were few, a consistent pattern of results to each of the questions was found. That is, the rejection group showed the most positive scores on each question while the varied monitoring group was second and the standard monitoring group was poorest.

The interpretation of these results is as follows: First, we assume that all of the routine behaviors which participants were instructed to monitor had previously grown automatic, thus providing the performers with little if any perceived control. Second, it is our assumption that alternative expressions of behavior are intrinsic to all activities. Such alternatives include possible variations in the topography of the behavior as well as in the effort and intensity with which it is performed. Presumably, the explicit monitoring of these behaviors interferes with automaticity, forcing the subject thereby to consider alternative forms of behavior which in turn require a purposeful choice, i.e., the making of distinctions among alternatives. Third, based on our earlier discussion of the relative effectiveness of choice versus rejection, we predicted that the perception of control would be strongest for the rejection condition (Monty et al., 1979). Presumably, the process of rejection forces a more complete consideration of the alternatives, thus resulting in the highest level of perceived control.

In a debriefing following the conclusion of the experiment, some of the subjects in the standard monitoring condition indicated that responding to the same questions every day for two weeks was extremely boring. At that point, we suggested to the participants that the true source of their boredom resided in their repeated choice of the same alternative without variation. We also observed that following training, some participants began to wear more coordinated combinations of clothing while others reported that they had grown more attentive to their environments, even responding with surprise to the presence of certain "novel" features of their accustomed environments.

These results are similar to those of Drew and Waters (1985), namely, that simple behaviors can be used to enhance the perception of control. More importantly, such effects generalized to a variety of behaviors, thus providing the potential for still further increase in control and motivation.

Benefits of Control in Institutional Settings

In a study with intermediate and skilled-care nursing home residents, Ryden (1984) investigated some of the factors which contribute to morale. She showed that the sense of control largely determined the level of morale in these patients. Moreover, the perception of control had very pervasive effects in this setting, even moderating the relationship between physical health and morale. That is, presumably the belief about control had a moderating effect upon the patients' responses to their own compromised health status. Perhaps the most interesting findings derive from the patients' reports and indicate that the primary contributors to the perception of control were based on freedoms related to eating and grooming. Thus, in conformity with previous studies (e.g., Drew & Waters, 1985), the perceived freedom to perform the most routine of activities determines the extent to which patients perceive freedom or infringements upon their perception of control.

In an interventional study in an institutional setting Rodin (1980) provided patients with a button which was effective for a limited (15 minutes) period of time each day in summoning the presence of a nurse. Initially, patients used the button more frequently than necessary; with time, however, button pressing decreased. There were occasional bursts of activity which Rodin suggested might have provided patients with a test of the availability of control. Results of the manipulation showed that general health and sociability increased in the experimental group, although no quantitative support was presented for her contentions. Rodin suggested that the mere presence of a button *could be* used to lessen the perceived stress associated with institutionalization. Reductions in perceived stress were significantly correlated with increased feelings of control.

THEORETICAL CONSIDERATIONS

The general theoretical approach employed in the present chapter is compatible with Bandura's (1984) notion of reciprocal causality. That is, while the behavior of the individual may be effective in controlling the environment, environmental changes can have a reciprocal effect on behavior. For example, environmental changes in response to behavior can provide feedback to the individual about their competence with respect to the environment. Changes in competence may in turn influence the individual's level of motivation. Increased levels of motivation may potentiate additional behaviors or increase the effectiveness of behavior, which in turn can increase competence and motivation. Similarly, ineffective behavioral-environment interactions can have a reciprocal effect and thus lower levels of competence and motivation.

The notion that individuals may learn from their own behavior is not a novel idea. More importantly, this feature can be exploited to increase the perception of control in the aged. However, whether control has a positive or negative effect on behavior depends on how it was made available to the individual. That is, for control to enhance motivation it must be earned by the individual (Revesman & Perlmuter, 1981). Only if the individual perceives responsibility for the outcome will the perception of control be enhanced. Conversely, the gratuitous awarding of control to the individual also implies that it can be lifted. Thus, arbitrarily providing control or the non-contingent rewarding of behavior (Winefield, 1983) each can reduce the individual's perception of control. Non-contingent rewards may lead the individual to develop a sense of resignation, which in turn can overwhelm their belief about the *potential* effectiveness of their behavior. As the perception of control decreases, the individual becomes more vulnerable to a variety of stressors (e.g., Glass & Singer, 1972).

Still, another source of motivation derives from the use of language by the individual or by society in the form of stereotypes. Words can alter motivation. The use of stereotypes or deprecatory labels such as those associated with aging, can provide individuals with self-fulfilling prophecies that can result in diminished levels of performance, and this in turn can reduce the perception of control and competence.

Throughout this discussion we have made reference to the assumption that control is illusory and yet it possesses motivational qualities. How can these two features be reconciled? We will attempt within a very brief space to sketch three basic features of control and motivation which allow individuals to develop and support beliefs about their perception of control, borrowing largely from Commons and Armstrong-Roche (1985).

First, the illusory aspect of control is related to the belief that people, at least in western culture, have with respect to their freedom of action. For example, Commons and Armstrong-Roche (1985) suggested that people can report a sense of knowing what they are going to do in the next moment. Hence they may conclude that they have free will.

Second, the motivational aspect of control may derive from the assumption that people commonly make about the causes or attributions for their behavior. That is, people may believe that any behavior which they *will*, can and does occur. Willing is the *sine qua non* of behavior. As Commons and Armstrong-Roche (1985) pointed out, this assumption is untestable because of its inherent circularity. Any behavior which occurs, is willed! On the other hand, when people experience non-contingencies between behavior and outcomes, they may feel that their free will has been diminished because the relationship between thoughts and behavior and its effects on the environment are no longer predictable.

Third, people often believe that what they are going to do is a reflection of their own thoughts; their thoughts derive from themselves. Thus, the self may be perceived as the first cause of behavior. With respect to the self as the first cause of behavior, again circular reasoning supports this notion so that it remains unassailably believable, i.e., untestable. That is, people may believe that the self is the author of thoughts because it is difficult to think back to an earlier occurring origin for behavior.

Although the relationship between choice and control, as discussed in this chapter, may not be self-evident (Chan, Karbowski, Monty, & Perlmuter, 1986) it is our assumption that when individuals are permitted to make autonomous choices they may perceive that they are the authors of their own behavior. Such an outcome strengthens their beliefs about control, thus incrementing further efforts at control, through a motivational mechanism.

EFFICACY AND ITS EFFECTS ON MOTIVATION

Condiotte & Lichtenstein (1981) have shown that when individuals entered a program designed to produce a cessation in smoking, their judgments about the probability that they would resist the tendency to smoke in certain situations was correlated with the degree of abstinence in those situations. Similarly, as Schunk and Carbonari (1984) pointed out, people do not violate diets because they lack the ability to resist, rather it is because they no longer desire to exert the necessary effort. Hence it may be proposed that the effort to control behavior derives not from external factors but rather from the individual's beliefs about the likelihood that they will resist certain competing tendencies. In other words, self-efficacy may provide motivation to conform to either internal or external stringencies. Moreover, such beliefs about efficacy may derive from the individual's perception of freedom. When freedom is compromised, the necessary motivation to effect a certain behavior is likewise diminished. Thus, we come full circle in the present analysis. Self-efficacy and perceived freedom provide the necessary conditions for self-imposed restrictions upon behavior in conformity with internally or externally originated demands.

THE SELF AND THE PERCEPTION OF CONTROL

In the next experiment we examined the role of the self in community dwelling aged who were participants in a day treatment program (for a more complete discussion see Perlmuter, Monty, & Chan, 1986). These subjects read a story which contained a number of blank spaces placed immediately in front of certain verbs. One group was instructed to complete the blanks with either "he" or "she" depending on the subject's gender while a second group was instructed to fill the blanks with the letter "I." Either type of insertion was reasonable with respect to the meaningfulness of the story. After reading the story both groups submitted to a recognition memory test followed by a series of questions about their perceptions of control and willingness to be involved in future research, etc. Questions were answerable with a seven-point scale.

Results showed that recognition was similar in both groups, but on the questionnaire, the "I" group produced responses which were significantly more positive with respect to questions of control, willingness to participate and even lead future activities than the "he/she" group.

Presumably when subjects write "I," they have an increased tendency to perceive control. Such effects presumably derive from the feedback associated with the use of "I" as the first cause.

EPILOGUE

When today is perceived as one long day which began yesterday; when the menu of last night's supper is seen as routine and immediately forgettable; when the appropriateness of dress is a decision of no consequence; when even a purposeful activity to be carried out leaves the performer with the question as to what was intended and why, such a series of events provide a message to the individual which presages helplessness, thereby serving to fulfill the negative societal promise of old age.

Are there alternatives and are they attainable? The present research provides an affirmative answer to both of these questions. Especially for the isolated aged, the perception of control and competence are often derived solely from self-appraisals. Thus, it becomes important to provide the aged with a sense of intentionality, purpose, and control. Such is attainable by encouraging a belief in control—a belief, however, that must be based on experience with control.

This chapter has shown repeatedly that control and motivation are intrinsically linked. Moreover, the aspects of behavior which can be used to enhance control are those which are available to almost all individuals, namely, those centered on eating, dressing, and other basic routines.

Perhaps it would be safe to conclude that "control cannot be taught it must be caught." That is, the individual must learn from his/her behavior the extent to which control is available. Indeed individuals can discover control in the basic and simple activities which support daily life.

Moreover, choices which are provided to the individual can induce a perception of control. Such choices, however, must be drawn from options which are similar and for which the outcomes associated with each are probabilistic, not certain and not chance. Thus, even a medical regimen could be used to foster perceptions of control if the available choices are properly presented.

The antithesis of control is found in the performance of behaviors which are carried out automatically or which the individual deems trivial as a result of environmental influence. Automaticity vitiates control, while triviality renders it worthless, even if discovered.

ACKNOWLEDGMENTS

Preparation of this chapter was supported in part by Grant AGO 2300 from the National Institute on Aging, V.A. Medical Research Services, and in part by the Behavioral Research Directorate, Human Engineering Laboratory.

REFERENCES

Atkinson, J. W. (1957). Motivational determinants of risk-taking behavior. *Psychological Review*, *64*, 359–372.

Bandura, A. (1984). Representing personal determinants in causal structures. *Psychological Review*, *91*, 508–511.

Chan, F., Karbowski, J., Monty, R. A., & Perlmuter, L. C. (1986). Performance as a source of perceived control. *Motivation and Emotion*, *10*, 59–70.

Commons, M. L., & Armstrong-Roche, M. (1985). When and why the free will illusion occurs. Paper presented at the Annual Meeting of the Eastern Psychological Association, Boston.

Condiotte, M. M., & Lichtenstein, E. (1981). Self-efficacy and relapse in smoking cessation programs. *Journal of Consulting and Clinical Psychology*, *49*, 648–658.

deCharms, R. (1979). Personal causation and perceived control. In L. C. Perlmuter & R. A. Monty (Eds.), *Choice and perceived control*. Hillsdale, NJ: Lawrence Erlbaum Associates.

Drew, B., & Waters, J. (1985). Videogames: A strategy to improve perceptual-motor skills in the non-institutionalized elderly. Paper presented at the annual meeting of the Eastern Psychological Association, Boston.

Fleming, C. C., & Lopez, M. A. (1981). The effects of perceived control on the paired-associate learning of elderly persons. *Experimental Aging Research*, *7*, 71–77.

Glass, D. C. & Singer, J. E. (1972). Behavioral aftereffects of unpredictable and uncontrollable aversive events. *American Scientist*, *60*, 457–465.

Harvey, J. H., Harris, B., & Lightner, J. M. (1979). Perceived freedom as a central concept in psychological theory and research. In L. C. Perlmuter & R. A. Monty (Eds.), *Choice and perceived control*. Hillsdale, NJ: Lawrence Erlbaum Associates.

Hull, C. L. (1943). *Principles of behavior*. New York: Appleton-Century-Crofts.

Humphreys, M., & Revelle, W. (1984). Personality, motivation, and performance: A theory of the relationship between individual differences and information processing. *Psychology Review*, *91*, 153–184.

James, W. (1890). *The principles of psychology*. New York: Henry Holt.

Kahneman, D. (1973). *Attention and effort*. Englewood Cliffs, NJ. Prentice-Hall.

Kahneman, D., Slovic, P., & Tversky, A. (1982). *Judgment under uncertainty: Heuristics and biases*. Cambridge: Cambridge University Press.

Kausler, D. H. (1982). *Experimental psychology and human aging*. New York: John Wiley & Sons.

Kelley, H. H. (1967). Attribution theory in social psychology. In D. Levine (Ed.), *Nebraska symposium on motivation*. Lincoln, NE: University of Nebraska Press.

Kimble, G. A., & Perlmuter, L. C. (1970). The problem of volition. *Psychological Review*, *77*, 361–384.

Langer, E., & Rodin, J. (1976). The effects of choice and enhanced personal responsibility for the aged: A field experiment in an institutional setting. *Journal of Personality and Social Psychology, 34,* 191–198.

Maehr, M. L., & Kleiber, D. A. (1981). The graying of achievement motivation. *American Psychologist, 36,* 787–793.

McClelland, D. C. (1975). *Power: The inner experience.* New York: Irvington.

McClelland, D. C. (1985). How motives, skills, and values determine what people do. *American Psychologist, 40,* 812–825.

McGlinchey, R. E., Perlmuter, L. C., Sizer, N., & Nathan, D. M. (1985). Effects of aging and type II diabetes on decision making and perceived control. Unpublished Manuscript, Harvard School of Dental Medicine, Boston, MA.

Mills, J. (1970). Unpublished analysis of perceived choice. University of Missouri, Columbia.

Monty, R. A., Geller, E. S., Savage, R. E., & Perlmuter, L. C. (1979). The freedom to choose is not always so choice. *Journal of Experimental Psychology: Human Learning and Memory, 5,* 170–178.

Monty, R. A., Perlmuter, L. C., Libon, D., & Bennet, T. (1982). More on contextual effects on learning and memory. *Bulletin of the Psychonomic Society, 20,* 293–296.

Monty, R. A., Rosenberger, M. A., & Perlmuter, L. C. (1973). Amount and locus of choice as sources of motivation in paired-associated learning. *Journal of Experimental Psychology, 97,* 16–21.

Perlmuter, L. C., Au, R., & Monty, R. A. (1985). The motivational effects of choice on learning and memory in the aged. Unpublished manuscript, Harvard School of Dental Medicine.

Perlmuter, L. C., & Langer, E. J. (1982). The effects of behavioral monitoring on the perception of control. *Clinical Gerontologist, 1,* 37–43.

Perlmuter, L. C., & Monty, R. A. (1982). Contextual effects on learning and memory. *Bulletin of the Psychonomic Society, 20,* 290–292.

Perlmuter, L. C., & Monty, R. A. (1977). The importance of perceived control: Fact or fantasy? *American Scientist, 65,* 759–765.

Perlmuter, L. C., Monty, R. A., & Chan, F. (1986). Learning, choice, and control. In M. M. Baltes & P. B. Baltes (Eds.), *Aging and Control.* Hillsdale, NJ: Lawrence Erlbaum Associates.

Perlmuter, L. C., Scharff, K., Karsh, R., & Monty, R. A. (1980). Perceived control: A generalized state of motivation. *Motivation and Emotion, 4,* 35–45.

Perlmuter, L. C., & Smith, P. (1979). The effects of choice and control on paired-associate learning in the aged. Paper presented at New England Psychological Association, Boston.

Prohaska, T., Parham, I., & Teitelman, J. (1984). Age differences in attributions to casuality: Implications for intellectual assessment. *Experimental Aging Research, 10,* 111–117.

Revesman, M. E., & Perlmuter, L. C. (1981). Environmental control and the perception of control. *Motivation and Emotion, 5,* 311–321.

Rodin, J. (1980). Managing the stress of aging: The role of control and coping. In S. Levine & H. Ursin (Eds.), *Coping and health.* New York: Plenum.

Rodin, J., & Langer, E. (1977). Long-term effects of a control-relevant intervention with the institutionalized aged. *Journal of Personality and Social Psychology, 35,* 897–902.

Ryden, M. B. (1984). Morale and perceived control in institutionalized elderly. *Nursing Research, 33,* 130–136.

Schachter, S., & Singer, J. E. (1962). Cognitive, social, and physiological determinants of emotional state. *Psychological Review, 69,* 379–399.

Schunk, D. H., & Carbonari, J. P. (1984). Self-efficacy models. In J. D. Matarazzo, S. M. Weiss, J. A., Herd, N. E. Miller, & S. M. Weiss (Eds.), *Behavioral health.* New York: John Wiley & Sons.

Smith, J. (1970). Age differences in achievement motivation. *British Journal of Social and Clinical Psychology, 9,* 175–176.

Spence, K. W. (1956). *Behavior theory and conditioning.* New Haven, CT: Yale University Press.

Steiner, I. D. (1979). Three kinds of reported choice. In L. C. Perlmuter & R. A. Monty (Eds.), *Choice and perceived control.* Hillsdale, NJ: Lawrence Erlbaum Associates.

Weisz, J. R. (1983). Can I control it? The pursuit of the veridical answers across the life span. In P. B. Baltes & O. G. Brim, Jr. (Eds.), *Life span development and behavior.* New York: Academic Press.

White, R. (1959). Motivation reconsidered: The concept of competence. *Psychological Review, 66,* 297–323.

Winefield, A. H. (1983). Cognitive performance deficits induced by exposure to response-independent positive outcomes. *Motivation and Emotion, 7,* 145–155.

Zimbardo, P. G. (1969). *The cognitive control of motivation.* Glenview, IL: Scott, Foresman and Company.

THE ENHANCEMENT OF STUDENT MOTIVATION

Carole Ames

This chapter concerns the academic motivation of students within the context of the classroom. Further, like others in this volume, this chapter is concerned with how motivation can be enhanced. How the issue of "enhancement" is approached, however, depends on whether one views motivation from a quantitative or qualitative perspective (Ames & Ames, 1984). It is not that motivation is more or less important from either perspective, instead, it is that motivation is defined differently and is therefore important for different reasons.

From a quantitative perspective, motivation is associated with concepts such as energy, drive, intensity of behavior, and duration of behavior. Within this perspective, student motivation is sometimes operationalized as time on task or engaged time. Increments in the amount of time a child spends on a task as well as gains in achievement are taken as evidence of "enhanced" motivation. Motivation is important because it (along with other variables) contributes to and predicts more visible outcomes such as achievement.

Advances in Motivation and Achievement: Enhancing Motivation,
Volume 5, pages 123-148.
Copyright © 1987 by JAI Press Inc.
All rights of reproduction in any form reserved.
ISBN: 0-89232-621-2

From a qualitative perspective, the study of motivation is more concerned with the study of how students think—how they think about themselves, their task, and their performance. Emphasis is placed on the content and direction of students' cognitive processes, such as students' beliefs about the causes of success and failure, self-evaluations, reasons for learning, and learning strategies. Although these cognitions mediate and affect how much time a student is willing or likely to spend on a task as well as resulting achievement, they can be viewed as important educational outcomes in their own right, they are central to the initiation and maintenance of learning, and are directly implicated when we are concerned with the quality of student task engagement (Corno & Mandinach, 1983), self-worth (Covington & Beery, 1976), and continuing motivation (Maehr, 1976).

Thus, enhancing motivation can be easily interpreted as only a problem of "enhancing achievement" when a quantitative perspective is adopted. Those practices which are associated with high achievement or high test scores are also viewed as fostering desirable motivation patterns in students. From a quantitative analysis then, conditions or treatments observed to increase student performance on achievement tests are therefore "best bets" for enhancing motivation. In actuality, practices that contribute to high test performances may also promote motivational patterns that are not conducive to long-term learning (Dweck & Elliott, 1983; Pascarella, Walberg, Junker, & Haertel, 1981).

In contrast, a qualitative conception of "enhancement" focuses on ways of modifying or changing how a student thinks. Here we are concerned with how we can get students to adopt certain goals, selectively attend to certain types of information, process information differently, and interpret performance information differently. Conditions which contribute to perceptions of personal competence and specific metacognitive processes also develop in students the ability to initiate, direct, and maintain their learning (Wittrock, 1984). Thus, changes in cognitions result in changes in achievement-directed behaviors that have important implications for long-term learning as well as the type and extent of involvement in specific learning activities. It is this latter conception of motivation, as a qualitative construct, that is the focus of this chapter.

QUALITATIVE MOTIVATION

Research on achievement motivation has focused on a wide variety of cognitive-based processes, including, for example, attributions, self-efficacy and self-evaluations, learning strategies and achievement goals. This research has also addressed a range of issues, including how motivational processes can best be conceptualized, how these processes differ across individuals and change over time, and how they can be modified when they are maladaptive.

Over the last decade, research and writings about the causes or antecedents of student motivation have increasingly focused on the classroom and other contextual factors that influence learning. The social and evaluative context surrounding students' learning experiences has been shown to have significant consequences for a broad range of motivation processes, including, for example, how students approach a task, how they evaluate their performances, how they perceive their own competence, and how they relate to others. Research which has focused on how cognitive motivational processes can be modified, however, has focused on the individual student as the target for intervention (e.g., Dweck, 1975; Schunk, 1982, 1984a), and with few exceptions (e.g., deCharms, 1976, 1984), has not been concerned with how the social and evaluative structure of the classroom may moderate the effectiveness of specific training interventions. This is not to say that there has been no interest in changing environmental or instructional factors. There has, in fact, been considerable research on modifying the structure of the classroom (e.g., Johnson & Johnson, 1985; Slavin, 1978, 1983); however, this research has focused almost exclusively on achievement outcomes. This line of research has been consumed with the question as to what type of learning environment leads to greater or lesser achievement, and motivation, when it has been considered, has been discussed hypothetically as a covariate of achievement.

What is problematic in integrating these two lines of research is that, by and large, they have progressed independently. Research which has focused on modifying the cognitive-motivational processes of the individual student has not addressed the impact of what the student experiences in the classroom situation. Research which has focused on modifying the learning environment of the classroom has not examined the qualitative dimensions of motivation processes. Certainly, attempting to change instructional practices (i.e., how the classroom is structured for learning) may be viewed as more troublesome and obtrusive than individually directed training programs. However, it is argued here that modifying environmental factors such as the structure of the classroom is not merely an alternative way of attempting to enhance motivation, it is *necessary* to achieve optimal motivation patterns. Such a dilemma may seem easily reconciled by suggesting that both approaches (individual training and instructional environment modification) are needed (cf. McCombs, 1984). It is my contention, however, that the effects of classroom factors on student motivation have been heretofore underestimated and that changes in classroom structure *must* figure prominently in any model of motivation enhancement or change. The purpose of this chapter, then, is to examine the implications of current research for motivation training, beginning with a brief description of specific motivational processes that are seen as critical to the initiation and maintenance of long-term learning.

QUALITATIVE DIMENSIONS OF MOTIVATION

Achievement attributions. Children's achievement attributions are the reasons or explanations they give to explain their performance. Achievement events are presumed to trigger an attributional search in which students ask themselves "why" questions such as, "Why did I fail?", or judge the contribution of specific factors to their performance as in, "How smart was I in solving those problems?" This latter form of attribution question has been called an informational search (Whitley & Frieze, 1985) as opposed to the former causal search, although both forms of attribution, asking for cause vs. asking for information, reflect how an individual is processing information and responding to specific situational and performance cues.

The central tenet of an attributional model of achievement motivation is that these attributions mediate the effects of certain antecedent events (e.g., success, failure) and subsequent achievement responses. There is, of course, the question as to what kinds of information and experiences trigger attributions. Certainly some achievement events and outcomes are more likely than others to elicit attributions. In classroom situations, students repeatedly encounter a multitude of experiences (e.g., grades, evaluations, teacher feedback) that are personally important and relevant and that have implications beyond the immediate situation, and thus, presumably trigger attributional responses. These attributions have been found to have significant effects on a wide range of achievement responses, including, for example, task choices or preferences, persistence in the face of difficulty, and affective reactions (see Weiner, 1979, for review). Attributions have also been implicated in children's continuing motivation (Maehr, 1976), self-worth (Covington & Beery, 1976), personal efficacy (Schunk, 1984b), and the quality of their involvement in learning (Corno & Mandinach, 1983).

Although there are a myriad of causal factors that can be used to explain an event, attribution theory and research has typically implicated ability and effort as the factors having the more important consequences for subsequent achievement activity. Both ability and effort describe characteristics of a person, that is, they are internal as opposed to external factors. Ability, however, is also perceived as stable across time and related tasks, while effort is perceived as changing or variable. Children who have an *a priori* tendency to associate failure with lack of effort have been described as mastery-oriented in that they tend to persist on difficult tasks and adopt strategies that enable them to plan, direct, and execute appropriate task behaviors (Diener & Dweck, 1978; Dweck, 1975). In contrast, children who tend to associate failure with low ability have been identified as "at-risk." These children are more likely to give up when they become frustrated and become focused on the inadequacy of their ability. It is this latter group, those who focus on their ability following failure, which has been the target for motivation intervention. The high value placed on ability as a desirable personal characteristic suggests that negative ability attributions have significant negative consequences for one's self-worth and subsequent achievement activity (Covington, 1984).

Achievement goals.   Related to attribution concepts are students' reasons for learning (Nicholls, 1985) and their achievement-related goals (Maehr & Nicholls, 1980; Dweck, 1984). The issue here concerns *why* students choose to engage in academic tasks, rather than whether or not they do so or how much time they spend doing so, although students' goal orientation certainly has implications for the latter. According to Maehr and Nicholls (1980; see also, Maehr, 1983, 1984; Nicholls, 1979, 1983, 1984), for example, students may choose to participate in specific activities to gain external rewards, to develop their ability, or to demonstrate high ability by outperforming others or by achieving success with little effort. Students who have different types of achievement goals are likely to differ in a variety of achievement-related beliefs and behaviors, ranging from how they respond to the challenges of a specific situation to the likelihood that they will pursue similar tasks and activities in other situations at other times. Students who are interested in developing their ability and gaining mastery, have been described as task-oriented. These students are more likely to see success as contingent upon their effort and more likely to engage in difficult tasks with the intent of learning something new. Students who instead want to demonstrate that they have ability, have been described as ego-oriented; they are more likely to avoid difficult situations and engage in failure-avoiding tactics (procrastinating, not trying) when their ability is threatened (see Covington & Beery, 1976, for examples of failure avoidance).

Dweck (1984; see also, Dweck & Elliott, 1983) has similarly differentiated two forms of achievement motivation according to the type of goal that is being pursued. She characterizes one goal as learning-oriented, similar to the task-oriented students described above. Students who value learning are theorized to prefer challenging tasks and value effort and diligence. A second goal orientation paralleling an ego-orientation is defined as performance-oriented. Students who perceive performance as important are more likely to choose tasks that ensure success and reflect positively on their ability.

The basic assumption in these achievement goal analyses is that the pursuit of different goals is likely to influence a range of achievement behaviors not unlike those highlighted in the previous section on attributions. Achievement goals, however, also influence cognitions such as attributions by making certain types of information salient and by affecting how this information is then interpreted. Achievement goals, therefore, provide the primary schema within which one's experiences are given meaning. Implicit in the writing on achievement goals is a value judgment that a task or learning goal orientation is more likely to produce independent learning and sustained involvement in achievement activities (Dweck, 1984; Nicholls, 1979, 1984).

Self-efficacy. Self-efficacy is an individual's belief that he/she has specific performance capabilities (Bandura, 1982). Efficacy expectations, however, are distinct from outcome expectations. The latter are defined as an individual's belief that a given behavior will lead to a successful or desired outcome. This distinction is important because a teacher can try to increase a child's outcome expectation (e.g., "Everyone's story will be displayed on parents' night"), but the child may continue to doubt his/her ability to perform the necessary behavior (i.e., write a story). Self-efficacy, then, is essentially one's self-concept of ability about a specific task in a specific situation. It is an individual's judgment about and confidence in his/her ability to perform.

Self-efficacy beliefs are most directly influenced by performance accomplishments and have been shown to affect persistence, task choices, effort expenditure, and actual task performance (see Schunk, 1982, 1984a, 1984b). Attributional judgments also influence efficacy judgments (Schunk, 1982). A successful performance attributed to effort enhances self-efficacy and a poor performance attributed to lack of effort maintains a positive self-concept of ability. Actually, this effect (i.e., a positive relationship between effort attributions and self-concept of ability would be predicted from both an attributional and self-efficacy (social learning) theoretical framework. According to self-efficacy theory, however, it is self-efficacy, not the attributional judgment, which drives subsequent achievement responses. The basic model is that positive self-efficacy sustains task involvement, leading to skill development and performance accomplishments which, in turn, further enhances the child's sense of efficacy

Self-regulated learning. When students confront challenging c tasks in the classroom, successful accomplishment of those tasks require. metacognitive skills. Metacognitive activities such as planning, monitoring, and self-checking are viewed as essential to sustained learning (Brown, Campione, & Day, 1981; Brown, 1978). According to Corno and Rohrkemper (1985; see also, Corno & Mandinach, 1983), it is with these skills that learning and motivation become integrated processes. Many classroom tasks require a high level of acquisition (e.g., alertness to the task, self-monitoring) and transformation (processing, connecting, and manipulating information) activity and whether students adequately engage in these processes depends on how the task is presented, the kind of instruction, how the situation is structured, and certain characteristics (e.g., ability) of the learner. Self-regulated learning is "an effort put forth by students to deepen and manipulate the associative network in a particular area . . . and to monitor and improve the deepening process" (Corno & Mandinach, 1983, p. 95). Self-regulated learning includes specific cognitive strategies that are defined by the task and content as well as general or generic metacognitive strategies that can be used in a variety of learning situations. These latter processes include self-monitoring and self-planning skills, that is, the ability to plan, guide, and execute one's learning whenever an academic task is encountered.

It is this latter component, self-monitoring, of self-regulated learning that is of interest here because it involves generic learning strategies that are not content-specific and that are related to other motivation processes. Self-monitoring and self-instructional processes have been found to co-vary with effort attributions. Diener and Dweck (1978), for example, assessed internal speech patterns of mastery- and helpless-oriented children and found that these children differed not only in their attributional orientation but also in their tendency to engage in strategic thinking when they encountered failure. Only the mastery-oriented children, those with an *a priori* tendency to attribute failure to inadequate effort, responded to failure with increased problem-solving strategies and with self-monitoring and self-instructions. Similarly, Ames (1984) found a tendency for effort attributions and self-monitoring strategies to co-occur in certain types of situations. Although these task-directed cognitions have been associated with a tendency to make attributions to effort, it remains uncertain as to whether they are precipitated by effort attributions.

How self-regulatory processes are used depends on the students' sense of personal competence in a somewhat reciprocal manner (Corno & Mandinach, 1983). While perceptions of competence are viewed as necessary precursors to the effective use of self-regulatory skills (Bandura, 1981; Corno & Rohrkemper, 1985), training children in self-regulatory skills is also regarded as a way in which students can gain a sense of competence (Bandura & Schunk, 1981; Corno & Rohrkemper, 1985). The development of these learning skills or strategies, the ability to apply these skills appropriately, and the perceived need to use these skills are all necessary for a high level of task engagement, that is, for self-regulated learning. The likelihood that students will use these skills is dependent on their prior attributions (i.e., whether effort is seen as related to one's performance), their self-perceptions of competence as well as the presence of a facilitating environment. Thus, self-regulated learning is conceptualized as involving general metacognitive processes (e.g., self-monitoring, planning) and these processes are seen as skills that can be learned and that represent a knowing how to learn.

HOW THESE CONSTRUCTS ARE RELATED

As can be seen, attributions, achievement goals, self-efficacy, and self-regulated learning are interrelated processes. Within each paradigm, however, the variables of interest are juxtaposed with behavior in a different manner. For example, attribution theory presumes that attributions are evoked to explain certain events and predict subsequent achievement responses and behavior in an event →cognition→ action sequence. Both attribution and self-efficacy theory emphasize the central role of cognitions in achievement behavior. Self-efficacy theory, however, inserts efficacy judgments between cognition and action (although *a priori* efficacy judgments also influence attributions) such that efficacy judgments, rather that attributions, determine subsequent thought, affect, or action. Using an achievement goal analysis, perceived goals enter the sequence before attributions. The salience of certain goals over others influences how events are perceived and interpreted. Finally, self-regulated learning processes are sensitive to achievement goals, attributions and efficacy judgments. Each of these can have positive or negative influences on how students approach and become engaged in a learning task. Perceptions of competence, expectations of reward (outcome expectations), and perceptions that one's effort will lead to the desired outcome influence the use of self-regulatory processes and the probability of sustained achievement activity (cf. Thomas, 1980).

There is now research which has focused on how these processes can be modified when they are maladaptive. These interventions have utilized individual retraining, that is, modifying specific cognitions of the individual student. Examples of these approaches are described below.

INTERVENTIONS BASED ON COGNITION RETRAINING

Within an achievement context, these cognitive-based processes have all received considerable "retraining" attention. Attribution retraining is based on the premise that causal attributions mediate and influence subsequent achievement behaviors; and therefore, changes in an individual's attributions should result in changes in achievement responses. The intent of the retraining interventions, in general, has been to induce individuals to make effort, rather than ability, attributions for failure. Dweck (1975), for example, has shown that repeated cueing and social reinforcement can be used to redirect children's attributions. In a series of studies (Dweck, 1975), Carol Dweck and her colleagues have identified children with an *a priori* tendency to attribute failure to lack of ability and then taught them to attribute failure to a lack of effort instead. Across the retraining studies, the objective of the interventions has been to make these individuals think more like mastery-oriented individuals. Individuals selected for retraining have ranged from children to college-age students, and from these groups individuals have been targeted because they were low achievers (Chapin & Dyck, 1976), judged "helpless" by teachers (Dweck, 1975), or have demonstrated an attributional set to associate failure with low ability on a questionnaire (Andrews & Debus, 1978).

The short-term benefits of such retraining efforts have had demonstrated effects on children's persistence as well as changes in their attributional schema. However, whether changes in attributions or achievement behaviors transfer to classroom settings and to academic tasks has not been demonstrated. Although the Andrews and Debus study showed some extended training, those changes were demonstrated only for nonschool-related tasks (anagrams, circle designs) outside the regular classroom. In fact, all the attribution retraining studies have used achievement-related but nonacademic tasks and have been conducted in laboratory-like or individualized settings free from public evaluation and social comparison, two dominant features of classroom life. And, as will be discussed more later, redirecting a child's thinking toward effort may be more difficult to attain in the classroom.

Similar forms of interventions involving goal setting, modeling, and attributional refocusing have been employed in efficacy training. Again, in laboratory-like settings, children have been given some type of reward contingent on their performance (Schunk, 1983), observed a model verbalize positive self and task-evaluations while solving problems (Bandura & Schunk, 1981; Schunk, 1984a), or have had their performance attributed to effort (Schunk, 1982). In each study, the focus has been on redirecting how the child processes performance information. The findings from this research have been quite consistent in demonstrating significant increments in children's beliefs that they can perform the task, and some studies (Schunk, 1982, 1983) have also shown increments in children's actual performance. Unlike the attribution retraining efforts, academic tasks (math) have been used in the efficacy training. Children have been selected for training because they are low achievers, with the assumption that low achievement in math also implies a low self-concept of ability for math. Thus, the selection of subjects is based on quite different criteria within an attribution and self-efficacy paradigm, and the subjects selected for efficacy training would not necessarily be those who are targeted for attribution training. The benefits of self-efficacy training, however, have not been demonstrated for situations where social comparison is salient and when the child compares unfavorably. Because self-efficacy is sensitive to many sources of information, the effectiveness of any training approach may be negatively affected by the presence of other conflicting cues.

Research which has specifically targeted the self-regulatory skills has used strategy training, that is, making students aware and knowledgeable about specific metacognitive skills as well as teaching them how and when to use them (e.g., Brown, Campione, & Day, 1981). Clinically based approaches to modifying self-control (e.g., Meichenbaum, 1977) provide a compatible model. Corno and Mandinach (1983) discuss participant modeling as a technique to teach children these skills. Using this approach, a child is provided with a model of how to perform a particular task. In addition to demonstrating the correct procedure, this model also suggests to the child how to respond when difficulty is encountered. That is, the child is shown how to respond to problems when new strategies must be identified and implemented.

Consistent with a social learning approach (see Bandura, 1977), the child is coached and reinforced for applying these strategies in relatively "safe" settings following direct instruction or modeling. Oden and Asher (1977) have demonstrated long-term effects when they used a very similar approach to train children in specific social skills. Although self-regulation is concerned with the child's internal speech, self-regulation is hypothesized to respond to direct instruction much like overt social skills. Rohrkemper and Bershon (1983) suggest that teachers can directly instruct children to engage in more constructive and facilitative inner speech by telling children what to say to themselves when they approach the task, when they are doing the task, and when they encounter frustration or failure. According to Schunk (1984b), training children to use these skills also serves to develop a sense of efficacy.

Corno and Mandinach (1983), however, suggest that the problem children have in using these skills (self-monitoring) is as much a matter of enactment as lack of skill knowledge. Thus, even when children have the knowledge whether they will actually use self-monitoring skills in the classroom may be dependent on the demands of the setting. Certain demands (e.g., where the teacher provides all the cues, information, and choices) may obviate the need for these skills, and certain types of structures (e.g., when social comparison is emphasized) may even negatively affect the student's tendency to engage in self-monitoring.

Unlike the individually directed efforts at retraining or modifying children's attributions, self-efficacy, or self-monitoring strategies, research and writing on children's achievement goals has focused on the role of the environment, that is, how the context or structure of the performance setting makes different goals salient. In an experimental study by Elliott and Dweck (1981), the situation in which children were performing was manipulated to highlight either performance or learning goals. The performance goal was made salient by telling children that their performance was to be filmed and later evaluated by experts. For the alternative learning goal, children were merely told that the learning task might be helpful to them in their other studies and no film was mentioned. The inculcation of these different "reasons" had significant effects on children's subsequent task choices, the strategies they used in their performance, and their attributions. The point here being that different achievement goals were elicited as a function of how the situation was structured. Thus, unlike the previous approaches which focused on modifying children's thoughts with individual training interventions, the research on achievement goals suggests that children's cognitions can be, or perhaps should be, changed by modifying the environment, that is, modifying the structure (i.e., the salience of specific information) of the performance situation.

As we see, common to the efficacy, attribution, and strategy training paradigms is first the individual setting in which the training occurs, well protected from the realities of the classroom. Also common to these approaches is a presumption of what the "at-risk" child is thinking about. According to attribution theory, the "at risk" child *is* making attributions and the problem is that the child should be making effort, rather than ability, attributions. According to efficacy theory, the problem of the "at risk" child is that he/she negatively evaluates his/her ability and therefore lacks confidence in his/her ability to perform. According to self-regulatory theory the "at risk" child does not use self-monitoring strategies effectively. It may be the case that the child does not have these strategies in his/her repertoire or that the child merely does not know how and when to use them.

Again, interventions such as these are based on the premise that effective achievement behaviors are dependent on the form and pattern of existing thought processes. These interventions involve individual training and are primarily directed toward helping the student acquire new or reshape existing cognitive processes. But an implicit assumption in these motivation training efforts is that what goes on in the classroom *will/can* support the objectives of these interventions. That is, children will continue to attribute their performance to effort, maintain high self-efficacy, and use self-monitoring strategies in the classroom. Unfortunately, there is now much evidence to suggest that certain types of classroom structures and, in fact, the character of most classrooms, do not encourage or support these desired cognitions. Classrooms which make social comparison goals salient promote an ability attributional focus, provide a constant threat to one's self-efficacy, and undermine the use of self-monitoring skills.

CLASSROOM INFLUENCES

The Character of the Classroom

In the classroom, students work on academic tasks that are embedded in an organizational structure, and it is this structure which conveys explicit and implicit information about how students are to be evaluated, what are valued student characteristics, and how students are to relate to the task and to each other. The organizational structure, therefore, impacts a range of student-task, student-teacher, and student-student relations.

Just as classrooms differ according to how they are structured, there are certain similarities across classrooms that distinguish them from other types of work or performance settings. The classroom environment is characterized by a high frequency of contact and interaction among its members. Student participation is expected but not necessarily insured, the goals or objectives are often ambiguous, multifaceted. and externally defined, and the evaluative criteria are typically nonspecific. Further, classroom work is often perceived by students as normatively too difficult or too easy, uninteresting and repetitive, and not worth the effort required.

Be that as it may, as children progress through school, significant changes in the nature of the classroom are evident (Blumenfeld, Pintrinch, Meece, & Wessels, 1982; Eccles, Midgley, & Adler, 1984; Levine, 1983). In the early years of the elementary school, teachers are generally quite generous in giving stickers, stamps, and happy faces. These rewards are often noncontingent on the child's level of performance and are just as often given for behavior as academic work. Children are typically given chances to redo their work without negative consequence, and just completing one's work is as important as getting it done correctly. Students' social behaviors and interest (e.g., "shows an interest in . . .") are given status equal to academic performance on report cards. Parents of kindergarten and first grade children, in particular, express as much concern about how their child is behaving at school as with how they are performing. In these early years, the child's task of sorting out the meaning of teacher feedback is not always easy. A task of writing a sentence and drawing a picture to illustrate the meaning, for example, may elicit comments from the teacher on the artwork, rather than the match between the artwork and the sentence. Unintentional feedback such as this may influence the direction of children's efforts on subsequent tasks. But, even in the early years, social comparison is often imposed through ability grouping, specific "membership" in such things as the "wise owl club," and differential rewarding with stickers, stamps, and happy faces. Children are quite aware of who reads best, draws the best pictures, runs fastest, etc. Although young children tend not to be daunted by negative social comparisons, they gradually begin to use this information in forming judgments abut their own ability (Frey & Ruble, 1985). Although children may believe that they can get smarter, they also become aware that they may never be as smart as others.

As children progress through the elementary grades, their performance in the classroom becomes more public; that is, how students compare to others becomes more salient (Bossert, 1979). Children become more attuned to normative standards and begin to interpret performance and normative-based feedback as reflecting on their ability. As a consequence, children's perceptions of their own ability (particularly those who are doing less well than others) begins to decline (Entwistle & Hayduk, 1978; Stipek, 1981, 1984). As well, their judgments of their ability begin to reflect the teacher's evaluation of their ability (Nicholls, 1982). Whole class recitations, ability grouping, and public evaluations of ability, performance, and behavior become common. Evaluations of academic and social behavior become more frequent and increasingly based on social comparative standards. The increasing difficulty of schoolwork is compounded by more frequent experiences of normative failure, i.e., the perception that one is not doing as well as others. In a very real sense, the evaluative climate of the classroom becomes more competitive as children progress through school (cf. Eccles, Midgley, & Adler, 1984; Parsons, Kaczala, & Meece, 1982).

How does this evolving competitive structure influence student motivation? Considerable research suggests that a normative climate makes it difficult for the majority of children to focus on their effort and the value of trying hard, to maintain high self-efficacy, to think about self-monitoring processes, and to believe that learning something new is as important as performing better than others.

Research Evidence

If we accept the conclusion that the structure of most classrooms is competitive, that is, makes social comparison salient, what are the effects of a competitive structure on motivational patterns in students? Perhaps, most important, and having significant consequences for the motivational processes described herein, is the consistent finding that competition focuses children on evaluating their ability (Ames, & Ames, 1984; Blumenfeld et al., 1982; Nicholls, 1979).

In our work (e.g., Ames, Ames, & Felker, 1977; Ames & Ames, 1981), we have consistently found that when children are competing, they tend to make ability attributions for their performance. Success (relative to others) leads to inferences of high ability and failure (relative to others) to inferences of low ability. These effects occur whether children are responding to their own (e.g., Ames, Ames & Felker, 1977) or another's (e.g., Ames & Felker, 1979) performance. In contrast, when children have been focused on trying to improve their performance, they do not appear to engage in precipitous evaluations of their ability. In one study (Ames, 1984), for example, students were asked to identify what they were thinking following their performance in a competitive or individualized setting. Children who were focused on comparing their performance with another ("let's see who can solve the most puzzles") reported significantly more ability-related thoughts than children who focused on improving their performance. In contrast, those children who were focused on improving reported significantly more effort-related thoughts as well as more self-monitoring thoughts (e.g., "I will make a plan. I will work carefully"). Taken together, theses studies suggest that competitive and noncompetitive settings involve different demand features such that children become focused on evaluating their ability when competing but focused on thinking about their approach to the task when they are in noncompetitive situations.

In several studies, Covington and Omelich (1981, 1984; see also, Covington, 1984), have examined the effects of a normative vs. mastery-based evaluation system on college-age students' attributions and performance. They have typically compared a conventional normative-based evaluation system to a mastery approach which involves absolute standards and offers students an opportunity for improvement through multiple tries on the exams. Only in the mastery system has effort proved to be a salient factor in students' reported attributions.

In one recent study, Covington & Omelich (1984) contrasted a criterion-referenced with a norm-referenced system of evaluation and attempted to sort out the relative effects of the method of evaluation from the multiple trials component. They found that the mastery-based learning structure enhanced qualitative motivational factors related to sustained task involvement. Moreover, the multiple trials component, that is, giving students an opportunity to improve, was the factor that had the more significant impact on these motivational processes. A perceived need and opportunity for improvement in the mastery condition of this study, which is also characteristic of the noncompetitive conditions of many laboratory studies (e.g., Ames & Ames, 1981; Ames, 1984) seems to be an important factor differentiating a noncompetitive from a competitive situation. Although self-concept of ability is viewed as an important mediator of performance, they found that student self-concept of ability predicted performance only in the normative-based structure. According to Covington and Omelich, ''The salience of ability perceptions are diminished by the motivational climate of a mastery structure'' (1984, p. 1048). What these findings suggest is that a high self-concept of ability may be necessary for optimal performance in competitive situations (see also, Nicholls, 1979), but the ability-performance linkage may be severed by a noncompetitive structure.

Not only does goal structure influence the degree to which ability becomes the focus of student thoughts, research also suggests it influences the degree to which ability perceptions of high and low achievers become dichotomized and the degree to which these ability perceptions become shared and stable over time. Both experimental (e.g., Ames & Ames, 1981; Ames, Ames, & Felker, 1977) and field-based (e.g., Marshall & Weinstein, 1984; Weinstein, Marshall, Brattesani, & Middlestadt, 1982; Weinstein & Middlestadt, 1979) studies have shown that students' perceptions of their own and others' ability become dichotomized when social comparison is emphasized. There is also evidence that this perceived hierarchical distribution of ability and achievement is shared by teachers as well as students (Ames & McKelvie, 1982; Weinstein & Middlestat, 1979; Weinstein et al., 1982). In contrast, noncompetitive, particularly cooperative structures, have been found to create a climate for perceived similarity where students (and teachers) are less likely to translate performance differences into ability differences (Ames, 1981).

Evidence that these differential ability perceptions can become shared and stable over time is evident in the research of Rosenholtz and her colleagues (see Rosenholtz & Rosenholtz, 1981; Rosenholtz & Wilson, 1980; Rosenholtz & Simpson, 1984a, 1984b). In their work, they have differentiated elementary school classrooms by a cluster of characteristics related to the frequency of whole class instruction, opportunities for students to make choices, and evaluations using social comparative criteria. What they have found in classrooms which score high on these factors (unidimensional classrooms) is a greater degree of agreement among students about who are the capable and less capable students. They also found that students' perceptions of their own and their classmates' ability are more discrepant in these unidimensional than in the multidimensional classrooms (i.e., classrooms low on the above factors). Thus, when social comparison is salient, ability not only becomes a salient factor in one's attributional judgments, the perceived distribution of ability in the classroom also becomes polarized and shared.

Although this brief review only begins to tap the extensive research in these areas, it does point to a set of consistent findings. These findings suggest that certain classroom structures, namely those where social comparison is imposed, focus children's thoughts on their ability to perform, diminish perceptions of their ability, promote a hierarchical view of how ability is defined by how one performs relative to others. Thus, the dominant focus of attention of each child in the classroom is on ability.

The intended consequences of attribution retraining, that is, getting students to focus on the role of effort in their learning, may be impossible to maintain in classroom situations where social comparative information and evaluation makes ability a more salient factor than effort. Similarly, the propensity to engage in ability attributions in competitive situations may make it impossible for many students to maintain positive self-efficacy. Although those students who compare favorably may experience enhanced self-efficacy, in a competitive structure, only a few students fit into this category. Competition is a condition of inequality where one student's success has negative implications for the potential of another student achieving the same outcome. On the one hand, self-regulated learners may be expected to fare well even when the situation is less than optimal. That is, self-regulated learners are more likely to react to and interpret failure in terms of strategy ("I took the wrong approach to the problem") (Corno, Collins, & Capper, 1982). On the other hand, competition tends to undermine the tendency to engage in strategic thinking regardless of the students' ability (Ames, 1984).

IMPLICATIONS FOR MOTIVATION RETRAINING

The implications of these findings become evident when we realize the extent of social comparison even in the elementary school. Thus, the conditions of the classroom are more likely to impede rather than facilitate the transfer of attribution retraining, self-efficacy training, and strategic thinking to the classroom. When the classroom structure is such that social comparative goals are elicited, the objectives of these individual interventions are not likely to become manifest in the classroom.

When normative comparisons are salient and important, inculcating effort attributions may not be sufficient. It has been argued elsewhere (Ames, 1984) that outcomes in competitive situations are dependent on multiple necessary causes. That is, both effort and ability are seen as necessary for success. As a consequence, effort becomes the "double-edged sword" (Covington & Omelich, 1979), negatively implicating one's ability when failure is encountered. Further, because normative comparisons have a strong influence on perceptions of competence, even good students are likely to see themselves in a disadvantageous position. Strategic thinking or thinking about how to perform a task is not easy when one is encumbered by external pressures.

What is or should be the goal or objective of interventions aimed at enhancing student motivation? Is the goal to help students cope with the realities of increasing competition and social comparison in school? If so, the target for intervention should involve the individual child as in the above training paradigms, but the content of the intervention must also involve coping strategies. Here the focus should be more on training children how to deal with frustration and failure, particularly negative social comparison. Whether or not this training should include attributions, efficacy, or self-monitoring content is probably less important than the conditions of the training which at some point must approximate or simulate the types of social comparisons that are likely to be elicited in the classroom. As we look at the conditions of most training studies, we find that the students are generally performing in an individual setting, even experiencing some degree of success, and not having to compare their performance to others. These conditions of training actually approximate those conditions which have been found to elicit a mastery or task goal orientation where children *do* focus on their effort, *do* attend to performance changes over time, *do* think about generic performance strategies, and *do not* devalue their ability following failure. In other words, the conditions of the training itself may serve to facilitate the desired changes, but they are not likely to facilitate transfer.

If children are to learn how to cope, there is a need to develop in students a tolerance for failure and constructive responses to failure (cf. Clifford, 1984); but it is not just dealing with failure, it is dealing with failure when that failure implies that others are doing better than oneself. This training might include attributing failure to effort but should also include attributions to strategy use. When children *are* trying, failure should be seen as resulting from inappropriate strategy. Strategy, like effort, is controllable, but like other academic skills, strategy change may require new learning. The problem here is that even attributions to wrong strategy or skill assumes that the task is perceived as reasonable. This is not always the case particularly when students are given normatively defined tasks.

Coping must also include self-monitoring strategies that explicitly relate to these situations. Clifford (1984), who suggests that children need to learn to cope with failure and error-making, in the end, offers remedies that involve removing the negative consequences of making errors. In other words, she suggests that the context of the evaluative structure be modified. The implication here is that the goals or retraining may be better attained when the demands of the classroom structure are also changed.

If, on the other hand, our goal is to help students become mastery-oriented (that is focus on the role and importance of effort to learning), self-regulated, and confident in their ability to perform, current individual training efforts may not be sufficient. Let's look at why this might be the case. First, training children to focus on their effort when the normative structure of the classroom focuses them on their ability does not deal directly with the problem. Just because children are taught to think about effort or strategies in a protected setting does not mean that they will continue to do so in the classroom where social comparison is salient. In other words, I am suggesting that a social comparative structure, when imposed, makes children aware of their performance relative to others and focuses them on their ability. In these situations, children, regardless of their expectations or *a priori* attributional tendency, think less about the adequacy of their own effort or the appropriateness of a specific strategy. Monitoring one's own strategy or progress (e.g., ''I will concentrate. I will take my time.'') is less important than monitoring the performance of others.

The saliency of ability in competitive settings might suggest that a self-perception of high self-efficacy would be the key to optimal motivation. Indeed, high self-efficacy should lead to a belief that effort and appropriate strategy ought to produce the desired outcome. However, because competition is a situation where rewards are restricted and few can be "winners," the outcome expectations for most students must necessarily remain low. Thus, although initial performance patterns may be positively influenced by efficacy inducements, over time, these self-perceptions are going to be more responsive to negative social comparison experiences (Bandura, 1984). As reported earlier, self-concept of ability does, in fact, decline for many students as they progress through school presumably as a result of accumulated negative social comparisons. Thus, while the few who compare favorably may be "motivated," self-efficacy beliefs of the majority must suffer. It is also the case that these categories of "winners" and "losers" are likely to remain fairly stable over time. Those children who are targeted for training may find it difficult to modify upward their outcome expectations, to focus on internal standards for judging their performance, and to maintain perceptions of personal control. Those children who probably need such training are also the group least likely to benefit from this type of training in the long run.

If the effectiveness of individual training efforts is influenced by the structure of classrooms, interventions should perhaps be targeted at the classroom level instead. Moreover, it is suggested that many of the objectives of retraining programs may actually be attained by redirecting an individual's goals, that is, modifying the classroom structure in such a way that social comparative goals are not elicited. As suggested by others (e.g., Dweck, 1984; Nicholls, 1979, 1984; Maehr, 1984), when achievement goals are modified, cognitive-motivational processes also change. Thus, it is argued that modifying or changing the nature of the child's experience in the classroom provides a viable way of modifying students' goals. How, then, has the classroom been studied and what does this research suggest for classroom-level interventions?

RESEARCH ON CLASSROOM LEARNING ENVIRONMENTS

Research on classroom learning environments has varied considerably in methodology, including systematic observations, measures of student perceptions, and actual field interventions. Most of the research has evolved from early observational approaches which involved the systematic coding and tabulating of specific occurrences (e.g., frequency of teacher vs. student talk, frequency of positive vs. negative feedback) by some nonparticipant observer. In these observations, attention was also paid to the ecology or physical arrangement of the classroom, to the types of activities (seatwork, small group), and to the proportion of time children spent in these different activities. These observational analyses have typically characterized the classroom as involving more teacher talk than student talk, more passive than active tasks, and as being more teacher-centered than student-centered. Recommendations for educational reform evolved as much from value judgments (e.g., that teachers should talk less and students talk more) as from consistently strong empirical relationships.

Other more recent approaches to assessing what goes on in the classroom have relied on student perceptions of the environment (e.g., Fraser & O'Brien, 1985; Moos & Moos, 1978; Walberg, 1979). Here, it is believed that students' reports more accurately reflect how they are experiencing the classroom environment. To the end of determining the effects of the environment as mediated by student perceptions, several instruments were developed such as the Classroom Environment Scale (Moos & Trickett, 1974) and the Learning Environment Inventory (Anderson & Walberg, 1974). Instruments such as these were designed for the purpose of measuring classroom level characteristics in terms of the average perceptions of students. The subscales on these instruments have been developed through factor analytic methods and the nature of the research had been to determine the relationship between these various dimensions (e.g., competition, affiliation, control) and various student outcomes (achievement, satisfaction, absenteeism). By and large, these instruments have focused on student achievement and attitudes.

In this tradition, motivation has been regarded as a quantitative variable as assessed by time on task, dimensions of affect such as satisfaction (e.g., Trickett & Moos, 1974), or attitudes toward subject matter (e.g., Fraser, 1981; Fraser & Fisher, 1982). As a consequence, when we ask what kind of environment is favorable to the development of optimal motivation patterns, we must first note that the assessments of qualitative motivation factors have not been made. Even when looking at attitude as the outcome measure, attitude has correlated positively with many different dimensions of classroom environment depending on the instrument used and population. It seems that all the dimensions that represent some positive orientation (e.g., participation, involvement) have in one study or another correlated positively with achievement and other affective outcomes.

In this research on classroom climate, it is also difficult to sort out the dimensions of the classroom with student outcomes. Satisfaction, for example, has sometimes been considered a dimension of classroom climate (see Walberg, 1979) and at other times a student outcome (e.g., Trickett & Moos, 1974). As a consequence, satisfaction is, on the one hand, viewed as independent from other dimensions of climate, and on the other hand, hypothesized to relate to dimensions of climate.

Conclusions from many of these "climate" studies lead to characterizations of the optimal classroom that seem less than conceptually consistent. For example, Trickett and Moos (1974) conclude that the classroom must be challenging but also high on cohesiveness and satisfaction. Moos and Moos (1978) suggest a need to increase social support in competitive settings, implying that competition with social support makes it "different." The clear absence of any *a priori* conceptual framework compounds the difficulty of establishing meaningful relationships across various studies.

Nevertheless, specific intervention strategies have evolved from this descriptive research base, and they have generally focused on changing student attitudes. One such study (Fraser, 1981; see also, Fraser & O'Brien, 1985), examined differences between students' and teachers' perceptions of the classroom environment and compared these perceptions with the preferred environment. The intervention was directed toward bringing the perceived or actual environment into alignment with the preferred environment. The method involved giving teachers a variety of ideas that are closely tied to the items on the instrument. Fraser and O'Brien (1985) give an example of encouraging teachers to be more sympathetic and helpful toward students having difficulties as reflected in the item, "Some students feel bad when they don't do as well as others." From a motivational perspective, expressions of sympathy towards some students may actually lead them to infer that they lack ability (Weiner, Graham, Stern, & Lawson, 1982). Further, focusing on the teachers' attitude does not directly deal with the "bad feelings."

Aside from this, there is other research which questions the use of student preferences as a basis for structural intervention. Peterson and Janicki (1979), for example, found that some students actually performed worse on a delayed achievement test when they were assigned to a structural approach (small vs. large group) that matched their preference. Student attitudes were not related to their initial preferences or assignment. Cronbach and Snow (1977) have similarly concluded that using student preferences as a basis for instructional decisions does not improve learning. The validity of compatibility or matching models has not been established and the feasibility for practice seem less than economical.

Over the years, research on classroom learning environments has not yielded to a theoretical framework. As a result, the dimensions of the classroom that have been illuminated have been those that evolve from factor analytic studies. Interventions, therefore, are directed at specific dimensions, making the teacher or classroom more like or less like the characteristics of these dimensions. How various dimensions are interrelated remains unexplored. How these dimensions of classroom climate relate to qualitative aspects of motivation (attributions, self-efficacy, self-regulation) has not been studied. How these dimensions combine to reflect qualitatively different motivational climates or motivational goals has not been studied. Even when we try to identify dimensions consistently associated with positive attitudes or affect, there is little guidance. In large part, this must be attributed to the absence of a unified conceptual scheme that provides a raison d'etre for the specific dimensions that have been targeted. So the picture here is that these findings do not help us define an "effective" classroom environment or one that will elicit optimal motivation processes.

Other research on classroom learning environments has relied on more experi-
mentally based approaches (see Johnson & Johnson, 1985; Slavin, 1983, for re-
views). These studies have followed a general paradigm of manipulating the
evaluative and interpersonal dimensions of the classroom and then assessing stu-
dent outcomes such as achievement, interpersonal relationships, self-esteem,
and attitudes toward school. The efforts in this area have focused extensively on
the comparison between cooperative-based structures and competitive (or what
has been descirbed as traditional) classroom structures. A typical example would
involve comparing classrooms using a team learning approach to math with
classrooms teaching math as usual. Student achievement on standardized and
classroom tests and interpersonal attitudes would be compared.

The evidence favoring cooperative-based structures for enhancing interper-
sonal attitudes has been particularly persuasive. Motivation as an outcome, how-
ever, has rarely been measured, instead it has typically been inferred from
achievement; and even when it has been measured, it has been assessed as a
global attitude toward the classroom (e.g., Slavin, 1978) or toward oneself as in
self-esteem (e.g., Norem-Hebeisen & Johnson, 1981).

Thus, although an intervention strategy which targets the social/evaluative
structure of the classroom is suggested, research on classroom environments has
not studied cognitive motivational processes as outcomes. Research in this tradi-
tion is fraught with problems that relate to issues of causality and theoretical
grounding. Classrooms are found to differ across a vast array of dimensions,
whether these dimensions are interrelated (and many do seem to be correlated),
represent salient features of the classroom, or are important causes of motivation
is unclear. Although cooperative structures are highly touted in the literature, we
know very little about how cooperative goals influence the qualitative motiva-
tional processes discussed here.

RECOMMENDATIONS

So now, it is time to ask how should the classroom be structured? Clearly, there
are many ways of attaining an environment for learning that is more likely to
foster optimal motivation patterns. It has been suggested by some (Johnson &
Johnson, 1974, 1985) that competitive as well as individualistic and cooperative
structures should all be used in the classroom. It is merely a matter of how much
and when they should be used. The evidence presented here does not support
such a conclusion. Instead, it seems rather clear that competitive goal structures
(i.e., situations which focus children on evaluating their ability) do not contrib-
ute to desirable motivation patterns. In fact, there is little, if any, viable evidence
that a competitive goal structure in the classroom is associated with outcomes
that are indicative of positive self-worth, continuing motivation, or quality task
engagement. Eliminating an important source of negative motivation, therefore,

involves restructuring the classroom so that social comparison goals are not elicited.

Recent findings from the program of research initiated by Covington and Omelich (1984) suggests that a perceived opportunity for improvement may be an important factor that diminishes the impact of competitive evaluation. When students have a chance to improve their performance, error making and mistakes are more tolerated. Mistakes and errors become an acceptable part of learning and students should not be penalized for making errors. From the student's perspective, he/she may be more willing to take a risk and to engage in challenging tasks (see Dweck, 1984). Such an approach sets into motion a "proximal goal" orientation that is likely to enhance students' perceptions of self-efficacy. Further, putting an emphasis on improvement may serve to engender an "incremental" view of ability, that is, a belief that competence is developed through effort.

The most basic recommendation must be that the classroom should not focus students on comparing themselves with others. This social comparison involves blatant methods such as grading on a curve or posting students achievements to less obvious practices such as not informing students of evaluation criteria in advance. Often students know little about the standards for evaluation or whether they can have a chance to improve their performance. The public posting of "milestones" or progress encourages social comparison even when, as it is often argued, all students could have attained the goals if they had chosen to do so. In other words, instructional practices which actually impose social comparison standards as well as those which encourage or make social comparison salient should not be used.

This sounds easy enough to those of us who are not in the classroom, but to teachers this sounds like a formidable task. To reduce the salience of social comparison also requires that public comparison on ability, social behaviors, and achievement be reduced, if not eliminated; that mistakes and errors be viewed as a part of learning rather than an index of failure to learn; and that progress and improvement over time be given status or priority in evaluations. In part, this can only be accomplished when public evaluation, itself, is reduced (see also, Covington & Beery, 1976). The handling of individual differences in the classroom tends to focus more on differences in how students *perform* rather than differences in how students *learn*.

There are several related issues involved here. One concerns the "reasonableness" of the expectations. Using absolute standards can have negative consequences on student self-efficacy when the standards are perceived as unattainable. While students will give "herculean" effort once in a while, it too soon becomes a situation where, as one student described it, "The juice isn't worth the squeeze."

Enhancing students' perceptions of control by giving them choices has been emphasized in many interventions (e.g., deCharms, 1976; Ryan, Connell, & Deci, 1985; Wang, 1976). Choice on tasks or scheduling, for example, are viewed as fostering beliefs in personal control and increasing students' involvement. While this may hold true in individualized or noncompetitive settings, student choices tend to be determined by their goals and the kinds of attributions they make for their performance. Fyans and Maehr (1979), for example, found that students' task preferences tend to be compatible with their attributions. Thus, when students are focused on their ability as when they are competing, their task choices may not foster continued learning. In our own research (Ames, 1984), we have found that students' task choices in competitive settings depend on whether they have compared favorably or unfavorably with others. Students who compare unfavorably tend to avoid ability-related tasks where the outcomes are luck-determined. That students seek to avoid challenging tasks when social comparison is salient has also been discussed by Dweck (1984) and Nicholls (1983), among others. As a consequence, providing students with choices is not likely to have the intended consequences if the social/evaluative structure of the classroom makes social comparison salient. Nevertheless, in the context of cooperative or mastery-oriented structures, providing choices may enhance the quality of task engagement and foster independent learning activity. In the context of competitively oriented situations, student choices are likely to reflect an avoidance of challenge in preference for tasks and activities that insure success and that do not reflect negatively on one's ability.

CONCLUSION

Perhaps it is most advantageous to call for the necessity of both types of interventions—those involving individual training and those aimed at classroom/instructional practices. Changing the classroom structure may not help some students who lack certain self-regulatory skills and who have, as a result of many accumulated experiences, adopted a belief that they are not able and that achievement is a function of one's ability. Individual training programs can help these students learn new skills and new ways of processing and interpreting information. These students are then well-prepared to function and learn in a noncompetitive or mastery-oriented classroom; however, they may not function effectively in an "unfriendly" classroom. Modifying the evaluative/social structure of the classroom is also necessary; and may be sufficient to elicit optimal motivation patterns in most students.

There is need for research on alternative ways of organizing the classroom for learning that specifically addresses those motivation processes that reflect an ability to initiate achievement activity and a high level (quality) of task involvement. At the present time, we know more about how varying classroom conditions affect student achievement than we do about how these same conditions influence how students approach a task and how they process and interpret information as well as the quality of their involvement.

REFERENCES

Ames, C. (1981). Competitive versus cooperative reward structures: The influence of individual and group performance factors on achievement attributions and affect. *American Educational Research Journal, 18*, 273–287.

Ames, C. (1984). Competitive, cooperative, and individualistic goal structures: A cognitive-motivational analysis. In R. Ames & C. Ames (Eds.), *Research on motivation in education* (Vol. 1, pp. 177–208), New York: Academic Press.

Ames, C., & Ames, R. (1981). Competitive and individualistic goal structures: The salience of post performance information for causal attributions and affect. *Journal of Educational Psychology, 73*, 411–418.

Ames, C., & Ames, R. (1984). Systems of student and teacher motivation: Toward a qualitative definition. *Journal of Educational Psychology, 76*, 535–556.

Ames, C., Ames, R., & Felker, D. W. (1977). Effects of competitive reward structures and valence of outcome on children's achievement attributions. *Journal of Educational Psychology, 69*, 1–8.

Ames, C., & Felker, D. W. (1979). An examination of children's attributions and achievement-related evaluations in competitive, cooperative, and individualistic reward structures. *Journal of Educational Psychology, 71*, 413–420.

Ames, C., & McKelvie, S. (1982). Evaluation of student achievement behavior in cooperative and competitive reward structures. Paper presented at the annual meeting of the American Educational Research Association.

Anderson, G., & Walberg, H. J. (1974). Learning environments. In H. J. Walberg (Ed.), *Evaluating educational performance*. Berkeley: McCutchan.

Andrews, G. R., & Debus, R. L. (1978). Persistence and the casual perception of failure: Modifying cognitive attribution. *Journal of Educational Psychology, 70*, 154–166.

Bandura, A. (1977). *Social learning theory*. Englewood Cliffs, NJ: Prentice Hall.

Bandura, A. (1981). Self-referent thought: A developmental analysis of self-efficacy. In J. H. Flavell & L. Ross (Eds.), *Social cognitive development: Frontiers and possible futures*. Cambridge: Cambridge University Press.

Bandura, A. (1982). Self-efficacy: Toward a unifying theory of behavioral change. *Psychological Review, 48*, 191–215.

Bandura, A. (1984). Recycling misconceptions of perceived self-efficacy. *Cognitive Therapy and Research, 8*, 231–255.

Bandura, A., & Schunk, D. H. (1981). Cultivating competence, self-efficacy, and intrinsic interest through proximal self-motivation. *Journal of Personality and Social Psychology, 41*, 586–598.

Blumenfeld, P. C., Pintrinch, P. R., Meece, J., & Wessels, K. (1982). The formation and role of self-perceptions of ability in elementary classrooms. *Elementary School Journal, 82*, 401–420.

Bossert, S. T. (1979). *Tasks and social relationships in classrooms*. Cambridge: Cambridge University Press.

Brattesani, K. A., Weinstein, R. S., & Marshall, H. H. (1984). Student perceptions of differential teacher treatment as moderators of teacher expectation effects. *Journal of Educational Psychology, 76*, 236–247.

Brown, A. L. (1978). Knowing when, where, and how to remember: A problem of metacognition. In R. Glaser (Ed.), *Advances in instructional psychology* (Vol. 1). Hillsdale, NJ: Erlbaum.

Brown, A. L., Campione, J. C., & Day, J. D. (1981). Learning to learn: On training students to learn from texts. *Educational Researcher, 10*, 14–21.

Chapin, M., & Dyck, D. G. (1976). Persistence in children's reading behavior as a function of N length and attribution retraining. *Journal of Abnormal Psychology, 85*, 511–515.

Clifford, M. M. (1984). Thoughts on a theory of constructive failure. *Educational Psychologist, 19*, 108–120.

Corno, L., Collins, K. M., & Capper, J. (1982). *Where there's a way there's a will: Self-regulating the low-achieving student.* ERIC Document Reproduction Service No. ED 22 499.

Corno, L., & Mandinach, E. (1983). The role of cognitive engagement in classroom learning and motivation. *Educational Psychologist, 18,* 88–108.

Corno, L., & Rohrkemper, M. M. (1985). The intrinsic motivation to learn in classrooms. In C. Ames & R. Ames (Eds.), *Research on motivation in education* (Vol. 2, pp. 53–90). New York: Academic Press.

Covington, M. V. (1984). The motive for self-worth. In R. Ames & C. Ames (Eds.), *Research on motivation in education* (Vol. 1, pp. 77–113). New York: Academic Press.

Covington, M. V., & Beery, R. (1976). *Self-worth and school learning.* New York: Holt, Rinehart, & Winston.

Covington, M. V., & Omelich, C. L. (1979). Effort: The double-edged sword in school achievement. *Journal of Educational Psychology, 71,* 169–182.

Covington, M. V., & Omelich, C. L. (1981). As failures mount: Affective and cognitive consequences of ability demotion in the classroom. *Journal of Educational Psychology, 73,* 796–808.

Covington, M. V., & Omelich, C. L. (1984). Task-oriented versus competitive learning structures: Motivational and performance consequences. *Journal of Educational Psychology, 76,* 1038–1050.

Cronbach, L. J., & Snow, R. E. (1977). *Aptitudes and instructional methods.* New York: Irvington.

deCharms, R. (1976). *Enhancing motivation: Change in the classroom.* New York: Irvington.

deCharms, R. (1984). Motivation enhancement in educational settings. In R. Ames & C. Ames (Eds), *Research on motivation in education* (Vol. 2, pp. 275–310). New York: Academic Press.

Diener, C., & Dweck, C. (1978). An analysis of learned helplessness: Continuous changes in performance, strategy, and achievement cognitions following failure. *Journal of Personality and Social Psychology, 36,* 451–462.

Dweck, C. S. (1975). The role of expectations and attributions in the alleviation of learned helplessness. *Journal of Personality and Social Psychology, 31,* 674–685.

Dweck, C. S. (1984). Motivation. In R. Glaser & A. Lesgold (Eds.), *The handbook of psychology and education* (Vol. 1). Hillsdale, NJ: Erlbaum.

Dweck, C. S., & Elliot, E. S. (1983). Achievement motivation. In P. Mussen (Eds.), *Handbook of child psychology* (Vol. 4). New York: Wiley.

Eccles (Parsons), J., Midgley, C., & Adler, T. F. (1984). Grade-related changes in the school environment: Effects on achievement and motivation. In J. Nicholls (Ed.), *Advances in motivation and achievement* (Vol. 3, pp. 283–331). Greenwich, CT: JAI Press.

Elliot, E. S., & Dweck, C. S. (1981). Children's achievement goals as determinants of learned helplessness and mastery-oriented achievement patterns: An experimental analysis. Unpublished manuscript, Harvard University.

Entwistle, D. R., & Hayduk, L. A. (1978). *Too great expectations.* Baltimore: Johns Hopkins University Press.

Fraser, B. J. (1981). Using environmental assessments to make better classrooms. *Journal of Curriculum Studies, 13,* 131–144.

Fraser, B. J., & Fisher, D. L. (1982). Predicting students' outcomes from their perceptions of classroom psychosocial environment. *American Educational Research Journal, 19,* 498–518.

Fraser, B. J., & O'Brien, P. (1985). Student and teacher perceptions of the environment of elementary school classrooms. *Elementary School Journal, 85,* 567–580.

Frey, K. S., & Ruble, D. N. (1985). What children say when the teacher is not around: Conflicting goals in social comparison and performance assessment in the classroom. *Journal of Personality and Social Psychology, 48,* 550–562.

Fyans, L. J., & Maehr, M. L. (1979). Attributional style, task selection and achievement. *Journal of Educational Psychology, 71,* 499–507.

Johnson, D. W., & Johnson, R. T. (1974). Instructional goals structure: Cooperative, competitive, and individualistic. *Review of Educational Research, 44,* 213–240.

Johnson, D. W., & Johnson, R. T. (1985). Motivational processes in cooperative, competitive, and individualistic learning situations. In C. Ames & R. Ames (Eds.), *Research on motivation in education* (Vol. 2, pp. 249–286). New York: Academic Press.

Levine, J. (1983). Social comparison and education. In J. Levine & M. Wang (Eds.), *Teacher and student perceptions: Implications for learning.* Hillsdale, NJ: Erlbaum.

Maehr, M. L. (1978). Continuing motivation: An analysis of a seldom considered educational outcome. *Review of Educational Research, 46,* 443–462.

Maehr, M. L. (1983). On doing well in science: Why Johnny no longer excels; why Sarah never did. In S. G. Paris, G. M. Olson, & H. W. Stevenson (Eds.), *Learning and motivation in the classroom.* (pp. 179–210). Hillsdale, NJ: Erlbaum.

Maehr, M. L. (1984). Meaning and motivation: Toward a theory of personal investment. In R. Ames & C. Ames (Eds.), *Research on motivation in education* (Vol. 1, pp. 115–144). New York: Academic Press.

Maehr, M. L., & Nicholls, J. G. (1980). Culture and achievement motivation: A second look. In N. Warren (Ed.), *Studies in cross-cultural psychology.* New York: Academic Press.

Marshall, H. H., & Weinstein, R. S. (1984). Classroom factors affecting students' self-evaluation: An interactional model. *American Educational Research Journal, 54,* 301–326.

McCombs, B. L. (1984). Processes and skills underlying continuing intrinsic motivation to learn: Toward a definition of motivational skills training interventions. *Educational Psychologist, 19,* 199–218.

Meichenbaum, D. (1977). *Cognitive behavior modification.* New York: Plenum.

Moos, R. H., & Moos, B. S. (1978). Classroom social climate and student absences and grades. *Journal of Educational Psychology, 70,* 263–269.

Moos, R. H., & Trickett, E. (1974). *Classroom environment scale manual.* Palo Alto, CA: Consulting Psychologists.

Nicholls, J. G. (1979). Quality and equality in intellectual development: The role of motivation in education. *American Psychologist, 34,* 1071–1084.

Nicholls, J. G. (1982). The development of the concepts of effort and ability, perception of own attainment, and the understanding that difficult tasks require more ability. *Child Development, 49,* 800–814.

Nicholls, J. G. (1983). Conceptions of ability and achievement motivation: A theory and its implications for education. In S. G. Paris, G. M. Olson, & H. W. Stevenson (Eds.), *Learning and motivation in the classroom* (pp. 211–237). Hillsdale, NJ: Erlbaum.

Nicholls, J. G. (1984). Conceptions of ability and achievement motivation: In R. Ames & C. Ames (Eds.), *Research on motivation in education* (Vol. 1, pp. 39–77). New York: Academic Press.

Norem-Hebeisen, A., & Johnson, D. W. (1981). Relationship between cooperative, competitive, and individualistic attitudes and differential aspects of self-esteem. *Journal of Personality, 49,* 415–425.

Oden, S., & Asher, S. R. (1977). Coaching children in social skills for friendship making. *Child Development, 48,* 495–506.

Parsons (Eccles), J., Kaczala, C. M., & Meece, J. (1982). Socialization of achievement attitudes and beliefs: Classroom influences. *Child Development, 53,* 322–339.

Pascarella, E. T., Walberg, H. H., Junder, L. K., & Haertel, G. D. (1981). Continuing motivation in science for early and late adolescents. *American Educational Research Journal, 18,* 439–452.

Peterson, P. L., & Janicki, T. C. (1979). Individual characteristics and children's learning in large-group and small-group approaches. *Journal of Educational Psychology, 71,* 677–687.

Rohrkemper, M., & Bershon, B. L. (1983). The quality of student task engagement: Elementary school students' reports of the causes and effects of problem difficulty. *Elementary School Journal, 85,* 127–147.

Rosenholtz, R. S., & Rosenholtz, S. J. (1981). Classroom organization and the perception of ability. *Sociology of Education, 54,* 132–140.

Rosenholtz, S. J., & Simpson, C. (1984a). Classroom organization and student stratification. *Elementary School Journal, 85,* 1–17.

Rosenholtz, S. J., & Simpson, C. (1984b). The formation of ability conceptions: Developmental trend or social construction? *Review of Educational Research, 54,* 31–64.

Rosenholtz, S. R., & Wilson, B. (1980). The effect of classroom structure on shared perceptions of ability. *American Educational Research Journal, 17,* 75–82.

Ruble, D. N., Boggiano, A. K., Feldman, N. S., & Loebl, J. H. (1980). Developmental analysis of the role of social comparison in self evaluation. *Developmental Psychology, 16,* 105–115.

Ryan, R. M., Connell, J. P., & Deci, E. L. (1985). A motivational analysis of self-determination and self-regulation in education. In C. Ames & R. Ames (Eds.), *Research on motivation in education* (Vol. 2, pp. 13–51). New York: Academic Press.

Schunk, D. H. (1982). Effects of effort attributional feedback on children's perceived self-efficacy and achievement. *Journal of Educational Psychology, 74,* 548–556.

Schunk, D. H. (1983). Effects of effort attributional feedback on children's perceived self-efficacy and achievement. *Journal of Educational Psychology, 75,* 848–856.

Schunk, D. H. (1984a). Sequential attributional feedback on children's achievement behaviors. *Journal of Educational Psychology, 76,* 1159–1169.

Schunk, D. H. (1984b). Self-efficacy perspective on achievement behavior. *Educational Psychologist, 19,* 48–58.

Slavin, R. E. (1978). Student teams and comparison among equals: Effects on academic performance and student attitudes. *Journal of Educational Psychology, 70,* 532–538.

Slavin, R. E. (1983). *Cooperative learning.* New York: Longman.

Stipek, D. J. (1981). Children's perceptions of their own and their classmates' ability. *Journal of Educational Psychology, 73,* 404–410.

Stipek, D. (1984). The development of achievement motivation. In R. Ames & C. Ames (Eds.), *Research on motivation in education* (Vol. 1, pp. 145–176). New York: Academic Press.

Thomas, J. W. (1980). Agency and achievement: Self-management and self-regard. *Review of Educational Research, 54,* 179–223.

Trickett, E., & Moos, R. (1974). Personal correlates of contrasting environments: Student satisfaction in high school classrooms. *American Journal of Community Psychology, 2,* 1–12.

Walberg, H. J. (Ed.) (1979). *Educational environments and effects.* Berkeley: McCutchan.

Wang, M. C. (1979). *The self-schedule system for instruction-learning management and adaptive school learning environments.* Pittsburgh, PA: Learning Research and Development Center, University of Pittsburgh.

Weiner, B. (1979). A theory of motivation for some classroom experiences. *Journal of Educational Psychology, 71,* 3–25.

Weiner, B., Graham, S., Stern, P., & Lawson, M. E. (1982). Using affective cues to inter causal thoughts. *Developmental Psychology, 18,* 278–286.

Weinstein, R. S., Marshall, H. H., Brattesani, K. A., & Middlestadt, S. E. (1982). Student perceptions of differential teacher treatment in open and traditional classrooms. *Journal of Educational Psychology, 74,* 678–692.

Weinstein, R. S., & Middlestadt, S. E. (1979). Student perceptions of teacher interactions with male high and low achievers. *Journal of Educational Psychology, 71,* 421–431.

Whitley, B. E., & Frieze, I. H. (1985). Children's causal attributions for success and failure in achievement settings: A meta-analysis. *Journal of Educational Psychology, 77,* 608–616.

Wittrock, M. C. (1984). Student thought processes. In M. C. Wittrock (Ed.), *Handbook of research on teaching* (third ed.). New York: McMillan.

BELIEFS AND ACHIEVEMENT IN MATHEMATICS AND READING: A CROSS-NATIONAL STUDY OF CHINESE, JAPANESE, AND AMERICAN CHILDREN AND THEIR MOTHERS

Shin-ying Lee, Veronica Ichikawa, and Harold W. Stevenson

From the first years of elementary school, Chinese children receive higher scores on tests of reading achievement than do American children on comparable tests. In parallel tests of mathematics, the scores of both Chinese and Japanese children surpass those of American children (Stevenson, Lee, & Stigler, 1986). These findings are in line with those of several other reports of international studies of mathematics and science, indicating that Japanese junior high school and high

Advances in Motivation and Achievement: Enhancing Motivation,
Volume 5, pages 149-179.
ISBN: 0-89232-621-2

school students are at the top or close to the top of all the groups tested (Comber & Keeves, 1973; Husen, 1967). The consistently excellent test performance of Chinese and Japanese children from the first grade through high school has led to a great deal of interest in determining its nature and origins.

During the past several years our research group has focused its attention on Chinese, Japanese, and American elementary school children. Through studies of the early years of schooling we have attempted to gain a better understanding of variables that contribute to academic achievement. We have studied children in elementary school because of the importance of these early years as a base upon which future education must be built. By looking at other cultures, especially those that produce high levels of academic achievement, we have sought to increase our understanding of possible bases for the differences in children's performance in the three cultures and to obtain a clearer picture of ways in which the performance of American children might be improved.

We have discussed the role of such variables as intelligence, school curricula, and home and classroom practices as they relate to children's achievement in other papers. For example, one hypothesis that is appealing in its simplicity is that Japanese, and presumably Chinese, children have higher intellectual ability than American children (Lynn, 1982). This hypothesis receives no support when representative samples of Chinese, Japanese, and American children are tested on a battery of cognitive tasks (Stevenson, Stigler, Lee, Lucker, Kitamura, & Hsu, 1985). Differences in intellectual ability do not offer a convincing account of the differences in academic achievement. Differences have been found, however, in the rate and number of concepts introduced in mathematics curricula of the schools (Stigler, Lee, & Stevenson, 1982), in the amount of time children spent on homework and were assisted by their parents (Stevenson, Lee, & Stigler, 1986), and in the time teachers spent in teaching substantive material and children spent in attending to what their teachers are saying (Stevenson, Stigler, Lucker, Lee, Hsu, & Kitamura, 1986).

We focus on a different set of factors in this chapter: the belief systems that accompany cultural differences in educational and childrearing practices, which in turn have a close relation to what children learn from their school work. Two domains of belief are explored. First, we will discuss beliefs about the relative value of mathematics and reading, as reflected in the opinions of children and their mothers. Many clues appeared in our earlier research that indicate Chinese and Japanese parents and teachers place more emphasis on mathematics and Americans place more emphasis on reading in their goals for elementary education. These beliefs and the consequences of the beliefs are examined more thoroughly in this chapter. The second general domain concerns beliefs about the relative importance of effort and ability as they are related to effective performance. Would Chinese and Japanese parents and teachers devote so much time and energy to the education of their children if they did not believe this devotion would yield important benefits for their children? Would Chinese and Japanese children demonstrate such intense dedication to their schoolwork if they did not believe it was highly valued in their society and would pay off later in their lives?

Little empirical information is available about belief systems in these cultures and how these influence children's academic achievement. We, and others (e.g., Azuma, Kashiwagi, & Hess, 1981), have found that Japanese mothers place greater emphasis on the value of effort than do American mothers, and that American mothers, in turn, place greater emphasis on ability than do Japanese mothers in their explanations of successful performance in school. These variables merit further exploration, especially since they are closely related to theories of human behavior long espoused in Asian philosophies.

The malleability of human behavior has often been described in Chinese writings (Munro, 1977). According to this view, uniformity in human nature is assumed; differences that arise among people are believed to be primarily a result of life experiences rather than an expression of innate differences among individuals. Emphasis is placed, therefore, on the virtue of effort as the avenue for improvement and accomplishment. A similar theme is found in Japanese philosophy, where individual differences in potential are deemphasized and great importance is placed on the role of effort in modifying the course of human development. The common Japanese phrase, "yareba dekiru" (If you try hard, you can do it) is a statement typical of Japanese values. Effort and self-discipline are considered by Japanese to be essential bases for accomplishment. Lack of achievement is considered to be due to the failure to work with utmost self-exertion ("isshokemmei"), rather than to a lack of ability or to personal or environmental obstacles. Thus, a central theme of this chapter is that beliefs about achievement reflect underlying cultural values and that these differences in cultural values lead, in turn, to different levels of performance. We are especially interested in knowing the degree to which elementary school children have incorporated the cultural values into the beliefs they express. (It is impossible here to discuss the philosophical background of these views more thoroughly, but the interested reader can find additional information in a recent volume on child development and education in Japan edited by Stevenson, Azuma, and Hakuta [1986]; in earlier volumes by Cummings [1980], DeVos [1973], and Lebra [1976]; and in a volume about Taiwan by Wilson [1970].)

THE STUDY

We chose to study fifth-graders. By the fifth grade, children are familiar with expectations and practices related to their school work and are able to make ratings and judgments that are highly reliable. The children in this study were participants in a longitudinal study that began when they were in first grade. For the present study, children were given tests of reading and mathematics and were asked to fill out a questionnaire that dealt with their beliefs and attitudes about school. Their mothers were interviewed in great detail about their children's experiences in school and about their own beliefs, attitudes, and expectations about their children's schooling.

The sample.   The fifth-grade children included in the study were from the following cities: the Minneapolis metropolitan area (United States), Sendai (Japan), and Taipei (Taiwan). We purposely excluded ethnic status as a variable in our study of American children. The Minneapolis metropolitan area was chosen primarily because most children in Minneapolis are from English-speaking, white, native-born families. If we had chosen other large American cities, it would have been necessary to test many more children in order to evaluate the role of ethnic status and language background in accounting for our results.

After discussions with colleagues in Japan and the United States, it was agreed that the Japanese city most similar in size and other characteristics to Minneapolis was Sendai, located 240 miles northeast of Tokyo in the Tohoku region of Japan. At the time the initial study was begun (1980), only two large Chinese cities, Taipei and Hong Kong, were possible research sites. Taipei was chosen because it is a modern Chinese city comparable in size to the Minneapolis metropolitan area, and because Chinese is the dominant language, rather than both Chinese and English as is the case in Hong Kong.

The procedure for our initial selection of children in each city ensured that a representative sample would be obtained. In discussions with school authorities, ten schools representing different regions of the city and different socioeconomic levels were selected. From each school, two classrooms at grade one were randomly chosen for study. Data for the present study were obtained from a follow-up study of the children who had been in these first-grade classrooms. Six boys and six girls had been randomly selected as target subjects for our initial study. All of the children who could be located four years later (1984) when they were in fifth grade were included in the follow-up samples. These samples included 121 American, 164 Chinese, and 165 Japanese children. All children who remained in the original schools were tested, and in Minneapolis an effort was made to find children who had moved to other schools.

To assess whether the children in the follow-up samples were representative of the original samples, first-grade reading vocabulary, reading comprehension, and mathematics scores of children in the follow-up samples were compared to those of children not included in the follow-up samples. No differences between these two groups were found for first-grade reading or mathematics scores of the Chinese children, all $ps > .05$. The two readings scores did not differ for the American children, $ps > .05$, but the first-grade mathematics scores of the American children were higher for those in the follow-up sample, $p < .05$. The reading comprehension and mathematics scores of the two Japanese groups did not differ, $ps > .05$, but the first-grade reading vocabulary scores of the Japanese children in the follow-up sample were lower than those not included in the present study, p <.05. It seems reasonable to conclude that the follow-up samples are fairly representative of our original samples.

Measures in the follow up study. All children were given tests of reading and mathematics achievement that were constructed especially for our research. These tests have been described in detail elsewhere (i.e., Stevenson, Stigler, Lucker, Lee, Hsu, & Kitamura, 1982; Stigler, Lee, Lucker, & Stevenson, 1982). The two separate scores for the reading test were combined into a single score. The test consisted of sight reading of vocabulary items and answering questions about meaningful text. The mathematics score was derived from a single test. The tests were administered to one child at a time in Minneapolis and Sendai. In Taipei, it was necessary to test groups of five or six children at a time.

Before taking the tests, the children were asked to fill out a questionnaire under the supervision of an examiner. The questionnaire explored several areas, of which only two are discussed in this chapter. One area dealt with children's beliefs and attitudes about reading, mathematics, and their life in school. The second area concerned children's evaluations of the role of effort and ability in performance. Items in this area were adapted from items developed by Jacquelynne Eccles and her associates (Personal communication, 1984), or were constructed especially for this study. The interview with the mothers was wide-ranging, and only the portions dealing with their beliefs and attitudes about their children's education will be discussed here. Both the interview and the children's questionnaire were constructed by bilingual speakers of each language. Great care was given to the wording of the questions and statements so that the same meaning was conveyed in each language.

Nearly all of the items in the children's questionnaire involved rating scales. In each case, a 7-point rating scale, anchored by three descriptive statements, was used. Favorable or positive responses were given higher values on the scales. An examiner explained the procedure for rating until the children understood what they were to do. Many items in the interview with mothers were open-ended and scales had to be developed for coding these answers. Scoring was done by native speakers of each language. (Examples of items in the mother interview and the child questionnaire appear in later sections.)

ANALYSES

Our strategy in analyzing the data was to begin by examining between-country effects. That is, we sought to explore the structure of beliefs of the children and mothers in each country and then to see whether these beliefs paralleled the children's average levels of performance. Do Chinese and Japanese children, who perform relatively well in mathematics, have different attitudes about mathematics than American children? Do children's attitudes about reading and mathematics differ among the three cultures? We also wanted to explore the relation within each country between beliefs and children's achievement. As will be seen, differences among the countries were pervasive and the direction of the differences was consistent. Within each country, however, effects were often less clear. Beliefs that differentiated American, Chinese, and Japanese children or their mothers were not necessarily related to achievement within each country.

Sex effects were analyzed, but they were rarely significant either as a main effect or in interaction with country. Except in a few instances, neither these fifth-grade children nor their mothers responded differently to items according to the sex of the child. Nor did the relations between the responses and achievement scores tend to differ for boys and girls. Sex differences are not discussed, therefore, in this report.

CHILDREN'S ACHIEVEMENT

The children's scores on the mathematics and readings tests have been discussed in detail in Stevenson et al. (1982) and Stigler et al. (1982). A vivid way of illustrating the differences that exist among Chinese, Japanese, and American children is to look at the best and worst performers in our original sample of 720 first-graders from which our follow-up sample came. For this purpose, we selected the 100 children regardless of country who received the highest scores in mathematics and the 100 children who received the lowest scores. We repeated this procedure for the reading scores. If children in the three cultures performed comparably, approximately 33 children from each country should be among those obtaining the top and bottom scores.

Only 15 American children were among the first-graders who received the 100 highest scores in mathematics. Among those with the lowest 100 scores in mathematics, there were 58 American children. The 100 first-graders in the bottom reading group defined by vocabulary scores contained 47 American children, and the bottom group defined by scores in reading comprehension contained 56 American children. In the top groups in vocabulary and comprehension, there were 47 and 32 American children, respectively. In mathematics, therefore, American children were over-represented among the worst scorers and under-represented among the highest scorers. In reading, American children tended to be over-represented in both the high and low scoring groups.

Poor performance in mathematics persisted when the American children were in the fifth grade. The mean score obtained in the mathematics test given to the American children in the fifth-grade follow-up sample was significantly below that of the Chinese and Japanese children (see Table 1). Unfortunately, the fifth-grade reading vocabulary scores of the follow-up samples cannot be compared. Testing the Chinese children in small groups made it necessary for them to write out the pronunciation of the characters in phonetic script (*zhuyin fuhao*) in the

Table 1. Mean Achievement Scores in Mathematics
and Correlation between Scores at Grades 1 and 5

	Mean	SD	r (grades 1–5)
USA	44.9	6.2	.62
Taiwan	50.0	6.3	.57
Japan	51.0	6.6	.63

sight reading of vocabulary items. (American and Japanese children were tested individually and answered the questions orally.) The reading scores of the American children exceeded those of the Japanese children, $ps < .01$. There was strong consistency between the scores in first and fifth grades for children in all three countries. The correlation for sight reading of single words was .56 for each country; for reading comprehension, the correlations were .50, .53, and .41 for the American, Chinese, and Japanese children. As can be seen in Table 1, the correlations also were high for mathematics.

CHILDREN'S ATTITUDES AND BELIEFS

Responses to the questionnaire were analyzed to reveal possible cross-national differences in the children's ratings and the relation of these ratings to achievement scores. Two major domains are described: children's general attitudes about school and their evaluations of their own performance.

Attitudes about school. We begin by attempting to gain an understanding of children's attitudes toward school. The children were asked to rate how well they like math, language arts, school, and homework. (The term, language arts [English], was described as including reading, spelling, and writing. In Japanese the term used was *kokugo,* "the Japanese language," and in Chinese it was *guoyu,* "the Chinese language.") Ratings were made on scales ranging from "a little" to "a lot."

An unexpected pattern of ratings appeared for mathematics. We had assumed that Chinese and Japanese children, who perform well in mathematics, would express the more positive attitudes about mathematics. However, American children gave the highest ratings and Japanese children gave the lowest ratings to how well they liked mathematics (see Figure 1). This difference, as well as the difference between the American and Chinese children, was significant, $ps < .01$.

Chinese children expressed the greatest fondness for reading. They also gave higher ratings than the Japanese and American children to how well they liked school, $ps < .001$. This occurred despite the fact that Chinese fifth-graders spend approximately 40 hours a week at school, Japanese children, 37 hours, and

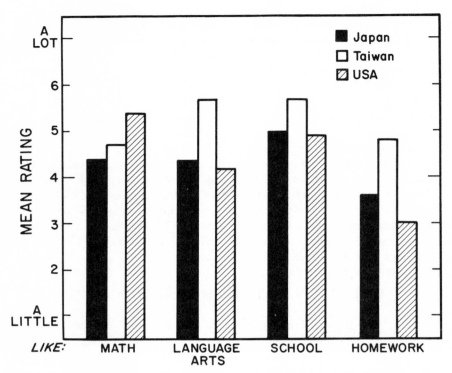

Figure 1. Children's ratings of how well they like math, language arts, school, and homework.

American children, only 30 hours. Similarly, Chinese children gave the highest ratings to how well they liked homework. Again, this occurred despite the fact that the average amount of time spent on homework each weekday night as estimated by the mothers was 115 minutes for the Chinese children, 57 minutes for the Japanese children, and 46 minutes for the American children.

One way of understanding what these ratings mean is to consider how they were interrelated. We can clarify what it means to like school by looking at the correlations between ratings on this variable and those for mathematics and reading. How well American children liked mathematics had no relation to how well they liked school, $r = .03$. The relation was significant for reading, $r = .34$, indicating that those who were more positive about reading also tended to be more positive about school than were those who liked reading less well. Different patterns were found in Taiwan and Japan. How well the Chinese and Japanese children liked school was positively related to how well they liked both mathematics and reading. (Correlations for Taiwan were .37 and .23, and for Japan, .27 and .42.) Mathematics appears to have a greater influence on the conception of school of Chinese and Japanese children than of American children.

Several other kinds of evidence strengthen the view that mathematics and reading have different roles in the three cultures. For example, in extensive observations of fifth-grade classrooms in Taipei, Sendai, and Minneapolis, we found that equivalent amounts of time were spent on reading and on mathematics in Chinese and Japanese classrooms, but that greater amounts of time were spent on reading than on mathematics in American classrooms (Stevenson, Stigler, Lucker, Lee, Hsu, & Kitamura, 1986). In addition, mathematics was very seldom emphasized in interviews with American mothers and teachers as something they wanted children to learn in elementary school. Both mothers and teachers suggested that if the curriculum were to be changed even more time should be spent on reading instruction (Stevenson, Lee, & Stigler, 1986).

Responses to several other questions also help to clarify the roles of reading and mathematics in the three cultures. The children were asked to rate their abilities in mathematics and reading (e.g., "How good at math are you?") and their own brightness (i.e., "If you were to rank all the students in your class from the brightest to the most stupid, where would you put yourself?"). American children's self-perceptions of their brightness were strongly related to their evaluations of their reading ability; Chinese and Japanese children were more likely to consider themselves to be bright if they perceived themselves as being skilled in mathematics. The correlation between the self-ratings of brightness and of mathematics ability was .37 in Taiwan and .46 in Japan. For the American children, the correlation was .20, a value that differs significantly from that for Japanese children, $p < .01$. When the self-ratings of brightness and of reading ability were compared, however, the correlation was .47 for the American children, but was .29 for the Chinese children and only .16 for the Japanese children. Again, the difference between the correlations for American and Japanese children was significant, $p < .01$.

A similar effect was found for the children's perception of their general effectiveness in school work (i.e., "If you were to rank all the children in your class from the worst to the best in school work, where would you put yourself?"). Points on the scale ranged from "the best" to "the worst." In Taiwan and Japan, these ratings were more strongly related to the children's ratings of their skill in mathematics than to their skill in reading. The difference between these correlations was evident in Taiwan ($rs = .53$ for mathematics versus .21 for reading) and in Japan ($rs = .47$ versus .25). These two correlations were the same in the United States; both were .41.

The evidence seems clear. Mathematics plays a central role in Chinese and Japanese children's conceptions of school, intelligence, and academic achievement. This is not the case for American children, who seem to regard reading as a more central component in their concepts of school and intelligence. It appears that American children believe that the major task of the elementary school years is to become literate, and give less attention to mathematics than they do to reading.

Relation to achievement.   Were the ratings of children's liking of math related to their achievement in mathematics? The answer was affirmative in all three countries. The more children said they liked mathematics, the higher were their scores on the mathematics achievement test (see Table 2). There is no clear basis for deciding the casual direction of this relationship, however. Doing well in mathematics may lead to more favorable attitudes about mathematics, or liking mathematics may lead to more vigorous efforts at studying mathematics.

How well the children liked language arts was significantly related to reading scores only for American children. Paradoxically, the ratings of how well both Chinese and Japanese children liked mathematics—but not of how well they liked reading—was significantly related to their reading scores.

As can be seen in Table 2, several other ratings also were related to the children's achievement scores. Ratings of how well the children liked homework was positively related to scores in both mathematics and reading for both Japanese and American children, but not for the Chinese children. Correlations of how well children liked school tended not to be related to their achievement scores.

Self-evaluations of ability and achievement.   Not only were there cross-national differences in the relation of the ratings to achievement scores, there also were significant differences in the children's self-evaluations. American children expressed more positive self-evaluations of their brightness and academic skills than Chinese and Japanese children. Japanese children tended to give themselves the least favorable ratings on these characteristics. The average ratings made by the children in each country appear in Table 3. All differences were highly significant, $ps < .001$.

Table 2.   Correlations of Mathematics and Reading Scores with Children's Attitudes

	USA	Taiwan	Japan
Mathematics			
Like			
School	.16	−.03	−.01
Homework	.30**	−.04	.19*
Mathematics	.30**	.23**	.46***
Reading	−.01	−.13	−.19
Reading			
Like			
School	.18*	.16	.06
Homework	.27**	.08	.20*
Mathematics	−.12	.24**	.22**
Reading	.19*	.12	−.03

*p < .05   **p < .01   ***p < .001

Table 3. Children's Self-Evaluations

	USA		Taiwan		Japan	
	Mean	SD	Mean	SD	Mean	SD
a. Brightness	3.8	1.1	3.3	1.2	2.9	1.0
b. School work	3.6	1.1	3.3	1.3	2.9	1.1
c. Ability in math	5.0	1.4	4.2	1.4	4.2	1.7
d. Ability in reading	4.8	1.2	5.1	1.1	4.2	1.4
e. Difficulty of math	3.5	1.4	3.6	1.5	4.0	1.6
f. Difficulty of reading	3.5	1.3	2.7	1.5	3.1	1.3

Note: For (a), 1 = the most stupid; 4 = average; 7 = the brightest; for (b), 1 = the worst; 4 = average; 7 = the best; for (c) and (d), 1 = not at all good; 4 = average; 7 = very good; for (e) and (f), 1 = very easy, 4 = neither easy nor hard; 7 = very hard.

All dfs = 2, 445–446; F(a) = 21.24, $p < .001$; F(b) = 10.66, $p < .001$; F(c) = 11.43, $p < .001$; F(d) = 23.79, $p < .001$; F(e) = 5.40, $p < .01$; F(f) = 30.81, $p < .001$.

American children's high self-evaluations extended to their ratings of their ability in mathematics. When asked to rate how good they thought they were in math on a scale where a rating of 4 was "average," the mean rating made by the American children was 5.0—above average. This was significantly higher than the self-ratings made by the Chinese and Japanese children, $ps < .001$. (It is important to note that American mothers also perceived their children as being good in mathematics. When these children were in first grade, the mean rating made by the American mothers of their child's mathematics abilities was 6.1 on a 9-point scale where a rating of 5 was "average." The mean ratings made by the Chinese and Japanese mothers were 5.9 and 5.7.)

Why should American children perceive themselves as being good at mathematics, when in cross-cultural comparisons they perform relatively poorly? One obvious possibility is that the mathematics curriculum in American schools is less difficult than the curricula in Japan and Taiwan. Children's ratings of how difficult they found mathematics gave some support to this interpretation. American and Chinese children thought mathematics was less difficult than did Japanese children, $ps < .01$. This assessment seems to reflect reality. In a recent analysis of textbooks from the three countries, Japanese textbooks were judged to be more difficult than Chinese and American textbooks (Stigler et al., 1982). The Japanese curriculum contained more concepts and skills and they were introduced earlier than in the curricula of Taiwan and the United States.

Self-ratings of reading ability were more in line with children's performance: Chinese children gave themselves the highest average ratings, followed by American, and then by Japanese children (see Table 3). Each mean differs from the preceding mean at the .01 level of significance.

It might appear from the preceding discussion that the American children did not have a clear idea about their level of academic achievement relative to other children. This was not the case. Even though the level of the ratings made by the

American children of their ability in mathematics were somewhat inflated, their perceptions of their status in relation to other children in their classrooms were as accurate as those of Chinese and Japanese children. That is, within-country correlations between self-perceptions of achievement in mathematics and actual scores on the mathematics test were very similar in the three countries. The correlations for the American, Chinese, and Japanese children were .43, .47, and .49, respectively.

The relation between children's perceptions of their reading skills and their scores on the reading test was lower than the corresponding value found for mathematics. In fact, the correlation between self-ratings and scores in reading for the Japanese children was only .05. For the American and Chinese children, the correlations were .36 and .34. It is not clear why the relation for the Japanese children should be so low. Lower correlations between self-evaluations and skill might occur if children obtain less direct evidence in their classrooms of how well they read than of how well they do in mathematics. If this were true, they would have less information to gauge how their skills compare to those of their classmates. This explanation still would not account for the lack of a significant relation for the Japanese children. Another possibility is that it is more difficult for Japanese children to assess their reading skill. Since Japanese children must learn to read Chinese characters (*kanji*), two syllabaries (*hiragana* and *katakana*), and romanized versions of Japanese words (*romaji*), all children may not share the same definition of what is meant by being good at reading.

Other perceptions.   Two other pieces of information support the argument that American children had a more positive evaluation of their school performance than the Chinese and Japanese children. American children believed their parents and teachers were more satisfied with their performance and they worried less about their own performance in school than Chinese and Japanese children.

One question concerned parents. Children were asked to evaluate whether they were doing as well in school as their parents wanted them to. A parallel question asked whether they were meeting their teachers' expectations. The scale ranged from "not very true of me" to "very true of me." A rating of four indicated the statement was "somewhat true of me." The average rating made by American children for the first statement was 4.8; it was 4.2 for the Chinese children, and 4.0 for the Japanese children. Corresponding means for the question about meeting the expectations of the teachers were 4.8, 4.0 and 3.6. The ratings of the American children were significantly higher than those of the Chinese and Japanese children, $ps < .001$. There is a small but interesting tendency in these means for the Chinese and Japanese children to believe that they are more successful in meeting their parents' expectations than in meeting those of the teacher.

In a second pair of items children were asked, "If you were absent from school for a few days, how much do you worry that you will be behind other students when you come back to school?'' and, ''How much do you worry that you will not be able to follow what the teacher teaches in class?'' A rating of four represented ''somewhat worried'' and a rating of seven represented ''very much worried.'' Ratings associated with both statements differed significantly, $ps < .001$. American children indicated the least worry and the Chinese children, the most. The means for the American children on the two statements were 3.8 and 3.9, and for the Chinese children, 6.3 and 5.9. The mean ratings by the Japanese children were 4.7 and 4.8. American children apparently had a greater sense of comfort about their school work than the Chinese and Japanese children.

Summary. It is useful to summarize the main findings obtained from the children's ratings. There obviously were large differences among the three cultures, both in the children's ratings of their attitudes about school and in the relative importance of reading and mathematics in their conceptions of academic performance and intelligence. American children believed they were performing at levels acceptable to their parents and teachers, and worried little about their school work. How well children liked mathematics was positively related to mathematics achievement in all three countries, but how well the children liked language arts was related to reading achievement only for the American children. American children gave themselves the highest ratings on ability in mathematics, brightness, and scholastic performance, and Japanese children gave themselves the lowest ratings. Children in all three countries had a good idea of where they stood relative to other children in mathematics, but evaluating reading ability seems to be more difficult, especially among Japanese children.

These results suggest two general conclusions about the poor performance of American elementary school children in mathematics. First, the poor performance appears to be due, in part, to the relative lack of importance given to mathematics in American conceptions of elementary school education. Mathematics seems to be a weak third in the American triad of reading, writing, and arithmetic. The second conclusion is related to the belief of American children that they were doing well in mathematics and that mathematics was not difficult. The likely consequence of such beliefs is that there is little motivation among American parents, teachers, and children to devote greater time and emphasis to mathematics, either at home or at school.

MOTHERS' BELIEFS AND PERCEPTIONS

We approached the mothers' attitudes about mathematics and reading in a manner somewhat different from that used with the children. We first explored the topic by asking the mothers the following question: ''For the average elementary school child, which subject do you think is more difficult, math or language arts?'' American mothers were nearly evenly divided between those that thought mathematics was more difficult and those that thought reading was more difficult (see Figure 2). Chinese and Japanese mothers had very different ideas from those of the American mothers. Most Chinese and Japanese mothers believed that mathematics was more difficult than reading.

These data are of special interest in view of the tasks faced by Chinese and Japanese children in learning to read. During the elementary school years Chinese children must learn to read at least 3000 characters; Japanese children must learn approximately 1000 characters in addition to three other scripts. Obviously, learning to read Chinese and Japanese is not an easy task, and is not a reasonable explanation of why so many mothers thought that reading was easier than mathematics. The mothers gave us other explanations of why math was more difficult. As is evident in Table 4, some mothers in each culture believed that mathematics was simply inherently more difficult. More American and Chinese than Japanese mothers believed that mathematics was more difficult because it required thinking, comprehension, and carefulness. The responses of few American mothers, but of nearly a quarter of the Japanese mothers indicated that they believed that mathematics was difficult because their children spent too little time on mathematics. On the other hand, a quarter of the responses of the American mothers indicated that they thought mathematics was difficult because children had little contact with math in their daily lives. Only one percent of the Japanese mothers mentioned the lack of daily usefulness of mathematics. Clearly, there were strong cultural differences in the mothers' interpretations of why their children faced difficulties in studying mathematics.

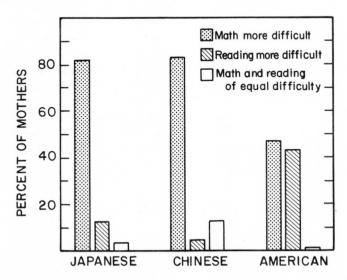

Figure 2. Mothers' ratings of relative difficulty of mathematics and reading for children.

Table 4. Percentage of Responses Made by Mothers Offering Various Reasons Why Mathematics Is More Difficult

	USA	Taiwan	Japan
Inherently more difficult	29	34	37
Requires thinking, comprehension	33	29	12
Child doesn't spend enough time	6	16	22
Less daily contact with math	25	6	1

A second approach to investigating mothers' attitudes about reading and mathematics was to ask them whether there were subjects in elementary school that needed more emphasis. Among American mothers, 57% answered affirmatively, as did 36% of the Chinese mothers and 46% of the Japanese mothers. The mothers then were asked to name these subjects. There was little indication that many American mothers were dissatisfied with the amount of time devoted to mathematics. More American mothers mentioned reading and language arts (38%) than mathematics (25%). Few Chinese mothers mentioned either of these subjects (less than 10%), but were more interested in giving more attention to subjects such as gym. The responses of the Japanese mothers were similar to those of the American mothers; 34% mentioned reading and language arts and 18% mentioned mathematics. These opinions are especially important in view of the large differences in the amounts of time children spend in language arts and mathematics classes in the fifth grade. On the basis of our observation of over 600 hours in the classrooms of Taipei, Sendai, and Minneapolis, we estimate that in the American fifth-grade classrooms 7.9 hours are spent each week in language arts classes and 3.4 hours in mathematics classes. The values for reading and mathematics classes in Taipei (11.1 and 11.7 hours) and Sendai (8.0 and 7.8 hours) are much larger and more similar to each other (see Stevenson, Stigler, Lucker, Lee, Hsu, & Kitamura, 1986).

Mothers' evaluations of their children's abilities. The mothers' evaluations of their children's abilities followed the pattern revealed by the children's ratings. American mothers had more favorable evaluations of their children's abilities than did Chinese and Japanese mothers. Mothers rated their children on seven attributes. In making the ratings, the mothers were to compare their child with other children the child's age. A rating of four was defined as "average"; one was "much below average" and seven was "much above average." On only one scale—persistence—did the American mothers fail to give their children higher average ratings than those given by the Chinese and/or Japanese mothers. Ratings of American mothers were higher than those of both Chinese and Japanese mothers for their children's ability to remember, express themselves verbally, and intelligence, $ps < .01$. Ratings were higher than those of Japanese mothers on the remaining three scales: learning, attention, and motivation, $ps < .01$. A second feature of the ratings should be noted. For a random sample of children, an average rating of four would be expected. It is obvious from the data in Figure 3, however, that average ratings in any of the three countries were rarely this low. Mothers in all three countries tended, on the average, to perceive their children as being above average.

Not only did the American mothers generally have the most favorable evaluations of their children, they also were the most satisfied with their child's current academic performance. American children believed this was the case, and their mothers' ratings were in line with this belief. Mothers were asked to choose among three points that represented being very satisfied, satisfied, or not satisfied with their child's present performance in school. Of the American mothers, 53% were "very satisfied" with their children's performance; only 8% of the Chinese mothers and 4% of the Japanese mothers were this pleased.

Within each culture, the mother's ratings were strongly influenced by their child's actual level of achievement. The reading and mathematics scores of the children differed significantly according to the ratings of satisfaction made by the mothers, $ps < .01$. The degree to which their levels of achievement differed is evident in Figure 4, where the mean z score derived from the combined mathematics and reading scores within each country are presented for mothers who were very satisfied, satisfied, or not satisfied with their child's level of achievement in school. In each case, the difference between mothers who were very satisfied and those who were not satisfied was approximately $1\frac{1}{2}z$ (standard deviation) units. It is noteworthy, however, that American children whose mothers were "not satisfied" were one standard deviation below the mean of the American children. This is a much more extreme score than was found for Chinese and Japanese children whose mothers were not satisfied with their performance. The mean for these children was less than a half standard deviation below the mean. The converse was the case for the children whose mothers were very satisfied with their achievement. American children whose mothers made this rating were only one-half a standard deviation above the mean for the American children, but the Chinese and Japanese children whose mothers were very satisfied with their achievement were one standard deviation above the mean. These data offer further evidence that American mothers appear to be much less demanding of their children in terms of their academic achievement than Chinese and Japanese mothers. That is, American children have to be performing very poorly for their mothers not to be satisfied with their performance, and they do not have to be much above average for their mothers to be very satisfied.

Generally, the mothers' evaluations give little support to suggestions that American parents are dissatisfied with American elementary schools. The American mothers in our sample generally were not only positive about their children's abilities and performance, they also were very satisfied with the job the school was doing in educating their child. When they were asked directly about their evaluations of their child's education, 81% of the American mothers, but

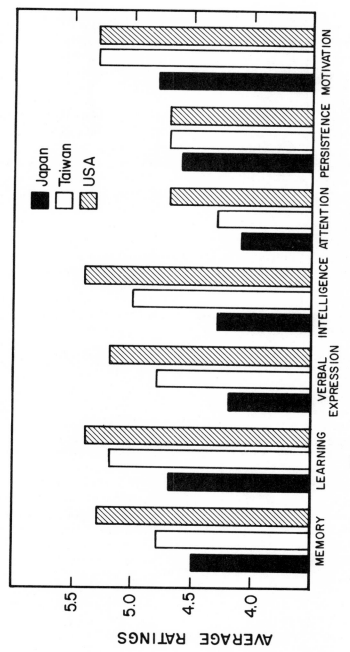

Figure 3. Mothers' ratings of children's abilities.

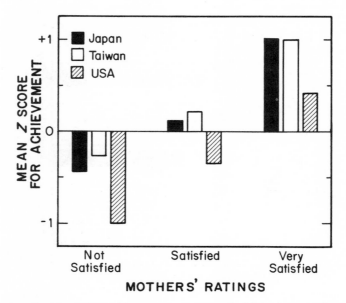

Figure 4. Standard (z) achievement scores of children according to their mothers' ratings of satisfaction with the child's achievement.

only 40% of the Chinese mothers and 36% of the Japanese mothers gave the school a rating of "excellent" or "good." Why American mothers and their children express such favorable perceptions is not clear. Positive attitudes would be more appropriate if American children demonstrated higher levels of achievement.

BELIEFS ABOUT ABILITY AND EFFORT

A second major purpose of this study was to investigate the relation of cultural beliefs and attributions about ability and effort to performance. In line with the cultural beliefs discussed earlier, we expected that Chinese and Japanese children would give greater emphasis to effort than the American children, and that the American children would give greater emphasis to ability than the Chinese and Japanese children. The predictions were generally confirmed.

Belief in the malleability of behavior characterized children in all three cultures. All three groups of children tended to reject the possibility that "If a person your age doesn't do well in math, there is probably nothing that person can do about it." Children believed that something could be done to help remedy poor performance. However, when it was proposed that everybody in the children's class "has about the same amount of ability," American children disagreed the most strongly and Chinese children showed the greatest degree of agreement (see Table 5).

Table 5. Mean Ratings Made by American, Chinese, and Japanese Children

	USA	Taiwan	Japan
a. Everybody in your class has the same amount of ability in math.	3.5	4.7	3.8
b. Everybody in your class has the same amount of ability in reading.	3.4	4.7	3.9
c. The best students in the class always work harder than the other students.	4.7	5.4	5.2
d. The best student in the class is always brighter than the other students.	3.8	3.6	4.6
e. If a person your age doesn't do well in math, there is probably nothing that person can do about it.	2.5	2.2	2.6
f. If a person your age doesn't do well in reading, there is probably nothing that person can do about it.	2.3	2.1	2.7
g. The tests you take can show how much or how little natural ability you have.	4.7	3.9	2.8

Note: 1 = strongly disagree; 4 = neither agree nor disagree; 7 = strongly agree. Country differences: dfs = 2, 444–446; $F(a) = 22.56, p < .001$; $F(b) = 26.60, p < .01$; $F(c) = 6.48, p < .01$; $F(d) = 18.25, p < .001$; $F(e) = 3.75, p < .05$; $F(f) = 6.17, p < .01$; $F(g) = 46.68, p < .001$.

Chinese children also were most likely to emphasize effort and least likely to emphasize native ability in their ratings of several other statements. The statement, "The best student in the class always works harder than the other students," elicited strongest agreement from the Chinese children and the least agreement from American children. For the statement, "The best student in the class is always brighter than the other students," Chinese children showed the least agreement. However, it was the Japanese children rather than the American children who showed the strongest agreement with the statement. Finally, the children were asked whether they agreed that "The tests you take can show how much or how little natural ability you have." Children who believe that performance reflects ability rather than effort would tend to agree with this statement. There were large differences of opinion among the children of the three countries. American children agreed with the statement, Chinese children disagreed, and Japanese children were more neutral.

It is apparent that interpreting the role of ability and effort in children's achievement is straightforward only for the Chinese children. They consistently showed the greatest rejection of ability and acceptance of effort as contributors to children's achievement. The evidence was not so consistent among American or Japanese children, although American children tended to give greater emphasis to the role of ability than did the children in the other two countries. Further clarification comes from questions about attributions that exist under conditions of success and failure.

The children were told, "Think about a time you did well on a test, or a time you did better than you usually do. Read each reason and then tell me how important it was for explaining why you did well on the test." The reasons were related to ability ("because I am talented"), effort ("because I studied very hard before the test"), task difficulty ("because the test was very easy"), and luck ("because I was lucky"). The same alternatives were offered for explanations of a situation where the child did not do well on a test.

The rank order of ratings was the same in all three countries under both success and failure conditions. Highest were the ratings of the importance of effort, followed by ratings of the importance of task difficulty, ability, and luck. Only one reversal to this pattern was found: Chinese children gave ability a slightly higher rating than task difficulty when the ratings were made for the failure condition. The mean ratings made by the children in each country and each condition are presented in Figure 5. It is evident that differences among countries existed primarily in the relative importance assigned to each of these attributes. It is helpful to summarize the major findings in somewhat greater detail before describing the analyses.

American children gave greater emphasis to ability as an explanation of success than did the Chinese and Japanese children, and the higher the American child's level of achievement, the greater was the emphasis given by the child to this explanation. The opposite was the case for the Chinese and Japanese children. They made lower ratings of the contribution of ability, and less emphasis was given to ability as the children's achievement scores increased. Effort was most strongly emphasized as the basis of success and lack of effort was emphasized as the basis of poor performance by the Chinese children. No differences among the three countries appeared when ability was considered as the basis for poor performance. Only the child's level of achievement was a significant factor. Low achievers in each country emphasized lack of ability to a greater degree than did average or high achievers. We will turn now to the analyses from which these conclusions were derived.

The two variables of central interest, ability and effort, were analyzed separately for success and failure conditions. Two independent variables were included in each analysis: (a) country and (b) the child's level of achievement according to the upper, middle, and lower thirds of achievement scores. The results of each analysis will be discussed in turn.

For the role of ability under conditions of success, there was a significant difference among the countries, $p < .001$, and a significant interaction between country and level of achievement, $p < .01$. Belief in the importance of ability increased among the American children according to their level of performance, decreased among the Chinese children, and remained stable for the Japanese children (see Table 6).

For the analysis of the role of effort under conditions of success, only the country effect was significant, $p < .001$. Chinese children gave the highest average ratings to effort (5.6), Japanese children gave the lowest (4.1), and American children were in between (5.4). The effects were very similar in the analysis of the role of effort in the failure condition. The mean rating made by the Chi-

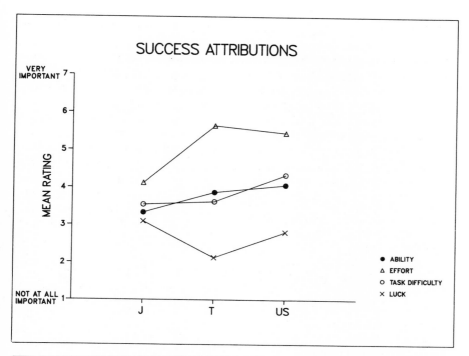

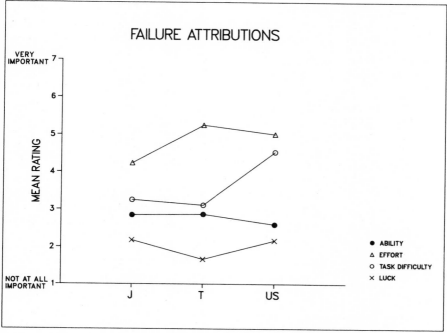

Figure 5. Children's ratings of attributions in success and failure.

169

Table 6.   Mean Ratings of the Role of Ability
in Successful Performance in Lower, Middle,
and Upper Thirds of Achievement

Achievement	USA	Taiwan	Japan
Lower third	4.0	4.4	3.4
Middle third	3.7	3.8	3.3
Upper third	4.5	3.1	3.3

nese children was 5.3; the mean rating for the Japanese children was 4.2; and it was 5.0 for the American children. It is not clear why the ratings of the Japanese children were so low. There was, in addition, a significant effect associated with level of achievement, $p < .01$. The higher the child's level of achievement in all three countries, the greater was the emphasis given to lack of effort as the cause of poor performance. The mean ratings were 4.5, 4.7, and 5.2 for children in the lowest, middle, and upper thirds in achievement.

In the analysis of the role of ability under conditions of poor performance, the only significant effect was found for the level of achievement. Low achievers in all three countries gave the most emphasis to the lack of ability as an explanation of poor performance and above average achievers gave the least emphasis, $p < .01$. The mean ratings for the low, average, and high achievers were 3.1, 2.8, and 2.5.

The analysis of the data derived from the ratings of the role of luck and task difficulty revealed that American children gave higher ratings to the role of difficulty of the task, both for doing well and doing poorly than did the Chinese children (see Table 7). Japanese children gave somewhat more emphasis to luck than did the Chinese or American children. It should be noted, however, that Japanese conceptions of luck and effort are not independent. It is commonly believed that hard work can result in improved luck. It may be more difficult, therefore, for Japanese children to separate their ratings of luck and effort than it is for the Chinese and American children.

Mothers' beliefs about effort and ability.   We also explored the mothers' beliefs about the role of effort and ability in their children's performance. We approached this task by asking the mothers several kinds of questions. For example, the mothers were told, ''Some parents talk about their children having 'ability.' We would like to find out your opinions about 'reading ability.' How about the following statements? (1) People tend to have the same amount of reading ability. (2) Any student can be good at reading if he/she tries hard enough.'' Two additional questions were: ''(1) To what extent do you believe that _____ was born with his/her reading ability? (2) To what extend do you think your child's environment and experiences determined his/her reading ability?'' Ratings were made on seven-point scales where a rating of four indicated neither

Table 7. Importance of Difficulty of Task and Luck under Conditions of Success and Failure

	Success			Failure		
	USA	Taiwan	Japan	USA	Taiwan	Japan
a. Difficulty of task	4.3	3.6	3.5	4.5	3.1	3.3
b. Luck	2.8	2.1	3.1	2.2	1.7	2.2

dfs = 2, 444–446; Success: *F*(a) = 8.78, *p* < .001; *F*(b) = 14.84, *p* < .001; Failure: *F*(a) = 30.25, *p* < .001; *F*(b) = 7.32, *p* < .01

agreement nor disagreement and the endpoints indicated strong disagreement or strong agreement. The items were repeated for ability in mathematics.

Mothers in the three countries showed significantly different beliefs about the role of ability and effort. American mothers did not agree that people have the same amount of ability in reading and mathematics. Ratings of the American mothers were lower than those of the Japanese and Chinese mothers, who tended to be more neutral in their opinions. When asked abut the role of effort, the Chinese and Japanese mothers agreed more strongly than the American mothers that any student can be good at reading and mathematics if he or she works hard enough. With one obvious exception apparent in Figure 6, differences between countries in the ratings were highly significant, *ps* < .001.

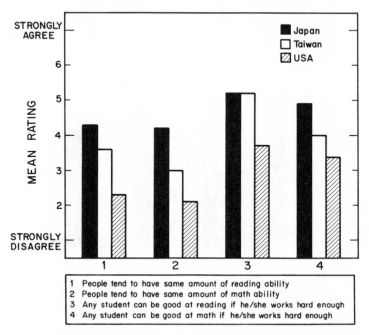

Figure 6. Mothers' ratings of four statements related to ability and effort.

In accord with the ratings for the preceding questions, American mothers expressed stronger beliefs than Chinese and Japanese mothers that their children were born with their math and reading abilities (see Figure 7). The means differed significantly for the ratings for both math and reading, $p < .001$.

Responses to another question provide additional evidence of cultural differences in beliefs about the contribution of ability to performance. Chinese and American mothers were asked when it was possible to predict a child's test performance at the end of the high school years. Ten percent of the Chinese mothers, but 38.1% of the American mothers believed that they could be predicted as early as the sixth grade. (This question was not included in the Japanese interview.) Here, as in other questions, American parents expressed stronger beliefs in the importance of ability as something that is acquired early in life.

Beliefs about the role of environment and experience on reading and mathematics ability also differed among the three groups of mothers, $ps < .01$. American mothers expressed stronger beliefs in the influence of environment and experience than did the Chinese and Japanese mothers (see Figure 7). It is not necessarily paradoxical that American mothers, who expressed stronger beliefs in the importance of native ability, should also express stronger beliefs in environmental influences. The role of environmental stimulation appears to be perceived differently in the three cultures. Chinese and Japanese mothers appear to

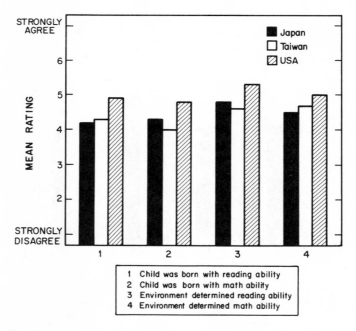

Figure 7. Mothers' ratings of four statements related to the role of innate ability and environment in children's performance.

give greater emphasis than American mothers to experiences related to academic performance, but American mothers are more likely to believe in the contribution of a generally stimulating environment to their child's development. Chinese and Japanese mothers spend more time working with their young children on homework than do the American mothers, but the American mothers spend more time reading to their children and taking them on outings (Stevenson, 1983). If having their child do well in school is the mother's major goal, the benefits of doing homework are obvious. The benefits of more general experiences such as hearing stories and visiting parks and museums are more indirect. We suspect that if the statement had included experiences more clearly related to academic achievement, Chinese and Japanese mothers would have made higher ratings than the American mothers.

An important question is whether mothers' beliefs were significantly related to their children's performance on the reading and mathematics test. Because belief systems may be closely related to parental education, we included the number of years of parental education as a variable in the regression analyses summarized in Table 8. However, even after controlling for the effects of parental education,

Table 8. Prediction of Scores in Mathematics and Reading from Mothers' Ratings of the Role of Various Factors in Mathematics and Reading Performance

	USA		Taiwan		Japan	
	partial r	*t*	*partial r*	*t*	*partial r*	*t*
	Mathematics					
Parental education	.23	2.42*	.24	2.51*	.20	2.45*
Same ability	.03		−.34	−3.66***	−.17	−2.06*
Effort	−.17		.07		.01	
Born with ability	.23	2.42*	.36	3.80***	.23	2.88**
Environmental factors	.17		−.08		.00	
	$R^2 = .20$		$R^2 = .29$		$R^2 = .14$	
	Reading					
Parental education	.36	3.30**	.43	4.63***	.16	
Same ability	.00		−.20		.00	
Effort	.12		−.01		−.09	
Born with ability	.22	2.34**	.24	2.42*	.10	
Environmental factors	.17		−.02		.10	
	$R^2 = .18$		$R^2 = .29$		$R^2 = .09$	

*$p < .05$ **$p < .01$ ***$p < .001$

mothers' ratings still made significant contributions to the prediction of children's scores on the achievement tests.

Generally, prediction of scores in mathematics was more reliable than was prediction of scores in reading, and the strength of the correlation was strongest in Taiwan. As is evident from the negative correlations in Table 8, the more strongly Chinese and Japanese mothers rejected the belief that people tend to have the same amount of ability, the higher were their children's scores in mathematics. On the other hand, agreement with the belief that their child was born with his or her mathematics ability was positively related to achievement in all three countries. Thus, even though Chinese and Japanese mothers of high achievers in mathematics rejected the belief that all children were born with the same ability in mathematics, they also believed that their child had been born with his or her ability in mathematics.

Mothers' ratings were much less closely related to the children's scores in reading. None of the partial correlations was significant in the analysis of the Japanese data. For American and Chinese mothers, the partial correlations related to mothers' belief in innate factors were significant. As was the case with predictions of mathematics scores, children's scores were predicted by the degree to which mothers accepted the statement that their child was born with his or her reading ability.

CHILDREN'S SCHOLASTIC MOTIVATION

We have examined children's attitudes and beliefs about school and both the children's and their mothers' beliefs about the role of effort and ability in academic achievement. Another way of examining the motivational basis for children's academic achievement is to ask them why they go to school and why they study. Children's reasons were assessed in two sets of items. In the first set, ratings were made of the degree to which four statements pertained to themselves. The phrase, "I spend as much time doing school work as I do because," was followed by four reasons: the time required to finish the work, pleasure in doing the work, following parental wishes, and avoiding punishment from the teacher. The second set of items began with the explanation: "Different students have different reasons for coming to school. How important for you are the following reasons for coming to school?" The reasons included liking schoolwork, meeting friends, special activities, parental wishes, general necessity, and learning. Ratings were made on scales which ranged from "not an important reason" to "a very important reason."

Factor analyses of the ratings from both sets of items were made separately for each country. Three factors, reflecting three sources of motivation, appeared in each analysis. The strength of the factor loadings of the items differed somewhat for each country, but in each case there were three distinct factors. The first was

Table 9. Items in Factors of Internal, External and Social Orientation

---

Internal

I spend as much time doing school work as I do because I like doing school work.

I come to school because I like the subjects we study there, like reading, math, social science, and natural science.

I come to school because I can learn many useful things from school.

External

I spend as much time doing school work as I do because it takes that much time in order to finish.

I spend as much time doing school work as I do because my parents want me to.

I spend as much time doing school work as I do because I don't want to be punished by the teacher.

I come to school because my parents want me to.

I come to school because students have to.

Social

I come to school because I like to see my friends there.

I come to school because I like the special activities we do there, like sports and band.

---

based on the child's interest in learning; the second, on external forces; and the third, on social aspects of school. The factors were labeled Internal, External, and Social Orientation. Items included in each factor appear in Table 9.

An index of each child's orientation was created by averaging the ratings of the items included within each factor. The mean of these values for each culture appear in Figure 8. The strongest internal orientation was among the Chinese

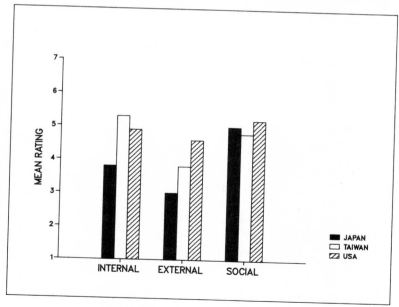

Figure 8. Children's ratings of motivation orientation.

children, and the strongest external orientation was among the American children. Differences among cultures were highly significant for these two factors, as were all comparisons of pairs of cultures, $ps < .01$. Ratings for the third factor, Social Orientation, also differed significantly among the three cultures. Chinese children placed somewhat less importance on social factors as a reason for attending school and studying than did the American and Japanese children. Regression analyses were conducted, but prediction of mathematics and reading scores from the internal, external, and social orientations generally were low, partial $rs < .20$. For Chinese children, however, an external orientation was negatively related to achievement in both reading and mathematics, partial $rs = -.32$ and $-.41$, $ps < .001$.

CONCLUSIONS

This chapter summarizes a portion of the results obtained in a follow-up study of Chinese, Japanese, and American children that was undertaken to provide information that might help to explain why American elementary school children perform less well in mathematics and reading than their peers in countries such as Taiwan and Japan. The emphasis in this report is upon cultural differences in beliefs and attitudes that are related to children's academic achievement. Two salient factors appear in our results:

1.   Americans appear to believe that developing skill in mathematics during the elementary school years is not as important as learning to read. Mathematics is not emphasized in American elementary schools and the mathematics curriculum is not difficult. American children's attitudes about school and their self-evaluations appear to depend much more strongly on their ability in reading than on their ability in mathematics. Moreover, American children believe they are doing well in mathematics and their mothers express satisfaction with the children's academic performance. As a consequence, the motivation of American children to apply themselves diligently to the study of mathematics does not appear to be as high as that of children in countries such as Taiwan and Japan, and American parents perceive less need to assist their children in mathematics or to seek changes in mathematics instruction than do Chinese and Japanese parents. The outstanding performance of Chinese and Japanese children in mathematics appears to be partly due, then, to the children's strong motivation for academic achievement, and to the importance of achievement expressed by their parents and teachers. Attitudes of Chinese and Japanese children about school are positive, expectations of parents and teachers for achievement are high, and large amounts of time are spent in instruction and practice.

In reading ability, American children exceed the level of performance of the Japanese children, but are not as skilled in reading as the Chinese children. In contrast to mathematics, where strengths and deficiencies can be attributed in part to motivational factors, the motivational factors related to performance in reading are much less clear. Other variables may be more highly related to reading scores. As we have pointed out elsewhere (Stevenson, 1983), American children, compared to Chinese and Japanese children, spend less time both in and out of school studying, and spend less time out of school reading for pleasure. It is likely that this limited practice in reading makes it difficult for some American children to acquire the reading skills expected of children their age. The less effective reading of Japanese children is related, we believe, to characteristics of the Japanese written language. Japanese contains three different scripts, which may increase the difficulty of early efforts at learning how to read.

2.   Although more emphasis was given to effort than to ability as a basis for achievement in all three countries, the relative strength of the belief in the importance of these factors differed among American, Chinese, and Japanese children and their mothers. Relative to their Chinese and Japanese counterparts, Americans placed greater emphasis on ability; correspondingly, Chinese and Japanese mothers and Chinese children placed greater emphasis on effort as an explanation for achievement.

In discussing the relation between beliefs and performance, the direction of causality cannot be clearly determined. It was impossible for us to ascertain whether the differences in beliefs were responsible for the children's performance, or whether the beliefs were direct reflections of performance. For example, children may work hard to the degree that they believe achievement is dependent upon effort, or they may believe that effort is important because they have been successful. Similarly, children may do better if they believe they have ability, or they may believe they have ability because of how well they have done. Each view may have special consequences. Children who attribute their success to effort may come to see themselves as hard workers, but children who attribute their success to ability may have more positive evaluations of themselves. These attributions may be closely related to the child's later sense of self-worth and confidence. Comparative studies of Chinese, Japanese, and American adolescents would make it possible to evaluate the long-term effects of these cultural differences in attributions. Because of the consistency of the effects we have reported, we would expect that the beliefs held by parents and children early in the child's life would contribute importantly to children's later achievement.

Many of the results described in this chapter could not be readily discovered in the study of children in a single culture. By using the same tests and interviews with large numbers of subjects in three diverse cultures, we believe we have obtained a clearer picture of the interrelation of beliefs and achievement than would have been possible if we had studied only American children. Furthermore, the findings of this study lead directly to suggestions about how the motivation of American children and parents for academic achievement might be enhanced.

Motivation depends upon information. As long as Americans continue to believe that American children are performing satisfactorily in mathematics and that mathematics is not difficult, it is unlikely that greater emphasis will be given to mathematics in American elementary school curricula. However, cross-national studies such as the present one may provide the information necessary for increasing this level of motivation. The deficiencies of American children in mathematical skills and knowledge are becoming strikingly clear. Hopefully, as parents, teachers, and other citizens recognize these deficiencies, and as the relevance of the deficiencies for future technological and scientific advances is acknowledged, the need for improving instruction in mathematics throughout the school years should become apparent. In contrast to the lack of emphasis on mathematics in American elementary schools, parents and teachers appear to be intensely motivated to provide ample opportunities for children to become proficient in reading. American children's attitudes reflect the impact of this difference in relative emphasis on reading and mathematics. The problem in American elementary schools seems to be that of convincing both teachers and parents that mathematics and science, as well as reading, merit the children's close attention.

Motivation for academic achievement may also be enhanced to the degree that students, as well as their parents and teachers, believe that increased effort pays off in improved performance. The willingness of Chinese and Japanese children, teachers, and parents to spend so much time and effort on the children's academic work seems to be explained partly by this belief. The situation often encountered when achievement is attributed to ability rather than to effort—as is often the case in American classrooms and homes—is that children are categorized early in their academic years according to their presumed level of ability. Although the self-evaluation of high achievers may be increased when they are described as having high levels of ability, the effect of categorizing the low achiever as having low levels of ability may be devastating. Once categorized and given a label as being a slow learner, poor in mathematics, or reading disabled, it may be difficult for a child to accept the possibility that improvement is possible and for parents to become motivated to devote themselves to assisting their children with their school work. Modification of these views is a necessary precursor to enhancing the child's motivation to work harder in school.

Finally, it has long been demonstrated in psychology that internal sources of motivation have more enduring strength and are less influenced by environmental conditions than are those that are more dependent upon external factors. Unless the child is strongly motivated to learn and the school environment facilitates this motivation, teachers and parents face an increasingly difficult burden in attempts to induce and sustain children's motivation for academic accomplishment. Increasing intrinsic motivation for academic achievement would appear to be a worthy goal for parents and teachers of American elementary school children.

ACKNOWLEDGMENTS

This chapter reports results from a collaborative study undertaken with S. Kitamura, S. Kimura, and T. Kato of Tohoku Fukushi College in Sendai, Japan, and C. C. Hsu of National Taiwan University in Taipei. The research was partially supported by NIMH grants MH 33259 and MH 30567, by grants from the Rackham School of Graduate Studies of the University of Michigan, and NSF grant 8409372.

REFERENCES

Azuma, H., Kashiwagi, K., & Hess, R. D. (1981). *Hahaoya no taido koudo to kodomo no chiteki hattatsu.* (The effect of mother's attitude and behavior on the cognitive development of the child: A U.S-Japanese comparison.) Tokyo: University of Tokyo Press.

Comber, L. C., & Keeves, J. (1973). *Science achievement in nineteen countries.* New York: Wiley.

Cummings, W. K. (1980). *Education and equality in Japan.* Princeton: Princeton University Press.

DeVos, G. (1973). *Socialization for achievement.* Berkeley: University of California Press.

Husen, T. (1967). *International study of achievement in mathematics: A comparison of twelve countries.* New York: Wiley.

Lebra, T. S. (1976). *Japanese patterns of behavior.* Honolulu: University of Hawaii Press.

Lee, S. Y., Stigler, J. W., & Stevenson, H. W. (1986). Beginning reading in Chinese and English. In A. Siegel & B. Foorman (Eds.), *Learning to read: Cognitive universals and cultural constraints.* Hillsdale, N.J.: Erlbaum.

Lynn R. (1982). IQ in Japan and the United States shows a growing disparity. *Nature, 297,* 222–223.

Munro, D. J. (1977). *The concept of man in contemporary China.* Ann Arbor: University of Michigan Press.

Stevenson, H. W. (1983). Making the grade. *Annual Report, Center for Advanced Study in the Behavioral Sciences,* pp. 41–51.

Stevenson, H. W., Azuma, H., & Hakuta, K. (Eds.) (1986). *Child development in Japan and the United States.* New York: W. H. Freeman.

Stevenson, H. W., Lee, S. Y., & Stigler, J. W. (1986). Mathematics achievement of Chinese, Japanese, and American children. *Science, 231,* 693–699.

Stevenson, H. W., Stigler, J. W., Lee, S. Y., Lucker, G. W., Kitamura, S., & Hsu, C. C. (1985). Cognitive performance and academic achievement of Japanese, Chinese, and American children. *Child Development, 56,* 718–734.

Stevenson, H. W., Stigler, J. W., Lucker, G. W., & Lee, S. Y. (1982). Reading disabilities: The case of Chinese, Japanese, and English. *Child Development, 53,* 1164–1182.

Stevenson, H. W., Stigler, J. W., Lucker, G. W., Lee, S. Y., Hsu, C. C., & Kitamura, S. (1986). Classroom behavior and achievement of Japanese, Chinese, and American children. In R. Glaser (Ed.), *Advances in instructional psychology.* Hillsdale, N.J.: Erlbaum.

Stigler, J. W., Lee, S. Y., Lucker, G. W., & Stevenson, H. W. (1982). Curriculum and achievement in mathematics: A study of elementary school children in Japan, Taiwan, and the United States. *Journal of Educational Psychology, 74,* 315–322.

Wilson, R. W. (1970). *Learning to be Chinese: The political socialization of children in Taiwan.* Cambridge, MA: MIT Press.

SOCIALIZING STUDENTS' MOTIVATION TO LEARN

Jere Brophy

This chapter focuses on a particular type of motivation called motivation to learn, especially as it applies to student attention to lessons and engagement in academic learning tasks in classrooms. It begins by defining motivation to learn and differentiating it from related concepts, summarizes related theory and research on the topic, and then describes principles for guiding teachers' efforts to stimulate such motivation to learn in their students.

DEFINITION OF MOTIVATION TO LEARN

Motivation to learn can be construed both as a general trait and as a situation-specific state. As a general *trait*, motivation to learn refers to an enduring disposition to value learning as a worthwhile and satisfying activity, and thus to strive for knowledge and mastery in learning situations. This trait is most characteristic

Advances in Motivation and Achievement: Enhancing Motivation,
Volume 5, pages 181-210.
Copyright © 1987 by JAI Press Inc.
All rights of reproduction in any form reserved.
ISBN: 0-89232-621-2

of individuals who find learning intrinsically rewarding—who enjoy or take satisfaction in expanding their knowledge of information, increasing their understanding of concepts or processes, or mastering skills. Similar levels of effort and persistence in learning situations may also be seen, however, in individuals who are motivated by a sense of duty ("If you are going to do a thing at all, do it right") or a desire to make the most of their time ("If you are going to have to put in the time on something anyway, you might as well do your best and get the most out of the experience").

In specific situations, a *state* of motivation to learn exists when task engagement is guided by the goal or intention of acquiring the knowledge or mastering the skill that the task is designed to teach. In classrooms, students reveal motivation to learn when they try to master the information, concepts, or skills being taught as they attend to lessons, read text, or work on assignments. Whether or not they find a particular task interesting or enjoyable, students who are motivated to learn that task will try to get the intended benefits from it by striving to make sure that they understand and will remember what they are supposed to learn. In contrast, students who are not motivated to learn the task will minimize their investment in it and do only as much as they believe that they need to do in order to meet performance standards that will insure access to reward or avoidance of punishment.

Several implications of this definition of motivation to learn need to be pointed out. First, the present approach fits within general social learning theory, and in particular, within *expectancy x value theory* (Feather, 1982) which posits that people's effort expenditure on tasks is a product of: (a) the value that they place on doing the task or reaping the benefits that it offers; and (b) the degree to which they expect to be able to succeed on the task if they apply themselves. This is the same general orientation to motivation shared by such approaches as those based on the concepts of achievement motivation (Dweck & Elliot, 1983), efficacy perceptions (Bandura, 1982; Bandura & Schunk, 1981), and causal attributions (Weiner, 1979). However, these formulations have been concerned mostly with the expectancy term of the expectancy x value formulation, whereas the present approach is focused on the *value* term (see Parsons & Goff, 1980, on this point). Thus, a focus on motivation to learn is not as much concerned with students' desire to achieve in the sense of competing with standards of excellence as with their desire to learn content and master skills. Similarly, it is not concerned as much with their perceptions of efficacy (focused on the self) as with their perceptions of the content to be learned and with their metacognitive awareness of their strategies for responding to the task. Finally, it is not concerned as much with students' attributions about the causes of success or failure as with their reasons for participating in academic activities in the first place. The present value-focused approach complements the various expectancy-focused approaches that are based on such concepts as locus of control (Stipek & Weisz, 1981; Thomas, 1980), sense of efficacy or competence (Bandura, 1982; Bandura & Schunk,

1981), personal causation (origin vs. pawn) perceptions (deCharms, 1976), or perceptions of covariation between effort and outcome (Cooper, 1979).

A second implication is the distinction between learning and performance: *learning* refers to the information processing, sense-making, and comprehension or mastery advances that occur during the acquisition of knowledge or skill; *performance* refers to the demonstration of such knowledge or skill after it has been acquired. Many approaches to the study of relationships between motivation and behavior ignore this distinction or deal only with performance. Such approaches are inappropriate for studying student motivation to learn, however, because of the heavily cognitive nature of classroom learning. With a few exceptions, such as penmanship or zoology dissection skills, school learning is primarily covert and conceptual rather than overt and behavioral. Thus, the term "motivation to learn" refers primarily to the motivation underlying these covert processes that occur during learning rather than to the motivation driving performance (reproduction or application of previously acquired learning).

A third implication concerns the criteria to be used in operationalizing and measuring the concept of motivation to learn in classrooms. Much motivation research has taken place in free choice or recreational settings where subjects could choose from a range of activities. Consequently, motivational measures in these situations tend to be based on time allocations (what activities the subjects choose to engage in and for how long). In classrooms, however, students usually are not free to choose how to allocate their time. Instead, they are expected to attend to lessons and work on assignments. Consequently, measures of student motivation to learn must reflect the *quality of student engagement in academic activities*. All students will attend to or work on the same required activities in a particular classroom, but students motivated to learn will attempt to get the intended academic benefits from those activities. To the extent that a choice is involved, it amounts to choosing to try to get the intended benefits from an imposed task, rather than choosing what to do in the first place.

Motives, Goals, and Strategies

Traditionally, psychologists have used motivational concepts to account for the initiation, direction, intensity, and persistence of behavior. *Motives* are hypothetical constructs intended to explain why people are doing what they are doing, and can be distinguished from related constructs such as *goals* (the immediate objectives of particular sequences of behavior) and *strategies* (the methods that the person is using to achieve the goal and thus satisfy or at least respond to the motive). Sometimes motives, goals, and strategies are easily distinguished from one another, as in the case of instrumental behaviors intended to satisfy tissue needs: A person responding to hunger (motive) goes to a restaurant (strategy) to get food (goal). At other times, however, motives, goals, and strategies are not so easily distinguished. This is especially true in conceptualizing the covert cog-

nitive activities involved in learning academic content, and thus in conceptualiz-
ing student motivation to learn as defined here.

This is most obvious when considering motivation to learn as a state that exists
in some degree in a particular school learning situation (as opposed to consider-
ing it as a general trait that distinguishes individuals). The term "student motiva-
tion to learn" as it applies to a particular school learning situation may be more
aptly described as a goal than as a motive. That is, all students who take a partic-
ular academic task seriously and attempt to get the intended knowledge or skill
benefits from it could be described as "motivated to learn" the task, even though
only some of these students might possess a generalized trait that could be called
motivation to learn (other students might attempt to get the intended academic
benefits from the task because they anticipate getting rewarded for doing so, be-
cause they anticipate needing the information or skills to prepare them for de-
sired careers, etc.). Although stemming from different motives, the learning
goals and associated strategies generated by these various students in response to
the task would be identical for all practical purposes, and thus could be described
as a situational state of "motivation to learn." Readers who desire a more clear
separation between motives and goals might wish to reserve the term "motiva-
tion to learn" for the motive and to use a term such as "mastery orientation"
(see Diener & Dweck, 1978) to refer to the learner's adoption of the goal of
mastery of the content or skill being taught in a given situation.

A further consideration complicating discussion of motivation to learn is that it
is difficult to maintain a clear separation between the motivational elements
(motives, goals) and the cognitive, executive, or strategic elements involved in
learning academic content (mathemagenic behaviors, information processing
skills, generative learning strategies, comprehension monitoring and repair strat-
egies, problem solving heuristics, etc.). These are easy to separate conceptually,
of course, but in practice, given the highly cognitive nature of intentional learn-
ing of semantically encoded meaningful content, there is an extremely high cor-
relation between the state of motivation to learn and the activation of cognitive
and metacognitive strategies for accomplishing such learning. In fact, it is
difficult to imagine how significant learning could occur without activation of
these strategies, and difficult to imagine how or why learners would activate such
strategies in particular situations unless they were responding to a generalized
trait of motivation to learn or at least had adopted mastery of the present task as a
goal.

In discussions of typical school learning situations, then, reference to a state of
student motivation to learn implies the presence not only of motivational ele-
ments (motives or goals), but also of learning and cognition elements (cognitive
and metacognitive strategies). Furthermore, reference to teachers' methods of
stimulating student motivation to learn (whether in the context of developing it as
a general trait or activating it as a situational state) implies not only methods of
inducing students to adopt mastery of content or skills as a goal, but also meth-

ods of inducing students to activate needed cognitive and metacognitive strategies (and if necessary, to teach them these strategies). The focus in this chapter is on specific learning situations within the school setting, so the term "student motivation to learn" will routinely imply student adoption of the goal of mastering the content or skills being taught (mastery orientation) and activation of the cognitive and metacognitive strategies needed to reach this goal. It will not necessarily imply that the student possesses motivation to learn as a highly developed generalized trait, however.

Socializing Student Motivation to Learn

Considered as either a general trait or a situational state, student motivation to learn is construed as an acquired competence developed through general experience but stimulated most directly through modeling, communication of expectations, and direct instruction or socialization by significant others (especially parents and teachers). The topic is approached here primarily from an interest in identifying strategies that teachers can use to stimulate student motivation to learn in their classrooms. Most of what follows will refer to motivation to learn as a situational state, although it is assumed that teachers' strategies that are effective for stimulating student motivation to learn in particular situations, if implemented consistently, will also stimulate development of student motivation to learn as a generalized trait.

RELATED THEORY AND RESEARCH

Until quite recently, theory and research on motivation had concentrated on the expectancy term rather than the value term within the expectancy × value theory approach, had treated motivation as a predictor variable or correlate in individual difference studies rather than as a dependent variable in experiments designed to induce change, and had not taken into account the highly cognitive nature of academic learning and the other factors that must be considered when conceptualizing motivation in the classroom setting. Consequently, although there is a large body of theory and research on the general topic of motivation, only a small portion of it applies specifically to the subtopic of motivation to learn in the classroom.

Theoretical Concepts and Models

Several theorists concerned with intrinsic motivation (Condry & Chambers, 1978; Kruglanski, 1978; Lepper, 1983) have demonstrated that a complete motivational analysis must address not only expectations and attributions concerning level of performance (Can I succeed on this task? Why did I achieve the

level of success that I achieved?), but also attributions concerning the reasons
why one is engaging in the task in the first place and expectations concerning
goals and objectives (What am I trying to accomplish here, and what benefits can
I expect to obtain from the experience?). These authors have shown that the qual-
ity of task engagement, and ultimately the amount or quality of achievement, is
higher when people perceive themselves as engaging in a task for their own rea-
sons (intrinsic motivation) than when they perceive themselves as engaging in
the task in order to please an authority figure, obtain a reward, escape punish-
ment, or respond to some other external pressure (extrinsic motivation).

Implications for teachers stemming from this line of theory and research in-
clude the suggestions that teachers allow students as many choices as possible,
that they introduce tasks and give feedback in ways that maximize students'
awareness of the potential value of the task for them and minimize their
awareness of the fact that the teacher is exerting authority over them and
requiring them to do the task (Brophy, 1981; Lepper, 1983), and that teachers
identify task elements that students find enjoyable and incorporate as many of
these elements as possible into classroom activities (Lepper & Gilovich, 1982;
Malone & Lepper, in press). These and other related ideas based on the notion of
maximizing students' intrinsic motivation for classroom activities are useful as
far as they go, but teachers' opportunities for implementing them in typical class-
room situations are limited because they must concentrate on seeing that their
students master the prescribed curriculum. Thus, most classroom activities are
required rather than optional, and must be done whether the students enjoy them
or not.

Jacquelynne Eccles (Parsons), in the process of studying girls' motivation and
performance in mathematics classes, has made several more general contribu-
tions to the conceptualization of motivation in the classroom. Parsons and Goff
(1980) have noted the need to consider the value that students place on activities
in addition to considering their expectations for success at those activities, and
Eccles and Wigfield (1985) have proposed a model suggesting that the value at-
tached to engaging in a task will depend on the degree to which such engagement
will fulfill needs, facilitate reaching goals, or affirm personal values. Underscor-
ing the point made above that motivation to learn cannot be equated with intrin-
sic motivation, Eccles and Wigfield suggest that subjective task value (the value
that a person places on engaging in a task) has three major components: attain-
ment value (the importance of doing well on the task in order to affirm one's
self-concept or fulfill achievement, power, or social needs), intrinsic or interest
value (the enjoyment one gets from engaging in the task), and utility value (the
role that engaging in a task may play in advancing one's career or reaching other
short- or long-term goals).

Brophy (1983a) presented a model for conceptualizing student motivation that
called for consideration of several qualitative aspects of such motivation in addi-
tion to its quantity. Distinctions were made between task-endogenous and task-

exogenous sources of motivation for task engagement, between the subjective focus on task value and the subjective focus on performance outcome, and between the affect associated with task engagement and the cognitions generated in guiding and responding to that engagement. Brophy argued that optimal task engagement is associated with a relaxed learning orientation rather than an intense level of arousal, with a focus on the task at hand rather than on the self or on task exogenous considerations, and with metacognitive awareness of what the task requires and how one is responding to it rather than with a focus on affective reactions.

Similar conceptualizations of optimal motivation to learn have been advanced by Maehr (1984) in his concept of personal investment in a task, by Nicholls (1984) in his emphasis on task involvement (in contrast to ego involvement), and by Corno and Mandinach (1983) and Corno and Rohrkemper (1985) in their discussions of the concept of self-regulated learning. Similar conceptions of student motivation to learn also underlie the advice offered by Keller (1983) concerning methods of building student motivation into instructional design, and the information and exercises included by McCombs (1984) in her motivational training program for college students.

Classroom Research on Student Motivation to Learn

The models offered in these recent theoretical writings agree in identifying the critical aspects of what is defined here as student motivation to learn, but despite this theoretical agreement and general recognition of the importance of the topic, there has not been much research on student motivation to learn in classroom settings. Furthermore, the data that do exist are not encouraging.

Anderson and her colleagues (Anderson, 1981, 1984; Anderson et al., 1984) observed first graders working on seatwork assignments and then interviewed them about what they had done, why they did it, and how they did it. Their data indicated that many students, especially low achievers, did not understand how to do their assignments. Yet, rather than ask the teacher or get help in some other way, these students were content to respond randomly or to rely on response sets that had nothing to do with the content they were supposed to be learning (using alternating or geometrical patterns for circling answers on multiple choice assignments; picking one from a list of new words to fill in the blank in a sentence without reading the sentence itself).

The low achievers seemed to be more concerned about completing their assignments than about understanding the content. As one said to himself when he finished a worksheet, ''I don't know what it means, but I did it.'' (Anderson et al., 1984, p. 20). High achievers completed most of their assignments successfully and showed less concern about getting finished on time, but even so, they seldom gave evidence of understanding the content related purposes of the assignments. Answers to questions about the purposes of assignments tended to be vague generalities ("It's just our work," or "We learn to read."), without reference to the specific content supposedly being learned or the skills being practiced.

Analysis of the teachers' presentations of assignments to the students suggested that teacher failure to call attention to the purposes and meanings of these assignments was a major reason for the students' low quality of engagement in them. Most presentations included procedural directions or special hints (Pay attention to the underlined words), but only five percent explicitly described the purpose of the assignment in terms of the content being taught, and only 1.5% included explicit descriptions of the cognitive strategies to be used when doing the assignment.

Other investigators have reported similar findings. Rorhkemper and Bershon (1984) interviewed elementary students about what was on their minds when they worked on assignments. They found that of 49 students who gave codable responses, two were concerned only about finishing, 45 were concerned about getting correct answers, and only two mentioned trying to understand what was being taught. Corno and Mandinach (1983) and Blumenfeld, Hamilton, Bossert, Wessels, and Meece (1983) have also expressed concern about the low quality of students' engagement in classroom tasks.

Doyle (1983) suggests that most students are preoccupied with maximizing their ability to predict, and if possible control, the relationship between their academic performance and the grade they will receive. In particular, he suggests that students will seek to avoid tasks that involve ambiguity (about precisely what will be needed to earn high grades) or risk (high difficulty levels or strict grading standards), and thus will avoid asking questions or seeking to probe deeper into the content because they want to stick with safe, familiar routines.

Brophy et al. (1983) observed reading and mathematics instruction in intermediate grade classrooms to test predictions about the relationships between the nature of the expectations about tasks that teachers established when introducing those tasks to their students and the levels of apparent task engagement (inferred from observation rather than measured directly through interviewing) displayed by the students once the tasks were begun. As expected, low levels of student engagement were observed on tasks that the teachers had introduced by communicating negative expectations (i.e., that the tasks would be boring or that the students would not enjoy them). However, task introductions in which teachers communicated positive expectations about the task were not associated with the highest levels of student engagement. Instead, student engagement was highest when the teachers launched directly into tasks without making any introductory statements about them at all. More generally, the evidence concerning the effectiveness of teachers' task introductions for eliciting student task engagement was disappointing: Only 14 of a possible 52 relationships reached statistical significance, and 12 of these were negative relationships. Thus, most relationships in-

dicated lower student engagement when teachers made some introductory state-
ment than when they did not.

Many of these negative relationships had been expected because they occurred
for task introductions that threatened punishment for poor performance, re-
minded the students of accountability pressures, or created negative expectations
about the task. However, negative relationships were also seen for task introduc-
tions expected to have positive effects on student motivation (teachers' projec-
tion of enthusiasm about the task or mention of the importance of the skills being
taught for success in our society), as well as for task introductions expected to be
perceived as neutral (challenging the students to set and strive to meet particular
goals).

Later analyses of these data by Brophy and Kher (1986) suggested that the task
introductions made by the teachers observed in this study probably did not have
much impact on student motivation to learn because: (a) statements likely to
stimulate student motivation to learn did not occur often enough; (b) when they
did occur, they were usually too short and sketchy to do much good; and (c)
whatever good they might have done was probably negated by other statements
likely to undermine motivation to learn.

Only about one-third of the teachers' task introductions included comments
judged likely to have positive effects on student motivation, and most of these
were brief general predictions that the student would enjoy the task or would do
well on it. In about 100 hours of classroom observation, only nine task introduc-
tions were noted that included substantive information about motivation to learn
as defined here:

- These are not elementary, high school, or college level words; these are
  living level words. You'll use them every day in life. If you plan to be a
  writer or enjoy reading, you will need these words.
- Remember: The essential thing is to do them correctly, not to be the first
  to finish.
- I think you will like this book. Someone picked it out for me, and it's
  really good.
- This is a really strange story. It's written in the first person, so that the
  person talking is the one who wrote the story about his experience. It has
  some pretty interesting words in it. They are on the board.
- The stories in this book are more interesting than the ones in the earlier
  level books. They are more challenging because the stories and vocabu-
  lary are more difficult. Reading improves with practice, just like basket-
  ball. If you never shoot baskets except when you are in the game, you are
  not going to be very good. Same with reading. You can't do without it.
- Answer the comprehension questions with complete sentences. All these
  stories are very interesting. You'll enjoy them.

- You girls should like this story because it is a feminist story. You boys will enjoy yours too. Your story is especially interesting. I want you to be sure to read it. It's a mystery, and you'll enjoy it.
- Percent is very important. Banks use it for interest loans, and so on. So it is important that you pay attention.
- You're going to need to know fractions for math next year. You will need fractions in the world to come.

Notice how minimal and essentially barren most of these remarks are. They do not go into enough detail to be very meaningful or memorable for most students, and many of them have a perfunctory quality suggesting that the teacher was going through the motions without much enthusiasm or conviction. Furthermore, whatever positive effect these remarks may have had was probably undercut by the facts that: (a) most of the teachers' remarks to the students concerned procedural demands and evaluations of work quality or progress rather than description of the task itself or what the students might get out of it; and (b) many of the rest included remarks such as the following, which depict academic tasks as boring and unrewarding:

- Today's lesson is nothing new if you've been here.
- If you get done by ten o'clock, you can go outside.
- Your scores will tell me whether we need to stay with multiplication for another week. If you are talking, I will deduct 10 points from your scores.
- This penmanship assignment means that sometimes in life you just can't do what you want to do. The next time you have to do something you don't want to do, just think: "Well, that's part of life."
- Get your nose in the book, otherwise I'll give you a writing assignment.
- You don't expect me to give you baby work every day, do you?
- You've been working real hard today, so let's stop early.
- You'll have to work real quietly, otherwise you'll have to do more assignments.
- My talkers are going to get a third page to do during lunch.
- We don't have a huge amount to do, but it will be time consuming.
- This test is to see who the really smart ones are.

Conclusions Regarding Socializing Student Motivation to Learn

Taken together, the theory and research reviewed above suggest that even though a theoretical consensus is developing concerning desirable features of student motivation to learn in classrooms, we are unlikely to see much of this desirable motivation developed until teachers are made aware of the need to stimulate such motivation to learn systematically when instructing and socializing their students, and are armed with strategies for doing so. Even assuming the development of effective strategies and teacher training methods, some powerful deterrents to success would have to be overcome: (a) most school activities are imposed requirements offering little opportunity for choice or autonomy, so that chances to take advantage of intrinsic motivation are minimal; (b) teachers must act as authority figures who control and sanction student behavior in addition to acting as helpful instructors, and resentments engendered in the process of enacting the authority figure role may sometimes undercut the effects of attempts to stimulate student motivation to learn; (c) teachers must assign grades, and students' concern about grades may interfere with their ability to concentrate on the task at hand and try to get the intended academic benefits from it; and (d) because of the familiarity and predictability of schooling, both teachers and students may become so adjusted to "the daily grind" that they begin to focus mostly on what needs to be done without much attention to why it is being done or what benefits are supposed to be derived from it.

On the other hand, there are some grounds for optimism. First, for reasons discussed in detail elsewhere (Brophy, 1983a) and alluded to briefly in this chapter, few teachers have received much information about student motivation to learn or about possible strategies for socializing such motivation in their preservice of inservice training. Typically, the information offered to teachers about motivational strategies focuses on controlling performance rather than on stimulating motivation to learn, and emphasizes the use of incentives, rewards, and grades rather than strategies designed to stimulate students to generate learning goals and the cognitive and metacognitive strategies needed to accomplish them. Thus, there is reason to believe that systematic emphasis on the latter strategies might have significant impact on teacher and student behavior.

Also, related teacher training efforts by others have achieved some success. deCharms (1976), for example, succeeded in causing both teachers and students to act more as origins and less as pawns in the classroom. More recently, Roehler, Duffy, and Meloth (1984) found that teachers could be trained to provide detailed explanation of content and to make sure that they called their students' attention to the purposes of academic activities, and that the students of these trained teachers showed significant increases in awareness of the purposes of activities, and more generally, in metacognitive awareness of their own information processing and learning progress when working on assignments. These successes suggest that training teachers in strategies for stimulating student motivation to learn would have similarly beneficial effects.

TEACHERS' STRATEGIES FOR SOCIALIZING STUDENT MOTIVATION TO LEARN

To provide a conceptual basis for such training, a literature review has been conducted to identify concepts, principles, and research findings related to the topic of socializing students' motivation to learn. For reasons described above, the most useful sources were those concerned specifically with motivation in the classroom, especially those that: (a) suggested strategies for building student motivation (not just using it as a predictor of individual differences in performance), (b) took into account task value (not just performance expectations), and (c) addressed the problem of motivating students' learning (not just controlling their later performance). The most useful sources were general works on motivation intended for teachers (Kolesnik, 1978; Wlodkowski, 1978), works on teacher expectation effects and socialization of students (Brophy, 1983b; Good & Brophy, 1984, 1986; Dusek, Hall, & Meyer, 1985), works on intrinsic motivation (Deci, 1975; Lepper & Greene, 1978; Malone & Lepper, in press), a chapter by Keller (1983) on including motivation in instructional design, works on stimulating active information processing and generative learning strategies in students (Good & Brophy, 1986; McCombs, 1984; Weinstein & Mayer, 1986), and research in industrial psychology dealing with factors that affect workers' attitudes toward their jobs (Hackman & Oldham, 1980).

When relevant sources were identified, the information they offered and its implications for teacher socialization of student motivation to learn were summarized and expressed in the form of principles or strategies to be recommended to teachers. Ideas from various sources that used different terminology but advocated essentially the same principle or strategy were combined in order to eliminate redundancy and identify a comprehensive yet manageably small set of basic principles. These principles, along with rationales explaining how and why they should work and elaborations or qualifications that need to be kept in mind when attempting to apply them in the classroom, have been organized into a master list.

The list is still being revised to eliminate redundancy, add additional strategies, and expand the material on qualifications and elaborations. The most recent version includes about 40 motivational strategies. Some of these are the traditionally emphasized strategies calling for attempts to control student performance through incentives or competition. Others involve attempts to develop in the students a sense of efficacy, a perception of effort-outcome covariation, a tendency to attribute performance outcomes to internal and controllable causes, and related perceptions and response tendencies suggested by a focus on the expectancy term of the expectancy x value theory of motivation. Along with the strategies based on incentives or competition, these strategies calling for development of success expectations are typically included among motivational principles suggested to teachers, and will not be discussed in detail here. Instead, the remainder of the chapter will focus on 24 strategies that form the basis for an experimental approach recently developed for application in junior high school social studies classes. These include 13 strategies for directly socializing students' motivation to learn, and an additional eleven strategies for developing it indirectly by capitalizing on existing intrinsic motivation in order to make academic activities more enjoyable for students. These 24 strategies are described below, after mention of four preconditions that must be in effect if the strategies are to succeed.

Preconditions for Stimulating Student Motivation to Learn

The following preconditions underlie the effective use of the motivational strategies to be described. *The strategies cannot work effectively if these preconditions are not in effect.*

1. Supportive environment. Anxious or alienated students are unlikely to develop motivation to learn academic content. Nor is such motivation likely to develop in a chaotic classroom. Thus, it is assumed that: (a) the teacher uses classroom organization and management skills that successfully establish the classroom as an effective learning environment; and (b) the teacher is a patient, encouraging person who makes students feel comfortable during academic activities and supports their learning efforts. The classroom atmosphere is business-like but relaxed and supportive. Students feel comfortable taking intellectual risks because they know that they will not be embarrassed or criticized if they make a mistake.

2. Appropriate level of challenge/difficulty. It is assumed that activities are of an appropriate difficulty level for the students. If the task is so familiar or easy that it constitutes nothing more than busy work, and especially if the task is so unfamiliar or difficult that the students cannot succeed on it even if they apply reasonable effort, no strategies for inducing student motivation to learn are likely to succeed. *Tasks are of appropriate difficulty level when the students are clear enough about what to do and how to do it so that they can achieve high levels of success if they apply reasonable effort.* When students encounter such tasks routinely, they will *expect to succeed* at them and thus will be able to concentrate on learning the tasks without becoming anxious or worrying about failure.

The simplest way to insure that students expect success is to make sure that they achieve it consistently; teachers can program students for success by beginning at their level, moving in small steps, and preparing them sufficiently for each new step so that they can adjust to it without much confusion or frustration.

Some students may need help in recognizing that they can succeed if they apply reasonable effort. Such students may not see the relationship between the degree of effort they put into their work and the degree of success they achieve. They may even believe that they lack the necessary knowledge or ability to succeed consistently, and may attribute the success they do achieve to chance factors (lucky guessing, easy assignments, etc.). Such students need to be: (a) reassured that they will be given work of appropriate difficulty level; (b) encouraged to attribute their successes to the combination of sufficient ability with reasonable effort; and (c) encouraged to attribute their failures to insufficient effort (if this is the case), or to confusion or reliance on inappropriate strategies (which can be overcome with additional teaching and practice).

3. Meaningful learning objectives.   One cannot expect students to develop motivation to learn if activities are essentially pointless in the first place. Therefore, it is assumed that activities have been selected with worthwhile academic objectives in mind. That is, they teach some knowledge or skill that is worth learning, either in its own right or as a step toward some larger objective. This would exclude the following activities: continued practice on skills already mastered thoroughly; memorizing lists for no particularly good reason; reading about something that is so foreign to the students' experience or is described in such technical or abstract language that it is essentially meaningless; looking up and copying definitions of terms that are never used in readings or assignments; and working on tasks assigned merely to fill time rather than to attain some worthwhile instructional objective.

Teachers may violate this precondition frequently if they confine their instruction to what is included in the curriculum materials. Some passages in most texts are so sketchy that, unless the teacher elaborates the material for the students, they will have no alternative but to memorize names, dates, definitions, locations, and other facts without developing much real understanding of what they are reading about.

4. Moderation/optimal use.   It is assumed that there is an optimal level for effective use of each motivational strategy. Strategies used too often or too routinely may lose their effectiveness, and any particular use of a strategy can become counterproductive if it goes on too long or gets carried to extremes.

Also, different activities will call for different numbers and kinds of motivational strategies. Where content is relatively unfamiliar and its value or meaningfulness to the students is not obvious, significant motivational effort involving several of the strategies described below may be called for. In contrast, little or no special motivational effort may be needed when the task involves something that the students are already eager to learn.

Strategies for Inducing Motivation to Learn

If the foregoing preconditions are in effect, the stage will be set for inducing student motivation to learn. The 13 strategies described in this section are the strategies most directly involved in stimulating student motivation to learn (or in activating it where it already exits). The first three general strategies establish the pervasive features of the learning environment to be established, and the next ten specific strategies are used when introducing and implementing particular classroom activities and follow up assignments. These are strategies for orienting students toward learning the content or mastering the skills that a task offers.

1. General modeling. Throughout all of their interactions with students, teachers should model interest in learning: let the students see that they value learning as a rewarding, self-actualizing activity that produces personal satisfaction and enriches one's life (Kolesnik, 1978). Teachers can share their interests in current events and items of general knowledge (and most especially, in aspects of the subject matter that they teach); can call attention to current books, articles, television programs, or movies on the subject; and can call attention to examples or applications of subject matter knowledge in everyday living, in the local environment, or in current events.

"Modeling" means more than just calling students' attention to examples or applications of social studies concepts taught in school. It means acting as a model—sharing one's thinking about such examples or applications so that one's students can see how educated people use information and concepts learned in school to understand and respond to everyday experiences in their lives and to news about current events elsewhere. Teachers can model by sharing their thoughts about: connections between concepts studied in school and events in their lives or in the news; insights or opinions about current events; questions that they are raising or predictions that they are making about how some current crisis will be resolved. Such modeling lets the students see how it is both stimulating and satisfying to understand (or even just to think or wonder about) what is happening in the world around us (Good & Brophy, 1984, 1986).

2. Communicate desirable expectations and attributions. Throughout all of their interactions with students, teachers can routinely project attitudes, beliefs, expectations, and attributions (statements about the reasons for students' behavior) that imply that the students share the teacher's own enthusiasm for learning. To the extent that teachers treat their students as if they already are eager learners, they will be more likely to become eager learners. Teachers can let students know that they are expected to be curious, to want to learn facts and understand principles clearly, to master skills, and to see their learning as meaningful and applicable to their everyday lives (Good & Brophy, 1984, 1986).

At minimum, this means avoiding suggestions that students will dislike working on academic activities or will work on them only in order to get good grades. Preferably, it also means treating students as active, motivated learners who care about their learning and are trying to understand.

3. Structure activities as learning experiences, not tests. It appears to be helpful if teachers make clear separations between instruction or practice activities and tests. Where instruction or practice activities include test-like items (recitation questions, practice exercises), these can be treated as opportunities for the students to work with and apply the material rather than as opportunities for the teacher to see who knows the material and who does not. If teachers are to expect students to engage in academic activities with motivation to learn (which implies a willingness to take risks and make mistakes), they will need to protect the students from anxiety or premature concern about performance adequacy.

It is necessary, of course, to evaluate student performance and assign grades using tests or other assessment devices. Until that point in the unit, however, the emphasis can be on teaching and learning rather than on performance evaluation, and students can be encouraged to respond to questions and performance demands in terms of "Let's assess our progress and learn from our mistakes," rather than "Let's see who knows it and who doesn't." When possible, teachers can give students opportunities to correct their mistakes or improve their responses by rephrasing the question or giving a clue (i.e., rather than just giving the answer or moving on to someone else). If it is necessary to give the answer or elicit it from another student, the teacher can include any explanation that may be needed to see that the first student "gets the point" and understands why the answer is correct. Teachers can have students correct their mistakes on seatwork and homework assignments as well. In general, teachers can encourage their students to treat each question and performance demand as an opportunity to check on their own understanding or apply what they are learning, and not merely as an opportunity to gain or lose points toward their grades (Good & Brophy, 1986).

These first three strategies are general ones that should pervade all classroom activities and teacher-student interactions. They involve socializing students to understand that the classroom is primarily a place for learning and that acquiring and applying knowledge and skills are important contributors to quality of life. The remaining strategies involve more specific words and actions to be used in introducing and implementing classroom activities and assignments.

4. Teacher enthusiasm.   Unless they are already quite familiar with a topic or assignment, students will look to the teacher for cues about how to respond. Consciously or not, the teacher will be modeling attitudes and beliefs about the topic or assignment, and students will pick up on these cues. If the teacher presents the topic or assignment with enthusiasm suggesting that it is interesting, important, or worthwhile, the students are likely to adopt this same attitude (Wlodkowski, 1978).

Enthusiasm when introducing academic activities should not be equated with pep talks or unnecessary theatrics. Instead, the teacher creates enthusiasm by identifying his or her own reasons for being interested in the topic or finding it meaningful or important, and then projecting these reasons to the students. Teachers can use dramatics or forceful salesmanship if they are comfortable with these techniques, but if not, a low key but sincere statement of the value that they place on the topic or activity will do just as well. The primary objective of teacher enthusiasm as a strategy for motivating students to learn is not to amuse, entertain, or excite the students, but to induce them to value the topic or activity.

5. *Induce task interest or appreciation.*   When introducing a task or activity, teachers can induce the students to value it by sharing their perceptions about how interesting or informative it is or how important the skills that it teaches are (Kolesnik, 1978). For example, they can mention applications of knowledge or skills to everyday living (especially applications that will allow students to solve problems or accomplish goals that are important to them) or mention new or challenging aspects that the students can anticipate (especially interesting or exotic ones).

6. *Induce curiosity or suspense.*   Teachers can stimulate curiosity or suspense by posing questions or doing "set ups" that make the students feel the need to resolve some ambiguity or obtain more information about the topic: ask them to speculate or make predictions about what they will be learning, or pose questions that successful completion of the activity will enable them to answer. Where relevant, teachers can show students that their existing knowledge is not complete enough to enable them to accomplish some valued objective, that their knowledge is internally inconsistent or inconsistent with certain new information, or that the knowledge they presently possess in scattered form can be organized around certain general principles or powerful ideas (Malone & Lepper, in press). In general, teachers can put their students into an active information-processing or problem-solving mode by posing interesting questions or problems that the activity will address (Keller, 1983).

7. *Make abstract content more personal, concrete, or familiar.*   Definitions, principles, and other general or abstract input may have little meaning for students unless made more concrete and specific. Teachers can promote personal identification with the content by relating experiences or telling anecdotes illustrating how the content applies to the lives of particular individuals (especially individuals whom the students are interested in and likely to identify with). They can also make abstractions concrete by showing objects or pictures or by conducting demonstrations, and can help students relate new or strange content to their existing knowledge by using examples or analogies referring to familiar concepts, objects, or events (Keller, 1983).

Sometimes the problem is not that the content is too abstract or unfamiliar for students to understand if it were explained sufficiently, but that there just is not enough explanation. For example, a seventh grade social studies text states that Russia exited World War I because "the revolution came and a new government took over." This brief statement does not supply enough details to enable students to visualize and understand the events surrounding the Russian revolution. To make the material more understandable to the students, a teacher would have to elaborate on it by explaining why and (especially) how the communists and others organized political and eventually military resistance to the czar's regime, killed or expelled the czar's family and key officials, and established a new government. With the benefit of such elaboration, the statement that "the revolution came and a new government was established" is transformed from a relatively meaningless statement that can only be memorized into a meaningful statement that students can explain in their own words because they can relate it to their prior knowledge and can visualize the events to which it refers.

8. Induce dissonance or cognitive conflict. In the case of familiar topics about which students may tend to think they already know everything there is to know, teachers can counter this tendency by pointing out unexpected, incongruous, or paradoxical aspects. They can call attention to unusual or exotic elements of the content to be learned, note exceptions to general rules, challenge the students to solve the "mystery" that underlies a paradox, or get the students to ask themselves "How can that be?" about strange but true phenomena (Keller, 1983).

9. Induce the students to generate their own motivation to learn. Besides stimulating motivation to learn in the students by using other strategies, it is possible to induce students to generate such motivation to learn for themselves. Teachers can ask them to think about the topic in relation to their own interests and preconceptions or ask them to identify questions that they would like to get answered, to list their particular interests in the topic, or to note things that they find to be surprising. Besides generating motivation to learn for particular topics, such exercises are useful for helping students to understand that motivation to learn must come from within themselves—that it is a property of the learner rather than the task to be learned (McCombs, 1984; Ortiz, 1983).

10. State learning objectives and provide advance organizers. When introducing a task, teachers can call the students' attention to the nature of the task and the academic benefits that they should receive from engaging in it. This will help them to establish a learning set to guide their response to the task. In order to be concrete and specific, and in order to provide the students with guidelines for goal setting and self-assessment, it is helpful to phrase objectives in terms of what the students should be able to do when they complete the task successfully rather than merely in general terms describing what the task is about. Statements of learning objectives are especially important for skill development tasks (in contrast to knowledge development tasks) (Good & Brophy, 1986).

11. Provide informative feedback. Teachers should give students feedback about their progress in understanding content or mastering skills. Where such feedback does not occur automatically in the process of engaging in a task, teachers can supply it by monitoring and correcting performance, providing answer keys, allowing students to give feedback to one another, or some other method.

Ideally, feedback should occur during or as soon as possible following the performance, so that students do not develop and "practice" erroneous concepts or strategies. Feedback should be clear, specific, and constructive. It should include recognition of progress made or partial successes achieved, and should be presented in ways that encourage and provide guidance for continued learning efforts.

If difficulties are attributed to causes, such difficulties should be attributed not to lack of sufficient ability on the part of the student but to lack of effort (if this is clearly the case) or (more likely) to confusion about what to do or reliance on an ineffective strategy for doing it. Most such feedback should be private rather than public, and focused on learning what is being taught rather than on the student as a person (Brophy, 1981).

12. Model task-related thinking and problem solving. The information-processing and problem-solving strategies that are used when thinking about curricular content and responding to academic tasks will be invisible to students unless teachers make them overt and observable by modeling them. Therefore, when teaching particular content, and especially when demonstrating skills or problem-solving strategies, teachers should not just tell the students what to do using the typical second- or third-person language of instruction. In addition, they should model the process by showing the students what to do and thinking out loud as they demonstrate. Such modeling should include the thinking that goes into selecting the general approach to use, deciding on options to take at choice points, checking progress as one goes along, and satisfying oneself that one is on the right track. Teachers can model recovery from false starts and from use of inappropriate strategies on occasion as well, so that students can see how one can develop a successful strategy even when one is not sure about what to do at first (Diener & Dweck, 1978).

This kind of cognitive modeling (thinking out loud so that students can observe one's information-processing and problem-solving strategies) appears to be powerful not only as an instructional device but as a way to socialize student motivation to learn. In addition to modeling the particular strategies needed for the task at hand, it is a way to show students what it means to approach a task with motivation to learn, and to model some of the general beliefs and attitudes associated with such motivation (patience, confidence, persistence in seeking solutions through information processing and rational decision making, benefiting from the information supplied by mistakes rather than simply giving up) (Good & Brophy, 1984, 1986).

13. Induce metacognitive awareness of learning efforts. When opportunities arise, teachers can train their students to be aware of their goals during task engagement, to monitor the strategies they use in pursuing these goals, to note

the effects of these strategies as they are used, and to monitor their own re-
sponses to these events as they unfold. In particular, they can train the students to
respond to errors as cues for analysis and concentrated efforts, rather than as cues
for becoming frustrated and giving up.

When motivated to learn, students do not merely let input "wash over them"
and hope that some of it will stick. Instead, they process the input actively by
concentrating their attention, making sure that they understand, integrating new
information with existing knowledge, and encoding and storing this information
in a form that will allow them to remember and use it later. The mere intention to
learn in this fashion is not sufficient to insure such learning. In addition, students
must possess and use cognitive and metacognitive skills for learning and study-
ing effectively. Some of these are specific to particular subject matter or types of
task, but some are general strategies that students will find useful for almost any
kind of learning or studying (Good & Brophy, 1986; McCombs, 1984; Wein-
stein & Mayer, 1986).

a. *Actively preparing to learn*. Teachers can teach their students to prepare
to learn actively by mobilizing their resources and approaching tasks in thought-
ful ways: getting mentally prepared to concentrate on the task; previewing read-
ing or listening tasks by noting their nature and objective; developing a plan be-
fore trying to respond to complex performance tasks.

b. *Committing material to memory*. Teachers can teach students to memo-
rize by repeating, copying, or underlining key words; making notes; or using
imagery or other mnemonic strategies.

c. *Encoding or elaborating on the information presented*. Usually it will not
be appropriate (or even possible) for students to rely on rote memory to retain
information verbatim, so they will need to be taught strategies for learning the
gist of the material: Paraphrasing and summarizing information to put it into their
own words; relating it to what they already know; and assessing their understand-
ing by asking themselves questions about the material to see if they can answer
them knowledgeably.

d. *Organizing and structuring the content*. It is helpful to identify or impose
organizational schemes that structure the content by dividing it into sequences or
superordinate-subordinate clusters: noting the main ideas of paragraphs, outlin-
ing the material, and noting whole-part, rule-example, question-answer, and
generalization-elaboration structures. Teachers can help their students to see that
they can use these structural elements as bases for organizing and remembering
what they learn.

e. *Monitoring comprehension*. Teachers can teach their students to remain
aware of the instructional objectives, the strategies they use to pursue them, the
relative success of those strategies, and the remediation efforts they undertake if
the strategies have not been effective. They can also teach strategies for coping

with confusion and errors: backing up and rereading, looking up definitions, identifying previous places in the text where the confusing point is discussed, searching the recent progression of topics for clues to the information that has been missed or misunderstood, retracing steps to see if the strategy has been applied correctly, and generating possible alternative strategies.

f. *Maintaining appropriate affect.* Teachers can model and instruct students in ways of approaching academic activities with desirable affect (relaxed but alert and prepared to concentrate; ready to enjoy or at least take satisfaction from engaging in the task) but not undesirable affect (anger, anxiety, etc.), and can model self-reinforcement for success and coping skills for responding to frustration and failure (reassuring self-talk, refocusing of attention on the task at hand, using the strategies listed at the end of the previous paragraph).

Task Design and Selection Strategies

It was noted previously that motivation to learn resides in the student rather than in the task to be learned, and that it should be possible to stimulate students to be motivated to learn any worthwhile task, whether or not they find the task enjoyable. It is for these reasons that motivation to learn a task has been differentiated from liking for the task, and that the strategies described above have been classified as the strategies involved most directly in socializing students' motivation to learn.

Nevertheless, given tasks that are equally appropriate from a curriculum and instruction point of view, it is preferable that students work on tasks that they find interesting and enjoyable rather than tasks that they find boring or irritating. This is the goal of the strategies described below. These strategies involve capitalizing on students' existing intrinsic motivation by selecting or designing tasks that they will find attractive or enjoyable. Although these strategies will not directly stimulate student motivation to learn, they should produce heightened task engagement sustained by the fact that students enjoy the actual processes involved in doing the task.

14. Adapt tasks to students' interests. Whenever a variety of activities could be used to accomplish particular curriculum objectives, teachers can take advantage of students' existing interests by designing or selecting activities that match those interests—activities that the students enjoy or that deal with topics that the students find interesting or important (Good & Brophy, 1986; Kolesnik, 1978). Task enjoyment also will be affected by Strategies 15–24.

15. Choice. Within the constraints imposed by the instructional objectives, teachers can offer their students choices of alternative tasks or alternative ways to meet requirements. If the students might take undesirable choices if left completely on their own, they can be provided with a menu of choices to select from or required to get approval of their choice before going ahead with it (Malone & Lepper, in press).

16. Novelty/variety. Students faced with the same routine and the same type of task each day will soon become bored. Therefore, teachers should try to be sure that something about each task (its form, its content, the media involved, or the nature of the responses it demands) is new to the students or at least different from what they have been working on recently (Keller, 1983). It is worth remembering that a steady diet of routine and predictable lessons followed by routine and predictable assignments soon becomes "the daily grind."

17. Autonomy. Although sometimes "there is only one right way" to do a task, most tasks can be designed to allow for some autonomous decision making and creativity by students. Most students feel unduly pressured if they perceive that every move they make is being prescribed and monitored by the teacher. In contrast, they are likely to experience heightened intrinsic motivation and commitment to the task when they perceive that they will have opportunities to exercise autonomy and creativity in deciding how to organize their time and effort in order to meet task requirements (Good & Brophy, 1986).

18. Activity/manipulation opportunities. Students tend to prefer activities that allow them to interact with the teacher or with one another, to manipulate materials, or in some way to respond actively rather than merely to listen or read. Ideally, these opportunities will often go beyond the simple question-answer formats seen in typical recitation and seatwork activities in order to include projects, experiments, discussions, role play, simulation, and creative applications (Good & Brophy, 1986).

Even within traditional recitation and discussion formats, teachers can create more active student involvement by going beyond factual questions to stimulate students to discuss or debate issues, offer opinions about cause and effect relationships, speculate about hypothetical situations, or think creatively about problems. In this way, students are led to think actively about the content instead of just memorizing facts and concepts.

19. Feedback features. Students tend to enjoy tasks that allow them to make responses and get immediate feedback better than tasks that do not allow for active response or that allow active response but do not provide immediate feedback that can be used to guide subsequent responses. Therefore, tasks designed to allow students to make active responses which will trigger immediate feedback are especially desirable (Malone & Lepper, in press).

So-called "self-correcting" materials have such feedback features built in. Teachers can build them into more typical classroom activities by leading the group in going through the task, circulating to provide feedback during independent seatwork times, or arranging for students to get feedback from answer keys or from discussing the work with one another. Also, teachers can break up otherwise lengthy lectures or presentations by interspersing recitation and discussion activities or follow-up assignments that allow students to make responses and get feedback.

20. Creation of finished products. Industrial workers enjoy jobs that allow them to create a product that they can point to and identify with more than jobs that do not result in finished products that provide tangible evidence of the fruits of their labor (Hackman & Oldham, 1980). Students are likely to respond similarly to academic tasks. That is, they are likely to prefer tasks that have meaning or integrity in their own right over tasks that are mere subparts of some larger entity, and they are likely to experience a satisfying sense of completion or accomplishment when they finish such tasks. Ideally, task completion will yield a finished product that the student can use or display.

21. Fantasy/simulation features. Where more direct application is not feasible, teachers can introduce fantasy or imagination elements that will engage students' emotions or allow them to experience events vicariously. Or, they can set up role play or simulation activities that allow students to identify with various characters or to deal with the content in direct, personalized ways. Ideally, such fantasy/simulation activities will confront students with problems they need to solve by drawing on the knowledge and skills they have been learning (Malone & Lepper, in press).

Simulation exercises include, but are not confined to, full-scale drama, role play, simulation games, or other "major productions." Other simulation activities are more modest and can be incorporated into more typical everyday instruction. These include brief simulation exercises or invitations for students to bring fantasy or imagination to bear in thinking about the content. In lessons on the USSR, for example, while leading the group in reading through and discussing the text a teacher might ask the students to imagine and talk about what it would be like to seek housing in a country where the government owned all of the property, or to get accurate information about current world events in a country where all of the media are controlled by the government. These brief fantasy/simulation exercises do not take much time or require special preparations, but they can be quite useful in stimulating students to relate to the content more personally and to take a greater interest in it.

22. Game-like features. Practice and application activities for almost any kind of content can be presented as games or structured to include features typically associated with games or recreational pastimes: "test yourself" challenges, puzzles and other problem-solving activities, and the like. Some such activities involve clear goals but require the student to solve problems, avoid traps, or overcome obstacles in order to reach these goals. Others challenge students to "find the problem" (i.e., to identify the goal itself, in addition to developing a method of reaching the goal). Others involve elements of suspense or hidden information that emerges as the activity is completed (puzzles that convey some message or provide the answer to some question once they are filled in). Still others involve a degree of randomness or some other method of inducing uncertainty about what the outcome of one's performance is likely to be on any given trial (Malone & Lepper, in press). Ideally, such game-like elements will complement, and not detract from, the academic benefits of the activity.

23. Higher level objectives/divergent questions. It is important that students learn basic facts, concepts, and definitions. However, a steady diet of activities that concentrate on these lower level knowledge and comprehension objectives soon becomes boring for most students. Therefore, there should be frequent activities or parts of activities devoted to higher level objectives (application, analysis, synthesis, or evaluation). Also, in addition to convergent questions designed to elicit a particular correct answer, there should be questions designed to elicit opinions, predictions, suggested courses of action or problem solutions, or other divergent thinking. Such questions and activities allow students to respond more actively and creatively to the content than do activities built around convergent questions about facts, definitions, or concepts (Wlodkowski, 1978).

Exposure to higher level objectives/divergent questions also helps make the material more meaningful and understandable to the students. If they are only exposed to facts without much explanation or integration, and if questions and assignments only require them to regurgitate these facts, students won't have much opportunity (let alone motivation) to make sense of the material by processing it actively, putting it into their own words, and relating it to their prior knowledge and experience. Therefore, this strategy is especially useful when the text provides only vague or sketchy coverage of the topic and orients the students more toward rote memorizing than toward learning with understanding.

24. Opportunities to interact with peers. Many students particularly enjoy activities that allow them to interact with peers. Teachers can build peer interaction into whole class activities such as discussions, debates, role play, or simulation. Peer-oriented students are likely to find such activities more enjoyable than whole class activities that allow them to interact only with the teacher. In addition, however, teachers can include activities that allow students to work together in pairs or small groups to tutor one another, discuss issues, develop suggested solutions to problems, or work as a team participating in simulation games or producing some group product (a report, display, etc.).

In addition to being more enjoyable because of the social aspect, such peer interactive activities may carry useful instructional and motivational benefits if the following conditions are met: (a) the activities are sufficiently structured around academic objectives to make them worthwhile learning experiences and not merely occasions for socializing; and (b) conditions are arranged so that everyone participates actively and has a substantive role to play in carrying out the group's activity (rather than having one or two students dominate the interaction or do all the work while others just watch) (Slavin et al., 1985).

ONGOING RESEARCH

The 24 motivational strategies presented above are theoretically useful for improving the quality of students' task engagement by stimulating their motivation to learn or by capitalizing on their intrinsic motivation to engage in enjoyable activities. Furthermore, each strategy is supported by at least some research. However, the supporting research usually was not conducted in classroom settings and thus did not take into account the public nature of teacher-student interaction, the implied competition for grades, the fact that school tasks are imposed rather than self-chosen, and all of the other factors that differentiate classroom learning situations from free-choice recreational situations. Thus, additional research is needed to see if teachers working under the usual classroom constraints can improve students' task engagement using these strategies. The author's current program of research is designed to generate such information.

Ultimately, the applicability and effects of each individual strategy will have to be studied separately in a variety of classroom settings. As a first step, however, a teacher training program that includes all 24 strategies treated as parts of a single package has been developed and used with junior high school teachers to see if systematic implementation of the strategies will significantly affect student motivation.

The 24 strategies described above are being implemented by seventh and eighth grade social studies teachers participating in an ongoing experimental study. The teachers address the same content using mostly the same methods and materials and the same schedule of lessons, assignments, and tests in two class sections, except that they introduce motivational elements into the experimental sections that are not introduced into the control sections. The basic rule of thumb is that at least one thing that is different or extra will be introduced into the plans for the experimental section each day. It is left up to the individual teachers to decide which of the principles are most appropriate for implementing in their classes, although all teachers are urged to place primary emphasis on principles 1–13 that deal directly with student motivation to learn, and only secondary emphasis on principles 14–24 that deal with intrinsic motivation.

Treatment implementation is monitored in two ways. First, teachers keep brief records of their plans for differentiating instruction between the two class sections each day, and these records will be coded for the nature and extent of special instructional elements planned for the experimental sections. Also, each teacher is observed one to two times per week by observers who visit both the experimental and the control sections that day and take detailed descriptive notes of what occurred in each section and later write comparative notes describing the similarities and differences observed.

Experimental effects on motivation will be assessed through class attendance and tardiness data and changes in students' responses to a motivational questionnaire administered early and again late in the semester. Effects on achievement will be assessed by comparing each teacher's two sections' performance on tests and assignments. A report describing the degree to which the principles were implemented in these classrooms and the effects of such implementation on student motivation and achievement will be prepared. In addition, the teacher's planning records and the observers' classroom descriptions will be analyzed to identify additional motivational principles, additional qualifications or elaborations on principles already identified, and good examples (at least for junior high school social studies instruction) of specific applications of these principles.

Because the study is presently in progress, findings cannot yet be reported. However, two observations gleaned from interactions with the teachers during the training workshops and visits to classes held early in the semester are worth noting here. First, there is great variation in the degree to which teachers already were implementing these principles before they became involved in our study. Some teachers routinely present relatively dull and predictable lessons and assignments that soon become "the daily grind," but others teach the same subject matter to similar students in much more varied and interesting ways that incorporate most of the above strategies and others besides. Previous research at the elementary grades rarely revealed the kind of excellent instruction (at least, from the perspective of stimulating student motivation to learn) that is observed routinely in several of these junior high social studies classes. This is probably due at least in part to the richer subject matter knowledge and disciplinary training that secondary teachers receive as subject matter specialists, although differences in the cognitive sophistication of the students and in the nature of the curriculum undoubtedly are also relevant. The larger point here is that as research on secondary instruction begins to accumulate, researchers studying teaching may have to make more and more qualifications on the notions of classrooms, teachers, and schooling that have been developed from research done almost exclusively at the elementary grade levels.

The second observation is that student motivation is intimately linked with curriculum and instruction, so that the content to be learned will affect the degree to which students can reasonably be expected to generate and follow through on motivation to learn as defined in this chapter. Inspection of the textbooks used in the social studies classes under observation suggests that certain passages, and sometimes even substantial portions of lessons, are so vague or sketchy as to preclude learning with genuine comprehension, thus leaving the students with no choice but to attempt to memorize a few names, dates, definitions, or isolated facts. In these situations, making the material more *meaningful* to the students by providing more information or supplying analogies, examples, or anecdotes that make the content more concrete and visualizable is fundamental to stimulating their motivation to learn, even more so than using strategies such as trying to stimulate curiosity or develop appreciation for the importance of the content. As one of the teachers noted, a skillful teacher thinks of the text as an outline to be filled in rather than as a complete and self-contained curriculum.

CONCLUSION

This chapter has defined the concept of student motivation to learn and differentiated this concept from related concepts, summarized related theory and research on the topic, presented lists of strategies (developed from a literature review) for stimulating students' motivation to learn or for capitalizing on their existing intrinsic motivation, and described the rationale and procedures for an initial experiment designed to test the feasibility and effects of implementing these strategies in typical classroom situations.

The experiment described above will provide information about the effectiveness of this particular set of principles for teachers who want to stimulate student motivation to learn by socializing their students in the classroom. Whatever its outcomes, however, the experiment will be just one element in what ultimately must become a much larger body of work on motivation in the classroom. In order to complement the work that is already available, additional studies are needed that have the following characteristics:

First, such research will focus on student motivation under typical classroom conditions. In defining and measuring such motivation, it will focus on quality of engagement in academic activities, recognizing that the choices available to students do not concern self-determination of what to do so much as whether or not to commit themselves and try to make the best of externally imposed activities that must be done at some level in any case.

Second, such research will complement the large volume of work on success expectations by focusing on the value that students place on a task because of the benefits they expect to derive from engaging in it or from accomplishing its objective. Similarly, in addition to considering the setting of performance goals and the attribution of performance levels (success or failure in reaching those goals) to causes, such research will consider students' specification of learning goals and attributional thinking about why they are engaged in academic activities in the first place (Why am I engaging in this activity, and what am I supposed to get out of it?).

Third, given the heavy cognitive component in most school learning activities, such research will focus on motivating original learning (not just later performance), and on the more cognitive, strategy-generation aspects of effort (not just the affective, task-liking, or persistence aspects).

Finally, such research will consider student motivation to learn as a dependent variable to be manipulated rather than merely as a correlate or predictor variable, and will be designed to identify strategies that teachers can use to stimulate such motivation to learn in particular situations and to socialize its development as a more general trait in their students.

ACKNOWLEDGMENTS

This work is sponsored in part by the Institute for Research on Teaching, College of Education, Michigan State University. The Institute for Research on Teaching is funded primarily by the Program for Teaching and Instruction of the National Institute of Education, United States Department of Education. The opinions expressed in this publication do not necessarily reflect the position, policy, or endorsement of the National Institute of Education. (Contract No. 400-81-0014).

The author wishes to thank June Smith for her assistance in manuscript preparation.

REFERENCES

Anderson, L. (1981). Short-term student responses to classroom instruction. *Elementary School Journal, 82,* 97–108.

Anderson, L. (1984). The environment of instruction: The function of seatwork in a commercially developed curriculum. In G. Duffy, L. Roehler, & J. Mason (Eds.), *Comprehension instruction: Perspectives and suggestions* (pp. 93–103). New York: Longman.

Anderson, L., Brubaker, N., Alleman-Brooks, J., & Duffy, G. (1984). *Making seatwork work* (Research Series No. 142). East Lansing: Michigan State University, Institute for Research on Teaching.

Bandura, A. (1982). Self-efficacy mechanism in human agency. *American Psychologist, 37,* 122–147.

Bandura, A., & Schunk, D. (1981). Cultivating competence, self-efficacy, and intrinsic interest through proximal self-motivation. *Journal of Personality and Social Psychology, 41,* 586–598.

Blumenfeld, P., Hamilton, B., Bossert, S., Wessels, K., & Meece, J. (1983). Teacher talk and student thought: Socialization into the student role. In J. Levine and M. Wang (Eds.), *Teacher and student perceptions: Implications for learning* (pp. 143–192). Hillsdale, NJ: Erlbaum.

Brophy, J. (1981). Teacher praise: A functional analysis. *Review of Educational Research, 51,* 5–32.

Brophy, J. (1983a). Conceptualizing student motivation. *Educational Psychologist, 18,* 200–215.

Brophy, J. (1983b). Research on the self-fulfilling prophecy and teacher expectations. *Journal of Educational Psychology, 75,* 631–661.

Brophy, J., & Kher, N. (1986). Teacher socialization as a mechanism for developing student motivation to learn. In R. Feldman (Ed.), *Social psychology applied to education.* Cambridge: Cambridge University Press.

Brophy, J., Rohrkemper, M., Rashid, H., & Goldberger, M. (1983). Relationships between teachers' presentations of classroom tasks and students' engagement in those tasks. *Journal of Educational Psychology, 75,* 544–552.

Condry, J., & Chambers, J. (1978). Intrinsic motivation and the process of learning. In M. Lepper & D. Greene (Eds.), *The hidden costs of reward: New perspectives on the psychology of human motivation* (pp. 61–84). Hillsdale, NJ: Erlbaum.

Cooper, H. (1979). Pygmalion grows up: A model for teacher expectation communication and performance influence. *Review of Educational Research, 49,* 398–410.

Corno, L., & Mandinach, E. (1983). The role of cognitive engagement in classroom learning and motivation. *Educational Psychologist, 18,* 88–108.

Corno, L., & Rohrkemper, M. (1985). Self-regulated learning. In R. Ames & C. Ames (Eds.), *Research on motivation in education* (Volume 2). Orlando, FL: Academic Press.

deCharms, R. (1976). *Enhancing motivation: Change in the classroom.* New York: Longman.

Deci, E. (1975). *Intrinsic motivation.* New York: Plenum.

Diener, D., & Dweck, C. (1978). An analysis of learned helplessness: Continuous change in performance, strategy, and achievement cognitions following failure. *Journal of Personality and Social Psychology, 36,* 451–462.

Doyle, W. (1983). Academic work. *Review of Educational Research, 53,* 159–199.

Dusek, J. B., Hall, V. C., & Meyer, W. J. (Eds.) (1985). *Teacher expectancies.* Hillsdale, NJ: Erlbaum.

Dweck, C., & Elliot, E. (1983). Achievement motivation. In P. Mussen (Ed.), *Handbook of Child Psychology* (fourth edition, Volume 4, pp. 643–691). New York: Wiley.

Eccles, J., & Wigfield, A. (1985). Teacher expectations and student motivation. In J. Dusek, V. Hall, & W. Meyer (Eds.), *Teacher expectancies* (pp. 185–226). Hillsdale, NJ: Erlbaum.

Feather, N. T. (Ed.) (1982). *Expectations and actions.* Hillsdale, NJ: Erlbaum.

Good, T. L., & Brophy, J. E. (1984). *Looking in classrooms* (third edition). New York: Harper and Row.

Good, T. L., & Brophy, J. E. (1986). *Educational psychology: A realistic approach* (third edition). New York: Longman.

Hackman, J. R., & Oldham, G. P. (1980). *Work redesign.* Reading, Mass: Addison-Wesley.

Keller, J. (1983). Motivational design of instruction. In C. Reigeluth (Ed.), *Instructional-design theories and models: An overview of their current status* (pp. 383–434). Hillsdale, NJ: Erlbaum.

Kolesnik, W. B. (1978). *Motivation: Understanding and influencing human behavior.* Boston: Allyn and Bacon.

Kruglanski, A. (1978). Endogenous attribution and intrinsic motivation. In M. Lepper & D. Greene (Eds.), *The hidden costs of reward: New perspectives on the psychology of human motivation* (pp. 85–107). Hillsdale, NJ: Erlbaum.

Lepper, M. (1983). Extrinsic reward and intrinsic motivation: Implications for the classroom. In J. Levine & M. Wang (Eds.), *Teacher and student perspectives: Implications for learning* (pp. 218–317). Hillsdale, NJ: Erlbaum.

Lepper, M., & Gilovich, T. (1982). Accentuating the positive: Eliciting generalized compliance through activity-oriented requests. *Journal of Personality and Social Psychology, 42,* 284–259.

Lepper, M., & Greene, D. (Eds.) (1978). *The hidden costs of reward: New perspectives on the psychology of human motivation.* Hillsdale, NJ: Erlbaum.

Maehr, M. (1984). Meaning and motivation: Toward a theory of personal investment. In R. Ames & C. Ames (Eds.), *Research on motivation in education* (Vol. 1, pp. 115–144). Orlando, FL: Academic Press.

Malone, T., & Lepper, M. (in press). Making learning fun: A taxonomy of intrinsic motivations for learning. In R. Snow & M. Farr (Eds.), *Aptitude, learning, and instruction: III. Conative and affective process analysis.* Hillsdale, NJ: Erlbaum.

McCombs, B. (1984). Processes and skills underlying continuing intrinsic motivation to learn: Toward a definition of motivational skills training and interventions. *Educational Psychologist, 19,* 199–218.

Nicholls, J. (1984). Conceptions of ability and achievement motivation. In R. Ames & C. Ames (Eds.), *Research on motivation in education* (Vol. 1, pp. 39–73). Orlando, FL: Academic Press.

Ortiz, R. (1983). Generating interest in reading. *Journal of Reading, 27,* 113–119.

Parsons, J., & Goff, S. (1980). Achievement motivation and values: An alternative perspective. In L. J. Fyans (Ed.), *Achievement motivation: Recent trends in theory and research* (pp. 349–373). New York: Plenum.

Roehler, L., Duffy, G., & Meloth (1984). The effect and some distinguishing characteristics of explicit teacher explanation during reading instruction. In J. Niles (Ed.), *Changing perspectives in research in reading: Language processing and instruction.* (Thirty-third Yearbook of the National Reading Conference). Rochester, NY: National Reading Conference.

Rohrkemper, M., & Bershon, B. (1984). Elementary school students' reports of the causes and effects of problem difficulty in mathematics. *Elementary School Journal, 85,* 127–147.

Slavin, R., Sharan, S., Kagan, S., Lazarowitz, R., Webb, C., & Schmuck, R. (Eds.) (1985). *Learning to cooperate, cooperating to learn.* New York: Plenum.

Stipek, D., & Weisz, J. (1981). Perceived personal control and academic achievement. *Review of Educational Research, 51,* 101–137.

Thomas, J. (1980). Agency and achievement: Self-management and self-regard. *Review of Educational Research, 50,* 213–240.

Weiner, B. (1979). A theory of motivation for some classroom experiences. *Journal of Educational Psychology, 71,* 3–25.

Weinstein, C., & Mayer, R. (1986). The teaching of learning strategies. In M. C. Wittrock (Ed.), *Handbook of Research on Teaching* (third edition). New York: Macmillan.

Wlodkowski, R. J. (1978). *Motivation and teaching: A practical guide.* Washington, D.C.: National Education Association.

DEVELOPMENTAL INTERVENTION AND MOTIVATION ENHANCEMENT IN THE CONTEXT OF SPORT

Steven J. Danish, Douglas A. Kleiber,
and Howard K. Hall

The manner in which various motivational orientations are socialized through childhood has been the subject of careful analysis in this volume and elsewhere. But relatively little attention has been given to changes in motivational orientation which occur after childhood (cf. Kleiber & Maehr, 1985), and even less to the way in which motivational processes formed and utilized at one period may be influential in adjusting to the problems which come with subsequent periods. Fundamental to models of life-span development is the recognition that the importance of various contexts changes with age. School loses its salience for most after high school and college, while after retirement, work becomes less impor-

Advances in Motivation and Achievement: Enhancing Motivation,
Volume 5, pages 211-238.
Copyright © 1987 by JAI Press Inc.
All rights of reproduction in any form reserved.
ISBN: 0-89232-621-2

tant. But it is likely that the habits and patterns shaped in one context have an impact beyond that context. This is an underlying assumption of research dealing with the influence of school experience on subsequent work patterns and the influence of work values on satisfaction with retirement.

Like school and work, sport is a context which emphasizes training and performance, but where the first two are explicitly linked to the process of socialization for adult roles, the suggestion that ''sport builds character'' (or anything else) is usually suspect. Indeed, those given to testing such assertions empirically (e.g., Ogilvie & Tutko, 1971) as well as other social critics (Lasch, 1979) point to a greater potential for degradation of individual character than for its enhancement in sport. Nevertheless, it is the prevailing assumption here that the experimental character of sport gives it a potential for a kind of motivation training which may promote positive adjustment to other circumstances and the effective formulation of future directions. As it may lead one's thinking in this respect it may also serve a preventive role in facilitating adjustment to life changes. And if such a salutary pattern of influences is more accurately the exception rather than the rule, it nonetheless bears examination as a pattern which has implications for the enhancement of motivation and development more generally.

The purpose of the chapter, then, is twofold. First, we will develop a framework to examine the relationship of motivation to performance within a developmental perspective. We will use sport as a context for understanding this framework because sport provides a concrete context for the expression of competence. We rarely have an opportunity to see the degree of personal competence attained as clearly as we do in sports, and so it becomes an important area of inquiry for those interested in studying optimal development. Second, we will use the framework as a means of understanding how to enhance motivation and performance and optimize development. While the focus will again be on the context of sport, it is with the matter of ''life beyond sport'' that this chapter is ultimately concerned.

As part of the development of the framework we will discuss and integrate several disparate literatures. In addition to examining research on motivation, performance and life-span development, we will consider work on the nature of sport and on goal setting. It is hoped that this particular juxtaposition of previously separate subjects will lead to new possibilities for effective intervention.

THE RELATION OF MOTIVATION TO PERFORMANCE AND DEVELOPMENT

Motivation

Motivation may be characterized in many ways, but in examining social motivation (including, but not limited to, achievement motivation), *direction, intensity,* and *persistence* are among the most important behavior manifestations (cf.

Maehr, 1984). Direction refers to the choice one makes among a set of alternatives. It is the exercise of will in expressing what one wants to do (Deci, 1980). To the extent that the choices reflect some intentionality they are likely to be governed by goals and incentives. If the choices one makes are responsive to the goals and incentives that are culturally sanctioned, the individual is likely to be regarded as "highly motivated," while the choice to respond to a less socially valued goal may lead—quite mistakenly—to an attribution of low motivation. Such differences are really the result of the direction of investment rather than the level of motivation (Maehr, 1984).

Intensity is more clearly a dimension of *level* of motivation and while the incentives that produce arousal may vary considerably, intensity refers to the extent to which one is activated. Clearly, performance is influenced by intensity and activation. Some is necessary, a lot—depending on the activity—may be too much. It is also important to note that optimal arousal is itself an endogenous reward. Much of the early work on intrinsic motivation (cf. Day, Berlyne, & Hunt, 1971) recognized that behavior oriented toward the production of additional stimulation is a natural concomitant of suboptimal arousal. The information flow produced by curiosity and exploratory behavior is sufficient reward to maintain such behaviors.

The third behavioral characteristic of motivation is persistence. What are the factors that enable one to stay with a task, ignoring other possibilities, enduring in the face of hardship, and delaying gratification until the task is completed? Of special importance to our analysis is the matter of "continuing motivation," that which is reflected in behavior which transcends institutional conditions. Maehr (1976) developed this concept primarily in relation to education to characterize a basis for continuing interest in, and involvement with, academic subjects after finishing courses and completing programs. But the general idea applies to various aspects of life we experience. Where the external reward system supporting behavior is no longer controlling, how, or why, does one persist with related activities?

As Maehr (1984) rightly points out, though, persistence cannot be fully distinguished from direction. A lack of persistence may be indicative not of a decline in motivation but rather a change in direction. This again puts motivation in a developmental framework. Growth and aging necessitates a constant reprioritization. Goals change to match changes in incentives and values. Development involves motivational reorientation to a great extent (Kleiber, 1985; Veroff & Veroff, 1980), and persistence—in the face of changing life circumstances—may in fact be maladaptive. Motivation enhancement in this sense may be a matter of redirection of personal investment.

While direction, intensity, and persistence are behavioral characteristics that help us to identify and operationalize motivation, the problem of enhancement requires that an evaluative stance toward motivation be taken as well. How is motivation changed for the better? What impact would such changes have on subjective experience of well-being, effective performance, and progressive development? A broader interpretation of intrinsic motivation provides a criterion model with which to examine both ongoing experience and developmental change.

Recent interpretations of intrinsic motivation in terms of self-determination (Deci, 1980), and optimal experience (Csikszentmihalyi, 1978, 1982, 1985) rely on the rather extensive evidence of the positive effects of being self-directed and seriously involved in almost any activity. Whether it be work or play, the feedback from activities wherein competence is extended to meet expanding challenges contributes significantly to one's self-concept and sense of well-being. Moreover, because greater challenges are sought as abilities expand, the process is inherently growth-producing. The social appropriateness of an activity will obviously dictate its ultimate acceptability, but for an optimal experience to occur, an intimate relationship with the task at hand is essential; and this may dictate a choice among the many social rewards to which one is necessarily acculturated. For example, there is evidence that the "enjoyment" which is associated with intense absorption is also common in delinquent and criminal activities (e.g., Csikszentmihalyi & Larson, 1978).

In developing a model of enjoyment, Csikszentmihalyi (1975) describes several conditions which contribute to the experience. His model is based on the concept of "flow," an experience of intense absorption which devotees of various activities, from rock climbing to surgery, readily recognized. These flow-producing activities have a clear structure and provide unambiguous feedback. The participant feels in control but somewhat challenged; the activity is complex enough to demand complete attention while still being within the realm of the participant's competence. The centering of attention on the action and the merging of action and awareness is accompanied by a loss of self-consciousness and ego-involvement. As soon as one steps back for self-appraisal and/or comparison with others, flow is lost and task involvement is made more difficult. But to the extent that task involvement is maintained, subjects report feelings of enjoyment based on a growing sense of competence. The perception of competence is a direct consequence of task involvement rather than being mediated by a secondary interpretation process.

This distinction is an important one as demonstrated in several recent analyses of achievement motivation. Maehr and Nicholls (Maehr, 1984; Maehr & Nicholls, 1980; Nicholls, 1979, 1984) have differentiated several goals common to the achievement context. Most common are the *ego goals* of comparison-based contexts. With ego goals, satisfaction and the perception of success come as a result of the outcome of performance as compared with some standard or comparison group of fellow participants. The competitive structures of most school classrooms reinforce this type of goal. Less common is the goal of social solidarity or *approval*. One performs for the social effects on a group. In this case, as Maehr (1984) puts it, "Faithfulness is more important than demonstrating competence."

However, closest to the conceptual framework of intrinsic motivation we are considering is what these researchers call *task goals*. Nicholls (1980) refers to it as

> endogenous task involvement . . . where the development or exercise of new understandings or skills is the goal of the action, rather than the means to some goal, and where attention is focused on the task, rather than the self or any task-irrelevant incentive.

Nicholls (1979) ties this orientation directly to intellectual development, provides evidence of such motivation in highly proficient and creative adults and shows its connection to other work on intellectual development. Our concern here is to go beyond the intellectual and look at the role of this type of motivation in adjusting to life transitions and in serving development more generally.

Another important body of research of relevance is that dealing with the matter of *overjustification*. Where such intrinsic motivation and task-oriented behavior exists it has been shown to be susceptible to the distracting and compromising influence of exogenous rewards (Deci, 1975; Kruglanski, 1975; Lepper & Greene, 1978). The addition of extrinsic rewards and sanctions has been regularly shown to have an undermining effect on interests previously sustained by the inherent demands of the activity on an individual's competence. Only when rewards are more contingent on performance, providing information about one's competence, does intrinsic motivation survive. But in a developmental perspective, the ability to maintain an orientation to tasks which allow intense involvement and all its benefits may be subject to the social reward systems—in school and elsewhere—that one has to grow into, through, and out of (cf. Condry, this volume). What survives of that orientation, if anything, may be a function of the individual or of the particular experience. But there is another question here as well. If one is successful at committing to tasks through a devotion to the process, is there a potential for disregarding alternatives? Motivational reorientation is a matter of direction finding which necessitates an open psychological stance. The possibility of foreclosing around activities, however enjoyable and task-involved, must be examined in light of broader developmental issues.

Performance

While performance is often seen as evidence of motivation (cf. Maehr, 1984; this volume), it is usually the result of some combination of effort and ability. It is even conceivable that a high level of performance—especially when judged in a normative sense—may be the result primarily of well-developed skills and abilities rather than the effort invested. But when judging the motivational component of performance we are considering the extent to which effort is applied in the interest of task accomplishment. To enhance performance, whether in academic examinations, the production of automobiles or shooting free throws, we concern ourselves as much with ensuring adequate investment in the task as we do with the training of task-specific abilities. In fact, the willingness to be trained probably is dependent on the investment in the task.

The enhancement of performance is, in a general sense, then, the shaping of personal investment (cf. Maehr & Braskamp, 1986). Performance enhancement begins *before* the task is confronted. A child who would give up some of her social activities to be involved in an early morning and after school competitive swimming program must consider the alternatives and make a choice. Such a choice involves a self-examination of personal predispositions and potentials if it is to be enduring, because at the beginning the actual experience of the task can only be anticipated. When choices are made which reflect these individual orientations, personal investment is enhanced.

When a task is actually confronted, the intensity of motivation will influence actual performance. The relationship between intensity of motivation (arousal) and performance has been the subject of a great deal of research (see Landers, 1980, for a review), but it can be concluded that for most tasks the relationship is curvilinear; a low level of arousal may not be "energizing" enough for task completion and will hinder a high level of performance. Conversely, a high level may be disruptive to performance. To the extent that the task requires sustained concentration, a moderate level of arousal that focuses attention is optimal. Thus, enhancing performance involves the management of intensity to create the optimum amount for the full investment of attention to the task or set of tasks. Arousal affects concentration which affects attention which determines investment.

The advantage of tasks which have endogenous rewards—i.e., are intrinsically motivating by virtue of being interesting, challenging, and "flow-producing"—is that attention is given more readily and intensity is governed more naturally. One does not have to struggle to raise or lower arousal if his/her abilities are well-matched with, and effectively employed in relation to, the demands of an activity. The challenge to a teacher, supervisor or coach, then, is to arrange or control circumstances to provide and protect that match. However, this is an ongoing process; as one's abilities improve, greater challenges are required to maintain that intensity. If greater challenges are not present, intensity drops and one becomes bored. Of course, the opposite can also occur; a mentor's zeal for providing greater challenges or one's own ambitiousness can result in a situation of excessive demand which is anxiety-producing and makes concentration and investment extremely difficult. Performing a new gymnastics routine at a regional tournament or playing a difficult piece of music in front of a discerning audience may each be excessively challenging. In some performance situations the stakes may be so high, there may be so much at risk, or so much to be accomplished, that concern about the outcome of performance is an everpresent distraction. In sum, it is important to recognize that developing appropriate task involvement is dependent on a number of factors including the developmental level of the individual and the environment in which the task is to be performed. Further, it is necessary to be sensitive to the fact that neither the developmental level nor the environment is static.

It is the importance of the future in many situations that also makes focusing on the present difficult. While optimal arousal, concentration and optimal intensity may be disrupted by outcome considerations, persistence may also be undermined. There is considerable evidence (e.g., Deci, 1975; Lepper & Greene, 1975, 1978) that the interest one has in an activity and the willingness to persist in it are compromised by extrinsic rewards such as money, praise, and recognition. Although there are circumstances where extrinsic rewards may heighten intensity to an optimal level—having a ''stake'' in something insures invested attention—preoccupation with outcomes reflects a reallocation of attentional resources that may change the overall orientation to the task. Even though compelling outcomes may perpetuate a high level of task performance and ensure task persistence, it is virtually inevitable that one then becomes somewhat dependent on those outcomes. Failure to achieve those outcomes may be a source of discouragement and disinvestment.

Therefore, while direction, intensity, and persistence may all be enhanced with extrinsic rewards, if enjoyment of and investment in the task itself are important, and if persistence is desired beyond or in the absence of extrinsic rewards, one must be sensitive to their overjustifying, undermining effects. This is problematic in all achievement paradigms which emphasize the setting of long-term goals and the delay of gratification.

To reiterate, persistence or continuing interest is a matter of direction, and changing personal incentives, changing task attraction, is just that—a change in direction. Thus, motivation enhancement is also a matter of reorientation, and where one is concerned with such things as education, graduation, vocational preparation, career change, and retirement a developmental perspective on enhancing motivation must allow for change.

Relating Motivation and Performance to Development

Enhancing motivation simply to enhance performance may be shortsighted. To the extent that performance is maintained and enhanced by contingencies external to the task itself, intrinsic interest may falter when these contingencies are no longer in operation. This is the problem of overjustification referred to earlier. However, the impact motivation has on performance does not occur in a vacuum. The level of both motivation and performance are at least somewhat dependent on the stage of development of an individual. What is motivating for an individual will differ across the life-span. Similarly, what constitutes optimal performance will be influenced by one's development. For these reasons an understanding of development is critical. Newman and Newman (1979) describe a psychosocial stage theory of development based on five organizing concepts: stages of development, developmental tasks, the psychosocial crises, the central processes for resolving the crises, and coping behaviors. It is assumed that the psychosocial development taking place at any one stage has an impact on the subsequent stages. Newman and Newman (1979) attach developmental tasks (Havighurst, 1953) to each stage. These tasks are a set of skills that are acquired as one gains mastery over the environment. In general, the tasks reflect skills necessary for motoric functioning, intellectual development, social and interpersonal behaviors, and emotionality. Mastery of skills associated with later stages of development is enhanced by competency in skills which are acquired at earlier life stages.

As one progresses through the stages certain demands or social expectations are placed upon the individual by society. The effort to adjust to these demands is the psychosocial crisis. These efforts produce a state of tension which provokes action. The action is the use of the set of developmental skills just recently acquired. Successful achievement or learning of a task promotes happiness and suggests that the individual will likely be successful at hurdling other developmental tasks. Failure to acquire skills necessary for successfully embracing a task can lead to personal unhappiness, societal disapproval, and difficulty in managing later developmental tasks.

For every crisis there is a difference between the level of skill of the individual and the expectations society has for skill performance. To resolve each crisis a different central process is required. Table 1 describes the different life stages, developmental tasks, psychosocial crises, and central processes as depicted by Newman and Newman (1979).

It becomes apparent, then, that the directions one chooses are related to what developmental task is being confronted and that life transitions such as graduation from school or retirement from work will be especially disquieting. What is particularly difficult during such transitions is how to facilitate the redirection or generalization of motivation. Whether personal investment in an activity is predominantly intrinsic or extrinsic, if it is activity-specific it may have the effect of foreclosing on other interests and directions for development. In fact, to the extent that an activity is highly involving, i.e., enjoyable and "flow-producing," it can have an almost addictive quality that has a narrowing effect (Csikszentmihalyi, 1975, p. 139). When sources of similar experience are not examined, motivation in the one context will not generalize.

Nevertheless, discouraging serious investment in such specialized activities, however irrelevant to subsequent life tasks and roles, is probably shortsighted. A concerted focus on *any* activity is what developmentalists call "selective optimization" (Baltes & Baltes, 1980); skills are built, a sense of competence is formed, and sources of personal gratification are identified. With this in mind,

Table 1.   A Psychosocial Theory of Development

Life Stage	Developmental tasks	Psychosocial crises	Central process
Prenatal (conception to birth)			
Infancy (birth to 2 years)	1. Social attachment 2. Sensorimotor intelligence and primitive causality 3. Object permanence 4. Maturation of motor functions	Trust vs. mistrust	Mutuality with the caregiver
Toddlerhood (2–4)	1. Self-control 2. Language development 3. Fantasy and play 4. Elaboration of locomotion	Autonomy vs. shame and doubt	Imitation
Early school age (5–7)	1. Sex role identification 2. Early moral development 3. Concrete operations 4. Group play	Initiative vs. guilt	Identification
Middle school age (8–12)	1. Social cooperation 2. Self-evaluation 3. Skill-learning 4. Team play	Industry vs. inferiority	Education
Early adolescence (13–17)	1. Physical maturation 2. Formal operations 3. Membership in the peer group 4. Heterosexual relationships	Group identity vs. alienation	Peer pressure
Later adolescence (18–22)	1. Autonomy from parents 2. Sex role identity 3. Internalized morality 4. Career choice	Individual identity vs. role diffusion	Role experimentation
Early adulthood (23–30)	1. Marriage 2. Childbearing 3. Work 4. Life-style	Intimacy vs. isolation	Mutuality among peers
Middle adulthood (31–50)	1. Management of the household 2. Child-rearing 3. Management of a career	Generativity vs. stagnation	Person-environment fit and creativity

Table 1.   (Continued)

Life Stage	Developmental tasks	Psychosocial crises	Central process
Later adulthood (51–)	1. Redirection of energy to new roles 2. Acceptance of one's life 3. Developing a point of view about death	Integrity vs. despair	Introspection

*From Newman and Newman (1979), pp. 30–31.

the task of those who would attempt to enhance motivation developmentally would include helping the individual in that identification process and finding alternatives for similar sources of competence and satisfaction in contexts more compatible with changed or anticipated life circumstances.

Support for such an approach comes from the work of Csikszentmihalyi and Larson (1984) on the activities and experience of adolescents. Using experience sampling techniques (electronic pagers and self-report forms), they were able to examine the subjective experience associated with the various activities of adolescents. When all the activities were examined, they found that the combination of challenge, concentration, intrinsic motivation, and positive affect was best reflected in art and hobbies, and sports and games. They called these "transitional activities" because they require discipline and concentration at the same time that they are enjoyable, and thus serve as a kind of "template" for the examination of adult alternatives. The assumption here, obviously, is that work and adult involvement more generally can be intrinsically rewarding as well as extrinsically supported (see also, Csikszentmihalyi, 1981).

Motivation enhancement in the developmental sense, then, has less to do with intensity than direction. With respect to maintaining interest and investment in the face of life course changes, persisting in spite of events which are both expected and unexpected, the activity must continue to provide satisfaction and meaning. Those activities which are complex enough to offer new challenges as one's skills are increased are more likely to be maintained. And this property, by virtue of association with growing competence, makes such an activity constitutive of one's identity (cf. Csikszentmihalyi 1985; Kelly, 1983).

But motivation may also be a matter of redirection of interests. Perseveration on tasks which are no longer rewarding is likely to lead rapidly to symptoms of maladjustment. The common problem of "burnout" reflects this pattern. Danish, Arthur, and Conter (1986) discuss a variety of rewards found in activities that may gradually be lost or insufficiently available in the first place. And, of course, as one's life circumstances change, so will personal needs and sources of satisfaction. Formerly rewarding activities may no longer be available or may require a variety of new considerations. It is important, then, for teachers, parents, supervisors, coaches, etc., as well as those involved in developmental intervention, to treat a decline in motivation relative to an activity sensitively. What has been lost? Can the activity be restructured or revised to regain what was lost? Can the satisfactions of that activity be found in others? Or are the goals themselves changing in meaning and importance, thereby suggesting new patterns of personal investment (cf. Maehr, 1984)? While we discuss approaches which promote generalization or redirection in a later section, let us comment briefly here on the context of sport, where motivation and performance are at a premium.

Sport as a Performance Context

For some, sport is an opportunity to prove oneself; for others it can be a place where one begins to know oneself. Either way sport provides participants with immediate and specific feedback about their performance. There is a clear beginning and end and an opportunity to evaluate one's progress toward a goal. This opportunity is infrequent in other life experiences because the criteria for evaluation are rarely so readily available. Sport provides an environment which is more personal, concrete, time-limited, and intense than others. An athlete's behavior can be characterized as an example of "selective optimization" (Baltes & Baltes, 1980). Individuals have a limited amount of time and energy to invest in life activities. Based on an evaluation of environmental demands, one's motivation, skills, and biological capacities, individuals select a pathway upon which to focus. Athletes have determined that maximal effort should be focused on behaviors judged to be essential for optimal athletic performance. What remains to be examined is how such decisions are actually shaped in the context of sport, how, or to what degree, the motivation is redirected as life circumstances change, and how that process can be facilitated.

GOALS AND THE ENHANCEMENT OF MOTIVATION IN SPORT AND LIFE

If one wishes to understand another, it is essential to understand his or her goals. Goals are for an individual what a program is for a computer. Goals determine the direction, intensity, and persistence of a set of behaviors. In a previous section we have described the relationship between motivation and performance. Goals are the mechanism which drives both motivation and performance. It is surprising then that goals have been so infrequently studied. Perhaps it is because individuals do not always identify goals. While this may be true in some areas, it is not true in sports where almost all athletes set goals.

How Goals Influence the Direction of Activity

The most common environment for the study of goals has been the workplace. Locke et al. (1981) did an extensive review of goal setting as a "motivational tool" in the workplace. Although many of these studies were laboratory or analog in nature, goals were found to have a beneficial effect on performance in over 90% of the studies reviewed. Perhaps the most consistent finding to emerge was that for goal setting to be effective, goals must be specific and challenging. Further, it was found that performance was enhanced when feedback was provided in relation to the goal.

Locke et al. (1981) suggests that goals influence performance in four ways. First, goals direct attention and subsequent action causing an individual to focus on the specific important elements of the task. Second, goals mobilize an individual's effort level, and since different goals require different levels of effort, the individual must evaluate how much effort is required to perform the task and expand effort in direct proportion to the difficulty of the task. Third, not only do goals lead to immediate effort, but prolonged effort or persistence will result as the individual strives to attain the goal. These first three effects of goal setting are considered to influence motivation directly. The fourth mechanism, termed "strategy development," has an indirect effect and is considered to be a more cognitive mechanism involving creative problem solving in order to reach the goal.

To view goals simply as a "motivational tool" which affects performance is limited and mechanistic in perspective. The orientation of Locke et al. (1981) toward motivation is to consider only the intensity and persistence of behavior and to overlook the direction. It is true that intensity and, to some degree, persistence can be enhanced by specific performance criteria and feedback. As noted earlier, sport has these performance characteristics and is thus a natural context for these processes. However, what is equally as important here is to understand how and what goals are selected so that we may understand the direction of the investment and the nature of investment change. Since many of the studies Locke et al. review are laboratory studies, the motivation is manufactured and therefore may not exist in a free choice environment. How to increase one's "motivation" to change the direction of his or her behavior is a different issue and one which has presented problems to behavioral scientists for some time.

Those interested in health behavior, for example, have studied how to influence individuals to adopt healthier behaviors. The *health beliefs model* (Rosenstock 1966; Rosenstock & Kirscht, 1979) derived from this research is based on two elements: the individual's psychological state of readiness to take a specific action and the extent to which a particular course of action is believed to be beneficial. Whether individuals will act is dependent upon how vulnerable or susceptible they feel to a particular health condition and the extent to which they feel that contracting the condition will have serious consequences. The major determinants, then, are the perceived susceptibility, the perceived seriousness, the perceived benefits of taking action, and the perceived barriers to taking action. According to this model, for a change to take place it must be based on a *want* or *need*, not an *ought to*, *should*, or *have to*. In other words, the decision to direct one's energies toward a specific end comes from within rather than as a result of pressure from without.

Kelman (1958) identified three levels of motivation. The first level, *compliance*, is synonymous with the terms "should" or "ought to." Compliance occurs when an individual's motivation is to gain external rewards or avoid punishment. The performance of the behavior is seen as required, and maintenance is not likely to occur in the absence of external contingencies.

A higher level of motivation is *identification*. Behaviors are performed and skills learned because others are doing similar behaviors. Satisfaction is derived from conforming. Problems occur with maintenance when the individual leaves the learning environment and moves to a natural environment.

The highest level of motivation is *internalization*. Internalization occurs when behaviors are performed because the rationale for performance agrees with the individual's value system. Since performance is intrinsically rewarding, maintenance is likely in diverse environments.

Making a commitment to athletic excellence involves a lifestyle change for most individuals. Such changes involve a significant expenditure of energy, including changes in the way one lives, spends time, relates to others, and fits into the community. No matter how attractive making a commitment to be a great athlete seems, unless it is accompanied by some internal rewards for making this commitment, persistence is unlikely.

How Goals Affect Intensity in Sport

While the decision to apply one's energies toward a specific end is dependent primarily on the direction of the motive, the level of success is much more a result of the intensity and persistence. And it is our belief that the level of intensity and persistence one is willing to invest in an activity is largely a function of the reason a goal was chosen, or, in other words, the understanding the individual has about why attaining the goal is important.

In sports, it is quite common to hear coaches complain about an athlete's performance under circumstances where the coach thought the situation or the environment would be highly motivating. Examples of such situations might be a championship game, having important recruiters observing, or performing in front of a large audience. But the extent to which these environments are arousing, is largely a function of different achievement goals. As was noted earlier, three categories of goals have been associated with achievement contexts

(Maehr, 1984; Maehr & Nicholls, 1980; Nicholls, 1979): ego goals, approval goals, and task goals.

Roberts (1985) suggests that it is the athletes' expectations of how they will perform that affects the perception of precompetitive stress. He concludes that for those athletes adopting an ego-oriented ability goal, precompetitive stress will depend upon their perceptions of their abilities. The impetus for the effort will be to maximize the probability of attributing high ability and minimize the probability of attributing low ability to oneself. Such a view leads the athlete to use social comparison processes to gain information regarding how his or her ability compares with other athletes. Thus, the major concern of the athlete centers around validating competence (Dweck & Elliott, 1983) with success and failure being determined by how well the abilities are demonstrated. If an athlete feels confident about his or her ability and expects to experience success, he/she will experience little precompetitive stress. If, however, the athlete is not confident or is unsure about his/her ability, he or she will experience significant precompetitive stress due to the uncertainty about whether the performance will come up to expectations.

For those individuals holding social approval-based achievement goals, stress will be experienced when their goal of gaining the approval of significant others is not accomplished. Sometimes athletes perform not for the purpose of demonstrating ability in comparison to others, but to gain approval from significant others such as the coach, spectators, parents, or friends. In contrast to other forms of achievement goals, those with social approval goals focus on the attribute of effort. Success and failure will be determined by others' evaluation of the athlete's level of effort.

Task-oriented individuals will perceive stress only when insufficient effort or commitment to the goal of individual mastery is evident. These athletes are not concerned with the demonstration of competence to others, but rather with increasing competence and developing mastery. The focus of the evaluation is not social comparison (winning) but individual mastery or improvement regardless of the performance outcome. Success and failure are not determined by assessing the competence of others but by making personal comparisons with one's own previous standards of performance.

The achievement goals adopted by athletes, then, affect their perception of stress, and knowledge of these achievement goals may explain individual differences in stress experienced by athletes. Being able to adopt a focus on individual task mastery would appear to be the most appropriate solution to the problem of the stress of competition. If athletes feel stress and pressure, it is likely that they are focused on the implications of failing to reach a goal, rather than the task at hand. A number of cognitive techniques and strategies are used by athletes to reduce stress associated with performance. However, these strategies simply reduce anxiety to an optimum performance level thereby allowing the athlete to direct attention to the task. Although they may indirectly affect goal-oriented striving by shifting the focus of attention back to the task, they are more difficult—and more important—for those who have ego-oriented and approval-oriented goals than for those with task-oriented goals.

A technique for reducing anxiety more generally is that of relaxation. The purpose of relaxation strategies is to create a physiological calming of the body and promote a shift in attention from anxiety-provoking thoughts to a relaxation set. Numerous specific relaxation techniques have evolved, the genre having originated with Jacobsen's (1938) progressive relaxation technique. He proposed that anxiety and relaxation are states that are incompatible, and in order to relax one must be able to distinguish tension from relaxation. This particular technique therefore requires athletes to progressively tense and relax muscle groups enabling them to become sensitized to the state of relaxation. In order to utilize this technique in competition, the athlete must practice the skill to be able to relax as soon as tension is recognized.

A technique frequently utilized in unison with relaxation to reduce anxiety is imagery. Suinn (1976) refers to mental imagery as "a covert activity whereby a person experiences sensory-motor sensations that reintegrate reality experiences" (p. 256). Similar in meaning to mental practice it involves more than simply visualizing the activity but rather using tactile, auditory, emotional, and muscular sensations, mimicking any sensory-perceptual experience. While the theoretical rationale for the imagery-performance relationship has been well documented in the psychological literature, the underlying premise in using imagery to control anxiety is that a person's thoughts and cognitions exert a profound influence upon overt behavior. Both Meichenbaum's (1977) stress inoculation program and Smith's (1980) stress management program use imagery in dealing with anxiety-producing situations. Briefly, both stress inoculation and stress management involve identifying feelings of anxiety, learning relaxation skills, and utilizing imagery to cope with visualized situations of various levels of stress.

Another technique which is utilized to control heightened arousal is what Mahoney (1979) refers to as "calming self-statements" and Weinberg (1984) terms "positive self-talk." Traditionally incorporated with relaxation, individuals engage in making these positive self-statements in an attempt to raise their confidence and reassure themselves that they have the ability to reach their achievement goal.

A fourth skill which may assist in controlling anxiety but which is also affected by increased anxiety is attentional focus. Nideffer (1976) defines attention as having two dimensions. The first he terms "width" which falls on a continuum from broad to narrow and refers to the amount of information one can attend to in a stimulus field. Direction also falls on a continuum from internal to external and refers to whether the individual is focusing on internal or external stimuli. He suggests that individuals have different attentional styles and that different sporting tasks require certain styles or a certain flexibility in order to shift the focus of attention. Nideffer (1976) notes that increased anxiety has the effect of interfering with the ability to shift from one type of focus to another and will produce an involuntary narrowing in attention. Von Schoyk and Grasha (1983) also state that increased anxiety or arousal reduces the scanning ability of the individual.

Since performance errors are often due to inappropriate attentional focus particularly when under stress, athletes need to be able to redirect their attention upon the task. In teaching athletes appropriate attention skills, Nideffer (1976) outlines a technique called "centering" which is designed to control stress, anxiety, and arousal. It is based on relaxation, deep breathing, and principles of mind-body interaction adopted from Eastern culture. However, similar cognitive skills aimed at developing attention control and stress management have been outlined by Mahoney (1979).

How Goals Affect Persistence

The strategies and techniques described above are all important in the management of arousal and intensity in sport performance. Motivation is enhanced when arousal is optimal and attention is properly focused. However, these strategies and techniques do not increase the persistence of ongoing effort an athlete is willing to invest in an activity. What one wants to get from a performance or athletic involvement will have a direct impact on arousal and concentration.

Motivation enhancement within sport has typically involved coaches and teachers adopting behaviorally based rewards and punishments including the incentive of recognition or more elaborate and sophisticated contingency management techniques (McKenzie & Rushall, 1974) in order to sustain effort, encourage persistence, and enhance performance. Many of these behaviorally based strategies may be considered successful if the criterion for success is a change in behavior to meet externally set performance requirements. However, if the aim of such strategies is to promote continued interest and develop enduring motivation toward participation in physical activity, then such techniques may not be totally appropriate. As was noted earlier, the use of external contingencies serves to undermine the individual perception of personal responsibility and self-determination and may result in a decrease in intrinsic motivation when the contingencies are withdrawn. Interpreted in terms of continuing motivation to participate in sport, an athlete is less likely to be motivated toward continued participation over the life-span if he or she perceives solely extrinsic factors to be motivating achievement striving.

To the degree that coaches and instructors are concerned with promoting continued interest in sport over a considerable period of time, it is essential that they understand what achievement means to the individual athlete. Achievement motivation is concerned with goal-directed striving (Dweck, 1984) which implies that an athlete's motivation to perform will depend upon the particular achievement goal held. Ewing (1981) and Roberts (1984b) suggest in fact that athletes may have multiple goals. For example, some athletes may play tennis to demonstrate how skillful they are whereas they play golf to improve their personal game and play softball to gain recognition from their peers. This implies that although it may be important for the athlete to achieve in each setting, the subjective understanding of achievement in each sport will be different and consequently, the criteria for evaluating success and failure will differ with respect to the specific achievement goal held. Maehr and Nicholls (1980) state accordingly that success and failure are best understood as psychological states which are based upon one's interpretation of outcomes with respect to achievement goals. In other words, what constitutes success and failure will differ for different athletes and it is essential to understand the individual athlete to understand how to intervene in the process or whether to intervene at all.

But, if persistence in the activity is what is desired, emphasizing task goals rather than ego goals is indicated. Encouraging athletes to strive for personal excellence rather than victory reduces the likelihood that they will make debilitating, ego-involved ability judgments which could lead to dropping out of sport altogether when victory is elusive. Striving to achieve personal mastery allows athletes whose perceptions of ability are low to emphasize effort and improvement in order to achieve rather than focusing on low ability. In addition, for those whose perceived ability is high, applying effort now becomes acceptable in order to reach ever higher personal standards. On the other hand, when an athlete maintains an ego-oriented conception of ability, success and failure are interpreted in terms of demonstrating ability in comparison to others. In this case, there is a much greater likelihood of perceived failure as the athlete has little control over an opponent's performance. However with a mastery focus, success and failure are interpreted in terms of personal standards over which the athlete has full control. Therefore, the athlete is personally responsible for achievement, and effort and persistence are associated with what is accomplished. If continued motivation is the aim, then perhaps the most effective method of heightening motivation and increasing achievement striving for all athletes would be to emphasize task involvement.

In sum, then, if we wish to enhance motivation, the activity must provide satisfaction and meaning and continue to do so as the individual develops. Those activities which are complex enough to offer new challenges as one's skills increase are more likely to be maintained. Moreover, the ability of an activity to be challenging will become associated with the individual's increasing competence thereby becoming part of his/her developing identity. Therefore, it seems evident that identifying one's achievement goals when developing strategies to enhance motivation is essential both in and out of sport.

The Influence of Development on Goals

As individuals develop and encounter new developmental tasks (Havighurst, 1953) and psychosocial crises (Erikson, 1963) what is important to them is likely to change (see also Newman & Newman, 1979; and Table 1). With the changes often come new life goals. These goals are the result of a redirection of interests and lead to either a shift in the commitment to a specific activity or to a change in the meaning that involvement in an activity has. For some individuals, however, the transition to a new life stage does not evolve into the development of life goals or a shift in commitment. For these individuals a redirection of interests is not desired and the thought of ''retiring'' from an activity is distasteful. Still others find themselves caught in the same activities despite changing internal and external circumstances. When previously satisfying tasks are no longer rewarding, ''burnout'' is likely. In this section we will examine some of the factors which precipitate problems with retirement and burnout.

How Retirement is Affected by Developmental Tasks

Historically, retirement has been an age-related event. In fact, though, retirement really relates to ending involvement in an activity. The activity may be vocational or avocational, but if it is rewarding and meaningful for the individual, he or she may not be willing to stop. Athletes, as a group, often have a difficult time retiring (Danish, 1982; Hill & Lowe, 1977; McPherson, 1977). Perhaps it has something to do with their youth, because the half-life of an athlete is so short, and the fact that retirement is usually reserved for older adults. However, it may also be due to psychosocial rewards associated with the activity, the achievement goals adopted by athletes, their self-evaluations, or some combination of these things.

Inevitably, one intensely involved in athletics sees that intensity wane (Hill & Lowe, 1977). Age alone will dictate that. Sport, at least in its institutionalized form, is characteristically youthful, taking advantage of the peaks in physical fitness which come, for most sports anyway, before one is 30 years old. For many, this time is accompanied by fear and anxiety about the future. While the transitions to any new life stage are anxiety-producing, the psychosocial development of athletes may be a special case (Kleiber, 1983).

Petitpas (1981) compared a sample of college freshmen and senior athletes and nonathletes with a number of instruments measuring ''psychosocial maturity.'' He found senior nonathletes to be significantly more mature than the senior athletes and concluded that athletes become too invested in athletics and do not have sufficient time to engage in exploratory behavior crucial to identity development.

Unfortunately, comparisons were not made with other groups of nonathletes highly committed to certain activities, either extracurricular (e.g., drama, music) or curricular (e.g., medicine). Such investments may simply be examples of selective optimization. As a result, energy is focused on one area to the exclusion of others and the individual becomes somewhat narrowed. The individual, in this case an athlete, may assume that his or her skills and capacities are limited and that the particular activity (sport) provides the only outlet to success. The failure to project success in other activities may interfere with the maturation process in some respects.

There is considerable evidence that the central mediating influence on goal-oriented striving is the self-perception of ability held by a person (Covington & Omelich, 1979; Dweck, 1980; Nicholls, 1979; Roberts, 1975; Roberts, Kleiber, & Duda, 1981). When this perception is a comparision-oriented evaluation, three assessments are necessary. First, the relative ability of another must be assessed; second, an assessment of one's own ability relative to another must be made; and third, the effort level of both parties must be assessed. For an individual to hold an ability-oriented goal where the object is to demonstrate ability or avoid demonstrating lack of ability, the implication of having low perceived ability has serious performance and self-evaluation consequences. For one to invest effort and persist at a task in which he or she feels failure is probable, does not happen often. Roberts (1984a, b) has noted that in athletic situations, athletes will apply little effort in such instances so as to prevent their lack of ability being made obvious. This means that few options are open to such individuals. The options include comparing oneself with other low ability individuals so that some success is possible, or comparing oneself against high ability individuals where failure is almost certain and therefore does not necessarily imply a lack of ability. Because neither of these options can be guaranteed in sport where opponents are often preselected prior to competition, many athletes will choose to exit from the achievement setting and seek out other achievement domains where their ability goals may be fulfilled (Ewing, 1981; Feltz et al., 1982; Roberts, 1984a b; Roberts et al., 1981). However, they may enter this new environment with little confidence that they can succeed, given their most recent experience with failure.

On the other hand, when individuals have higher perceptions of their abilities, failure is incongruent with their perceptions and they will be unwilling to redirect their goals. Unfortunately, neither will they be likely to invest considerable effort where the comparison situations are not in doubt. In other words, when individuals know that not much effort is required to achieve the goal of demonstrating ability, not much effort will be expended. In her research on success, optimal challenge, and pleasure, Harter (1978) found that pleasure and feelings of mastery coincided with optimal challenges. When situations are structured such that no challenge exists, success may have little meaning.

In sum, having ego-oriented goals is likely to cause retirement problems for athletes from several perspectives. First, if they do not feel as able in sports as others, they may retire but feel less than fulfilled personally. So while they begin new pursuits, this beginning may be accompanied by a lack of satisfaction because of limited success with previous life goals and a lack of confidence about their ability to be successful in future activities. Second, if athletes feel more able than others they may not feel the need to expend much energy in their athletic activities. Consequently, they may begin to feel less satisfied with their activities but unable to develop alternative sources of satisfaction because of a fear of having to compete in arenas where they have less ability.

While we have related the espousal of ego-oriented achievement goals with retirement "problems," difficulty with retiring exists for others as well. To better understand these difficulties it is important to develop a perspective about how one has gained or benefited by involvement in an activity. For example, Danish (1983) surveyed some 300 men and women athletes from 20 sports and had them identify the satisfactions and rewards from participating in sports. These rewards included:

> making a commitment and sticking with it; learning to win and lose; working with people whom you don't necessarily like; learning patience; becoming disciplined; being in shape; having opportunities to travel; a break from studies; a sense of belongingness to a special group; having a challenge; being able to go to school; fame; respect; opportunity to prove yourself; success experiences—sense of accomplishment; participating in games and having fun; discovery and creativity; money to live on; self-control; taking orders; communication skills; drive and dedication—pushing oneself to limits; learning one's own limitations; and to compete without hatred (p. 231).

The list includes all three types of achievement goals: ego or social comparison goals; approval or social support goals; and task mastery goals. We will discuss in more detail later the ease or difficulty with which different achievement goals can be transferred from sports to nonathletic activities. However, it is most important to note that giving up an activity will be difficult without assurances that the reward will be available in the new activity. The fact that such assurances are rare is what makes life transitions a difficult and anxious process.

Burnout from a Developmental Perspective

The problems individuals experience with the transition from work to retirement or to some other form of work are most acute when individuals are meeting many of their needs in the activity they are leaving. The example of retirement from sports for athletes is an apt example where many of the life satisfactions for the athlete are involved in sports participation. In a sense, the problem of "burnout" is just the opposite: in unfulfilling retirement, work is meeting too many needs for an individual to want to stop; in burnout, not enough needs are being met for the individual to want to continue (cf. Cherniss, 1980). *Burnout, then is the failure to achieve work-related life goals* (Danish, Arthur, & Conter, 1983).

Because burnout results from a lack of "job" satisfaction, it is often assumed that the cause is a poor match between job selection and the individual's personal needs (Herzberg, 1966, 1968). However, what makes someone feel satisfied and fulfilled at age 16, for example, is not necessarily the same at 30. It is too often overlooked that needs change across the life-span and that frequent reappraisal may be necessary, for careers are one very important way we seek to fulfill our needs and find meaning for our existence (Sarason, Sarason, & Cowden, 1975).

However, burnout is not a phenomenon confined to the workplace. Casady (1975) has described housewife burnout and it is now a reasonably common occurrence in sport. Bjorn Borg made the following statement upon his retirement:

> I haven't got the right motivation . . . Tennis had to be fun if you want to get to the top and I don't feel that way anymore. [I found out after a year away] how nice and fun life can be without tennis, how there are so many other life values. (Laird, 1983, p. B-3)

Another statement from Lori Kosten, a tennis phenom at seven who felt she was a victim of burnout at 15, depicts a similar theme:

> I woke up to a world of all the super things happening. Headlines, traveling from state to state, missing school, meeting people, winning, being a fighter, wanting things and never being satisfied. Almost from the beginning of my life I was a star. Then when it ended and I couldn't take it anymore I said 'I'm sick of fighting. I want to live.' (McDermott, 1982, p. 84).

Compare these statements with that of a woman intercollegiate athlete who was asked to describe the meaning of sport participation for her: "Through the intellectual and physical exercises involved in sport, women discover their physical potential, test their ambition and realize their ability to create their own destiny." Thus, we begin to see how sport has different meaning for different people. A similar point was made when we examined the rewards and satisfactions athletes gained from participation in sport. Some athletes are seeking growth and self-satisfaction; others are seeking to win. While the latter may be temporarily rewarding, it is not sustaining. When one's self-perception depends on a particular successful outcome then the failure to demonstrate high abililty relative to others—which almost inevitably comes for an aging athlete—is likely to lead to disillusionment.

INTERVENING TO ENHANCE MOTIVATION

Distinguishing among the three manifestations of motivation, namely direction, intensity, and persistence, adds greatly to the complexity of the concept. Too often when motivation is viewed unidimensionally, the cause and effect relationship between motivation and performance seems almost obvious—when an individual's performance is not up to expectation, it is because of lack of motivation. By examining the relationship between the intensity or level of the motivation and performance, it becomes evident that too much intensity may also interfere with performance. We have described several interventions designed to moderate intensity, many of which fit under the rubric of "stress management." We have focused our discussion on how these strategies can enhance sport performance, but they are applicable wherever intensity can affect performance. Such situations are common in the workplace and in interpersonal interactions where "making the right impression" is an important element.

The most difficult characteristic of motivation to alter is direction. It is our contention that to understand the direction(s) one wishes to pursue, an understanding of that individual's goals are necessary. Moreover, if we are talking about life goals we must recognize that goals change across the life-span as an individual's needs change. Thus, to understand an individual's goals, we must put them in a developmental perspective. For this reason we have delineated tasks and psychosocial crises. We have also placed development within a life events/life transition framework.

If one wishes to develop an intervention to enhance an individual's ability to choose or alter directions, the major component must be goal setting. In the developmental intervention to be described, goal setting is the focal point.

Life Development Intervention

Life Development Intervention (Danish & D'Augelli, 1983) is consistent with other preventive mental health practices but is unique in its use of a life-span developmental framework and its emphasis on *personal competence*. Life development intervention works to help people encounter routine and unexpected life circumstances by developing personal competence in life planning. The intent is to encourage individuals to be producers of their own development, to be active problem solvers and planners, and to develop a sense of self-efficacy. Personal competence is defined as the ability to do life planning, to be self-reliant, and to seek the resources of others in coping. Developing personal competence involves having a series of skills, both interpersonal and intrapersonal. By interpersonal skills we are referring to the ability to relate effectively to others in a variety of different ways. By intrapersonal skills we are referring to the ability to set goals, acquire knowledge, make decisions, take risks, develop self-control, and understand oneself (Danish, D'Augelli, & Ginsberg, 1984).

The focal point of the life development intervention framework is the ability to identify and set life goals. Most intervention systems stress the alleviation of problems. Goals usually are defined in terms of eliminating a given problem; less occasionally they are viewed as being able to attain some state that is opposite to a problem (for example, having confidence rather than reducing self-deprecation). The underlying issue is empowerment (Rappaport, 1981). What skills, if any, do individuals want to learn? How would they like to cope with a specific event; what are their life goals? Having individuals identify their goals and develop plans to attain them is an empowering act.

Goal setting is a difficult process. Setting goals involves a considerable expenditure of energy. If the goal is not set in a way that is clear and makes attainment possible, the energy expended may be in vain. Goal assessment involves three parts: goal identification, goal importance, and delineation of the barriers to achieving the goal. Goals must involve the identification of a specific positive behavior and be under the control of the goal setter. When goals are negative ("don'ts") so much attention may be focused on the behavior to be avoided that it usually provokes anxiety. The determination of a specific, positive behavior provides an opportunity for individuals to initiate action and then to evaluate whether these actions are effective in goal attainment. When the goals are identified using these guidelines, they will most likely be task-oriented achievement goals instead of ego or social comparison goals such as winning or performing better than a teammate. When what is identified is an outcome rather than a performance quality, the behaviors actually necessary for goal attainment are frequently ignored. An important dimension in the goal setting process, then, is to distinguish performance goals from outcome goals.

In addition to setting positive, task-oriented, and behaviorally stated goals, the importance of the goal must be determined. Goals that are more important to significant others or are "should" or "ought to" goals are less likely to be attained.

Once the goal has been set and its importance determined, the process of goal attainment can begin. To understand what is required to attain the goal, it is necessary to recognize what barriers and roadblocks exist to goal achievement. In other words, what is preventing the individual from achieving the goal? Four roadblocks have been identified—a lack of knowledge, a lack of skill, an inability to assess the risks involved in changing behavior, and a lack of social support. A lack of knowledge refers to a lack of information or facts which prevent the goal from being achieved. For example, an individual may not know what duties are involved in a certain job. When individuals lack skills they know what to do but not how to do it. For example, an inability to identify task-specific qualities of performance may interfere with establishing a task orientation. Recognizing and evaluating subtle changes of performance are skills that are refined with experience and training. Some individuals know what and how to achieve their goal but are afraid to initiate the necessary actions because of the risk involved. Risks are the benefits of an action minus the costs. When the costs outweigh the benefits the risk is too great and actions are rarely taken. Thus, individuals may want to retire from sports and may know how, but fear they will fail and do not take the risk. The final roadblock has to do with the lack of social support. Even when individuals know how to and are willing to change, the lack of support from important people in their lives may inhibit action. For example, the individual wishing to pursue a new career may even be willing to risk rejection; however, the lack of support from present friends may impede goal achievement. Social support is especially crucial in persisting with a new behavior.

Individuals who cannot reach their goals typically experience one of these four roadblocks, and may experience more than one (Danish, 1983; Danish & D'Augelli, 1980, 1983; Danish, D'Augelli, & Ginsberg, 1984; Danish, Galambos, & Laquatra, 1983; Danish, Smyer, & Nowak, 1980).

Often when individuals do not reach the standard expected of them it is blamed on their lack of motivation. However, if goals have been set which are "wants" and not "shoulds," and are specific in nature, this explanation is inappropriate. When goals are "wants" they are important to the goal setter and the "direction" of behavior is not at issue. When goals are specific, the persistence of behavior will likely increase because what constitutes success will be clear. An alternative explanation for the failure to reach goals which are important to the goal setter is the barriers which have been delineated. Instead of attributing it to lack of motivation, it is more likely a result of a lack of mental skills such as self-monitoring ability, having self-control, being assertive, and talking positively to oneself, or to an inability to take risks. The latter is especially likely when individuals adopt an ego or social comparison achievement orientation. When such an orientation is chosen, the fear of demonstrating low relative ability may be debilitating.

Sport as a Point of Departure

We have used sport as a context to understand the relationship between motivation, performance, goal setting, and development. Sport provides a context to study "typical performance" for when participants are concentrating on their physical performance, their basic orientation toward life is on display. For example, we can observe how they deal with stress, success, failure, and life transition. By examining their achievement orientation we can determine their goals.

When one studies sports and athletes for awhile, it becomes evident that what sets competent athletes apart is their mental preparation. The better athletes concentrate more effectively, talk to themselves more positively, set clearer goals and develop more well-defined plans to attain the goal. Too often when we watch sports we become overly enamored with the athlete's physical abilities and lose sight of the mental skills. The importance of these mental skills is not exclusive for athletes. These skills are *life* skills and they are what determines the level of excellence reached. The excellence of athletes is the same that is required in business, the arts, or the sciences. It is evident that excellence in athletics requires physical skills in the same way that talent is necessary in the arts; however, while ability is necessary, it is not sufficient. Because sport has such a clear beginning and end and a way to evaluate progress, it has importance as a metaphor for life. And it is that which we really seek to understand—how to develop excellence in life.

When we understand what is necessary to reach excellence, we are in a position to intervene, if we wish, and if the individual wants us to. Teaching goal setting within a life development intervention framework provides a means for focusing on the positive, enhancing performance in whatever domain the goal setter chooses. As a result, excellence, however it is defined and in whatever domain, becomes an attainable goal.

REFERENCES

Baltes, P. B., & Baltes, M. M. (1980). Plasticity and variability in psychological aging: Methodological and theoretical issues. In G. Gurski (Ed.), *Determining the effects of aging on the central nervous system* (pp. 41–66). Berlin: Shering.

Burton, D. (1983). Evaluation of goal setting training on selected cognitions and performance of collegiate swimmers. Unpublished doctoral dissertation, University of Illinois, Urbana-Champaign.

Casady, M. (1975, May). Runaway wives: Husbands don't pick up the danger signals their wives send out. *Psychology Today, 8,* 42.

Cherniss, C. (1980). *Professional burnout in human service organizations.* New York: Praeger.

Covington, M. V., & Omelich, C. L. (1979). It's best to be able and virtuous too: Student and teacher evaluative response to successful effort. *Journal of Educational Psychology, 71,* 688–700.

Csikszentmihalyi, M. (1975). *Beyond boredom and anxiety.* San Francisco: Jossey-Bass.

Csikszentmihalyi, M. (1978). Intrinsic rewards and emergent motivation. In M. R. Lepper & D. Greene (Eds.), *The hidden costs of reward: New perspectives on the psychology of human motivation* (pp. 205–218). Hillsdale, NJ: Lawrence Erlbaum Associates.

Csikszentmihalyi, M. (1982). Toward a psychology of optional experience. In L. Wheeler (Ed.) *Review of personality and social psychology* (Vol. 3, pp. 13–36) Beverly Hills: Sage.

Csikszentmihalyi, M. (1981). Leisure and socialization. *Social Forces, 60,* 332-340.

Csikszentmihalyi, M. (1985). Emergent motivation and the evolution of the self. In D. Kleiber & M. Maehr (Eds.), *Motivation and adulthood* (pp. 93–119). Greenwich, CT: JAI Press.

Csikszentmihalyi, M. & Larson, R. (1978). Intrinsic rewards and school crime. *Crime and Delinquency, 24,* 322–335.

Csikszentmihalyi, M. & Larson, R. (1984). *Being adolescent.* New York: Basic Books.

Danish, S. (1982). Retirement counseling for college athletes: A life development approach. Unpublished manuscript.

Danish, S. (1983). Musings about personal competence: The contributions of sport, health and fitness. *American Journal of Community Psychology, 11,* 221–240.

Danish, S., Arthur, T., & Conter, J. (1983). Understanding and intervening in burnout: Enhancing worker satisfaction. Unpublished manuscript.

Danish, S. J., & D'Augelli, A. R. (1980). Promoting competence and enhancing development through life development intervention. In L. A. Bond & C. Rosen (Eds.), *Primary prevention of psychopathology* (Vol 4, pp. 105–129). Hanover, NH: University Press of New England.

Danish, S. & D'Augelli, A. (1983). *Helping skills II: Life development intervention.* New York: Human Sciences Press.

Danish, S. J. & D'Augelli, A. R., & Ginsberg, M. R. (1984). Life development intervention: Promotion of mental health through the development of competence. In S. Brown & R. Lent (Eds.), *Handbook of counseling psychology* (pp. 520–544). New York: Wiley.

Danish, S., Galambos, N., & Laquatra, I. (1983). Life development intervention: Skill training for personal competence. In R. D. Felner, L. A. Jason, J. N. Moritsugu, & S. S. Farber (Eds.), *Preventive psychology: Theory, research and practice.* New York: Pergamon Press.

Danish, S., Smyer, M., & Nowak, C., (1981). Developmental intervention: Enhancing life event processes. In P. Baltes & O. Brim (Eds.), *Life span development and behavior* (Vol. 3, pp. 339–366). New York: Academic Press.

Day, H. I., Berlyne, D. E., & Hunt, D. E. (Eds.), Intrinsic motivation: A new direction in education. Montreal: Holt, Rinehart and Winston of Canada, Limited.

Deci, E. L. (1975). *Intrinsic motivation.* New York: Plenum.

Deci, E. L. (1980). *The psychology of self-determination* Lexington, MA: Heath.

Duda, J. L. (1981). A cross-cultural analysis of achievement motivation in sport and the classroom. Unpublished doctoral dissertation, University of Illinois, Urbana-Champaign.

Dweck, C. S. (1980). Learned helplessness in sport. In C. H. Nadeau, W. R. Halliwell, K. M. Newell, & G. C. Roberts (Eds.), *Psychology of motor behavior and sport—1979* (pp. 1–11). Champaign, IL: Human Kinetics.

Dweck, C. S. (1984). Motivation. In R. Glaser & A. Lesgold (Eds.), *The handbook of psychology and education* (pp. 289–305). Hillsdale, NJ: Erlbaum.

Dweck C. S., & Elliot, G. S. (1983). Achievement motivation. In P. Musser (Gen. Ed.) & E. M. Hetherington (Vol. Ed.), *Handbook of child psychology, IV*. New York: Wiley.

Ellis, M. (1973). *Why people play*. Englewood Cliffs, NJ: Prentice-Hall.

Erikson, E. (1963). *Childhood and society*. New York: W. W. Norton.

Ewing, M. E. (1981). Achievement orientation and sport behavior of males and females. Unpublished doctoral dissertation, University of Illinois, Urbana-Champaign.

Feltz, D. L., Gould, D., Horn, T. S. & Petlichoff, L. (1982). Perceived competence among youth sport participation and dropouts. Paper presented at NASPSPA Conference, College Park, Maryland.

Harter, S. (1978). Effectance motivation reconsidered, toward a developmental model. *Human Development, 21,* 34–64.

Havighurst, R. (1953). *Developmental tasks and education*. New York: Wiley.

Herzberg, F. (1966). *Work and the nature of man*. Cleveland: World Publishing.

Herzberg, F. (1968). One more time: How do you motivate employees? *Harvard Business Review, 46,* 53–62.

Hill, P., & Lowe, B. (1974). The inevitable metathesis of the retiring athlete. *International Review of Sport Sociology, 9*(3–4), 5–29.

Jacobsen, E. (1938). *Progressive relaxation*. Chicago: University of Chicago Press.

Kelly, J. R. (1983). *Leisure identities and interactions*. London: Allen and Unwin.

Kelman, H. (1958). Compliance, identification and internalization: Three processes of opinion change. *Journal of Conflict Resolution, 2,* 51–60.

Kleiber, D. (1983). Sport and human development: A dialectical interpretation. *Journal of Humanistic Psychology, 23,* 76–95.

Kleiber, D. A. (1985). Motivational reorientation in adulthood and the resource of leisure. In D. Kleiber & M. Maehr (Eds.), *Advances in motivation and achievement, Vol. 4: Motivation and adulthood* (pp. 217–250). Greenwich, CT: JAI Press.

Kleiber, D. A., & Greendorfer, S. L. (1983). Social reintegration of former college athletes (Report No. 3). Unpublished manuscript, Champaign, IL.

Kleiber, D., & Maehr, M. (Eds.) (1985). *Advances in motivation and achievement, Vol. 4: Motivation and adulthood*. Greenwich, CT: JAI Press.

Kleiber, D. A., & Roberts, G. C. (1981). The effects of sport experience in the development of social character: An exploratory investigation. *Journal of Sport Psychology, 3,* 114–122.

Kruglanski, A. W. (1975). The endogenous-exogenous partition in attribution theory. *Psychological Review, 82,* 387–406.

Laird, J. (1983, January). Bored Borg announces retirement. *Centre Daily Times,* B-3.

Landers, (1980). The arousal-performance relationship revisited. *Research Quarterly for Exercise and Sport, 51,* 77–90.

Lasch, C. (1979). The degradation of sport. In *Culture of narcissism*. New York: W. W. Norton.

Lepper, M. R., & Greene, D. (1975). Turning play into work: Effects of adult surveillance and extrinsic rewards on children's intrinsic motivation. *Journal of Personality and Social Psychology, 31,* 479–486.

Lepper, M. R., & Greene, D. (Eds.) (1978). *The hidden costs of reward: New perspectives on the psychology of human motivation*. Hillsdale, NJ: Erlbaum.

Lepper, M. R., Greene, D., & Nisbett, R. G. (1973). Undermining children's interest with extrinsic rewards: A test of the "overjustification hypothesis." *Journal of Personality and Social Psychology, 28,* 29–37.

Locke, G. A., Sarri, L. M., Shaw, K. N., & Latham, G. P. (1981). Goal setting and task performance: 1969–1980. *Psychological Bulletin, 90,* 125–152.

Maehr, M. L. (1976). Continuing motivation: An analysis of a seldom considered educational outcome. *Review of Educational Research, 46,* 443–462.

Maehr, M. L. (1984). Meaning and motivation: Toward a theory of personal investment. In R. Ames & C. Ames (Eds.), *Research on motivation in education, Volume 1: Student motivation.* (pp. 115–144) New York: Academic Press.

Maehr, M. L., & Braskamp, L. A. (1986). *The motivation factor: A theory of personal investment.* Lexington, MA: D. C. Heath.

Maehr, M. L. & Nicholls, J. G. (1980). Culture and achievement motivation: A second look. In N. Warren (Ed.), *Studies in cross-cultural psychology*(Vol. 3, pp. 221–267). New York: Academic Press.

Mahoney, M. J. (1979). Cognitive skills and athletic performance. In P. C. Kerdall & S. D. Hallon (Eds.), *Cognitive-behavioral interventions: Theory, research and procedures* (pp. 423–443). New York: Academic Press.

McDermott, B. (1982, November). The glitter has gone. *Sports Illustrated, 57,* 82–96.

McKenzie, T. L., & Rushall, B. S. (1974). Effects of self-recording or attendance and performance in a competitive swimming training environment. *Journal of Applied Behavior Analysis, 7,* 199–206.

McPherson, B. (1977). The occupational and psychological adjustment of former professional athletes. Paper presented at the American College of Sports Medicine Annual Meeting, Chicago.

Meichenbaum, D. (1977). *Cognitive behavior modification: An integrative approach.* New York: Plenum.

Newman, B., & Newman P. (1979). *Development through life.* Homewood, IL: Dorsey Press.

Nicholls, J. G. (1979). Quality and inequality in intellectual development: The role of motivation in education. *American Psychologist, 34,* 1071–1084.

Nicholls, J. G. (1980). Striving to determine and develop ability: A theory of achievement motivation. Paper presented at a symposium on Attributional Approaches to Human Motivation, University of Bielefeld, West Germany.

Nicholls, J. G. (1984). Achievement motivation: Conceptions of ability, subjective experience, task choice, performance. *Psychological Review, 91*(3), 328–346.

Nideffer, R. M. (1976). Test of attentional and interpersonal style. *Journal of Personality and Social Psychology, 34,* 394–404.

Ogilvie, B., & Tutko, T. (1971). Sport: If you want to build character, try something else. *Psychology Today, 5,* 61–63.

Otto, L., & Alwin, D. (1977). Athletics, aspirations and attainments. *Sociology of Education. 50*(2), 102–113.

Petipas, A. (1981). The identity development of the male intercollegiate athlete. Unpublished doctoral dissertation, Boston University, Boston, MA.

Rappaport, J. (1981). In praise of paradox: A social policy empowerment over prevention. *American Journal of Community Psychology, 9,* 1–26.

Roberts, G. C. (1975). Win-loss causal attributions of Little League players. *Movement, 7,* 315–322.

Roberts, G. C. (1984a). Achievement motivation in children's sport. In J. Nicholls (Ed.), *Achievement motivation in childhood* (pp. 251–279). Greenwich, CT: JAI Press.

Roberts, G. C. (1984b). Toward a new theory of motivation in sport: The role of perceived ability. In J. M. Silva & R. S. Weinberg (Eds.), *Psychological foundations of sport* (pp. 214–228). Champaign, IL: Human Kinetics.

Roberts, G. C. (1985). The perception of stress: A potential source and its development. In M. Weiss

& D. Gould (Eds.), *The 1984 Olympic Scientific Congress proceedings, Vol 10: Sport for children and youth.* Champaign, IL: Human Kinetics.

Roberts, G. C., Kleiber, D. A., & Duda, D. L. (1981). An analysis of motivation in children's sport: The role of perceived competence in participation. *Journal of Sport Psychology, 3,* 206–216.

Rosenstock, I. M. (1966). Why people use health services. *Millbank Memorial Fund Quarterly, 44,* 94–127.

Rosenstock, I. M., & Kirscht, J. P. (1979). Why people seek health services. In G. C. Stone, F. Cohen, & N. E. Adler (Eds.), *Health Psychology.* San Francisco: Jossey-Bass.

Sarason, S., Sarason, E., & Cowden, P. (1975). Aging and the nature of work *American Psychologist, 30,* 584–592.

Smith, R. E. (1980). A cognitive-affective approach to stress management training for athletes. In C. H. Nadeau, W. R. Halliwell, K. M. Newell & G. C. Roberts (Eds.), *Psychology of motor behavior and sport—1979.* Champaign, IL: Human Kinetics.

Spink, K. S., & Roberts, G. C. (1980). Ambiguity of outcome and causal attributions. *Journal of Sport Psychology, 23,* 237–244.

Stevenson, C. L. (1975). Socialization effects of participation in sport. *Research Quarterly, 46,* 287–301.

Suinn, R. M. (1976). Visual motor behavior rehearsal for adaptive behavior. In J. Krunboltz & C. Thomas (Eds.), *Counseling methods* (pp. 360–366). New York: Holt.

Veroff, J., & Veroff, J. (1980). *Social incentives.* New York: Academic Press.

Von Schoyk, S. R., & Grasha, A. F. (1983). Attentional style variations and athletic ability: The advantages of sports' specific test. *Journal of Sport Psychology, 3,* 149–165.

Weinberg, R. S. (1984). Mental preparation strategies. In J. M. Silva & R. S. Weinberg (Eds.), *Psychological foundations of sport* (pp. 145–156). Champaign, IL: Human Kinetics.

ENHANCING MOTIVATION FOR INVOLVEMENT IN VOLUNTARY EXERCISE PROGRAMS

Leonard M. Wankel

Motivation for involvement in vigorous physical activity has emerged as an important area of study in recent years. The rapidly escalating costs of health care, together with the recognition that many of the most serious diseases present in modern societies are due to self-selected lifestyle factors, has focused increased attention on preventive health measures (Lalonde, 1974; U.S. Department of Health and Human Services, 1983). One important aspect of these shifting priorities in health care has been the recognition of the importance of physical activity to health.

Considerable evidence has been provided to document the importance of regular physical activity to both physiological and psychological health (Berger, 1982; Breslow & Engstrom, 1980; Folkins & Sime, 1981; Kannel & Sorlie,

Advances in Motivation and Achievement: Enhancing Motivation,
Volume 5, pages 239-286.

1979; Martin & Dubbert, 1982; Paffenberger, Hale, Brand, & Hyde, 1977). Notwithstanding this empirical evidence and the fact that most people are aware of the health benefits of regular activity, approximately one-half of the population remains sedentary (Canada Fitness Survey, 1983; Fitness Ontario, 1981a, 1983; Martin & Dubbert, 1982). Further, of those who are active many do not exercise at a sufficient intensity or duration to garner any significant health benefits. Moreover, commonly 50% of those who do initiate an exercise program withdraw within six months (Dishman, 1982; Gale, Eckhoff, Mogel, & Rodnick, 1984; Morgan, 1977; Oldridge, 1982; Ward & Morgan, 1984).

In this context, motivational research pertinent to the applied field of exercise adherence takes on considerable importance. It is the purpose of this chapter to address significant issues pertaining to regular involvement in exercise. After reviewing the extant literature with respect to factors affecting exercise involvement, current issues facing this area of research will be discussed and future directions for research and practice will be suggested. The chapter has been structured into five major sections. The first three respectively address the personal, situational, and programmatic factors that affect exercise involvement. Section four addresses interventions which have been employed in an attempt to motivate more regular engagement in activity programs. The fifth and last section provides a discussion of a number of difficulties or problems which have plagued the existing research, identifies significant issues and offers a number of suggestions for future research. These suggestions span issues pertaining to advancing theoretical knowledge of exercise adherence motivation as well as advancing the practical benefits of the research.

PERSONAL FACTORS AFFECTING EXERCISE INVOLVEMENT

Personal factors affecting exercise behavior might be classified into three major groupings: (a) demographic factors, (b) physical factors, and (c) psychological factors.

Demographic Factors

Gender.   Although sex differences in physical activity involvement might appropriately be discussed under the classification "physical factors," because of the major role that learning and cultural factors play in shaping individuals' activity engagement patterns, male-female differences in activity involvement will be considered here in terms of gender differences.

Traditionally males have been thought to be more physically active than females; however, recent North American surveys indicate few gender differences in terms of amount of involvement. For example, the Canada Fitness Survey

(1983) indicated that 57% of males and 55% of females, fourteen years of age and older, were physically active. "Active," in this study, was defined as participating in vigorous activity at least three times per week over at least a nine-month period. Similarly, the 1980 Gallup Poll figures from the United States indicated that 70% of American males and 71% of females reported doing some daily exercise for fitness.

The report on physical activity involvement in Ontario in 1983 (Fitness Ontario, 1984) indicated that although nearly as many females (56%) as males (58.5%) were active, more marked gender differences were evident in the intensity of exercise involvement. Averaged over the spring and fall sampling points, 29% of males exercised at a high intensity level (as assessed in standardized metabolic equivalent units [METS]), whereas the comparable value for females was 23%. These differences were more pronounced in the fall (November) than in the spring (June) survey.

Intensity differences were paralleled by differences in the popularity of various activities for the two sexes. More males than females participated in jogging (Gallup Poll, 1983; Canada Fitness Survey, 1983) and in team sports (Fitness Ontario, 1981a). More women than men participated in organized exercise classes, swimming, bicycling, and walking (Fitness Ontario, 1981a).

Further references to gender implications for motivating exercise involvement will be made in the sections pertaining to program interventions and theoretical integration. At this point it is sufficient to state that gender is a factor which affects activity involvement both in terms of intensity of involvement and activity choice.

Age. There is a general decrease in activity involvement with increased age. According to a 1982 survey conducted in the United States (Gallup Poll, 1983), the percentages of different age groups that participated in daily fitness-related activities were as follows: 25–39 year olds, 50%; 30–49 year olds, 44%; 50-;64 year olds, 39%; 65 years and older, 48%. A similar decline with age was evident in the numbers involved in jogging: 13–15 year olds, 53%; 16–17 year olds, 50%; 18–24 year olds, 30%; 25-29 year olds, 24%; 30–49 years olds, 12%; 50–64 year olds, 6%; and 65 years and older, 2%. The Canada Fitness Survey (1983) provides similar information on Canadians. According to this survey the percentages of different age groups that participated in exercise three or more times per week over at least a nine-month period were as follows: 10–14 year olds, 75%; 15–19 year olds, 68%; 20–39 year olds, 54%; 40–59 year olds, 47%; and 60 years of age and older, 53%.

Although these statistics are interesting in that they provide information on current participation patterns for different age groups, caution must be exercised in interpreting them. These are correlational data and thus no causal interpretation of the effects of age on activity is warranted. As McPherson (1984) indicates, there are a number of different explanations that might account for the

observed negative relationship of age and activity involvement. One factor
which influences activity involvement at different age levels is the confounding
of age with life cycle effects. Adult involvement in leisure activities is
significantly altered by such life cycle changes as marriage, parenthood, and
children achieving independence (Dixon, 1985; Kelly, 1974). Beyond this, cul-
tural norms as to what types and levels of activity are appropriate for different
age groups as well as actual physical limitations for different age groups un-
doubtedly influence involvement. Although no adequate theory to account for
age changes in activity has been proposed to date, as McPherson notes . . .
"Physiological and medical evidence suggests that most older adults have the
ability to engage in some type, and to some degree of physical activity" (p. 18).
Hence the decreased engagement of older adults in physical activity might
largely be ascribed to factors other than basic physiological limitations. Nielsen
(1974) presents evidence, obtained from interviews with seniors, which is con-
sistent with this interpretation.

Marital status.   More single than married persons participate regularly in
vigorous physical activity. The respective "active" figures for married and
single respondents to the Canada Fitness Survey were 49% and 63% while they
were 45% and 60% in the 1977 American Gallup study. Although the decreased
involvement of married persons in physical activity may reflect the amount of
their discretionary activity which is family oriented, displacing at least to some
extent personal involvement (Kelly, 1974); these figures undoubtedly also reflect
the confounding effects of age. This would be especially true for the Canadian
study where the sample frame included individuals fourteen years of age and
over.
   Despite these overall trends, there are reversals in given programs. Olson and
Zanna (1982) found that married as opposed to single participants participated
more regularly at two selected health centers. Although the reason for this was
not obvious, it would appear that particular facilities or programs might cater to
certain target groups more than others and this might result in attendance patterns
which differ from overall norms.

Education level, occupational status, income level.   The interrelated demo-
graphic factors education level, occupational level, and income level are also re-
lated to activity involvement. According to the 1977 Gallup Poll, 59% of
college-educated Americans participated in daily physical activity while the cor-
responding figures for high school-educated and grade school-educated individu-
als were 47% and 30% respectively. With respect to occupational status, 56% of
professional and business people, 57% of clerical and sales workers and 45% of
manual workers reported participating in daily physical activity. Similar patterns
are evident in the data provided by the Canada Fitness Survey. According to that
study the percentages of different education groups participating in regular phys-
ical activity (at least three times per week over at least a nine-month period) were

as follows: university degree, 64%; college or university diploma, 58%; high school, 56%; elementary school education, 41%. The corresponding figures for different occupational groupings were: managerial/professional people, 60%; white-collar workers, 53%; blue-collar workers, 48%. Studies of structured exercise programs, be they employee fitness programs (e.g., Cox, 1984) or post-cardiac programs (e.g., Oldridge, 1982) have also found executive and managerial personnel to be much more likely to participate than blue-collar workers.

Kirshenbaum and Sullivan (1983) in an analysis of the so-called "Fitness Boom" in the United States drew a rather negative conclusion as to the extent of the boom and how widespread it was across various demographic groups. They state:

> . . . This boom is in large part illusory. To begin with it's much more of a factor in some social, economic and age groups than others. The much ballyhooed growth in the number of private health clubs and employee fitness programs has been paralleled by a less widely recognized decline in the availability of traditional fitness programs in parks, recreation departments and, above all, schools. This shift from public to the private sector is reflected in the fitness boom demographics: Participants in it are more likely to be rich than poor, executives than blue-collar workers, white than non-white, college graduates rather than high school graduates, adults rather than children. (p. 63)

Credit rating, a factor which is probably related to economic and occupational status, has also been shown to be positively correlated with exercise adherence (Heinzelmann & Bagley, 1970; Massie & Shephard, 1971). Aside from a simple economic explanation for this positive relationship, another possible explanation is that a person who pays his/her bills regularly and who maintains a responsible job, may also be more responsible toward other behaviors including regular involvement in physical activity.

Smoking abstinence.   A number of studies have reported a negative relationship between smoking and remaining active in an exercise program (Massie & Shephard, 1971; Nye & Paulsen, 1974; Oldridge, Donner, Buck, Jones, Andrew, Parker, Cunningham, Kavanagh, Rechnitzer, & Sutton, 1983; Olson & Zanna, 1982; Sidney & Shephard, 1976). In addition, epidemiological evidence indicates an inverse relationship between smoking and physical activity involvement (Criqui, Wallace, Heiss, Mischel, Schonfeld, & Jones, 1980). This relationship might suggest that a number of different desirable health practices tend to go together. Evidence consistent with this interpretation is provided by the Canada Fitness Survey (1983) wherein it was reported that physically active individuals placed more importance than did sedentary individuals on such health-related behaviors as getting adequate sleep, not smoking, controlling stress, and maintaining proper weight. Similarly, an evaluation of a community fitness campaign (Fitness Ontario, 1982) found that changes in physical activity could best be predicted from a generalized perception of lifestyle change which included changes in smoking and drinking behaviors and more effective weight control.

These observations are supportive of attempts to promote general positive health practices or healthy lifestyles. In such an approach, a more holistic perspective of health is adopted which includes an integration of such aspects as nutrition/ diet, stress management, exercise/fitness, smoking cessation, and drinking moderation, rather than promoting the individual health behaviors separately.

Exercise history.   According to Dishman, Sallis, and Orenstein (1985) past participation in a particular exercise program is the single best predictor of future participation in that program. They report a study by Frankel (1984) wherein it was found that this factor accounted for between 30% and 50% of the variance in participation across the first few months of a supervised exercise program. Similarly, Morgan et al. (1984) found that employees who joined a new employee fitness program had already established stronger exercise habits than those who chose not to join the program.

There is also some evidence to indicate that good program adherence is positively related to involvement in active leisure pursuits (Franklin, in press; Oldridge, 1979; Teraslinna, Partanen, Koskela, & Oja, 1969). Also, Bayles et al. (1984) reported a positive relation between adherence to a walking exercise program and preprogram levels of involvement in stair climbing and walking. Dishman (1981), on the other hand, found no relationship between program adherence and preprogram level of exercise intensity, duration, or frequency.

Early involvement in sports has not been shown to be strongly related to exercise involvement. Although Harris (1970) found that middle-aged males who participated in a fitness program were likely to have had a background in sports, other studies of self-reported levels of current physical activity have not found consistent differences between former interscholastic and intercollegiate athletes and nonathletes (Dishman, 1985). One study, Montoye et al. (1957), reported that nonathletes were more active than former athletes during middle age. Research has not found earlier participation in sport to affect adherence to cardiac rehabilitation exercise programs (Dishman, 1981; Dishman, Sallis, & Orenstein, 1985; Morgan, 1977). Evidence does indicate however that a negative experience during early physical education and sport involvement can be a significant barrier to later involvement in activity as an adult (Department of Youth, Sport, and Recreation, Victoria, Australia, 1975; Fitness Ontario 1981b).

It would appear that although exercise history may influence current involvement, the relationship may be modified by more current factors. That is, current lifestyle and environmental factors may intervene to strengthen or interfere with earlier developed exercise habits. More recent exercise involvement patterns should be more predictive of current practices as fewer intervening influences would have an opportunity to interfere. On the other hand, early patterns may not be strongly related because of the effects of considerable personal and environmental changes. Research in the area of leisure involvement indicates that while engagement in some leisure activities shows continuity across different age periods of the life-cycle, engagement in others shows marked differences (Kelly, 1974, 1977; Yoesting & Burkhead, 1973). In other words, there is evidence for both continuity and change in leisure practices over the life-cycle. Engagement in physical activity as one form of leisure behavior might be expected to reflect similar patterns.

In summary, a number of demographic factors have been shown to be related to involvement in physical activity. These studies are almost exclusively of a correlational nature, however, and thus have not established causality in the relationship. Further, a number of these demographic factors are interrelated and it has not been clearly established which of these factors are most important to the observed relationships with physical activity involvement.

Physical Factors

In their predictive research on exercise adherence, Dishman and associates (Dishman & Gettman, 1980; Dishman, Ickes, & Morgan, 1980) found that body weight and body composition were predictive of program adherence especially when utilized in conjunction with a measure of self-motivation. Generally, persons who were overweight tended to be more prone to withdrawing from an exercise program. A number of other researchers (Franklin, 1984; Massie & Shephard, 1971; Pollock et al., 1982) have also reported significant attendance differences with body weight and composition differences while others (Bruce, Frederick, Bruce, & Fisher, 1976; Oldridge et al., 1983; Ward & Morgan, 1984) have reported no differences. Frankel (1984) found that even in a gentle walking program up to 70% of the obese subjects ceased their involvement within one year. In addition, obese individuals have been seen to be less likely to become involved in alternative activity programs (Brownell, Stunkard, & Albaum, 1980).

Measures of aerobic fitness have not effectively predicted exercise adherence (Dishman, 1981; Dishman & Gettman, 1980; Franklin, 1984; Morgan, 1977; Oldridge, 1982). In the large Canada Life corporate fitness program, it was found that neither initial nor continuing participants were particularly fit (Shephard, in press). In fact, the non-compliers and dropouts, especially the males, were more fit than the adherers. These unexpected results might be attributable to the fact that the promotion and pattern of progression of the program were geared primarily to the unfit.

While noting the general lack of predictability of exercise adherence from physical characteristics, Dishman (1986) suggests that physical characteristics may affect exercise behavior indirectly by interacting with psychological or setting influences. He states:

. . . Biologic factors may influence behavior by interacting with psychological or setting influences to effect behavioral states that are reinforcing or aversive; these might include exercise sensations or chronic changes in disease symtomatology. This remains tenable but untested. However, data show that the common practice of relativizing exercise intensity to a standardized proportion of metabolic tolerance is ineffective in equating perceived discomfort during exercise (Ingjer & Dahl, 1979) and that low intensity activity may permit (Ballantyne et al., 1978; Pollock et al., 1977) but does not ensure (Gwinup 1975; Oldridge et al., 1983) increased adherence (p.106).

In sum, current information provides little basis for using physical capacities or characteristics as a factor for exercise prescription to enhance adherence. It would appear that psychological factors such as the participants' perceptions of the activity situation and their expectations concerning it might be of greater relevance.

Psychological Factors

Knowledge of and beliefs about exercise.   As would be expected, individuals who join physical activity programs generally believe that regular exercise results in significant health benefits (Teraslinna et al., 1969; Wankel, 1980). Probably because of this generally homogeneous perspective in terms of positive beliefs and attitudes about exercise, such measures have not been effective predictors of exercise adherence (Wankel, 1985). That is, while most if not all individuals joining activity programs have positive beliefs about the health value of exercise, they all do not persist in the programs. Evidence indicates that people generally, even those who chose not to join programs and who are inactive, also believe that exercise is beneficial (Canada Fitness Survey, 1983; Perrin, 1979). Moreover, survey studies report that most people indicate that increased knowledge (information) about exercise would not increase their participation (Canada Fitness Survey, 1983; The Perrier Study, 1979). Although most individuals, active and inactive, believe that they should engage in more activity (Fitness Ontario, 1981a; General Mills Study, 1979), increased information about the value of exercise is not likely to increase participation. This interpretation perhaps should be qualified with respect to what type of knowledge is referred to. Although it is unlikely that general knowledge about the benefits of exercise would be useful as this information is generally well accepted, more specific information pertaining to how, when and where to exercise might be useful (Olson & Zanna, 1982; Wankel, 1980). The importance of specific types of information and situational factors, which influence beliefs concerning likely outcomes from a program and the level of control over these outcomes, will be discussed in later sections pertaining to locus of control, self-efficacy, attitudes, and situational factors which influence activity choice.

Personality factors.   Although a number of researchers have related various personality measures to aspects of exercise involvement, there has been a lack of systematic research in this area. Most studies have been of an isolated one-time nature with no systematic follow-up on the results of earlier studies. Similar to most of the personality research in other areas, there has been a general lack of a sound theoretical framework. Rather, there has been a tendency to conduct exploratory studies, utilizing various personality measures to determine whether different groups such as exercisers or nonexercisers, adherers or dropouts, differ on certain personality measures.

The results of many of these investigations have been inconsistent. Whereas Blumenthal, Williams, Wallace, Williams, & Needles (1982) and Young and Ismail (1977) reported extroversion to be positively related to exercise adherence, Massie and Shephard (1971) reported a negative relationship. Similarly, with respect to ego strength, Blumenthal et al. reported a positive relationship while Dishman, Ickes, and Morgan (1980) reported no relationship to exercise adherence.

Other studies have reported differences between groups involved in exercise to varying extents. Brunner (1969) found that regular exercisers, those who exercised at least three times per week, differed from spasmodic exercisers, those who exercised less than three times per week, in their scores on the Adjective Check List. The regular exercisers scored significantly higher on intraception, number of favorable adjectives, defensiveness, achievement, dominance, and self-confidence while the spasmodic exercisers scored higher on succorance and counselling readiness. In a similar study, Keith, Spurgeon, Blair, & Carter (1974) compared the Motivation Analysis Test (MAT) profiles of a group of physically active individuals with those of a group of inactive individuals. The active individuals scored higher on mating erg (sex drive) and the narcissism sentiment erg (sensual indulgence) and lower on superego sentiment (conscience) than did the sedentary individuals. Finally, Young and Ismail (1977) compared the personality profiles (Cattell 16PF) of a group of regularly active individuals, a group of individuals who had been inactive but became and remained active and a group of newly active individuals who dropped out. The consistently active group scored lower on Factor 0 (guilt) than did the other groups throughout the four-year period of the study. The newly active exercise group scored lower on Factor Q (conservative temperament) than the regularly active group, initially, but at the end of the four-year study period, the groups were not different.

Until these results have been replicated across different situations with different population groups, they must be considered extremely tentative. Moreover, given the general ineffectiveness of personality trait orientations for explaining behavior in other areas (e.g., Martens, 1975; Mischel, 1968; Rushall, 1973), this would not seem to be a profitable approach to pursue in exercise adherence research.

Research with a more delimited measure of personality, the Self Motivation Inventory (SMI) has similarly produced mixed results. Whereas some studies have found the inventory to discriminate effectively between adherers and dropouts across a variety of activity programs including athletic conditioning (Dishman, Ickes, & Morgan, 1980; Martin, 1981; Olson & Zanna, 1982; Stone, 1983) and cardiac rehabilitation (Franklin, in press); other researchers have not found the SMI to effectively differentiate between adherers and dropouts in an adult fitness program (Gale et al., 1984; Snyder & Spreitzer, 1984; Ward & Morgan, 1984) or in interscholastic sport (Robinson & Carron, 1982). Previous research by the author and his colleagues (Wankel, Yardley, & Graham, 1985) did not find level of self-motivation to have a significant effect on frequency of attending an adult physical activity program.

In their original work with the SMI, Dishman, Ickes, and Morgan (1980) combined the SMI with body weight and composition measures in a psychobiologic model to predict exercise adherence. They found that the model resulted in a 40% improvement over chance in retroactive accounting for program dropouts and a 16% improvement in accounting for adherers. Ward and Morgan (1984) utilized the psychobiologic model in a prospective study to predict exercise behavior. The model resulted in a 87% accuracy for males and 91% accuracy for females in predicting adherence (39% improvement over chance in accuracy of prediction). The model was not effective in predicting dropouts, however; it actually resulted in less accurate predictions of who would drop out than could have been made strictly on the basis of chance. In this study, participants were defined as adherents if they completed 32 weeks of exercise training while those who missed more than two consecutive weeks of exercise sessions for reasons other than sickness, travel, or injury were defined as dropouts.

These conflicting results, with respect to adherence and dropping out may indicate that different processes are involved in the two and that the SMI is more attuned to the former. Replication of these results through further research, however, is needed to establish the value of this instrument.

Research within the delimited focus of social learning theory, utilizing the Rotter Internal-External Locus of Control Scale, has been similarly inconclusive. Although within the orientation of this theory it would be predicted that internals, because they believe that they are more in control of their own destiny, would tend to adhere to exercise regimens more consistently than would externals, research results have not provided strong support (Morgan, 1977). Beyond the general Locus of Control Scale, a more specific Health Locus of Control Scale (Wallston et al., 1976) similarly has not proven to be of much utility for differentiating between those who demonstrate good exercise adherence and those who do not (Morgan, 1977). O'Connell and Price (1982) did find that internality as assessed by a later version of the Health Locus of Control (Wallston, Wallston, & DeValis, 1978) was related to participation in a corporate fitness program.

Despite these disappointing results with personality type measures pertaining to locus of control, the importance of the concept pertaining to an individual's perceived ability or capacity to influence significant desired outcomes pertaining to exercise remains viable. However, the emphasis may need to shift from a stable trait-like conception to a more dynamic state conception which is sensitive to the influence of situational information as well as personal dispositions.

Bandura's theory of self-efficacy (1977) adopts such a dynamic orientation. According to Bandura (1982), self-efficacy is one's perceived judgement of "how well one can execute courses of action required to deal with prospective situations" (p. 122). Bandura distinguishes between outcome expectancy and efficacy expectancy. The former refers to a belief that particular actions/behaviors will result in specific outcomes while the latter refers to a belief that the individual is capable of performing the requisite action/behavior. Bandura suggests that these latter perceptions of self-efficacy have important implications for the selection, intensity, and duration of behaviors. Applying these concepts to exercise adherence may help to explain the divergent results pertaining to the relationship between beliefs pertaining to the value of exercise and actual engagement in physical activity. While two individuals may both believe that participation in an aerobics program will produce desirable outcomes (similar outcome expectancies), if one individual perceives that he/she has the time, resources, and physical skills to successfully participate in the class while another does not (different efficacy expectancies), the actual exercise behaviors of the two might be expected to differ considerably.

Although little research has been conducted which directly tests the importance of self-efficacy to exercise adherence, there is some supportive evidence. Albinson (1981) reported that self-efficacy was related to the participation of adolescents in physical education classes while May and Albinson (1980) found that self-efficacy influenced the selection of physical activities by women. Also, the work by Sonstroem and his colleagues pertaining to attitudes and physical activity involvement, to be discussed presently, is consistent with self-efficacy predictions. This research has indicated that there is a significant relationship between one's estimate of his/her physical abilities and the attraction to physical activity (Sonstroem, 1978; Sonstroem & Kampper, 1980). Further, research pertaining to continued involvement in youth sports (Feltz & Petlichkoff, 1983; Roberts & Duda, 1984) indicates the primary importance of the related concept "perceived competence."

In concluding this section pertaining to personality influences on physical activity, it may be noted that general trait orientations have not been shown to be very useful for explaining exercise behavior. Although it can be argued that these generally inconsistent results might be due to the use of inappropriate tests in some studies and the failure to separate studies according to types of activity programs and subject groups when reviewing the results, it is the author's opinion that there are basic limitations to the trait orientation. Rather than attempting to use personality measures to match individuals to exercise type or program format as some authors (e.g. Shephard, in press) have suggested, it is the author's view that other more specific measures such as program interests, goals or expectancies, exercise history, and perceived competence in certain activities would be more valuable.

This discounting of the predictive value of general personality measures in no way questions the value of considering personal dispositions. While acknowledging the importance of situational and program factors to be discussed in the ensuing sections, it is maintained that how these factors will influence an individual's exercise behavior will depend upon his/her subjective perception and reaction to those factors. Thus more dynamic state-like personal factors have considerable importance and must be considered in concert with other factors. Such dynamic, interaction approaches will be discussed further in the concluding section of the chapter.

In the next section, however, attention is turned to another psychological construct, attitude, which has been studied in relation to physical activity behavior.

Attitude toward physical activity. Attitude, like personality, is a psychological construct; however, it differs in that it has a specific reference object. Whereas personality traits are general predispositions which are posited to influence behavior across widely divergent contexts, attitudes are generally delimited to a more specific focus. Triandis (1971) defines attitude as "an idea charged with emotion which predisposes a class of actions to a particular class of social situations" (p.2). Adapting this definition to physical activity or exercise, a suitable definition might be: the thoughts or beliefs, and the accompanying emotional feelings which an individual has about some aspect of physical activity or exercise which predisposes the individual to engage in activity or exercise in given social situations.

The research literature pertaining to attitudes toward physical activity or exercise may be grouped into four major categories for discussion purposes. The first, is a general grouping of early research on attitude toward some aspect of physical activity, physical education, or related stimulus object. A variety of attitude scales, generally of a Likert-type, were employed and indicated that most subject groups held positive attitudes. However, due to a variety of conceptual and methodological limitations much of this research contributed little to clarifying the importance of attitudes to physical activity behavior (Albinson, 1975; Kenyon, 1971).

The research of Kenyon (1968a, b) in conceptualizing the distinctive dimensions of physical activity and in developing a scale for measuring these dimensions made a valuable contribution beyond the earlier, less systematic research. A major value of this research was in elucidating the different conceptual meanings commonly held for physical activity and in identifying the relative instrumental strengths of different dimensions for different groups (Alderman, 1969; Kenyon, 1968a, 1970). Further, large-scale cross-national research did indicate that there was a relationship between attitudes as assessed by the Attitude Toward Physical Activity (ATPA) scale and involvement in physical activity (Kenyon, 1970).

Subsequent adaption of the ATPA for use with children in the form of the Children's Attitudes Toward Physical Activity Scale (CATPA) (Simon & Smoll, 1974) was also useful for identifying differing attitudes between different population groups. As with the adult instrument, a major contribution of the CATPA was to provide a reliable, internally consistent measure of the different conceptual dimensions of physical activity. Despite these methodological advances, neither the ATPA nor the CATPA have been shown to have much predictive value for identifying groups or individuals who will be differentially involved in physical activity (Dishman, 1986; Dishman & Gettman, 1980; Morgan et al., 1984). This might be at least partially attributable to the general lack of specificity in the scales. They focus on the various instrumental values of the general concept ''physical activity;'' whereas, most measures of involvement in activity are situation-and/or activity-specific. This issue will be discussed in greater detail later.

Robert Sonstroem and his associates (Neale, Sonstroem, & Metz, 1969; Sonstroem, 1982; Sonstroem & Kampper, 1980; Sonstroem & Walker, 1973) have developed a theoretical model and corresponding attitudinal measures more directly focused on explaining involvement in physical activity. According to this model, involvement in physical activity influences an individual's estimate of his/her physical ability which in turn influences the person's attraction or liking for physical activity and actual involvement.[1] Research evidence has generally supported these predictions with respect to physical activity in general. Dishman (1978), Neale et al. (1969), and Sonstroem (1978; Sonstroem & Kampper, 1980) have all reported a significant relationship between the estimates that individuals make of their abilities and their attraction to physical activity. On the other hand, Dishman (1978) reports a study wherein no significant relationship was found.

With respect to the predicted relations of attraction to physical activity and actual involvement, several researchers have reported supportive findings when the reference is physical activity in general (Neale et al., 1969; Sonstroem, 1974; 1978; Sonstroem & Walker, 1973). Sonstroem (1978) has further reported that this significant relationship is stable even when the effect due to the estimate of physical ability is partialled out. Attraction to physical activity, however, has not been shown to be an effective predictor of participation in a particular physical activity program (Dishman & Gettman, 1980; Morgan, 1977; Sonstroem & Kampper, 1980). This may be at least partially attributable to different levels of specificity in the attraction and involvement measures, a point which has been given considerable emphasis in the work of Martin Fishbein and I. Ajzen.

Fishbein and Ajzen (Ajzen & Fishbein, 1977; Fishbein, 1973; Fishbein & Ajzen, 1974) have suggested that the low relationship frequently reported between attitudinal and behavioral measures may at least partially be attributable to the lack of specificity in the two measures, or alternately, differences in specificity of the measures. An extensive review of the attitude-behavior literature supported this position. It was found that when the attitude measure corresponded in level of specificity to the behavior measure, there was a good predictive relationship (Ajzen & Fishbein, 1977).

Fishbein and Ajzen (1975; Ajzen & Fishbein, 1980; Fishbein, 1980) have developed a theory of reasoned action to predict and explain voluntary behavior. According to this theory the most immediate determinant of behavior is the individual's specific behavior intention (BI), that is, the intention to perform a specific act in the given situation. This behavioral intention is, in turn, determined by two factors, the individual's attitude toward performing the act and the individual's subjective norm. Attitudes are conceptualized and operationalized in an expectancy value orientation as the sum of the individual's beliefs about the probability of certain desired consequences resulting from the behavior. The subjective norm similarly is viewed as a composite of individual normative beliefs, the individual's beliefs concerning what significant others important to him/her think about his/her engaging in the specific behavior. In operationalizing the model, the normative beliefs for each relevant other are weighted by the strength of the individual's motivation to comply with that significant other's views. Symbolically the overall prediction model can be represented as:

$$BI = [\Sigma Aact]wo + [\Sigma NB(mc)]w1$$

where B = behavior; BI = behavior intention; ΣAact is the sum of the individual's attitudes toward performing the act; ΣNB(mc) is the sum of the individual's perceptions of important other's beliefs concerning his/her engagement in the act weighted by his/her motivation to comply with their beliefs; w0 and w1 are weights which are empirically derived by entering the assessed values of B1, ΣAact and ΣNB(mc) into the regression equation.

Although it is acknowledged that other factors such as environmental constraints, demographic variables, personality traits, and other attitudes can affect behavior, in terms of the model these factors are seen as having only indirect effects. That is, they affect behavior only to the extent that they influence one of the attitude, normative belief, or motivation to comply components. Figure 1, taken from Ajzen and Fishbein (1980) illustrates the posited relationship of various variables to behavior. Although some research has questioned the completeness of the model (e.g., Bentler & Speckart, 1979; Zuckerman & Reis, 1978), evidence has been provided to indicate that the theory of reasoned action can predict a number of different areas of voluntary behavior with some accuracy (Ajzen & Fishbein, 1969, 1970, 1977, 1980; Davidson & Jaccard, 1975; Fishbein, 1972; Jaccard & Davidson, 1972).

Limited research has been conducted to test the utility of the theory of reasoned action in an exercise context. In an initial attempt, Wankel and Beatty (1975) utilized the model in an attempt to explain attendance behavior in an employee fitness program. Limited support for the theory was derived. A correlation of .11 was found between behavioral intentions (intention to attend the program at least twice per week) and actual attendance behavior. The multiple correlation of the sum of the attitudinal measures and the sums of the normative

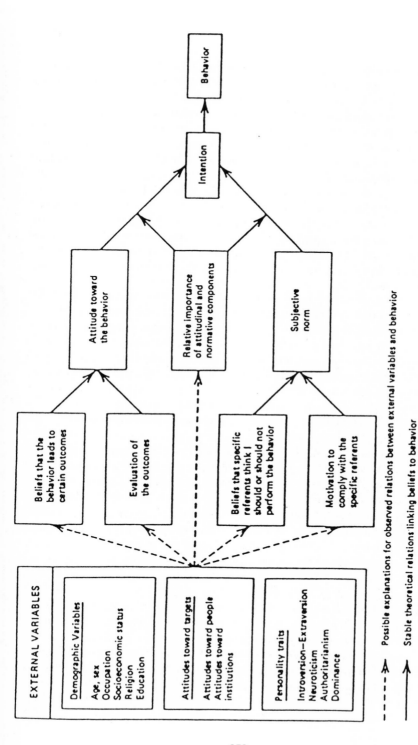

Figure 1. Indirect effects of external variables on behavior.

Source: From Ajzen, I. & Fishbein, M. (1980). *Understanding attitudes and predicting social behavior.* Reprinted by permission of Prentice-Hall, Englewood Cliffs, New Jersey.

- - - →   Possible explanations for observed relations between external variables and behavior

———→   Stable theoretical relations linking beliefs to behavior

253

LEONARD M. WANKEL

belief measures pertaining to one's friends times the strength of motivation to comply with their views was .26. The prediction of behavioral intention to exercise on one's own was somewhat more effective with a multiple correlation of .47. In interpreting the results, the authors suggested that the reason for better prediction of the behavior intention for exercising on one's own than for exercising in the program was probably due to the lack of variability in both the behavioral intention and attitudinal measures for within the program. In the case of both measures, scores were very high and variability was probably limited by a ceiling effect. Support for such an interpretation is evident in the observation that the better prediction for exercising on one's own was accompanied by lower overall means and greater variability for both the attitude and behavior intention measures. A lack of specificity in the wording of the scale items plus some inconsistency between the wording of the behavior intention measures and the attitudinal and normative belief measures may also have contributed to the weakened predictions.

In a more adequate test of the model, Riddle (1980) found strong support for the predictive utility of the model in an exercise context. She found that behavior intention (BI) correlated .82 with the actual behavior, jogging at least three times per week, over a two-week period. In addition, the multiple regression of attitude toward the behavior and the sum of normative beliefs times the motivation to comply was .742. The attitude component was the strongest single predictor of BI having a simple correlation of .643 while that for NB(Mc) was .157. The author points out that the direct belief statements for operationalizing the model also effectively differentiated between joggers and non-exercisers and could serve as a basis for future behavior change attempts.

Godin, Cox, and Shephard (1983) found that the multiple regression of attitude toward the act of exercising and social norms pertaining to exercising with the intention to exercise was .503. Individual regression coefficients indicated that the attitude component contributed most to the prediction (R = .505, P <.001) while the social norm added relatively little (R = .147, N.S.). Contradictory to the predictions from the theory of reasoned action, it was found that current activity habits added significantly to the prediction of exercise behavior intentions independent of the attitude and social norm effects (R = .592, r = .304, p < .001).

Olson and Zanna (1982) incorporated measures based on Fishbein's theory of reasoned action into their interview schedule used in interviewing participants and dropouts from commercial fitness centers. They did not, however, analyze the results in such a way as to test the predictive model. Rather, they simply performed a series of univariate comparisons to determine whether dropouts and participants differed in their responses to different items. They found that for both males and females regular exercise program attenders in contrast to dropouts and irregular attenders, reported a stronger desire to comply with important others, stronger social norms, and greater intentions to exercise. In addition, for males but not females, regular attenders had more favorable attitudes toward attending regularly than did irregular exercisers or dropouts.

An obvious conclusion to this section on attitudes and physical activity or exercise is that there is a need for further research. Although over the years considerable research has been conducted on various aspects of attitudes toward physical activity, it is only in recent years that research focused upon specific attitudinal measures designed to predict relevant exercise behavior has been undertaken. The relative effectiveness of the "theory of reasoned action" for predicting relevant behaviors in other areas, as well as some promising results using this approach in the exercise and physical activity domain, suggests that this is one theoretical orientation which definitely warrants further investigation by exercise adherence researchers.

Exercise goals.   People commonly report two major reasons, health benefits and enjoyment or pleasure, for participation in vigorous physical activity (Canada Fitness Survey, 1983; Miller Lite Report of American Attitudes Toward Sport, 1983; Palm, 1978; Perrin, 1979; Statistics Canada, 1978). The relative emphasis placed upon these two major goal categories varies according to the particular type of activity program. If the program emphasizes social and recreational sports, naturally enjoyment is given high priority. On the other hand, a program designed primarily to develop aerobic fitness will tend to attract individuals who are most interested in seeking health benefits.

It is important to distinguish between reasons for initial involvement in an exercise program and those related to continued involvement. Heinzelmann and Bagley (1970) in their study of post-cardiac male adults found that whereas health-related factors (desire to feel better, lessen chance of heart attack) were the primary reasons for joining the exercise program, program and leadership-related factors were most frequently reported to be reasons for remaining in the program until its end. Similarly, Perrin (1979) reported that new participants most frequently reported health benefits to be their main reason for being involved in physical activity; whereas long-term participants emphasized enjoyment of the activity as their primary reason for being involved.

In a retrospective interview study of an employee fitness program (Wankel, 1985) found that continuing participants and dropouts alike rated anticipated health benefits (e.g., lose weight, reduce anxiety, prevent cardio-vascular disease) as the most important reasons for joining the program. The two groups did not differ in the reported importance of those health-related goals. With respect to such non-health-related goals as competition, curiosity, enjoyment, recreational skills, and going out with friends, however, the continuing participants scored higher than the dropouts. These differences in goals, together with the more positive reaction of the continuing participants than the dropouts to the program, may help to explain the different adherence patterns.

While the above studies may suggest that non-health-related goals may be more important than health-related goals for long-term adherence, this is not always the case.

Olson and Zanna (1982) in a study of commercial fitness centers and Morgan et al. (1984) in their study of an employee fitness program found that those motivated for enjoyment had poorer adherence than did those motivated primarily for health benefits. These conflicting results probably indicate that neither type of goal has a guaranteed advantage to adherence, the key factor is probably how well the individual's goals are fulfilled by the program and the individual's resultant satisfaction with the program. Danielson and Wanzel (1977), and Olson and Zanna (1982) have reported the achievement of exercise goals to be positively related to exercise adherence.

In summary, a number of personal characteristics have been shown to be related to exercise involvement. The following summary statement from the 1980 U.S. Gallup Poll provides a description of the typical active individual.

> Those most likely to say they exercise daily are basically the upscale socioeconomic groups, the college educated, those in the upper and upper-middle income brackets, and professional, business people, and others in white collar positions. In addition, young people (under 30 years old) are more likely to say they exercise than are their elders, men are more likely than women, and people living in the Northeast and far West are more likely than middle westerners and southerners. (p. 111)

However, caution must be exercised in interpreting such descriptions. It must be remembered that most of the information, from which this portrayal was formulated, was obtained from correlational, cross-sectional studies. As such, the data provide a description of who participates at a given time but they do not provide an explanation as to why these individuals participate and why others do not. In other words, the information pertaining to what personal characteristics are related to exercise involvement is descriptive, not prescriptive. It indicates what is but not why it is or what should be.

This would seem to be a critical distinction for exercise leaders to make so that they do not simply provide programs to perpetuate these patterns. The author has argued this case in a recent paper (Wankel, in press).

> It is important, however, that program planners and organizers be cognizant of these patterns and question to what extent their program practices lead to or reinforce these patterns. Care must be taken to ensure that participation patterns are not interpreted as reflecting demand characteristics when in fact they may simply reflect the supply of opportunities. One implication is that in planning programs, information is needed from individuals and groups not represented in current programs. By basing program planning largely on input from current program participants, as is too frequently the case, a built-in bias is established which perpetuates current participation patterns (p. 14).

In the next section, attention is shifted from a focus on personal factors to a consideration of environmental/situational factors which have been shown to influence exercise involvement.

ENVIRONMENTAL/SITUATIONAL FACTORS

The discussion of environmental or situational factors which affect exercise adherence will be discussed under two headings: (a) social support, and (b) location and convenience factors.

Social Support

A number of self-report studies of program participants have indicated that the support of family and/or friends is important to exercise involvement and program adherence. Large-scale surveys pertaining to factors affecting exercise involvement have indicated that the support of family and friends is one of the most effective means of encouraging greater participation in vigorous physical activity (Canada Fitness Survey, 1983; Fitness Ontario, 1981a).

With respect to program adherence, Heinzelmann and Bagley (1970) found that 80% of men whose wives had positive attitudes towards an exercise program had excellent patterns of adherence while the corresponding figure for men whose wives had neutral or negative attitudes was only 40%. Similarly, a large multicenter Canadian cardiac rehabilitation exercise study has found spousal support to be an important factor affecting program adherence (Andrew et al., 1981; Andrew & Parker, 1979; Oldridge, 1984).

In a study of adult male continuing participants and dropouts from an experimental employee fitness program, Wankel (1985) found that continuing participants reported receiving more social support from a variety of different sources. The adherers reported receiving significantly higher levels of support from nonwork friends and work supervisors, and marginally greater levels of support from their families than did the dropouts. The two groups did not differ in their reported levels of support received from friends at work.

Social support can be valuable in at least two important ways. First, from a motivational point of view the support of significant others such as family, friends, and co-workers is important. As previously discussed with respect to Fishbein and Ajzen's theory of reasoned action, considerable evidence has been accumulated to indicate that normative beliefs are one of the major determinants of behavior intentions and actual voluntary behavior. Beyond this, the support of family and friends might involve more direct support through modifying home and work schedules and obligations to accommodate the exercise program and through shared transportation to the exercise site. The recognition of the importance of significant others to the success of an individual's program has led to a number of attempts to develop the support of these groups. A minimal approach is to inform significant others about the program. Heinzelmann (1973) states:

> Those persons who serve as significant others should be adequately informed about the nature of the program and be involved in the program on a continuing basis to ensure that their reac-

tions provide social support, and reinforce the individual's participation, rather than influence
it negatively (p. 279).

A common means of attempting to build spousal support for members in-
volved in a program is to schedule periodic educational/social events which in-
clude spouses. Other programs provide opportunities for spouses and perhaps
other family members to exercise together. Although these programs will not ap-
peal to all, they do build in the advantage of having members from the same
household mutually reinforcing each other's attitudes and involvement in the
program. Recognition of the importance of social support to program attendance
has resulted in attempts to structure and build social support networks to encour-
age involvement (Wankel, 1984; Wankel, Yardley, & Graham, 1985). These
programs attempts will be discussed later with the discussion of program inter-
ventions.

Location and Convenience Factors

Lack of time is consistently reported to be the major barrier to increased activ-
ity involvement (Canada Fitness Survey, 1983; Fitness Ontario, 1983). It is note-
worthy that this is as true, or more so, for regular exercisers as it is for sedentary
individuals (Canada Fitness Survey, 1983; Perrier Study 1979). This observation
probably reflects the general truism that "there is never enough time for every-
thing," so whether or not an individual participates in a given activity probably
depends to a large extent on the scheduling of the activity and the priority placed
on that particular activity.

Evidence does support the importance of time scheduling of exercise programs
as well as the convenience of the program in terms of exercise location. Wanzel
(1977; 1978) reported that 42.5% of the dropouts from an industrial exercise pro-
gram gave as their reason for leaving that the program was located too far away
from their home. Over 40% of the respondents indicated that disruption of their
daily schedule was a reason for dropping out. In a related Finnish study,
Teraslinna et al., (1969) found that involvement in an exercise program was af-
fected by its proximity to one's place of work. A number of other researchers
have reported similar results from cardiac rehabilitation or prevention programs
(Andrew et al., 1981; Kavanagh et al., 1973; Wilhelmson, Sanne, Elmfeldt,
Grimby, Tibblin, & Wedel, 1975).

Wankel (1985) found that more dropouts than adherers reported "inconven-
ient time" and "inconvenient location" as factors disliked about a program.
Consistent with the importance of convenience, Gettman, Pollock, and Ward
(1983) reported that adherence to unsupervised exercise was better than for a
regular instructor-led program and had the advantage of flexible time scheduling
for the participant. Olson and Zanna (1982) found that regular attenders, in con-
trast to dropouts, reported that it was easier for them to fit exercise into their
lifestyle and reported experiencing less unexpected, disruptive events.

Contradictory evidence is presented by Gettman, Pollock, and Ward (1983) who reported that continuing unsupervised exercise participants actually lived further from the site than did dropouts. Also, Olson and Zanna (1982) found that regular exercisers in their study lived further from the fitness centers at which they exercised than did the dropouts and irregular attenders. Although these observations may just confirm the perception that for many people inconvenient location or time are just rationalizations for less acceptable reasons, such as lack of commitment or loss of interest, the important point is that regardless of the validity of these factors for lack of involvement, the perceptions of lack of time and convenience are important factors related to withdrawal. Therefore, in attempting to promote greater involvement, program organizers must take these perceptions seriously and attempt to assist individuals to develop strategies to overcome these perceived barriers. One such strategy might be to provide programs at a variety of localities and times to counteract the lack of availability arguments. Another approach might be to make individuals aware of their priorities, when programs are available, or how they might schedule different events to facilitate involvement. In this regard, Goodrick, Warren, Hartung, and Hoepfel (1984) have indicated how time management training might be useful.

> Participants would learn how to assess their use of time using diaries, how to schedule and set priorities, how to discover the cause of exercise procrastination and to think about what value they place on being physically fit relative to other uses of time (p. 49).

PROGRAMMATIC FACTORS AFFECTING EXERCISE INVOLVEMENT

Group Versus Individual Programs

A number of authors have noted the importance of positive social interaction for facilitating regular involvement in an activity program (Faulkner & Stewart, 1978; Heinzelmann 1973; Kindl & Brown, 1976; Massie & Shephard, 1971; Perrin, 1979). Heinzelmann and Bagley (1970), in their study of adult males, found that 90% of the participants in the program indicated that they preferred to workout either in a group or with another person. These figures may be inflated by a self-selection bias on the part of those who joined the cardiac prevention program, however, as Perrin (1979) in a survey of physical activity participants in Waterloo county, Ontario, found that 35% of the active participants exercised alone, 35% exercised with family members or one or two friends, while 27% exercised with larger groups. On the basis of these observed preferences, Perrin made an important observation. He noted that there were distinct groups of individuals with discrete exercise format preferences, and consequently, "diverse programs are necessary to encompass individuals with different exercise preferences'' (1979, p. 51). Similar considerations were emphasized by Massie and Shephard (1971) in their study of group and individual exercisers.

Gender may be one factor which influences those format preferences. Wanzel (1977) in his study of drop-in exercisers at an employee fitness center found that 62% of the female exercisers came to the center with a friend or spouse. The comparable figure for males was 26%. This greater tendency for females than males to come to an exercise program or center with someone else can also be commonly observed at commercial clubs and community-run programs.

Although the role of a fitness class or center as a venue for meeting people has been noted (Waters, Whitman, Martin, & Gram, 1977) there is little systematic information available to document the importance of this factor to exercise adherence. In their study of two fitness centers, Olson and Zanna (1982) found that fewer female dropouts than continuing participants reported making friends at the facility. Male participants and dropouts did not differ in their responses to the question. In view of the rapid growth and expansion of private and commercial fitness centers and their prominent role in the North American activity delivery system, more systematic research should be conducted on them to document their motivational appeal and their effectiveness in promoting regular activity and fitness.

Although a number of factors, such as group identification and commitment, social reinforcement for engagement in a desired activity, competitive stimulation, and the opportunity to engage in team activities have been suggested to underlie the motivational effects of group exercise (Brawley, 1979), there is an absence of systematic research to identify or evaluate the importance of these various factors. Some experimental research has been conducted on program interventions to enhance regular involvement. This research will be discussed in a later section devoted to program interventions.

Intensity of Exercise

Although certain exercise guidelines are essential to have a proper training effect (American College of Sports Medicine, 1978), it is questionable if such specifications are most advisable from an adherence perspective. There is no direct evidence bearing on this question; however, Dishman (1982) has indicated that the intensity of exercise which is optimal from a physiological training perspective is not likely the optimal level for adherence. Further, there is evidence to indicate that it is the subjective experience of exercise intensity rather than the objective level which is most important to adherence. Ingjer and Dahl (1979) found that exercise participants who reported greater physical discomfort tended to discontinue a program even when exercise intensity had been standardized for each participant on the basis of assessed maximum oxygen uptake.

Pollock et al. (1977) reported that excessive exercise volume can result in increased program attrition due to injury. They found that an intensity level of

85%–90% of maximum heart rate for 45 minutes, three hours per week resulted in a 17% injury dropout rate for 20- to 35-year-old untrained males. The comparable rate for subjects exercising five days per week for 30 minutes was 6%. They further noted that injuries were unlikely with less duration and frequency at the same intensity.

Although reduced exercise volume results in fewer injuries and thus fewer unavoidable dropouts, it does not in itself guarantee high adherence rates. Oldridge et al. (1983) have reported that in a three-year study of post-myocardial infarction patients, both low volume exercisers (50% VO2 max, one day/week) and high volume exercisers (65%–85% VO2 max, two to six days/week) had a comparable 45% dropout rate. Further, although Ballantyne et al. (1978) reported that walkers had a lower dropout rate than participants in a more vigorous program, Gwinup (1975) reported a high (68%) dropout rate from an employee walking program for obese females.

It would appear that a number of factors may interact to influence the effect of exercise intensity on adherence. Too intense exercise may result in injury which would limit involvement. Discomfort due to intensity might negatively affect motivation while in a converse fashion, if a subject perceives that the exercise intensity is too low or the program too infrequent to produce health benefits, the likelihood of dropping out may be increased (Oldridge et al., 1978). In essence it would appear that it is the individual's perception of the situation which is most important to adherence. The individual must perceive that the activity regimen is of a suitable duration, intensity, and frequency to result in the desired benefits while at the same time it is not perceived as being too costly in terms of time, effort, and discomfort.

While these interpretations would appear to "make good sense," it must be acknowledged that there is little empirical support to substantiate them. Thus, this is another area requiring further research attention; however, in the meantime it would appear warranted to suggest that an exercise leader should pay close attention to an individual's perceived and preferred exercise intensity and not to insist adamantly on prescribing a work rate based exclusively on percentage of maximum capacity or some other physiologically determined criterion.

Type of Activity

A number of authors have suggested that the inclusion of sport or recreational activities can enhance enjoyment and facilitate adherence (Heinzelmann & Bagley, 1970; Perrin, 1979; Wankel, 1985). As in the case of exercise intensity, however, there are likely to be individual differences in this regard. If the individuals perceive the recreational activities not to be effective in terms of health benefits and if they prefer other recreational activities or different settings to those offered in the program, they are likely to discontinue. There is no magic in any particular type of activity. Different individuals prefer different activities;

hence, it would seem important, if recreational activities are to be included, that the participants be given some choice of activities. Beyond the importance of actual choice of activities for enjoyment, evidence indicates that the perception of choice is important to enjoyment and commitment to an activity. This research will be discussed in the ensuing section on program interventions as will research pertaining to the importance of challenge and environmental stimuli.

PROGRAM INTERVENTIONS TO ENHANCE EXERCISE ADHERENCE

Although correlational studies are instructive for gaining an initial insight into what factors are associated with involvement, they are not able to establish causal relationships. Hence, it is important that controlled experimental investigations be carried out to establish the causal effect of different program factors on attendance. Although several problems characteristic of field research plague the area, a beginning has been made in investigating the importance of different factors. Investigations which have been carried out can be grouped into the following categories: reinforcement approaches, antecedent stimulus manipulations, decision-making approaches, and interventions to structure social support.

Reinforcement Approaches

Epstein, Wing, Thompson, and Griffiths (1980) found that both a weekly attendance contract, which provided for a one-dollar weekly deposit return contingent upon participation, and an attendance lottery (coupons which provided a chance to win a prize were awarded for each class attended) significantly enhanced attendance of a 25-day (five week) jogging program. The two interventions both resulted in 64% attendance while the control group attended 40% of the classes. Wysocki, Hall, Iwata, and Riordan (1979) found that behavioral contracts providing for earning back personal items which had been placed on deposit, by accumulating specified numbers of points on Cooper's (1977) aerobic points system, resulted in increased levels of aerobic exercise. Although four of the original subjects withdrew from the study in the initial stages, seven of the remaining eight participants doubled their aerobic points by the end of 10 weeks. In addition they all maintained an improved level at the end of a 12-month period.

In a case study, Kau and Fisher (1974) found that spouse-administered reinforcement effectively increased a woman's aerobic exercise. Martin, Dubbert, Katell, Thompson, Raczynski, Lake, Smith, Webster, Sikora, and Cohen (1984) investigated the relative effectiveness of individual-based and group-based feedback and praise. It was found that the individual feedback which was provided during the running program was more effective than the group-based feedback and praise provided at the end of the running period. This was true both for program attendance (77.2% vs. 65.8%) and for continued involvement in activity three months after termination of the treatment program (54% vs. 17%).

Two studies have examined the effectiveness of self-control training programs for exercise behavior. In a case study of a young adult woman, Turner, Polly, and Sherman (1976) found that a program consisting of self-contracting, self-monitoring, and self-reward and punishment resulted in increased reported exercise behavior and improved fitness over a five-month period. In a case study of three overweight adult males, Keefe and Blumenthal (1980) found that a program of self-set, easily attainable goals coupled with self-reinforcement resulted in increased involvement and "marked improvement" in physical fitness over a two-year period. All three subjects improved from "poor" levels of fitness to either "high" or excellent levels. In addition, all three had developed positive exercise habits so that by the end of two years they no longer relied upon the self-control techniques. The natural reinforcements obtained from the activity effectively replaced the programmed reinforcements.

In sum, these studies indicate that reinforcement approaches can effectively result in increased exercise behavior, at least for selected individuals. Further, in a number of these studies, the increased activity level was maintained over an extended time period. This is important in that a frequent criticism of reinforcement approaches to behavior change is their lack of long-term effectiveness. It is possible as suggested by Wysocki et al. (1979) and Keefe and Blumenthal (1980), that after a period of regular involvement, the intrinsic rewards of exercise may take over from the original external reinforcers to maintain behavior. A weakness of this research is the general case study orientation using small numbers of non-representative subjects and selected therapists/leaders. This, together with the early attrition of a number of subjects in the Wysocki et al. study questions the generalizability of the results. Further, research with more representative leader and participant samples is required to address this question.

Antecedent Stimulus Conditions

Although many exercise programs use a variety of poster boards and media messages to remind people about their programs and to encourage regular involvement, there is little systematic evidence pertaining to the effects of antecedent stimuli upon exercise behavior.

In one field study, Brownell, Stunkard, and Albaum (1980) found that the strategic placement of cartoon posters, which encouraged stair climbing, beside escalator/stairways in public buildings, resulted in increased use of stairs. The percentage of subjects using the stairs rather than the escalators increased from 6.3% during baseline conditions to 14.4% during the poster board treatment phase. In a second study the authors found that the effects of the treatment remained largely undiminished for one month after termination of the treatment but that effects had largely dissipated by a three-month follow-up observation.

Oldridge and Jones (1983) found that participants in a cardiac rehabilitation exercise program who agreed to sign a statement of intent to comply with an exercise regimen had significantly better adherence than both a control group and those members who refused to sign the agreement. The percentage attendance of the scheduled classes over six months for the three groups were 65%, 42%, and 20% respectively.

Thompson and Wankel (1980) investigated the influence of perceived activity choice upon attendance. It was found that even when actual activity choice was controlled, the perception of choice, manipulated by telling some individuals that their choices had been honored while others were told that program factors necessitated the assignment of specific activities, resulted in better exercise attendance by the "choice" group over a ten-week period. The choice group attended the activity center an average of 1.69 times per week while the no-choice group had an average attendance of 1.25 times per week. It was also found that those in the perceived choice condition expressed greater intentions to continue exercising after termination of the study than did those in the no-choice condition.

In summary, there have been few systematic studies investigating the effects of antecedent stimulus conditions on exercise behavior. There is some evidence, however, to indicate that situational factors, either in the form of information suggesting different levels of control or choice in the situation as well as environmental stimuli which produce either distracting or informative cues, can affect adherence.

Goal-Setting and Cognitive Strategies

In an interview study of participants in an employee fitness program, Danielson and Wanzel (1977) found that achievement of exercise goals was correlated with exercise adherence. Similarly, Olson and Zanna (1982) found that dropouts from commercial fitness programs reported obtaining fewer of their goals than did continuing participants. In addition, continuing participants were more satisfied with their progress toward goals and felt more positive about the outcomes realized from the exercise program. Martin et al. (1984) found that flexible, self-set distance exercise goals resulted in better attendance and three-month maintenance of running behavior than did fixed, progressive, instructor-set goals. The class attendance rate for self-set goals was 83.7% while it was 67.8% for fixed, progressive, instructor-set goals. Forty seven percent of the self-set goal subjects were still exercising three months after the end of the program in contrast to only 28% of the fixed goal subjects. With respect to type of exercise goals, the same authors found that when individualized feedback/reinforcement was provided by an instructor during the running sessions there was no difference in the adherence of participants receiving distance-based goals and those receiving time-based goals. However, when no such individualized feedback was available, time-based goals resulted in better attendance (69%) than did distance-based goals (30%).

In a third study, Martin et al. (1984) found that distal (six-week) goal-setting was associated with greater mean program attendance (83% vs. 71%) and three-month maintenance behavior (67% vs. 33%) than was more frequent proximal (weekly) goal selection. This result is contrary to that of Danielson and Wanzel (1977) who found that successful exercise adherers in a drop-in employee fitness center tended to set shorter term goals than did drop-outs.

Clarification of the importance of the time focus of goals to exercise adherence must await further research; however, the importance of goal difficulty seems clear. Dishman (1985) reports that some individuals set unrealistically high goals so that they are "doomed to failure from the outset." The importance of realistic but challenging goals to both performance and satisfaction has been demonstrated in a number of research areas (Locke et al., 1981).

Pennebaker and Lightner (1980) found that the amount of external and internal information made available to exercise participants significantly affected the enjoyment of the activity and/or exercise performance and the perception of fatigue. In a laboratory study, the type of stimulus information provided via an auditory tape to subjects walking on a treadmill affected reported levels of fatigue. Subjects who were provided dissociative stimuli in the form of music and traffic noises reported less fatigue than did subjects who underwent similar levels of exercise but who were provided with associative auditory input in the form of taped heart rate sounds. In a follow-up field study, runners' reactions to running on a cross-country course were compared to those for running on a lap course. In terms of performance, the participants ran a standardized distance faster on a cross-country course than on a lap track. These performance differences were paralleled by different affective reactions. Participants reported experiencing greater boredom and frustration when running laps and indicated a clear preference for running on the cross-country course.

Weinberg et al. (1984) carried out a follow-up study to further examine the effects of associative and dissociative strategies as well as positive self-talk on endurance performance. In a study of distance run in a 30-minute interval, they found no significant difference in the performance of subjects instructed in using the three strategies. The authors suggest that the failure to obtain differences between the conditions might be due to the homogeneous nature of the subjects—all were trained runners who could run 1 1/2 miles in 10 minutes or less. In a second study it was found that dissociation and self-talk strategies resulted in better performance of a muscular endurance task, horizontal leg lift, than did an association strategy.

In their studies of adherence to a running program, Martin et al. (1984) also investigated the effects of associative and disassociative cognitive strategies on adherence. Individuals in the associative strategy condition were instructed to focus their thoughts on their internal body feedback; whereas, individuals in the dissociative strategy condition were instructed to focus their thoughts on the external environment. It was found that the dissociative group had significantly better attendance (76.6%) than the associative group (58.7%) over the 12-week program. The dissociative group was also superior in long-term maintenance behavior at both three-month (87.5% vs. 37.5%) and six-month (67% vs. 43% of those physically able) follow-up points.

Further research is required to more clearly delineate the particular conditions under which different cognitive strategies result in better exercise program adherence. Another cognitive intervention to enhance exercise adherence is that based upon the decision-making process pertaining to initially getting involved in an exercise program.

Decision-Making Approaches

Involving potential participants in the decision-making process has been shown to influence exercise involvement. Heinzelmann (1973) cites research by Heinzelmann and Bagley which found that a small group discussion and decision-making approach was more effective than a large lecture approach for recruiting adult males to an exercise program. Faulkner and Stewart (1978) found that a small group discussion combined with an individual fitness test was more effective in recruiting participants for an employee fitness program than was a fitness test alone, a poster-brochure awareness campaign or an educational seminar approach.

A decision balance-sheet technique has been effectively used to assist individuals to explore the potential outcomes from an exercise program and to facilitate exercise adherence. In essence, this technique involves an interviewer assisting an individual to complete a balance-sheet grid with the following categories: utilitarian gains or losses (instrumental effects) to self; utilitarian gains or losses for significant others; self-approval or disapproval; approval or disapproval of significant others; others. After completing the grid, the individual reports his/her responses aloud to the interviewer who verbally reinforces desired responses. Hoyt and Janis (1975) found that a telephone-administered decision balance-sheet procedure facilitated attendance of a university-operated fitness program for females. Class participants who completed an exercise program-related balance-sheet attended 84% of the classes over a seven-week period while participants who completed an irrelevant balance-sheet pertaining to smoking cessation attended 41% of the classes, and subjects in a control condition, who did not receive any balance-sheet treatment, attended 40% of the classes.

Wankel and Thompson (1977) extended the application of the decision balance-sheet (DBS) technique to a commercial health club drop-in program with participants who had been inactive for a period of at least one month. Two separate balance-sheet conditions were employed: a full balance-sheet procedure, identical to that utilized in the Hoyt and Janis study, and a positive-only balance-sheet which deleted reference to any anticipated negative outcomes. In addition, a regular club telephone call-up condition and a control (no treatment) group condition were employed. It was found that the two balance-sheet treatments resulted in better program attendance than did the two other conditions. The mean number of workouts over the one-month period for members of the respective groups were: full DBS, 1.3; positive-only DBS, 1.5; regular club telephone check 0.7; control 0.2.

Graham (1979) reported in Wankel (1984), and Wankel, Yardley, & Graham (1985) investigated whether the decision balance-sheet might be differentially effective for individuals with different levels of self-motivation. Participants in community-based fitness programs were categorized as high or low self-motivated on the basis of their scores on the Self-Motivation Inventory (Dishman, Ickes, & Morgan, 1980). Half of the participants within each level of self-motivation category were administered a decision balance-sheet via telephone, while the others formed the no-treatment, control condition. It was found that the decision balance-sheet resulted in marginally improved attendance. There was no significant interaction effect of level of self-motivation with the treatment and no significant self-motivation main effect. Hence, although the general utility of the decision balance-sheet technique was supported it was not found to be especially effective for low self-motivated individuals as had been predicted.

Hoyt and Janis (1975) offered two possible explanations for the decision balance-sheet treatment effects upon increased exercise behavior. First, they suggested that the treatment might result in an inoculation effect. That is, by encouraging the individual to consider possible negative outcomes of the decision, the technique might assist the individual to deal more effectively with any negative consequences which might be encountered. Second, they suggested that by causing the individual to systematically consider the potential positive consequences of his/her decision (e.g., to participate regularly in an exercise program), the technique might have a self-persuasion effect similar to that found in studies of role playing effects upon attitudes (e.g., Collins & Hoyt, 1972; Janis, 1968). Both Hoyt and Janis (1975) and Wankel and Thompson (1977) provide evidence to indicate that it is self-persuasion rather than emotional inoculation which is primarily responsible for the effectiveness of the balance-sheet treatment.

It would appear that the interviewer/counselor plays a critical role in the success of the decision-balance technique. Janis (1983) has incorporated the DBS technique into his general model of effective counseling to facilitate behavior change. This model will be discussed with other theoretical orientations in the last section of this chapter.

Structured Social Support

As previously indicated, surveys and self-report studies pertaining to factors facilitating regular involvement have frequently reported the support of various "significant others" to be important to exercise adherence (Andrew et al., 1981;

Canada Fitness Survey, 1983; Fitness Ontario, 1981a, 1983; Heinzelmann & Bagley, 1970).

Based on this evidence, Wankel and Yardley (1982; reported in Wankel, 1984; Wankel, Yardley & Graham, 1985) designed a program to develop social support for encouraging regular attendance in an exercise program. The program consisted of leader, class, buddy (partner), and home support elements. Exercise leaders were informed of how they could assist in implementing the program and they were encouraged to show an ongoing interest in the exercise behavior of the participants. They were also asked to regularly encourage the participants to establish and maintain their home and buddy support systems, to attempt to develop a positive class atmosphere, and to ensure that the class attendance and social support charts were systematically marked. The program was introduced to the participants at their first exercise class by one of the researchers. Self-instruction booklets on the program as well as self-monitoring attendance and social support charts were provided to each participant for recording relevant behaviors. Results indicated that exercise class participants who received the social support program attended more of the classes (68%) than did those who did not receive it (60%). Evaluative feedback indicated that participants considered the leader support, buddy in class support, and the general class support to be the most valuable aspects of the overall program.

In a follow-up study Wankel and Kreisel (1983; reported in Wankel, 1984), compared the effectiveness of the structured social support intervention with a group decision balance-sheet treatment and a no intervention-control condition. The social support treatment resulted in better attendance than either of the other conditions. The percentage attendances for the respective conditions were 65.2%, 56.2% and 54.4%.

Subjective feedback from exercise leaders in these two studies indicated that the effectiveness of an exercise-buddy system depended upon the familiarity of the individuals assigned to be exercise buddies. Empirical support for this observation was obtained in a study conducted within a commercial health club (Wankel, 1984). New members joining the club were categorized into two groups—those who joined alone and those who joined with another person. Individuals within the two categories were then randomly assigned to either a structured social support treatment condition or to a control condition. The exercise records of the members indicated that individuals joining the club with someone who became their exercise buddy exercised at the club significantly more often than did those who joined alone and were assigned a buddy, or those who joined with someone but did not receive the social intervention. The attendance of individuals in the alone-control condition did not differ significantly from the other three groups. The mean attendance figures for the four groups over a 12-week period were: joined together-treatment, 14.0; joined together-control, 6.2; alone-treatment, 7.0; alone-control, 9.5.

In conclusion, a number of interventions have been found to be effective in facilitating more regular exercise adherence. A variety of reinforcement techniques, antecedent stimuli manipulations, contracting, goal-setting, cognitive techniques, decision-making and social support interventions have been found to enhance program attendance. Further, a comparison of the magnitude of the different treatment effects reveals that a variety of interventions may have similar effects. Table 1 presents a summary of program intervention studies and their effects upon exercise adherence. To facilitate a comparison of results across studies, wherever possible the intervention effects have been reported in terms of percentage attendance of an exercise program. Such a standardized measure, although not perfect, does facilitate a comparison of the results of different studies. Further reference will be made to this consideration in the final section of this chapter when the problem presented by the inconsistent definitions of adherence across studies is discussed. From Table 1 it can be observed that most of the program interventions resulted in attendance increases of between 10% and 20%. Occasionally, interventions have resulted in program attendance rates more than double the baseline rates.

The relative similarity of exercise participation effects for a variety of program interventions across studies, especially the similarity of results for different treatment effects within the same study, raises the question as to whether all of these results may not simply be due to a common component of social reinforcement (Dishman, 1986) or a Hawthorne effect (Green, 1977; Godin & Shephard, 1983; Wankel, Yardley, & Graham, 1985).

Although such explanations cannot be discounted in all cases, the fact that some studies have demonstrated treatment effects while including conditions to control for Hawthorne-type effects (Hoyt & Janis, 1975; Thompson & Wankel, 1980) questions this interpretation. In an earlier report (Wankel, Yardley, & Graham, 1985), the author and his colleagues favored an explanation based upon the similarity of treatment approaches adopted and the multidimensional nature of motivation to account for similar treatment effects.

> A more probable interpretation for the consistently positive but weak results is the general similarity of the research approaches utilized in the various studies. These studies have all been field experiments where emphasis was placed on experimental control and a standardized intervention. This emphasis necessarily reduces the intensity of the treatment intervention which may account for the relatively weak impact. The fact that quite different treatments (e.g. perceived choice, focussed decision-making, social support) have all had positive effects may simply indicate that motivation is multidimensional and many different approaches may accomplish the same end. The relative consistency of results across different treatment interventions in the exercise area is paralleled by results of research pertaining to different smoking cessation treatment programs (Hunt & Bespalec, 1974) (pp. 154–155).

The issue of *why* various treatment approaches work is an issue requiring further study. This will be discussed further, along with other problems and issues facing research in the area, in the final section of this chapter.

Table 1. Effectiveness of Different Interventions
for Enhancing Exercise Adherence

Treatment	Study	Subjects	Magnitude & Duration of Effect
I REINFORCEMENT			
a. monetary reinforcers: weekly attendance contract vs. attendance lottery vs. control	Epsetin et al. (1980)	N = 41; females	64% vs. 64% vs. 46% attendance (25 day/ 5 week program)
b. material reinforcers	Wysocki et al. (1979)	N = 12; males & females	7 of 8 participants doubled aerobic points level in 10 weeks; maintained improved level over 12 months
c. spouse administered personal reinforcers	Kau & Fisher (1974)	N = 1; female	good adherence; fitness improved
d. individual feedback & praise vs. group feedback & praise	Martin et al. (1984)	N = 33; males & females	77.2% vs. 65.8% attendance; 54.8% vs. 17% maintenance at three months
II SELF-CONTROL			
e. self-control training; monitoring, rewarding, punishing	Turner et al. (1976)	N = 1; female	regular adherence attained; improved fitness level over 5 months
f. self-set goals & self reinforcement	Keefe & Blumenthal (1980)	N = 3; males	all Ss improved from "poor" to "good" or "excellent" fitness levels; maintained over 2 years
III ANTECEDENT STIMULUS CONTROL			
g. Cartoon poster advocating stair use not escalator	Brownell et al. (1980)	general population present in public buildings	stair users rose from 6.3 to 14.4%; effects maintained for 1 month but dissipated by 3 months
h. perceived activity choice vs. no-choice	Thompson & Wankel (1980)	N = 36; females	improved average attendance over 6 week period (M = 1.69 vs. = 1.25).
i. signing contract to comply with exercise regimen	Oldridge & Jones (1983)	N = 120; males CR program	better adherence over 6 months; signers = 65% non-signers = 20%; control = 42%
IV GOAL-SETTING OR COGNITIVE TRAINING			
j. flexible self-set goals vs. fixed, progressive, instructor set goals	Martin et al. (1984)	N = 34; males & females	better attendance over weeks (83.7% vs. 67.8% and 3 month maintenance (47% vs. 28%)

Table 1. (Continued)

Treatment	Study	Subjects	Magnitude & Duration of Effect
k. assigned progressive distance goals vs. time-based goals	Martin et al. (1984)	N = 33; males & females	no difference when individual praise & FB present; better attendance when it was not (69% vs. 33%)
l. distal goal-setting (6 week) vs. proximal goal setting (weekly)	Martin et al. (1984)	N = 24; males & females	better attendance (83% vs. 72%) and 3 month maintenance (67% vs. 33%)
m. dissociative strategy vs. associative strategy	Martin et al. (1984)	N = 16; males & females	better attendance (77% vs. 59%) and better 3 month maintenance (67% vs. 33%)
V DECISION MAKING APPROACHES			
n. Decision Balance-sheet DBS vs. irrelevant, DBS vs. control	Hoyt & Janis (1975)	N = 50; females	Better attendance over a 7 week program; 84%; 41%; 40%
o. DBS vs. "positive only" DBS; club call-back & control	Wankel & Thompson (1978)	N = 100; females	improved average attendance of exercise club (M = 1.3; M = 1.5; M = .7; M = .2).
p. DBS vs. control	Graham (1979) reported in Wankel (1984) and Wankel et al. (1985)	N = 52; females	improved class attendance over 5 weeks; 58% vs. 45%
VI STRUCTURED SOCIAL SUPPORT			
q. Structured social support; class buddy, & home support plus attendance & support monitoring	Yardley reported in Wankel (1984) and in Wankel et al. (1985)	N = 186; females	improved class attendance over 9 classes; 68% vs. 60%
r. Structured social support (SSS); class, buddy & home support plus attendance & support monitoring	Wankel & Kreisel (1983) reported in Wankel (1984)	N = 134; males & females	improved class attendance; SSS = 65.2%; group DBS = 56.2%; control = 54.5%

The preceding review has discussed a number of personal, situational, and programmatic factors which are related to regular exercise involvement. Such descriptive information is informative as to what groups of individuals are likely to be active and what types of conditions are likely to facilitate involvement. It does not, however, provide much clarity as to why certain groups are active.

Further, such general approaches add little to our ability to determine if a given individual will be active or under what conditions that individual will be active.

While intervention studies have extended the correlational survey studies by indicating that some preceding treatment conditions can result in changes in exercise behavior, these studies have also been quite limited. Although they have established that certain interventions do facilitate involvement, little has been done to identify which interventions are most advantageous for certain groups of individuals. Further, it is left for future research to delineate the delimiting conditions for the effectiveness of certain interventions in terms of time-frame, activity scope, and population groups.

The concluding section of this chapter will discuss a number of issues which face researchers in the exercise engagement and adherence area.

PROBLEMS, ISSUES, APPLICATIONS, AND FUTURE DIRECTIONS

This discussion of some of the difficulties plaguing exercise adherence research, issues that must be addressed and recommendations for future research will be organized under four main topic areas: (a) measures of exercise involvement/adherence; (b) the lack of sound theoretical frameworks for adherence research; (c) the need to differentiate between initial and long-term involvement; and (d) the practical implications of past research and suggested directions for future research.

Measures of Exercise Involvement/Adherence

One of the factors impeding progress in the exercise adherence field, as in other areas of adherence research (cf. Gordis, 1979; Oldridge, 1982), has been the absence of an acceptable standardized measure of adherence. Various researchers have utilized different definitions and measures with the result that it is difficult, if not impossible, to accurately compare the results of different studies. Frequently, individuals withdraw from programs and are classified as dropouts although they continue to exercise on their own outside the program. Also it has been common practice to not differentiate between those individuals who are forced to withdraw from programs, because of injury or other unavoidable reasons, and those who withdraw simply because of a change in interest level. This practice tends to be self-defeating in studies designed to investigate the effects of motivational treatments upon exercise involvement; by increasing the error variance in the involvement measure it decreases the probability of obtaining statistically significant treatment effects (Wankel, 1984). Although no totally satisfactory measure of adherence is readily available, a number of suggestions for overcoming the limitations of previous measures have been offered (Martin & Dubbert, 1982; Wankel, 1984). Martin and Dubbert (1982) suggest that percentage of overall classes (scheduled events) attended be adopted as a standard measure. This practice, which was followed in reporting the results in Table 1, does facilitate inter-study comparison. It does not, however, control the above-described confounding effect of injury and unavoidable absences.

In a previous article (Wankel, 1984), the author suggested the utilization of some system of "excused absences" to provide a more accurate measure of "discretionary absences" that better reflect motivation or commitment. Adherence then would be defined in terms of percentage attendance of possible classes with excused absences controlled for. Two different methods of identifying and discounting excusable absences were proposed.

> Self-reports are one obvious means of identifying reasons for absenteeism, but the questionable validity of such self-report measures requires the use of cross-validation procedures. If a buddy system is being employed, the buddy can serve as an information source as to why the partner is absent. Even when a formal buddy system is not in place, individuals frequently tend to come to class with someone else, and these individuals might provide useful information concerning the other's absence. Spouses or other family members can also be used to obtain useful information concerning an individual's absence. Regardless of which particular approach is considered, discretion must be exercised in gathering the data so as not to antagonize the individual. These procedures should probably be worked out with the participants before beginning the study.
>
> Another way of determining unavoidable absences is to schedule make-up classes, wherein individuals would not be considered absent from a class if they attended a make-up session. This might effectively take care of short-term unavoidable absences; however, extended unavoidable absences would still remain a problem. Perhaps a composite approach that used make-up sessions together with a system of self-report "excused absences" for extended absences would be most effective. (p. 132)

Obviously, some modification would be required for defining exercise adherence in unstructured, spontaneous exercise contexts. Perhaps in such cases the number of workouts in the specified time period would be an appropriate measure of adherence. Alternately, a minimum number of workouts per week may be specified (e.g., the three times per week guideline for fitness programs advocated by the American College of Sports Medicine) and conformity to this standard would indicate adherence. Overall adherence to such spontaneous individual programs could then be specified in terms of a ratio of number of weeks in which the involvement standard was met. This utilization of percentage of classes attended or ratio of weeks in which exercisers met the criterion level would overcome the numerous quite arbitrary practices currently used to dichotomize study participants as adherers and dropouts.

Lack of a Theoretical Framework for Adherence Research

The bulk of research pertaining to factors affecting exercise involvement has been of a descriptive nature with no coherent theoretical framework. Although this research has established that a number of factors are related to exercise involvement, little progress has been made in developing an integrating theory drawing these factors together to explain involvement. While some attempts have been made to apply a health belief model (e.g., Becker, 1974) to exercise behavior (Oldridge, 1979; Morgan et al., 1984; Olson & Zanna, 1982); these attempts have not had much success in differentiating between those who participate regularly in exercise and those who do not. Similarly, attempts to develop an empirically derived model for predicting exercise adherents or dropouts from various psychological, social, and physical factors have not been highly successful. As discussed in the earlier section pertaining to the effects of personal factors on exercise involvement, the work of Dishman and colleagues on a psychobiologic model (Dishman, Ickes, & Morgan, 1980; Dishman & Gettman, 1980) showed some initial promise but later results have been quite mixed.

As indicated in the review of the attitudinal literature, two models have received considerable attention in attempting to predict exercise involvement. While Sonstroem's model of physical estimation and physical attraction for physical activity has been shown to have some promise for predicting activity involvement, a more fruitful approach would appear to be that based upon Fishbein and Ajzen's theory of reasoned action. The general success of this theoretical orientation for predicting a variety of different voluntary behaviors, together with the promising results obtained in applying it to exercise contexts by Riddle (1980) and Godin, Cox and Shephard (1983) suggest that this is a viable research orientation that warrants further systematic study.

With respect to the intervention research designed to promote adherence or more regular involvement, two basic theoretical orientations have been adopted. On the one hand, a number of studies have adopted a behavioral orientation. Various reinforcement techniques and antecedent stimuli manipulations have been shown to facilitate involvement. On the other hand, other studies have adopted a more cognitive orientation. In the main, such cognitive techniques as goal-setting, perceived-choice, decision-making interventions, and attitude change programs have been introduced as specific techniques in individual studies without reference to any integrating, overall theoretical orientation. In essence, techniques which have been shown to result in effective behavior change in other areas have been applied in selected exercise settings.

A number of these techniques, however, (e.g., reinforcement techniques; decision balance-sheet; structured social support) have been incorporated by Irving Janis (1983) into a model of short-term counseling and helping behavior. As the exercise leader may be viewed as a counselor or a person in a position to help the participant achieve his/her exercise goals, this model of short-term counseling/ helping behavior would appear to be an appropriate approach for integrating a number of techniques/factors which have been studied in isolation in various exercise adherence studies. Table 2, adapted from Janis (1983), indicates how some of the techniques which have been utilized to enhance exercise adherence (refer to Table 1) can be integrated into Janis' three-phase model of how leaders/

Table 2. Critical Phases and Key Variables that Determine the Motivating Power of Counselors as Change Agents

		Interventions that Have Been Studied in Exercise Adherence Research
Phase 1: Building up motivating power	1. Encouraging clients to make self-disclosures *versus* not doing so.	
	2. Giving positive feedback (acceptance and understanding) *versus* giving neutral or negative feedback in response to self-disclosure	— decision balance-sheet technique
	3. Using self-disclosures to give insight and cognitive restructuring *versus* giving little insight or cognitive restructuring	
Phase 2: Using motivating power	4. Making directive statements or endorsing specific recommendations regarding actions the client should carry out *versus* abstaining from any directive statements or endorsements	— signed commitment (contract) statements
	5. Eliciting commitment to the recommended course of action *versus* not eliciting commitment.	
	6. Attributing the norms being endorsed to a respected secondary group *versus* not doing so	
	7. Giving selective positive feedback *versus* giving noncontingent acceptance or predominantly neutral or negative feedback	— reinforcement techniques
	8. Giving communications and training procedures that build up a sense of personal responsibility *versus* giving no such communications or training	
Phase 3: Retaining motivating power after contact ends and promoting internalization	9. Giving reassurances that the counselor will continue to maintain an attitude of positive regard *versus* giving no such reassurances	— structured social support
	10. Making arrangements for phone calls, exchange of letters, or other forms of communication that foster hope for future contact, real or symbolic, at the time of terminating face-to-face meetings *versus* making no such arrangements	— exercise partners

Table 2.   (Continued)

	Interventions that Have Been Studied in Exercise Adherence Research
11. Giving reminders that continue to foster a sense of personal responsibility *versus* giving no such reminders.	
12. Building up the client's self-confidence about succeeding without the aid of the counselor *versus* not doing so	— self-efficacy training

Adapted from Janis, I. L. (1983). *Short-term counseling: guidelines based on recent research.* New Haven, CN: Yale University Press, p. 27. Permission to reprint granted.

counselors can develop motivating power to assist individuals in seeking a desired behavior change (e.g., more regular involvement in exercise). Consideration of Janis' theory may provide useful guidelines for planning a more systematic program of exercise adherence research than the apparent isolated techniques which have been investigated to date.

Initial Versus Long-Term Involvement

Whereas a number of treatment interventions have been shown to effectively enhance short-term adherence, their long-term effectiveness has generally not been established. Accordingly, there is a need to investigate the long-term effectiveness of the different approaches. Evidence from other behavior change areas indicates that the most efficient reinforcement contingencies for behavior change are not the most efficient contingencies for maintaining those changes over the long term. Further, evidence from smoking cessation research indicates that whereas behavioral approaches might be most effective for facilitating initial stopping, attitudinal change programs might be more effective for long-term abstinence (Best & Block, 1979). Self-report data from long-term exercisers similarly indicates the importance of attitudinal and enjoyment factors. Hence it is recommended that research be conducted to systematically investigate what factors are related to the enjoyment of exercise. Although there has been a lack of specific research in this area, research pertaining to intrinsic motivation and enjoyment may provide some useful suggestions (Csikszentmihalyi, 1975; Deci, 1975; Wankel, 1980, 1985, in press).

A beginning in this direction was made in research conducted by Wankel (1985) wherein it was found that continuing participants, in contrast to program dropouts, placed higher emphasis on nonhealth goals (e.g., to develop recreational skills, to go out with friends, to release competitive drive, to satisfy curiosity) and had more positive reactions to the program and reported developing more friendships within the class. Future research into the importance of enjoyment for exercise involvement might benefit from research pertaining to intrinsic motivation and enjoyment (Csikszentmihalyi, 1975; Deci, 1975). In addition, a sociological model proposed by Snyder and Spreitzer (1979), wherein enjoyment is viewed as one of five determinants of commitment to leisure sport involvement, warrants consideration as a potentially more comprehensive view of involvement since it places enjoyment into context with other factors. Snyder and Spreitzer (1984) provide evidence, from a questionnaire study of exercise adherers and dropouts, which indicates the importance of intrinsic enjoyment to adherence.

Aside from this emphasis upon the importance of situational and enjoyment factors for long-term involvement, Dishman (1982) has suggested that various physical and psychological factors may be differentially important at different time periods. Dishman suggests that there may be distinct stages in the overall process of exercise involvement and different variables may be needed to predict or account for involvement at any one stage. Some support has been provided for this position by the research of Ward and Morgan (1984). These authors, using a psychobiologic prediction model patterned after that used in the earlier research of Dishman and associates (Disman, Ickes, & Morgan, 1980; Dishman & Gettman, 1980), found that different factors entered into the multiple regression equations to predict adherents at 10 weeks, 20 weeks, and 32 weeks after initiation of the program. It will require further research to establish whether there are consistent identifiable stages in overall exercise involvement and whether certain factors are consistently related to involvement during these different stages.

A further finding in the Ward and Morgan (1984) study was that there were different prediction equations for males and females at various stages in the period of involvement. Therefore, further research in investigating the influence of various personal and situational factors on adherence at different time points should also take gender into consideration and investigate whether similar factors are involved for males and females.

Practical Implications of Past Research and Directions for Future Research

As indicated in the review of intervention techniques (refer to Table 1 for a summary) a variety of techniques have been shown to facilitate exercise adherence but no one technique has been shown to be consistently superior. Therefore, an exercise leader wishing to introduce some intervention into an exercise program in order to facilitate adherence may choose from a variety of potential techniques. In making such a choice the leader should consider a number of factors. Foremost among these might be the resources needed to implement each potential technique, the leader's skills and preferences relevant to each, the number of participants in the exercise class, and the class members' preferences for the various interventions. In a previous report, the author and his colleagues (Wankel, Yardley, & Graham, 1985) offered the following recommendation:

. . . the leader should select the technique or techniques that he/she feels most comfortable with and which seem(s) most appropriate to the particular program.

If there are relatively few subjects and considerable staff resources probably one of the behavioral methods which seem to provide more powerful effects than the group based interventions would be advisable. Where limited resources are available one of the group based interventions such as those investigated in this study (*decision balance-sheet, structured social support*) would be appropriate. A vital consideration in any intervention is the cooperation of the participants. Obviously, if they resist the intervention it will be nonproductive at best and counter productive at worst (p. 155).

Martin and Dubbert (1982) after an extensive review of the adherence literature recommended the development of an optimum treatment package for enhancing exercise adherence. In this regard they state:

. . . the optimal treatment package should probably include a very convenient location (e.g., neighborhood-based programs), group-based, lower intensity exercise with enthusiastic participant therapists, ample modeling, feedback and social reinforcement, flexible, participant-influenced exercise goalsetting, and extensive family/social involvement. The program should also be tailored to individual needs, for example, personal health goals/limitations, body composition, skill level, need for social approval versus independent pursuit of goals, and desire for variety or competition versus comraderie (Oldridge, 1977; 1982). Choice, either perceived or actual, appears to be important to adherence to exercise (Thompson & Wankel, 1980) as well as other behaviors (Kirschenbaum, Tomarken & Ordman, 1982). In respect to the overly competitive individual (e.g., Type A), we recommend that very highly competitive activities be allowed only in addition to a more relaxed, enjoyable fitness training/maintenance program (p. 1013).

Although the above summation would seem to be a reasonable recommendation for the exercise leader on the basis of current research information, there is a need for further research to refine such "an optimal package." Research of two types is needed to assist the exercise leader in providing the most effective programs from a motivational point of view. First, clinical research is necessary to assess which combination of treatments can provide the optimal package for given exercise programs in given situations. Second, controlled experimental research is needed in order to systematically investigate the effectiveness of various treatment components.

This is the classical trade-off of clinical and experimental research. Whereas the former emphasizes a powerful treatment by building in a number of components at the expense of being able to understand which particular components produce the desired effects, the latter emphasizes experimental control and random assignment of treatments in order to identify causal effects. Further, whereas the clinical approach focuses upon producing desired results for the particular client group involved, the basic experimental orientation is to identify treatment variables which have generalizable effects to other populations. There is a need for both kinds of research in the area of exercise adherence so that both powerful and generalizable treatments might be developed.

ACKNOWLEDGMENTS

The author expresses his appreciation to W. Bedingfield, B. Nielsen, and J. Sefton for their helpful comments on an earlier draft of this chapter.

NOTES

1. Although Sonstroem's model also pertains to other factors such as how physical activity affects perceived ability and self-esteem, this aspect will not be discussed as it is not germane to the present discussion.

REFERENCES

Ajzen, I., & Fishbein, M. (1969). The prediction of behavioral intentions in a choice situation. *Journal of Experimental Social Psychology. 5,* 400–416.

Ajzen, I., & Fishbein, M. (1970). The prediction of behavior from attitudinal and normative variables. *Journal of Experimental Social Psychology, 6,* 466–487.

Ajzen, I., & Fishbein, M. (1977). Attitude-behavior relations: A theoretical analysis and review of empirical research. *Psychological Bulletin, 84,* 888–918.

Ajzen, I., & Fishbein, M. (1980). *Understanding attitudes and predicting social behavior.* Englewood Cliffs, N.J.: Prentice-Hall.

Albinson, J. (1975). Attitude measurement in physical education: A review and discussion. In B. S. Rushall (Ed.), *The status of psychomotor learning and sport psychology research* (1.11-1.37). Dartmouth, N.S.: Sport Science Associates.

Albinson, J. G. (1981). Self-efficacy of adolescents and their participation in physical education classes. Unpublished manuscript, Queen's University, Kingston, Ontario.

Alderman, R. B. (1969). A sociopsychological assessment of attitude toward physical activity in champion athletes. *Research Quarterly, 40* (3), 1–9.

American College of Sports Medicine. (1978). Position statement on the recommended quantity and quality of exercise for developing and maintaining fitness in healthy adults. *Medicine and Science in Sports, 10,* vii-x.

Andrew, G. M., Oldridge, N. B., Parker, J. O., Cunningham, D. A., Rechnitzer, P. A., Jones, N. L., Buck, C., Kavanagh, T., Shephard, R. J., Sutton, J. R., & McDonald, W. (1981). Reasons for dropout from programs in post coronary patients. *Medicine and Science in Sports and Exercise, 13,* 164–168.

Andrew, G. M., & Parker, J. O. (1979). Factors related to dropout of post myocardial infarction patients from exercise programs. *Medicine and Science in Sports, 7,* 376–378.

Ballantyne, D., Clark, A., Dyker, G. S., Gillis, C. R., Hawthorne, V. M., Henry, D. A., Hole, D. S., Murdoch, R. M., Semple, T., & Stewart, G. M. (1978). Prescribing exercise for the healthy: Assessment of compliance and effects on plasma lipids and lipoproteins. *Health Bulletin, 36*(4), July, 169–176.

Bandura, A. (1977). Self-efficacy. Toward a unifying theory of behavioral change. *Psychological Review, 84*(2), 191–215.

Bandura, A. (1982). Self-efficacy mechanisms in human agency. *American Psychologist, 37*(2), 122–147.

Bayles, C., LaPorte, R., Petrini, A., Cauley, J., Slemenda, C., & Sandler, R. B. (1984). A comparison of compliers and non-compliers in a randomized exercise trial of 229 post-menopausal women. *Medicine and Science in Sports and Exercise (abstract) 16,* 115.

Becker, M. H. (1974). The health belief model and personal health behavior. *Health Education Monographs, 2*, 326.

Bentler, P. M., & Speckart, G. (1979). Models of attitude behavior relations. *Psychological Review, 86*, 452–464.

Berger, B. G. (1982). Psychological effects of running: Implications for personal significance and self-direction. In J. T. Partington, T. Orlick, & J. Salmela (Eds.), *Sport in perspective* (pp. 140–144). Ottawa: Coaching Association of Canada.

Best, J. A., & Block, M., (1979). Compliance in the control of cigarette smoking. In R. B. Haynes, D. W. Taylor, & D. L. Sackett (Eds.), *Compliance in health care*. Baltimore: John Hopkins University Press.

Blumenthal, J. A., Williams, R. S., Wallace, A. G., Williams, R. B., & Needles, T. L. (1982). Physiological and psychological variables predict compliance to prescribed exercise therapy in patients recovering from myocardial infarction. *Psychosomatic Medicine, 44*, 519–527.

Brawley, L. R. (1979). Motivating participation in the fitness group. *Recreation Research Review, 6*, 35–39.

Breslow, L. A., & Enstrom, J. E. (1980). Persistence of health habits and their relationship to mortality. *Preventive Medicine, 9*, 469–483.

Brownell, K., Stunkard, A., & Albaum, J. (1980). Evaluation and modification of exercise patterns in the natural environment. *American Journal of Psychiatry, 137*, 1540–1545.

Bruce, E. H., Frederick, R., Bruce, R. A., & Fisher, R. (1976). Comparison of active participants and dropouts in CAPRI cardiopulmonary rehabilitation programs. *American Journal of Cardiology, 37*, 53–60.

Brunner, B. C. (1969). Personality and motivating factors influencing adult participation in vigorous physical activity. *Research Quarterly, 40*, 464–469.

Canada Fitness Survey. (1983). *Fitness and lifestyle in Canada*. Ottawa, Ontario: Fitness and Amateur Sport, Government of Canada.

Collins, B. E. & Hoyt, M. F. (1972). Personal responsibility for consequences: An integration and extension of the "forced compliance" literature. *Journal of Experimental Social Psychology, 8*, 558–593.

Cooper, K. (1977). *The new aerobics*. New York: Bantam Books.

Cox, M. H. (1984). Fitness and life-style programs for business and industry: Problems in recruitment and retention. *Journal of Cardiac Rehabilitation, IV, 4*, (part 1), 136–142.

Criqui, M. H., Wallace, R. B., Heiss, G., Mishkel, M., Schonfeld, G., & Jones, G. (1980). Cigarette smoking and plasma high-density lipoprotein cholesterol. *Circulation, 62*, 72–76 (Supplement).

Csikszentmihalyi, M. (1975). *Beyond boredom and anxiety: the experience of play in work and games*. San Francisco: Jossey-Bass.

Danielson, R. R., & Wanzel, R. S. (1977). Exercise objectives of fitness program dropouts. In D. M. Landers & R. W. Christina (Eds.), Psychology of motor behavior and sport (pp. 310–320). Champaign, Illinois: Human Kinetics.

Davidson, A. R., & Jaccard, J. J. (1975). Population psychology: A new look at an old problem. *Journal of Personality and Social Psychology, 31*, 1073–1082.

Deci, E. (1975). *Intrinsic motivation*. New York: Plenum.

Department of Youth, Sport and Recreation. (1975). *Attitudinal study: Fitness and recreation in Victoria*. Melbourne: Department of Youth, Sport and Recreation, Government of Victoria.

Dishman, R. K. (1978). Aerobic power, estimation of physical ability, and attraction to physical activity. *The Research Quarterly, 49(3)*, 285–292.

Dishman R. K. (1981). Biologic influences on exercise adherence. *Research Quarterly for Exercise and Sport, 52*, 143–159.

Dishman, R. K. (1982). Compliance/adherence in health-related exercise. *Health Psychology, 1*, 237–267.

Dishman, R. K. (1986). Exercise adherence. In W. P. Morgan & S. N. Goldston (Eds.), *Exercise and mental health* (pp. 98–157). Washington, DC: Hemisphere Publishing.

Dishman, R. K., & Gettman, L. R. (1980). Psychobiologic influences on exercise adherence. *Journal of Sport Psychology, 2,* 295–310.

Dishman, R. K., & Ickes, W. J. (1981). Self-motivation and adherence to therapeutic exercise. *Journal of Behavioral Medicine, 4,* 421–438.

Dishman, R. K., Ickes, W. J. & Morgan, W. P. (1980). Self-motivation and adherence to habitual physical activity. *Journal of Applied Social Psychology, 10,* 115–131.

Dishman, R. K., Sallis, J. F., & Orenstein, D. R. (1985). *Public Health Reports, 100(2),* 158–171.

Dixon, M. (1985). Psychosocial influences on male involvement in physical activity at mid-life: Theoretical considerations. Unpublished doctoral dissertation, University of Alberta, Edmonton.

Epstein, L. H., Wing, R. R., Thompson, J. K., & Griffin W. (1980). Attendance and fitness in aerobic exercise: The effects of contract and lottery procedures. *Behavior Modification, 4,* 465–479.

Faulkner, R. A., & Stewart, G. W. (1978). Exercise programmes—recruitment/retention of participants. *Recreation Canada, 36(3),* 21–27.

Feltz, D., & Petlichkoff, L. (1983). Perceived competence among interscholastic sport participants and dropouts. *Canadian Journal of Applied Sport Sciences, 8,* 232–235.

Fishbein, M. (1972). Toward an understanding of family planning behaviors. *Journal of Applied Social Psychology, 2,* 214–227.

Fishbein, M. (1973). The prediction of behavior from attitudinal variables. In C. D. Mortenson & K. K. Sereno (Eds.), *Advance in communication research* (pp. 3–31). New York: Harper & Row.

Fishbein, M. (1980). A theory of reasoned action: Some applications and implications. In M. M. Page (Ed.), *Nebraska symposium on motivation, 1979* (pp. 65–116). Lincoln, Nebraska: University of Nebraska Press.

Fishbein, M., & Ajzen, I. (1974). Attitudes toward objects as predictors of single and multiple behavioral criteria. *Psychological Review, 81,* 59–74.

Fishbein, M., & Ajzen, I. (1975). *Belief, attitude, intention and behavior: An introduction to theory and research.* Reading, MA: Addison-Wesley.

Fitness Ontario. (1981a). *Physical activity patterns in Ontario.* Toronto: Ministry of Culture and Recreation, Government of Ontario.

Fitness Ontario. (1981b). *Physical activity: Reaching adults who know, but don't do.* Toronto: Ministry of Culture and Recreation, Government of Ontario.

Fitness Ontario. (1982). The relationship between physical activity and other health-related lifestyle behaviors. A research report from the Ministry of Culture and Recreation, Sports and Fitness Branch, Government of Ontario. Toronto, Ontario.

Fitness Ontario. (1983). *Physical activity patterns in Ontario - II.* Toronto: Ministry of Tourism and Recreation, Government of Ontario.

Fitness Ontario. (1984). *Physical activity patterns in Ontario - IIa (1982–83 update).* Toronto: Ministry of Tourism and Recreation, Government of Ontario.

Folkins, C. H., & Sime, W. E. (1981). Physical fitness training and mental health. *American Psychologist, 36,* 373–389.

Frankel, H. M. (1984). Unpublished observations, Kaiser-Permanente, Center for Health Research, Portland, OR. Cited in Dishman, R. K., Sallis, J. F., & Orenstein, D. R. (1985). The determinants of physical activity and exercise. *Public Health Reports, 100(2),* 158–171.

Franklin, B. (in press). Exercise program compliance: Improvement strategies. In J. Storbic, H. Jordan, & D. Wison (Eds.), *Obesity: Practical approaches to treatment.*

Gale, J. B., Eckhoff, W. T., Mogel, S. F., & Rodnick, J. E. (1984). Factors related to adherence to an exercise program for healthy adults. *Medicine and Science in Sports and Exercise, 16,* 544–549.

The Gallup Poll. (1977). Exercise, pp. 1200–1202.

The Gallup Poll. (1980). Sports, pp. 109–111.

The Gallup Poll. (1983). Jogging/Exercise, pp. 16–17.

The General Mills American family report, 1978–1979: Family health in an era of stress. (1979). Yankelovich, Skelly and White, Inc., New York.

Gettman, L. R., Pollock, M. L., & Ward, A. (1983). Adherence to unsupervised exercise. *The Physician and Sportsmedicine, 11(10),* 56–66.

Godin, G., Cox, M., & Shephard, R. J. (1983). The impact of physical fitness evaluation on behavioral intentions towards regular exercise. *Canadian Journal of Applied Sport Sciences, 8,* 240–245.

Godin, G., & Shephard, R. J. (1983). Physical fitness promotion programmes: Effectiveness in modifying exercise behavior. *Canadian Journal of Applied Sport Sciences, 8(2),* 104–113.

Goodrick, G. K., Warren, D. R., Hartung, G. H. & Hoepfel, J. A. (1984, February). Helping adults to stay physically fit: Preventing relapse following aerobic exercise training. *JOPERD,* 48–49.

Gordis, L. (1979). Conceptual and methodologic problems in measuring patient compliance. In R. B. Haynes, D. W. Taylor, & D. L. Sackett (Eds.), *Compliance in health care* (pp. 23–45). Baltimore: Johns Hopkins University Press.

Graham, J. H. (1979). The effects of a decision of balance-sheet intervention upon exercise adherence of high and low self-motivated females. Unpublished M. A. thesis, University of Alberta, Edmonton.

Green, L. W. (1977). Evaluation and measurement: Some dilemmas for health education. *American Journal of Public Health, 67(2).* 155–161.

Gwinup, G. (1975). Effect of exercise alone on the weight of obese women. *Archives of Internal Medicine, 135,* 676–680.

Hanson, M. G. (1976). Coronary heart disease, exercise, and motivation in middle-aged males. Unpublished Ph.D. dissertation, University of Wisconsin, Madison.

Harris, D. (1970). Physical activity history and attitudes of middle-aged men. *Medicine and Science in Sports, 2,* 203–208.

Heinzelmann, F. (1973). Social and psychological factors that influence the effectiveness of exercise programs. In J. L. Naughton & H. K. Hellerstein (Eds.), *Exercise testing and exercise training in coronary heart disease.* New York: Academic Press.

Heinzelmann, F., & Bagley, R. W. (1970). Response to physical activity programs and their effects on health behavior. *Public Health Reports, 85(10),* 905–911.

Henderson, J. (1980). Rolling out the red carpet with F.I.T.N.E.S.S. In R. R. Danielson & K. F. Danielson (Eds.), *Fitness motivation: Proceedings of the Geneva Park workshop.* Toronto: ORCOL.

Hoyt, M. F., & Janis, I. L. (1975). Increasing adherence to a stressful decision via a motivational balance-sheet procedure: A field experiment. *Journal of Personality and Social Psychology, 35(5),* 833–839.

Hunt, W. A., & Bespalec, D. A. (1974). An evaluation of current methods of modifying smoking behavior. *Journal of Clinical Psychology, 30,* 431–438.

Ingjer, F., & Dahl, H. A. (1979). Dropouts from an endurance training program. *Scandinavian Journal of Sports Sciences, 1,* 20–22.

Jaccard, J. J., & Davidson, A. R. (1972). Toward an understanding of family planning behaviors: An initial investigation. *Journal of Applied Social Psychology, 2,* 228–235.

Janis, I. L. (1968). Attitude change via role playing. In R. P. Abelson et al. (Eds.), *Theories of cognitive consistency: A sourcebook.* Chicago: Rand-McNally.

Janis, I. L. (1983). *Short-term counseling: Guidelines based on recent research.* New Haven: Yale University Press.

Kannel, W. B., & Sorlie, P. (1979). Some health benefits of physical activity: The Framingham study. *Archives of Internal Medicine, 139,* 857–861.

Kau, M. L., & Fisher, J. (1974). Self-modification of exercise behavior. *Journal of Behavior Therapy and Experimental Psychiatry, 5,* 213–214.

Kavanagh, T., Shephard, R. J., Doney, H., & Pandit, V. (1973). Intensive exercise in coronary rehabilitation. *Medicine and Science in Sports, 5,* 34–39.

Keefe, F. J., & Blumenthal, J. A. (1980). The life fitness program: A behavioral approach to making exercise a habit. *Journal of Behavior Therapy and Experimental Psychiatry, 11,* 31–34.

Keith, J. A., Spurgeon, J. H., Blair, S. M., & Carter, L. W. (1974). Motivational differentials among physically active and inactive mature males as measured by the Motivational Achievement Test. *The Research Quarterly, 45(3),* 217–223.

Kelly, J. R. (1974). Socialization toward leisure: A developmental approach. *Journal of Leisure Research, 6,* 181–193.

Kelly, J. R. (1977). Leisure socialization: Replication and extension. *Journal of Leisure Research, 9,* 121–132.

Kenyon, G. S. (1968a). A conceptual model for characterizing physical activity. *Research Quarterly, 39,* 96–105.

Kenyon, G. S. (1968b). Six scales for assessing attitude toward physical activity. *Research Quarterly, 39,* 566–574.

Kenyon, G. S. (1970). Attitude toward sport and physical activity among adolescents from four English speaking countries. In G. Lushen (Ed.), *Sport and games in their cross-cultural appearances.* Champaign, IL: Stipes.

Kenyon, G. S. (1971). Individual adjustment in culture and society. In L. A. Larson (Ed.), *Encyclopedia of sport sciences and medicine.* New York: MacMillan.

Kindl, M., & Brown, P. (1976). The team approach—the effective treatment of obesity in the community. *CAHPER Journal, 43(1),* 39–41, 44.

Kirshenbaum, D. S., Tomarken, A. J., & Ordman, A. M. (1982). Specificity of planning and choice applied to adult self-control. *Journal of Personality and Social Psychology, 42,* 576–585.

Kirshenbaum, J., & Sullivan, R. (1983). Hold on there America. *Sports Illustrated, 7,* 60–74.

Lalonde, M. (1974). *A new perspective on the health of Canadians.* Ottawa: Information Canada.

Locke, E. A., Shaw, K. N., Saari, L. M., & Latham, G. P. (1981). Goal setting and task performance: 1969–1980. *Psychological Bulletin, 90,* 125–152.

Martens, R. (1975). *Social psychology and physical activity.* New York: Harper & Row.

Martin, J. E. (1981). Exercise management: Shaping and maintaining physical fitness. *Behavioral Medicine Advances, 4,* 3–5.

Martin, J., & Dubbert, P. (1982). Exercise applications and promotion in behavioral medicine: Current status and future directions. *Journal of Consulting and Clinical Psychology, 50,* 1004–1017.

Martin, J., Dubbert, P. M., Katell, A. D., Thompson, J. K., Raczynski, J. R., Lake, M., Smith, P. O., Webster, J. S., Sikora, T., & Cohen, R. E. (1984). The behavioral control of exercise in sedentary adults: Studies 1 through 6. *Journal of Consulting and Clinical Psychology, 52,* 795–811.

Massie, J. F., & Shephard, R. J. (1971). Physiological and psychological effects of training. *Medicine and Science in Sports, 3,* 110–117.

May, J., & Albinson, J. G. (1980). Self-efficacy as a factor in selection of physical activity for women. Paper presented at the Canadian Society for Psychomotor Learning and Sport Psychology annual conference, Vancouver, British Columbia.

McPherson, B. D. (1984, July). Sport, health, well-being and aging: Some conceptual and methodological issues and questions for sport scientists. Paper presented at the Olympic Scientific Congress, Eugene, OR.

The Miller Lite report on American attitudes toward sports. (1983). Milwaukee, WI, Miller Brewing Co.

Mishel, W. (1968). *Personality and assessment.* New York: Wiley.

Montoye, J. H., Van Huss, W. D., Olson, H., Pierson, W. R., & Hudec, A. (1957). *Longevity and morbidity of college athletes.* Indianapolis: Phi Epsilon Kappa.

Morgan, W. P. (1977). Involvement in vigorous physical activity with special reference to adherence. In L. I. Gedvilas & M. E. Kneer (Eds.), *National college physical education association proceedings*. Chicago: University of Illinois.

Morgan, W. P., & Pollock, M. L. (1978). Physical activity and cardiovascular health: Psychological aspects. In F. Landry & W. Orban (Eds.), *Physical activity and human well-being (Vol. 1)*. Miami: Symposia Specialists.

Morgan, P. P., Shephard, R. J., Finucane, R., Schimmelfing, L., & Jazmaji, V. (1984). Health beliefs and exercise habits in an employee fitness programme. *Canadian Journal of Applied Sport Services, 9*, 87–93.

Neale, D. C., Sonstroem, R. J., & Metz, K. F. (1969). Physical fitness, self-esteem, and attitudes toward physical activity. *The Research Quarterly, 40*(1), 743–749.

Nielsen, A. B. (1974). Physical activity patterns of senior citizens. Unpublished Master's thesis, University of Alberta, Edmonton.

Nye, G. R., & Poulsen, W. T. (1974). An activity programme for coronary patients: A review of morbidity, mortality, and adherence after five years. *New Zealand Medical Journal, 79*, 1010–1020.

O'Connell, J. K., & Price, J. H. (1982). Health locus of control of physical fitness-program participants. *Perceptual Motor Skills, 55*, 925–926.

Oldridge, N. B. (1979). Compliance in exercise rehabilitation. *The Physician and Sports-medicine, 7*, 94–103.

Oldridge, N. B. (1982). Compliance and exercise in primary and secondary prevention of coronary heart disease: A review. *Preventive Medicine, 11*, 56–70.

Oldridge, N. B. (1984). Compliance and dropout in cardiac exercise rehabilitation. *Journal of Cardiac Rehabilitation, 4*, 166–177.

Oldridge, N. B., & Jones, N. L. (1983). Improving patient compliance in cardiac rehabilitation: Effects of written agreement and self-monitoring. *Journal of Cardiac Rehabilitation, 3*, 257–262.

Oldridge, N. B., Wicks, J. R., Hanley, R., Sutton, J., & Jones, N. (1978). Non-compliance in an exercise rehabilitation program for men who have suffered a myocardial infarction. *Canadian Medical Association Journal, 118*, 361–364.

Oldridge, N. B., Donner, A., Buck, C. W., Jones, N. L., Andrew, G. A., Parker, J. O., Cunningham, D. A., Kavanagh, T., Rechnitzer, P. A., & Sutton, J. R. (1983). Predictive indices for dropout: The Ontario exercise heart collaborative study experience. *American Journal of Cardiology, 51*, 70–74.

Olson, J. M., & Zanna, M. P. (1982). Predicting adherence to a program of physical exercise: An empirical study. Report to the Ontario Ministry of Tourism and Recreation, Government of Ontario, Toronto, Ontario.

Paffenbarger, R. S., Hale, W. E., Brand, R. J., & Hyde, R. T. (1977). Work-energy level, personal characteristics and fatal heart attack: A birth-cohort effect. *American Journal of Epidemiology, 105*, 200–213.

Palm, J. (1978). Mass media and the promotion of sports for all. In F. Landry & W. Orban (Eds.), *Physical activity and human well being* (pp. 273–279). Miami, FL: Symposium Specialists.

Pennebaker, J. W., & Lightner, J. M. (1980). Competition of internal and external information in an exercise setting. *Journal of Personality and Social Psychology, 39*, 165–174.

The Perrier study: Fitness in America. (1979). Perrier-Great Waters of France, Inc., New York.

Perrin, B. (1979). Survey of physical activity in the regional municipality of Waterloo. *Recreation Research Review, 6*(4), 48–52.

Pollock, M. L., Gettman, L. R., Milesis, C. A., Bah, M., Durstine, L., & Johnson, M. (1977). Effects of frequency and duration of training on attrition and incidence of injury. *Medicine and Science in Sports, 9*, 31–36.

Pollock, M. L., Foster, D., Salisbury, K., & Smith, R. (1982). Effects of a YMCA starter fitness program. *The Physician and Sports Medicine, 10*, 89–102.

Riddle, P. K. (1980). Attitudes, beliefs, behavioral intentions and behaviors of women and men toward regular jogging. *Research Quarterly for Exercise and Sport, 51(4)*, 663–674.

Roberts, G. C., & Duda, J. A. (1984). Motivation in sport: The mediating role of perceived ability. *Journal of Sport Psychology, 6*, 312–324.

Robinson, T. T., & Carron, A. V. (1982). Personal and situational factors associated with dropping out versus maintaining participation in competitive sport. *Journal of Sport Psychology, 4*, 364–378.

Rushall, B. S. (1973). The status of personality research and application in sports and physical education. *Journal of Sports Medicine, 13*, 281–290.

Shephard, R. J. (in press). Exercise adherence in corporate settings—personal traits and program barriers. In R. K. Dishman (Ed.), *Exercise adherence and public health*. Champaign, IL: Human Kinetics.

Sidney, K. H., & Shephard, R. J. (1976). Attitude toward health and physical activity in the elderly: Effects of a physical training program. *Medicine and Science in Sports, 8*, 246–252.

Simon, J. A., & Smoll, F. L. (1974). An instrument for assessing children's attitudes toward physical activity. *Research Quarterly, 45*, 407–415.

Snyder, E. E., & Spreitzer, E. E. (1979). Lifelong involvement in sport as a leisure pursuit: Aspects of role construction. *Quest, 31(1)*, 57–70.

Snyder, E. E., & Sprietzer, E. E. (1984). Patterns of adherence to a physical conditioning program. *Sociology of Sport Journal, 1*, 103–116.

Sonstroem, R. J. (1974). Attitude testing examining certain psychological correlates of physical activity. *The Research Quarterly, 45*, 93–103.

Sonstroem, R. J. (1978). Physical estimation and attraction scales: Rationale and research. *Medicine and Science in Sports, 10*, 97–102.

Sonstroem, R. J., & Kampper, K. P. (1980). Prediction of athletic participation in middle school males. *Research Quarterly for Exercise nd Sport, 51*, 685–694.

Sonstroem, R. J., & Walker, M. I. (1973). Relationship of attitudes and locus of control to exercise and physical fitness. *Perceptual and Motor Skills, 36*, 1031–1034.

Statistics Canada. (1978). *Culture statistics: Recreational activities. Ottawa*.

Stone, W. (1983, August/September). Predicting who will drop out. *Corporate Fitness and Recreation, 31*–35.

Teraslinna, P. T., Partanen, T., Koskela, A., & Oja, P. (1969). Characteristics affecting willingness of executives to participate in an activity program aimed at coronary heart disease prevention. *Journal of Sports Medicine and Physical Fitness, 9*, 224–229.

Thompson, C. E., Wankel, L. M. (1980). The effects of perceived choice upon frequency of exercise behaviour. *Journal of Applied Social Psychology, 19*, 436–443.

Triandis, H. (1971). *Attitude and attitude change*. New York: John Wiley & Sons.

Turner, R. D., Polly, S., & Sherman, A. R. (1976). A behavioral approach to individualized exercise programming. In J. D. Krumboltz & C. E. Thoreson (Eds.), *Counseling methods*. New York: Holt, Rinehart and Winston.

United States Department of Health, Education and Human Services. (1983). Promoting health/preventing disease. Public health service implementation plans for attaining the objectives for the nation. Public Health Reports, (September—October; supplement).

Wallston, B. S., Wallston, K. A., Kaplan, G. D., & Maides, S. A. (1976). Development and validation of the health locus of control (HLC) scale. *Journal of Consulting and Consulting and Clinical Psychology, 44*, 580–585.

Wallston, K., Wallston, D., & Devalis, R. (1978). Development of the multi-dimensional health locus of control (MHLC) scales. *Health Education Monographs, 6*, 160–170.

Wankel, L. M. (1979). Motivating involvement in adult physical activity programs. *Recreation Research Review, 6(4)*, 40–43.

Wankel, L. M. (1980). Involvement in vigorous physical activity: Considerations for enhancing self-motivation. In R.R. Danielson & K. F. Danielson (Eds.), *Fitness motivation: Proceedings of the Geneva Park Workshop*. Toronto: ORCOL.

Wankel, L. M. (1984). Decision-making and social support strategies for increasing exercise adherence. *Journal of Cardiac Rehabilitation, 4,* 124–135.

Wankel, L. M. (1985). Personal and situational factors affecting exercise involvement: The importance of enjoyment. *Research Quarterly for Exercise and Sport, 56(3),* 275–282.

Wankel, L. M. (in press). Exercise adherence and leisure activity: Patterns of involvement and interventions to facilitate regular activity. In R. K. Dishman (Ed.), *Exercise adherence and public health.* Champaign, IL: Human Kinetics.

Wankel, L. M., & Beatty, B. D. (1975). Behavior intentions and attendance of an exercise program: A field test of Fishbein's model. in *Mouvement, actes du 7e Symposium Canadien en Apprentissage PsychoMoteur et Psychologie du Sport,* October. 381–386.

Wankel, L. M., & Kreisel, P. S. J. (1983). A comparison of the effectiveness of structured social support and group decision balance-sheet approaches to motivating exercise adherence. Unpublished research report prepared for Fitness and Amateur Sport, Canada, Project #218, Ottawa, Ontario.

Wankel, L. M., & McEwan, R. (1978). The effects of privately and publicly set goals upon athletic performance. In F. Landry & W. A. R. Orban (Eds.), *Motor learning, sport psychology, pedagogy and didactics of physical activity, (pp. 327–334). Miami, FL: Symposia Specialists.*

Wankel, L. M., & Thompson, C. E. (1977). Motivating people to be physically active: Self-persuasion vs. balanced decision-making. *Journal of Applied Social Psychology, 7,* 332–340.

Wankel, L. M., & Yardley, J. K. (1982, August). An investigation of the effectiveness of a structured social support program for increasing exercise adherence of high and low self-motivated adults. Paper presented at the Canadian Parks/Recreation Association National Conference, Saskatoon, Saskatchewan.

Wankel, L. M., Yardley, J. K., & Graham, J. (1985). The effects of motivational interventions upon the exercise adherence of high and low self-motivated adults. *Canadian Journal of Applied Sport Sciences, 10(3),* 147–156.

Wanzel, R. S. (1977). Factors related to withdrawal from an employee fitness program. Paper presented at the American Association for Leisure and Recreation National Conference., Seattle, WA.

Wanzel, R. S. (1978). Toward preventing dropouts in industrial and other fitness programs. *Recreation Canada, 36(4),* 39–42.

Ward, A., & Morgan, W. P. (1984). Adherence patterns of healthy men and women enrolled in an adult exercise program. *Journal of Cardiac Rehabilitation, 4,* 143–152.

Waters, H. F., Whitman, L., Martin, A. R., & Gram, D. (1977, May 23). Keeping fit: America tries to shape-up. *Newsweek,* 78–86.

Weinberg, R. S., Smith, J., Jackson, A., & Gould, D. (1984). Effect of association, dissociation, and positive self-talk strategies on endurance performance. *Canadian Journal of Applied Sport Sciences, 9(1),* 25–32.

Wilhelmson, L., Sanne, H., Elmfeldt, D., Grimby, G., Tibblin, G., & Wedel, H. (1975). A controlled trial of physical training after myocardial infarction: Effects on risk factors, nonfatal reinfarction, and death. *Preventive Medicine, 4,* 491–508.

Wysocki, T., Hall, G., Iwata, B., & Riordan, M. (1979). Behavioral management of exercise: Contracting for aerobic points. *Journal of Applied Behavior Analysis, 12,* 55–64.

Yoesting, D. R., & Burkhead, D. L. (1973). Significance of childhood recreation experience on adult leisure behavior: An exploratory analysis. *Journal of Leisure Research, 5,* 25–36.

Young, R. J., & Ismail, A. H. (1977). Comparison of selected physiological and personality variables in regular and non-regular adult male exercisers. *Research Quarterly, 48,* 617–622.

Zuckerman, M., & Reis, H. T. (1978). Comparison of three models for predicting altruistic behavior. *Journal of Personality and Social Psychology, 36,* 498–510.

MANAGING ORGANIZATIONAL CULTURE TO ENHANCE MOTIVATION

Martin L. Maehr

This chapter addresses the problem of organizational effectiveness.[1] It is concerned specifically with the role of management in increasing the effectiveness of the organization through enhancing motivation. While this chapter draws heavily on current research on work organizations, the central issues are of relevance to a broad array of "for profit" and "nonprofit" organizations: schools, social service organizations, as well as work organizations. Most, if not all such organizations have to be concerned with reaching certain goals—and surviving. Those who manage or lead these organizations have a common concern: what can be done to elicit the best efforts of the members of the organization toward the realization of the goals of the organization? Or, more specifically, what can those

Advances in Motivation and Achievement: Enhancing Motivation,
Volume 5, pages 287-320.
Copyright © 1987 by JAI Press Inc.
All rights of reproduction in any form reserved.
ISBN: 0-89232-621-2

who lead and manage do to enhance and focus the motivation of all concerned with the organization?

It is not at all unusual for managers and leaders to have little or no continuing or direct contact with the persons who do the basic work of the organization. The chief executive officers of large corporations, for example, do not regularly meet with the majority of their workers nor talk to them about their jobs. Characteristically, they can only deal with them through others, often through an elongated chain of command. As a result, they are hardly in a position to have much direct control over what goes on at the various work stations. In the nature of their jobs, they seldom see anyone who actually produces or sells the product that gives the company its *raison d'être*. Indeed, in many cases they may even try to avoid this knotty issue of worker motivation, commitment and morale, hoping perhaps that it will be handled by the personnel department or by automation. Yet, like leaders generally, they are, and have to be, concerned about the overall performance of the organization which they head. They are held accountable for any decline in worker productivity and with issues of motivation and morale. And, so, the question is inevitable . . . Is there anything that can be done by leaders and managers to affect what goes on ''in the trenches'' It is the purpose of this chapter to answer that question.

During the past several years our research group has concentrated a considerable portion of its efforts on this question. We have recently concluded an extensive study of motivation and achievement in the world of work and came to consider especially the question of why certain organizations managed to elicit the best efforts of their personnel—and why others did not. In this chapter I wish to consider two general conclusions that have emerged from this research. First, commitment, satisfaction, productivity, and the overall effectiveness of an organization are strongly associated with the kind of social psychological climate, the ''culture,'' that exists in the organization. Second, this climate, or what I prefer to call ''culture,'' is a controllable force. Specifically, it can be affected positively and negatively by what the leadership of the organization does. There are steps that can be taken by those who lead and manage which can and will affect organizational culture and in turn enhance motivation and overall performance in the pursuit of the goals of the organization.

The first purpose of this chapter is to present a summary of the research which leads to these assertions. A second purpose is to suggest how managers and administrators—leaders—can use this information in creating an organizational culture which optimizes motivation.

ON THE NATURE OF MOTIVATION

This chapter focuses on motivation as a prime mediating cause of organizational effectiveness. Before considering how organizations can affect motivation it is advisable to specify ''motivation,'' a term which has been subjected to a variety of definitions (cf. Deci & Ryan, 1985; Maehr & Braskamp, 1986; Kleiber & Maehr, 1985; McClelland, 1985b).

Motivation as Personal Investment

While few would ignore the possible importance of something generally termed "motivation" in determining organizational effectiveness, not all would agree on what this important something is. Commonly, it is assumed that motivation has something to do with inner states of the person such as needs, drives, psychic energies, or forces. Admittedly, when researchers or laypersons talk about motivation, that kind of language is often used. But these terms represent inferences from certain *behavioral patterns*. It is possible that disagreement and confusion about the nature and definition of motivation is a product of not considering precisely what it is that causes us to infer motivation. What is the observation, the perceived behavior, that causes us to believe that motivation is or is not present in a particular person or group?

References to motivation seem to encompass a wide variety of activities. Closer scrutiny of these references and activities, however, indicates that the term motivation is more precisely associated with a certain limited set of behavioral patterns. More precisely, it may be suggested that references to "motivation" tend to arise out of observations regarding five distinguishable behavioral patterns: choice, persistence, continuing motivation, intensity, and performance (cf. Maehr & Braskamp, 1986). Examples of these behavioral patterns in the case of on-the-job performance in a well-established work role are presented in Table 1.

On the surface these behavioral patterns may seem diverse. Yet, there is a certain commonality suggested therein. They each indicate how and to what extent individuals *invest* themselves in any given activity. Indeed, as we observe individuals apparently making choices, persisting at tasks, and exhibiting varying

Table 1.   Secretarial Behaviors Illustrative of Nature and Level of Personal Investment

General Categories	Illustrative Examples
Choice	Absenteeism
Persistence	Length of Service
Continuing Motivation	Participate Voluntarily in skill upgrading programs
	Takes work home on occasion
Activity Level	Pages typed
Performance	Overall performance rating of superior

levels of intensity, a convenient metaphor comes to mind. Persons can and do invest resources, such as money, in a variety of ways. They can and do also invest such personal resources as time and energy in a variety of ways. When observing the distribution of time and energy, one might suggest that the individual is in effect investing his/her personal resources in a certain manner. Observations of intensity possibly suggest that not only the direction but also the amount of resources is important. In any event the term *personal investment* is one that we have found to be convenient for summing up the kind of behavior that gives rise to motivational inferences.

It may also be noted that the use of the term personal investment is not just an attempt to be clever. There is more than style involved in the use of this term. In effect, a unique perspective on managing motivation is implicit in the term personal investment. The use of the term personal investment is designed to stress that motivation is particularly indicated by the kinds of choices that people make in their lives. Therewith, it is stressed that motivational "problems" are not, in the main, attributable to a *lack* in motivational potential. Rather, "motivational problems" are largely a matter of how people choose to invest their time and energy. Thus, when supervisors consider workers to be "un-motivated," they do so because they have observed that they are not directing their attention to assigned tasks. They are not *generally* passive or inactive. Indeed, in another context or on different types of jobs these same workers may be observed to show all the activity, persistence, and involvement that would elicit the characterization, "motivated." The point is that, for the most part, motivation cannot be appropriately viewed as something the person either has or doesn't have. Rather, people are differentially motivated depending on the situation. Boldly put, all exhibit these behaviors that reflect motivation under some conditions. Thus, the inevitable question of concern is—why in this but not that case? What is there about a particular job or job context that does not serve to elicit worker investment? There is not really anything "wrong" with the person—she is not lacking in drive, she is not lazy; she simply is not attracted to the task in this case. In such instances the manager may be well-advised to ask: What is there about the job or the job context that does not serve to elicit her investment?

Meaning Determines Personal Investment

The burden for change is placed especially on the situation. More particularly, the focus is placed on the *meaning* of the situation to the performer. What this situation means to the individual is the critical determinant of investment.

"Meaning" may mean different things. The theory of personal investment construes the term meaning to refer to certain thoughts and perceptions that the individual has in reference to a situation. Briefly, there are three types of thoughts that are especially important in this regard. First, there is the perception of options or action possibilities available in the situation. Individuals choose and act in terms of what they perceive as possible *and* acceptable. Thus, it may be impossible for an Iowa farmer on a third generation family farm to see himself as doing anything else but farming. It may be that he cannot see himself as successfully pursuing any other option; it may be that his own identity and that of his family is irrevocably tied to farming—it is the "right" thing to do and not to do it is to lose that identity. A personal investment perspective on motivation stresses the importance of considering such perceptions of options and alternatives in assessing the reasons for a course of action. They are a first and critical component of what is referred to as the meaning of the situation to the person.

A second meaning component consists of the thoughts that one has with reference to one's own person; broadly, one's self-concept. Maehr and Braskamp (1986) have suggested several aspects of selfhood that may be particularly important so far as motivation and personal investment are concerned. Included among these is a *sense of competence,* a belief in one's ability to do something if effort is put forth (cf. also, Covington, 1984; Nicholls, 1983; Nicholls & Miller, 1984).

Third and finally, there are reasons for, or personal goals in, performing the task. These are termed personal incentives and refer to the motivational focus of the activity: What does the person hope to get out of performing? What is defined as a "successful" or "unsuccessful" outcome? Examples of personal incentives commonly employed in current research on motivation and personal investment include seeking novelty or a challenge, doing better than others, pleasing one's peers, or obtaining financial benefits or rewards (cf. Braskamp & Maehr, 1985; Maehr, 1984b; Maehr & Braskamp, 1986).

Self-evidently, these three components are commonly featured in theories of motivation. They must be viewed as cognitions that operate collectively and interactively in mediating the personal investments that people make (cf. Maehr, 1983; Maehr, 1974b; Maehr & Braskamp, 1986).

Antecedents of Meanings and Personal Investment

Of course, there are a variety of factors that affect the meaning of the situation to the person. We can simplify this complexity of causes by referring to two basic causal categories: the *person* and the *situation.* And, as we concentrate specifically on personal investment in the world of work, we find it convenient to subdivide situation into *job* and *organization.*

Person.   First, it may be noted that individuals arrive at any specific situation with "experiential baggage." They have a history that has given them certain meaning biases, certain thoughts about themselves and about situations. They arrive at any scene with established beliefs about and definitions of success and failure. They vary in their sense of themselves as self-reliant and competent. And, they may also vary in their knowledge about, sensitivity to or preference for certain options. The point is that people are seldom, if ever, blank tablets so far as meaning is concerned. While these thoughts, perceptions—meanings— may at least have an initial effect on how they behave, personal investment theory stresses that they are cognitions. As such, they are in theory subject to change in response to changing contexts and circumstances. They are not qualities fixed in stone at an early age, though they do represent an important motivational bias.

Situation. Personal investment, then, is not solely and ineluctably determined by predispositions which a person brings to a situation. Personal investment is not just a function of "personality" or "character." It certainly is not something that is established irrevocably at an early age and which generalizes across all work and achievement contexts. It is sometimes tempting to suggest that some are simply more motivated than others and leave the discussion at that point. But such a simplistic analysis is misleading at best. In my opinion, it is downright wrong. Persons are motivated to a considerable degree depending on the situation. Thus, such features of the work context as well as the nature of the task to be done, with whom it is to be done and how it is to be done play a critical role in determining personal investment. One can design and redesign jobs to affect motivation and personal investment of workers (Hackman & Oldham, 1980). If, for example, the task is designed such that the worker has a wide degree of choice on how it will be done, a task personal incentive orientation is likely to emerge. Such an orientation should in turn lead to "internal motivation" (Hackman & Oldham, 1980) and to "continuing motivation" and commitment (Maehr, 1976; Maehr & Braskamp, 1986). Thus, it is not just what the person brings to the situation that is important; the nature of the situation itself is certainly also of importance. More specifically, one can identify features of the *job* and of the work *organization* that affect meaning and personal investment.

All in all, then, while personal predispositions may effect personal investment, personal investment theory stresses especially the importance of the performance context in defining meaning and personal investment.

A PERSPECTIVE ON MANAGEMENT

The term "management" refers to a variety of behaviors and responsibilities (see, for example, Mintzberg, 1973; Nadler, Hackman, & Lawler, 1979). Focusing particularly on its use in an organizational setting, the term management refers to a role that incorporates a variety of behaviors such as making decisions, resolving conflicts, exercising leadership, organizing work, exercising power. Basically, management focuses on the development and implementation of plans for the optimum use of available resources in furthering the purposes for which the organization exists. In this chapter the special concern is the optimum use of *human resources.* More specifically, the issue is, how does management enhance the personal investment of employees in accord with the organization's goals?

It should be evident that motivation is not a topic management can ignore. As one reviews studies of successful organizations, it is clear that those that are successful are successful largely because they are able to attract and retain the personal investment of their employees (see, for example, Peters & Austin, 1985; Peters & Waterman, 1982; Ouchi, 1981). Generally, managers and supervisors at all levels are expected to do something to enhance the motivation and personal investment of employees. Indeed, this may well be their primary task. Increasingly, there is a call for managers to be leaders (see, for example, Bass, 1985; Bennis, 1984; Sergiovanni & Corbally, 1984). It is implied that leadership means eliciting the "stuff" of motivation—involvement in the work at hand, commitment to the organization and concern with doing the job well. This chapter accepts that particular perspective on management as valid—as will become increasingly clear. The stress is on the manager—the leader—as motivator. The basis for the essential thrust of this chapter is that managers must direct themselves especially to eliciting the motivation—the personal investment—of all within the organization toward achieving the goals of the organization.

But how can this be done? What can leaders and managers do to enhance motivation and personal investment in accord with organizational goals? There is an ever-increasing literature directed toward answering such questions (see, for example, Bass, 1981, 1985; Kellerman, 1984; Yukl, 1981). This literature was alluded to in passing as the basic antecedents of personal investment were outlined. But more can and must be said in this regard on the way to making the special arguments of this chapter.

Strategies for Enhancing Motivation

Over the years a variety of strategies for initiating motivation change have been discussed, developed, and implemented. Reviewing what has been said in this regard one might suggest that in general there are thought to be three "pressure points" for change: the Person, the Job, and the Organization.

In the first case, one can view motivation as resting particularly in the individual and work on changing something about him or her. Or if change is not easy then one can concentrate on selecting the "right" persons; that is, persons who are judged likely to exhibit high motivation in the role assigned. In the main this has been the approach pursued by such notables in the area as David McClelland (1978, 1985a; McClelland & Winter, 1971).

The second and third possible pressure points for change involve the situation. In this case, the focus is not so much on the characteristics of individuals but on features of the situation that will bring about change. Within the broad category of "situation" one can specify two important subcategories. First, there is the *task*, the specific role to be played by the person, the job to be done. From the work of Hackman and Oldham (1980), as well as that of others, it is clear that there are a variety of things that can be done to change the task which will in turn affect motivation. Second, as will become increasingly evident in this chapter, the job situation, the task to be done or the role to be played, is not the sole determining feature of the context. The nature, structure, policies, goals, and values of the organization as a whole make a difference.

Most recently, the focus has been placed particularly on how individuals' thoughts about and perceptions of the situation mediate motivation. It is the *meaning* of the situation to individuals that determines motivation patterns. While persons do tend to bring a set of perceptual and cognitive biases to each new situation, these biases are, in principle, subject to change.

The pragmatic question for those who are in roles where they must manage motivation is whether it is more practical to change the situation or to select the persons who happen to hold the desired meaning biases. If the latter is chosen, enhancing motivation in an organization will involve especially a stress on

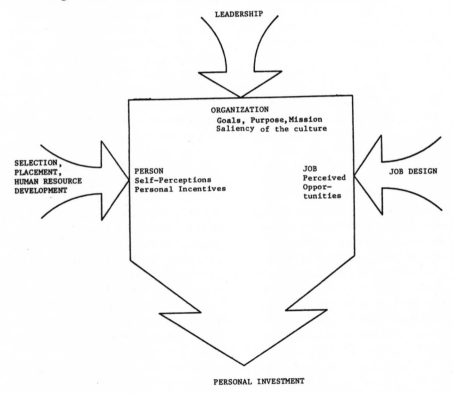

Figure 1. Pressure Points for Changing Personal Investment in an Organization

recruitment, personnel selection, or perhaps an emphasis on changing persons to fit job and organizational expectations. If the former strategy is pursued, then the stress is on changing the work situation—redesigning the job, changing the work climate, or designing the organizational culture to enhance motivation of all regardless of the motivational biases they may bring to the situation. An outline of perspectives and strategies that can be pursued in enhancing motivation in an organizational setting is presented in Figure 1.

While each of these strategies may have a role to play in managing motivation, I intend to focus on the possibility that leaders can have pervasive effects on the organizational context, the overall climate of the work place, which in turn will affect motivation and personal investment. Evidence will be presented in support of the argument that leaders can choose to play a special role in enhancing personal investment through establishing a culture that supports commitments to and encourages participation in the organization. What this means and how it can be done is the topic to which I now turn.

A CONCEPT OF ORGANIZATIONAL CULTURE

On the Concept of Culture

There is, of course, considerable precedent for specifying the concept of *culture*. This particular concept has been around for some time. More importantly, it is an established concept within the realm of social science theory and research. While that in no sense is meant to imply that there is universal agreement on the use of the term, there is firm basis for establishing a working definition that can ultimately prove useful in measurement and research. Following previous work (Maehr, 1974a), it may be suggested that culture is properly viewed in the first instance as a complex of norms extant within a given social organization or group. These norms, in turn, might be viewed as shared answers relative to basic questions confronting the organization or group. Norms are "answers" in the sense that they reflect a response to problems confronted by the group and the persons who compose that group; they reflect a choice that must be made in organizing individual and group behavior. But it should not be concluded that individuals are always fully cognizant of the problems that are being solved or the choices made. Often as not, a norm represents an unquestioned assumption about how things are to happen. It is an answer that is seen as inevitable.

The use of the term "culture," then, assumes that a certain group of individuals has been functioning in an interdependent fashion over a period of time. When such social interaction exists there will be normative products. That is, the group will arrive at ways of organizing itself, regularizing the behavior of its members, coordinating their functions, minimizing conflicts, etc. In sum, the group members work out ways of getting along among themselves. The answers that the group arrives at in this regard are a first type of normative product. A second type of normative product evolves out of concerns regarding how the group will relate to its environment. How will it survive in the wider world? Each social group arrives at some more or less agreed upon answers to such basic questions of existence. It produces guidelines or *norms* for dealing with, thinking about, and acting in reference to the problems of living. These norms, or *shared answers* to life's problems, are a critical if not *the* critical feature of a culture. Examples of such answers are beliefs about the nature of man—or the nature of employees. Are they basically trustworthy? Reliable? Responsible? Theories of management often revolve around such basic questions as well as questions regarding the nature of work: Is it a necessary obligation, a unique act? A necessary end? Or, is it a high calling, a means for self-definition and self-actualization, a social responsibility (cf. Maehr, 1974a, 1976)?

It is important to add that within any culture there is a need to communicate what the culture is, if indeed the culture is to persist and have relevance as a guideline for behavior. This is done in a variety of ways. Myths exist to describe heroes and, not incidentally, define what is worthy of emulation and worth striving for. Such heroes essentially define options, a range of possible behavior as well as suggest what one can hope for.

In a similar fashion, rituals and observances are not only designed to reinforce a view of the world in general, but also to encourage a notion of purposes in particular. This is what much of so-called religious life is about. But secular rites and rituals are often every bit as important as those found in churches and temples (see, for example, Boje, Fedor, & Rowland, 1982).

It is through the observation of rite and ritual that one can often best sense what the life of a social group is about. These activities reveal the basic answers of the group, its *culture*. They become opportunities for values to be expressed. Through these opportunities the group or organization expresses its purpose and describes its image. Thereby it says to all its participants: this is what we are striving for, what we want to be—*and* this is what will be recognized and rewarded. Thus, ritual, rite—*and* social observances of various types serve to reinforce meaning, particularly as they establish goals and define options.

In terms of personal investment theory it should be emphasized that culture provides general guidelines for establishing meanings. It defines options. It establishes the availability and desirability of goals and what is worth striving for. And within limits, it suggests ways in which individuals should define themselves as members of a social group. In this sense culture provides meaning for groups and individuals. Further, as culture establishes such meaning orientations it influences motivation and personal investment.

The Concept of Organizational Culture

It is on this tradition that concepts related to "organizational culture" tend to build. Thus, Whetten (1984) defines the culture of an organization as, "Taken for granted assumptions about shared beliefs, values and norms about the way things are (or should be) done around here." That is, he stresses the normative role of culture and notes the fact that shared expectations and guidelines for actions tend to exist within organizations that are in an important sense specific to and uniquely characteristic of that organization. Deal and Kennedy (1982) note this feature of organizations but also stress how these norms are communicated through rite, ritual, and myth. It is not only societies that sponsor rituals and create heroes for such purposes, organizations do this also. Example after example can be given of rituals that are standard in various companies, heroes who are promoted, and rites that are observed. And, as Deal and Kennedy point out, these events serve the purpose of defining the guidelines for all who participate in the organization. In a special way, they really define what is worth striving for within this context, what is expected and what will be rewarded. Friday afternoon "beer busts," as they apparently existed at Tandem Corporation (Deal & Kennedy, 1982), can serve to express a value of social interaction and of the worth of all in the organization. Thursday noon birthday lunches or coffee hours in an office can have similar effects. Such social events serve to point up the importance a company places on cooperative and effective social interaction on the part of all members of the organization. When such activities cut across levels of power and authority, one can also communicate the meaning that not only are all members of the organization important but also that all have a contribution to make. One may also communicate or reinforce the belief that mobility within the organization is a possibility. As these events occur in coordination with achievement or the striving to attain production goals, one can also encourage the belief that productivity is valued. To this it may be added that organizational culture can be thought of as providing a meaning base which guides personal investment. This occurs particularly as options are defined and incentives stressed. It also occurs as roles are assigned and status conferred.

The term "culture," then, is used to refer to the nature of an organization as a wholistic entity. As others (e.g., Goodenough, 1963, 1971; Schein, 1984, 1985) have suggested, the nature of a culture is best revealed in the norms of the group. It may be suggested further that norms can best be identified by the group members themselves. It is the "subjective culture" (Triandis et al, 1972) that is critical in understanding and predicting behavior, especially personal investment in the organization. While a broad range of norms must be considered as an integral part of organizational culture, consideration here can only be given to limited facets of the organizational culture. Given the present concern with motivation and personal investment, special attention will be devoted to those facets of the organizational culture which appear to be most important in this regard. Specifically, the focus will be on the shared perceptions of purposes and desired ends.

The Potential Utility of the Concept of Organizational Culture

There are a number of reasons for considering a construct such as organizational culture. Among these are the utility of the construct in approaching the potential problems of management. Managers and leaders need to develop a perspective of the organization that can be readily grasped by managers and leaders, grasped in such a way that they can operate effectively in terms of it. Thus, the use of the concept of organizational culture relates especially to an intention to describe an entity to which all of management can relate. The chief executive officer and senior level management of a corporation are particularly concerned with what they can do to enhance motivation and productivity. They are also concerned with commitment and morale. In most cases, however, they cannot or do not foresee the possibility of concerning themselves with specific job situations nor can they concern themselves with selecting all the "right" people. At best, they can select only a few. They can only directly affect the behavior of those with whom they must deal on a day-to-day, face-to-face, basis. And, that number is often quite limited.

Since senior level management cannot really expect to affect most workers in a direct and immediate fashion through job design or personnel selection, their attention is drawn to the effects of *organizational* changes on behavior. Basically, their concern is with how they can affect the overall context in which persons work and thereby, hopefully, influence morale and productivity. It is this problem of affecting the overall organizational context that the concept of organizational culture presumes to address.

ORGANIZATIONAL CULTURE, MEANING, AND PERSONAL INVESTMENT

Organizational Culture Can Be Assessed

While the study of organizational culture is still in its infancy, there are, nevertheless, several important conclusions that can be reached on the basis of results thus far. First, the concept of organizational culture appears to be viable. Previous research of a more ethnographic nature has indicated that companies may differ in shared assumptions, expectations, role relationships, and norms. For a variety of reasons, including sheer practicality in the use of the concept, it is important that recent research has also suggested that one can assess critical dimensions of organizational culture in a standardized and reliable fashion following accepted psychometric and survey research procedures (see, for example, Denison, 1984, 1985; Maehr & Braskamp, 1986). Indeed, one does well to note that while the concept of organizational culture is of relatively recent origin, there are precedents aplenty to guide the researcher in constructing psychometrically viable assessment procedures. A basis for the systematic assessment of culture generally is to be found, for example, in the work of Triandis et al. (1972). More specific to organizational culture per se, considerable work of relevance here has been conducted under such rubrics as organizational environments or climates (see, for example, Campbell, Dunnette, Lawler, & Weick, 1970; Cook, Hepworth, Wall, & Worr, 1981; James & Jones, 1974; Lawler, Hall, & Oldham, 1974; Schneider & Snyder, 1975; Stern, 1970).

In our research (Maehr & Braskamp, 1986), a specific attempt was made to focus the definition of organizational culture in such a way that it could be related specifically to motivational issues. In the course of our early work on motivation and personal investment in organizational settings, it became evident that individuals were not only willing to talk about themselves and their work, they were even more able and willing to talk about their workplace. Moreover, they seemed to be able to describe their place of work in terms of whether or not they could pursue options and incentives that were of importance to them. Often spontaneously, they could tell us not only about the incentives, rewards, and opportunities that existed in their specific job but could also tell us what the company as a whole seemed to be promoting or emphasizing. When they talked about incentives available in their job, these incentives seemed to parallel statements they were making about events that gave rise to a sense of success or satisfaction on their part. They expressed a greater or lesser degree of knowledge of what was stressed by the firm or company. They also could and did express how they personally related to company goals and incentive structures. Thus, we became increasingly fascinated by the possibility that goals and incentives structures evident to the employees or participants in an organization may be a most important feature of the organization—certainly so far as their own investment in the organization was concerned.

This is not to suggest that goals and incentives available within the organizational context are all that there is to the culture, but they apparently are a most important feature of anything that we may wish to define as organizational culture. In this regard it may be recalled that when the general nature of culture was discussed earlier, it was noted that the establishment and promotion of guidelines relative to what was worth striving for was an important dimension. Conceivably, one could specify such desiderata in terms of dimensions complementary to the designated personal incentive dimensions identified as important in human striving. And, in our work, we proceed to do just that. More specifically, we considered it logical to assume that different organizations would tend to emphasize different purposes and goals for working which would match the personal incentive dimensions that were seen as crucial in guiding personal investment.

Following this general line of reasoning, we then began to construct a series of questions about what was available to the worker in the organizational context, focusing especially on the pursuit of incentives and their availability. This eventuated in the development of a set of "organizational culture" scales, the technical features of which are set forth elsewhere (Braskamp & Maehr, 1985; Maehr & Braskamp, 1986). We were able to assess reliably the perceptions that individuals have of the company in which they work. Our work also indicated that the perceptions of the company paralleled the personal incentives that we had found to be associated with the behavior of individuals. That is, organizational values were found to match the personal incentives of persons. This complementarity of culture and person scales, of course, was not an altogether accidental finding, since we doubtless were biased in designing items so as to reflect compatible person and culture goals. But it is important that we could reasonably claim that individuals recognize categories of company goals which are comparable to the personal incentives that guide their personal investment.

In addition to identifying incentive dimensions that described organizations as they were perceived by workers, we also developed another type of scale for assessing organizations. There was reason to believe that the very saliency of an organizational culture in itself might be a critical factor. That was a point that was often made in ethnographic and other nonpsychometric studies (cf., for example, Deal & Kennedy, 1982; Peters & Waterman, 1982). Besides, it seems logical enough that companies may not only stress certain incentive possibilities or affirm certain purposes, goals, and values, but they may also stress, to a greater or lesser degree, what the company stands for. They may be more or less effective in communicating the *mission* (i.e., goals and purposes) of the organization. We chose also to assess the saliency of the culture directly by asking persons about their awareness of what the company stood for and what it promoted. As it turned out, this was a wise decision since the responses on the saliency scale proved to be quite interesting as well as useful in predicting certain patterns of behavior.

In summary, this basic approach and attendant efforts yielded reliably distinguishable dimensions of organizational culture. These dimensions are comparable to "personal incentives" which guide individual personal investment. Thus, as individuals may be guided especially by certain personal incentives, such as the intrinsic interest value of the job, so organizations may vary in the degree to which the work done there is interesting. They may vary in the stress on endeavoring to make work life challenging and in the degree to which the employee self-actualization is an object of concern. The organizational culture dimensions identified by Maehr and Braskamp (1986) are described and defined in Table 2.

In passing, it may be noted that these particular dimensions represent, of course, only one possible configuration of the dimension that may exist in organizations. They evolved from a specific attempt to understand the organization in terms of personal investment theory and therewith focus on dimensions that have been found useful in that context. Different dimensions have been designated by others (see, for example, Denison, 1984, 1985). But there is remarkable overlap in the research definition of appropriate organizational culture dimensions. Thus, while it would not be wise to assume that these dimensions are the final word on the topic, they may well be articulating major causes of organizational effects on motivation. At least, for now, that is a viable hypothesis.

Table 2. Description of the Four Organizational Culture Scales
and Sample Items

Description	Sample Items
Task	
Emphasis placed on excellence, doing the job right, trying new things, improving productivity.	Around here we are encouraged to try new things. Management expects us to be good productive workers.
Ego	
Emphasis on competition and contests among organizational units is encouraged, conflict is not to be avoided, overt recognition that there are powerful persons in the organization.	This organization establishes contests in which we compete for extra benefits. People spend a lot of time trying to know those who are in power.
Social	
Emphasis on a family feeling among the members, caring for and respecting each person as an adult, participation of all workers in decision making.	People have little trust in each other in this organization. In this organization, they really care about me as a person.
External Rewards	
Emphasis on giving each person attention, reinforcement, recognition, salary bonuses, and feedback about employee's work.	People here are always getting awards and extra benefits by doing good work. There are many incentives here to work hard.

Organizations Can Be Distinguished

It is important to note further that not only have certain possibly viable dimensions of organizations been identified but they have also been shown to reliably distinguish among organizations. Ethnographic studies and more informal analyses, of course, have argued extensively that organizations are different in their culture. But psychometric analyses have taken this a step further and begun to specify possible critical dimensions that in fact distinguish organizations. This has both theoretical and practical importance. Certainly, the ability to identify cultural dimensions through psychometric procedure enhances the utility of the concept. It makes it possible for managers to "diagnose" the organizational culture through standardized survey procedures much as they might assess employees' job satisfaction. Ethnographic research in organizations doubtless has its place. However, it is safe to assume that few managers would be inclined to hire an ethnographer to work in an organization for an extended period in order to sense the essence of the organization. So, the evolution of the possibility for standardized assessment is not only of theoretical interest but also of considerable practical significance.

In order to test the viability of these organizational culture dimensions, six companies were selected for intensive scrutiny. These companies were selected on the basis of extensive, independently derived, information that indicated that they varied in organizational culture. We then proceeded to administer the four-dimensional organizational culture scale to samples from each company to test whether this instrument could, in fact, distinguish these companies in a reasonable fashion. The companies selected for comparison are described in Table 3 and the pattern of results are summarized in Figure 2. Briefly, it was found that the organizational culture scales were able to distinguish companies as one might expect they should.

In addition to determining whether our scales could distinguish different companies in a reasonable and reliable fashion, we also explored the uniqueness and integrity of the construct as it was assessed through these scales. For example, we specifically considered whether the organizational culture scales assessed something different from that which one might obtain through averaging the personal incentive patterns of the people who worked in the organization. More informally put, we inquired whether the "personality" of the organization was something different than a mere summation of the personalities of the persons who happen to compose it.

Finally, we considered the pervasiveness of a perception of organizational culture across various levels in the work organization. The organizational culture construct itself implies some degree of generality across a social group, of course. But the degree to which the participants in this group adhere to a definition of the culture is in and of itself an interesting issue. For example, while there may be a broad base of agreement regarding what IBM or Proctor and Gamble are about, is there a slightly different understanding of the respective cultures in different organizational units within such organizations? Does the perception of organizational culture vary with the job held? Does it vary with status in the corporate hierarchy? Does it vary with being central or peripheral to the essential operations of the company?

Generally speaking, the results supported the conclusion that organizational culture is a viable construct in its own right. More specifically, evidence was found which indicated that perceptions of the particular job context was different from a perception of the broad organizational context or culture. Similarly, the organizational culture measure was something more than the summation of the personal incentives of the persons in the organization or the types of jobs performed.

Organizational Culture is Associated with Personal Investment

If organizations tend to have a distinctive organizational culture, does it have an influence on the worker? Specifically, how is organizational culture related to personal investment?

The "bottom line" in discussion of organizational culture has to be the effects

Table 3. Summary Description of Six Sample Organizations

Type of Company	Brief Description of Company	Type of Personnel Included in Sample
Commuter Airline	A family-owned company of 200 employees with $30 million annual revenue. Headquarters are located in relatively small midwestern city. Long history of safety.	Executives, Mechanics, Customer Service, Flight Crew
Health Care	A general care hospital of 200 beds located in a midwestern town of 35,000. It had recently initiated an agressive marketing campaign to increase its status within the community.	Executives, Department Directors, Middle Managers, Supervisors, Nursing Coordinators
Consulting Firm	A management consulting company which has grown to over 25 million annual sales in 20 years. The firm, which employs 360 persons and has its headquarters in a suburb of a large western city, has many affiliate offices throughout the world.	Executive, Sales, Research/Product Development
Trade Association	An established association that represents producers of a farm commodity. Headquarters are located in a large midwestern city, but branches are located throughout the world. The staff totals nearly 180 and the annual budget exceeds $15 million.	Executives, Middle Management
Manufacturing	The company, located in a small midwestern city, began as a family firm 60 years ago. Currently it has 600 employees and has revenue in data processing products exceeding $100 million. In the past 10 years the company has increased its sales by over 300%	Executives, Middle Management
Fast Food	The firm owns over 40 fast food restaurants under a franchise agreement with one of the largest national restaurant chains. The firm is located in a large East coast city, but owns restaurants in over 10 cities in 3 states. The firm is 10 years old with the original 3 owners still holding the leadership positions.	Executives, Middle Management

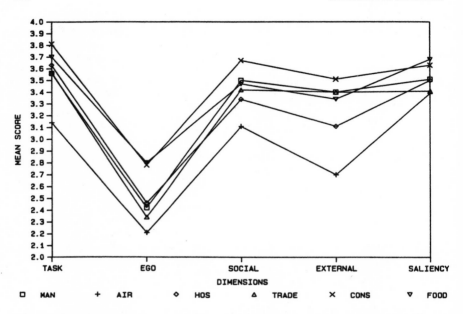

Figure 2. Average Scores on Organizational Culture and Saliency Scales of Employees in Six Organizations

on personal investment. There may be other reasons for defining and assessing organizational culture, but the ultimate question necessarily concerns whether variation in organizational culture eventuates in variation in personal investment. A next logical step in our research, then, was to relate these measures of organizational culture to measures of motivation and personal investment.

Generally, the results supported the hypothesis that differences in organizational culture were associated with differences in motivation and personal investment.

Saliency.   First, it was found that the very saliency of the organizational culture itself—apart from the specific content—seems to have important effects on personal investment. That is, when employees were aware that the organization stood for something, that it stressed certain values and goals, they were more likely to be personally invested in their work. As shown in Table 4, the workers' perception of the saliency of organizational culture is highly and positively related to both organizational commitment and job satisfaction.

This finding, of course, accords well with the ethnographic and more informal analyses of organizational culture. Deal and Kennedy (1982), Hackman, (1985), and Peters and Waterman (1982) have argued for the effects of making a company's values and mission salient to all who are involved in the corporate enterprise. Presumably, the good organizations *know* what they are about. This know-

Table 4. Correlations Among Organizational Culture, Saliency,
and Commitment

| | Organizational Culture | | | | | |
	Task	Ego	Social	External	Saliency	Commitment
Organizational Culture						
Task		00	81	76	65	64
Ego			−07	07	−12	−05
Social				81	67	67
External					62	67
Saliency						61
Commitment						

ing is present at all levels; it is not only knowledge privy to the leadership. Rather, a major function of leaders is to communicate the values and purposes to the other members of the organization. What we have found here is evidence that employees are likely to be more personally invested in the organization when the company's values are very self-evident and obvious to them. To put it differently, clear beliefs about the mission as well as the style of a company were associated with job satisfaction and organizational commitment. Thus, it appears that a strong organizational culture, regardless of what it is and how it is manifested, tends to elicit personal investment.

Organizational culture profile. Granted that the saliency of organizational goals and expectations is likely to be important, what possible effects might the different goals have? In this regard, the high correlations among the task, social, external rewards, and saliency organization culture dimensions might first of all be considered. Companies which communicate the value of challenge in work, social solidarity and make a point of recognizing and rewarding performance are also characterized by a salient culture. This may mean that it is as the company expresses itself clearly through these cultural dimensions that it will likely convey a sense of purpose and meaning to the employee. Perhaps it is through a special stress on these facets of the organizational culture that the mission of the organization is especially visible to the employee. And, as we shall soon see, it is to some extent the stress on these aspects of company life that organization commitment is engendered and job satisfaction enhanced. In any event, these are at the very least intriguing hypotheses about the nature of organizational culture and personal investment. Moreover, they are hypotheses that could effectively guide management practice.

But how might these different organizational culture goals influence personal investment directly? In order to determine this, a series of analyses was conducted. The purpose of these analyses was to determine the special effects of organizational culture apart from those that might be associated with the nature of the job or with individual differences in motivational orientation. In brief, it was found that three of the four organizational culture goal variables emerged as critical variables in predicting both job satisfaction and organizational commitment: task, social, and external. The ego culture goal variable appears to play no systematic role. The pattern of correlations presented in Table 4 reflects the general thrust of the results of the more complex multiple regression analyses that were conducted. Moreover, when we looked at these results more closely, scrutinizing individual items and examining interview protocols, we concluded that clear guidelines for management were evident. First, under the general rubric of task goals, it was clear that organizations that stressed excellence, innovation, and worker autonomy were most likely to elicit the personal investment of their workers. A stress on the contributions of the individual worker in improving the effectiveness of the organization was also found to be important. Thus, organizations that take seriously the possibility that employees at all levels are likely to have good ideas, were found to have satisfied and committed workers.

In examining more closely why the social aspects of the culture were associated, we found two things. First, employees were likely to be more personally invested in a place where people care about them and where their relationships with others is positive. But in the workplace at least, it seemed that it was important that this care also include the employer's keeping employees informed and involving them in decisionmaking. The latter finding is in accord with Denison's (1984, 1985) finding that *participation* was a critical organizational variable, one that led not only to high employee morale or organizational commitment but also to higher performance.

Finally, as we examined more closely what the overall association between the external goal dimension and personal investment might embrace, several things became evident. First, performance appraisal must eventuate in feedback to the employee. This feedback must not only be informative but also be visibly and logically tied to recognition and rewards. Such a pattern of results might suggest that one does well to maintain a strong merit-based system of performance evaluation and reward. But the results also suggested that some caution be exercised in introducing such a system. In our sample a stress on social competition within the organization was not a positive contribution to motivation and personal investment. Insofar as a merit-based or any other performance appraisal system emphasizes interpersonal competition, it may prove problematic—at least in the kind of organizations that were included in our organizational culture study sample. Moreover, somehow the evaluation-feedback process must stress the positive side of the individual's performance. One apparently does little to elicit the personal investment of workers by simply telling them they are worse than others. Rather, organizational commitment and job satisfaction seem to be enhanced when feedback and reward relate to the progress of the worker in a role. Additionally, if somehow supervisors can stress the positive side in evaluating performance, defining each work role as a special contribution to the overall enterprise, then worker motivation is likely to be enhanced.

All in all, what we seem to be picking up in these initial results on goal stresses within the culture of an organization is something very similar to what has been observed in a variety of studies on the effects of freedom, competition, and participation in a broad range of contexts with widely different individuals. Thus, the way our workers viewed evaluation and reacted to it appeared to be little different than the way students have been observed to react to evaluation and classroom climates stressing different performance goals (Ames, 1984; Ames & Ames, 1984; Covington & Omelich, 1984; Dweck, 1984; Dweck & Elliot, 1983; Maehr, 1983, 1984a). The sense that one has some autonomy as well as responsibility and plays a significant role seems as basic to the workplace as to other contexts.

Conclusion

Clearly, organizational culture is an entity that can be identified and assessed. It is not just a product of one's hunches or intuitions. While the research reviewed here is only in its initial stages, there are already important implications to be deduced—not only for further research but also for management practice. The continuing specification and study of organizations is, of course, necessary. Indeed, to a considerable degree the present chapter has suggested how that continuing work might proceed. But the promise of something more is already evident in the results. At the very least there is evidence that there is an organizational variable called organizational culture that is responsive to actions taken by management. What these actions might be will be suggested later in this chapter. At this point it suffices to underscore the significance of even these very preliminary results.

The Individual in the Organization

Inevitably, questions are raised regarding the "problem of the match" between person and environment. Specific to the present discussion, do individuals whose personal incentive profiles tend to match the goal profile of the organization also tend to be more invested in the organization?

Employing our data set, Mayberry (1985) conducted a series of sophisticated analyses directed toward answering this question. Briefly, Mayberry compared and contrasted a congruency (person-environment match) model with a separate components model for predicting job satisfaction and organizational commitment. That is, he first considered the effectiveness of personal incentives—organizational culture congruencies in predicting both job satisfaction and organizational commitment. The personal incentive-organizational congruency was indexed in terms of discrepancy scores on parallel personal incentive and organizational culture scales.

Having considered the effects of such congruencies, he next considered how organizational culture goals, irrespective of individual differences in personal incentive or personal incentive-cultural goal similarities/discrepancies, might serve to predict personal investment. He concluded that one could do at least as well or better in predicting job satisfaction and organizational commitment by simply looking at the scales measuring organizational culture without considering personal incentive orientations or personal incentive-organizational cultural discrepancies/similarities.

At first glance, these results may seem surprising. Matching models have held sway in a variety of different behavioral science research areas in recent years (see, for example, Endler, 1981; Miller, 1981). They have also played an important role in the analysis of organizational behavior as well (see, for example, Brousseau, 1983; Schein, 1978). Moreover, simple "common sense" would lead us to expect that congruency or matching models would ultimately prove most effective in predicting job satisfaction and organizational commitment. But these results suggest that the matching model is not always the most appropriate and useful one to employ. Nor are these findings readily attributable to the usual technical problems which beset congruency measures, since Mayberry used sophisticated scaling and analysis procedures that should have minimized the typical problems of enhanced error in combining two scales to form a congruency scale. Yet, it may well be that organizational culture, as it happened to be assessed in this particular research, does in fact have pervasive and widely generalizable effects on job satisfaction and organizational commitment.

If Mayberry's results are valid, then one is encouraged to focus on general facets of the workplace which are found to make a difference on employee behavior. One can focus on organizational culture variables and be confident of predictable efforts in the case of a broad spectrum of individuals. This makes these results directly applicable to the problems confronting the manager of a large organization. These results confirm ethnographic, case study, and even more informal observations of organizational processes to the effect that the organizational culture construct has important predictive and possibly causal validity so far as enhancing the personal investment of participants in the organization is concerned. Further, organizational culture seems to have a pervasive effect apart from the special needs and goals of individuals in reference to how they see their job or the organization as a whole.

In the final analysis, then, organizational culture dimensions by themselves deserve attention as antecedents of personal investment. That is not only an interesting but an important finding. If individual personal incentive or congruency measures were more predictive, we would have been confronted with a real problem in advising organizational leaders. What could they do except concern themselves with employee selection and placement? As has already been emphasized, most leaders can expect to have only a very limited influence on staffing. And, what influence they can have will in most cases not eventuate in immediate changes in overall motivation and personal investment. But our results indicated that organizational culture may be of greater importance in affecting personal investment. This presents a promising new opportunity for leaders.

ORGANIZATIONAL CULTURE IN SUMMARY

The popular media would have us believe that "excellent companies" possess what might almost be called a different personality. They are of a generally different character than "run-of-the-mill" companies. More generally, there is a widely held perception that all companies possess their own unique character. These intuitive hunches are essentially confirmed in the research reviewed in this chapter. Companies are different, and different in terms of characteristics that might appropriately be labeled in a collective fashion, "culture." That general finding is in itself interesting and supportive of further work in the general domain of organizational culture using not only ethnographic and case history methods but also psychometric procedures.

But the results also speak directly to the special needs of executives and managers at all levels. They speak to leaders of organizations in an important and very practical way. In this chapter it has been suggested that in today's world of management there is a need to understand organizations in wholistic terms and to identify pressure points for influencing overall motivation and productivity. Not only is the concept of an organizational culture viable for general purposes, it is a specifiable phenomenon. Moreover, there is a relationship between organizational culture and personal investment. Knowing something about the cultural facets of an organization allows us to predict job satisfaction and organizational commitment and probably performance. That is, at the very least, an important early step in determining how to change organizations, not only to improve work life but also to enhance overall effectiveness.

There is, indeed, reason for optimism relative to the concept of organizational culture and its usefulness in the realm of organization theory and practice. Certainly, there are a variety of specific issues that have gone unresolved; much research is still needed. But the evidence is such that one can begin realistically to construct items of advice and counsel for those who lead and manage.

MANAGING ORGANIZATIONAL CULTURE TO ENHANCE MOTIVATION

Granted that identifiable facets of the organizational culture do indeed lead to variations in personal investment on the part of those who participate in the organization. How does one change organizational culture so that personal investment is in truth enhanced? That, of course, is in many ways the ultimate question of this chapter. It is, however, not an easy question to answer. The foregoing review of research should have established a preliminary basis for giving counsel. But we need to draw more broadly on the literature, extrapolating from a variety of findings and theory in order to begin to come up with useful answers. There is no large literature which systematically evaluates controlled experiments in organizational culture change. Yet, the literature is quite rich in suggesting how one might put together a change program that would likely be effective. In this concluding section, it is the intention to splice these pieces together into an integrated set of hypotheses relevant to changing organizational culture so that personal investment is enhanced.

At the outset of this chapter, the dilemma confronted by leaders of large organizations was posed. On the one hand, they are concerned with enhancing motivation of personnel throughout the organization. On the other hand, they seem to be limited in what they can do in this regard. They are often only minimally involved with personnel selection and placement or job design—action areas which may have direct effects on employee motivation. More generally, it can be said that they have very little face-to-face contact with the vast majority of the employees. Typically, they do not even see most of their workers at work. They seldom have an opportunity to assess what their various jobs are like and to praise, reward, and encourage. As a result, they are often left with only a hope that something they do at the top will somehow filter down to the actual levels at which workers are chosen and placed, jobs designed and supervised, and performance appraised and rewarded. Is the hope that leaders can have a pervasive influence on motivation and personal investment in the organization a vain hope?

It is not! The evidence suggests that there is an organizational variable, organizational culture, that affects personal investment in a pervasive way. But the issue now is: can leaders consciously set about affecting organizational culture? And if so, how?

There is little doubt but that a strong organizational culture, a sense of mission, and the existence of a certain kind of work climate will encourage personal investment. Our research has confirmed the suggestions of others in making that basic point quite clear. The interest at this juncture is to build on what we know about antecedents of organizational culture in suggesting a course of action for leaders. How does one act so as to make the organization responsive? Specifically, what can the leadership of the organization do to create an organizational culture that influences the personal investment of employees?

Programmatic Objectives

An answer to such questions can, of course, only be approximated at this stage of our knowledge. However, it seems reasonably clear that a first step in this regard must involve establishing certain programmatic objectives. More specifically, one can basically summarize the possibilities for managerial effectiveness in affecting personal investment by concentrating on three programmatic objectives.

Establishing and communicating a "mission." As pointed out earlier, an organization is most likely to elicit the personal investment of workers when its objectives and values are clear *and* when they are effectively communicated to all those concerned. Good companies know what they are about and are able to communicate the mission across all levels of the organization. When the company is characterized by a clear and integrated set of objectives, expectations, and values—a "mission"—it is most likely to be effective. As employees become aware of this mission, they are likely to be personally invested in the activities and programs that are the organization.

So, the establishment and communication of what we have termed an "organizational mission" should be a first programmatic objective of leaders. Moreover, it is the leadership that bears major responsibility in this regard. It falls to the leadership of an organization to establish and communicate a mission. Indeed, it may well be that this is the major function of leaders so far as enhancing motivation and personal investment is concerned (cf., for example, Bennis, 1984; Schein, 1985).

Establishing salient incentives. If the organization is to elicit the personal investment of employees, it does well to make it clear that certain opportunities exist within the organization for pursuing selected personal incentives. The selection of precisely which personal incentives is important in the first instance. It apparently makes a difference in the way an organization operates when it is concerned with excellence and high achievement expectations for its members. Equally important is making sure that personal incentives are indeed salient.

The course of action envisioned in this programmatic effort may be viewed as complementary to the establishment of a mission. Thus, whereas a mission concerns primarily the relationship of the organization to the world at large, its place, its role in that world, communicating incentive opportunities relates especially to members of the organization. Of course, the two are not unrelated. It is probably only as individuals perceive that they can successfully pursue certain personal incentives within the organization that the overall mission of the organization is likely to have its motivational effects.

The existence and the importance of certain personal incentives within an organization emerges especially in our own research, although it most certainly has precedents elsewhere. In this regard, it may be recalled that organizations which were viewed as concerned with providing (1) interesting and challenging jobs (task dimension), (2) a positive social climate (social dimension), and (3) appropriate recognition and reward (external rewards dimension) were most likely to have satisfied and committed workers. Apparently, these three goal dimensions

of organizational culture are the most critical so far as enhancing personal invest-
ment is concerned.

Concern for the individual in the organization. The research on organiza-
tional culture indicates that successful organizations are characterized by a con-
cern for the persons who compose the organization. That concern includes an
interest in the total welfare of the individual. But most importantly, it is charac-
terized by a focus on enabling each person to actualize his or her potential—to do
their personal best. A more focused look at item responses in Maehr and Bras-
kamp (1986), for example, indicated that employees' belief that the organization
was indeed concerned with the welfare of the individual played a special role in
insuring job satisfaction and commitment. Workers apparently want an interest-
ing job, good social relationships in their workplace, and appropriate recognition
for work well done. But the commitment and the job satisfaction that is engen-
dered by these conditions is especially enhanced by the underlying perception
that this is a company that cares about its workers, cares about their welfare,
their personal growth, and the actualizing of their potential.

Therefore, the corporate leaders should not only define organizational values,
express a set of objectives, and communicate performance expectations, they
must also incorporate in what they say in this regard some clear expression that
they care about employees. To put it differently, the mission is not only "out
there"—corporate successes and achievements—but also resides in the quality
of concern for the corporate body. The mission desirably includes not only a col-
lection of reasons for existing in the wider society but also an expression of how
this body is to go about fulfilling this mission in society. An organization's con-
cern with the role of individual members in accomplishing organizational goals
is one of the most critical concerns.

How Can Such Objectives Be Achieved

It is difficult to suggest precisely what can be done to achieve such broad pro-
grammatic objectives. Yet, there are certain action domains that seem to be espe-
cially important in this regard. Therewith, there are certain courses of action
which seem to make a difference.

Diagnosis/assessment. A first course of action involves the establishment of
procedures for identifying the culture of the organization. Is it coherent? Is it
salient? Is it desirable? Implicit in this regard is a piece of advice that is straight-
forward and simple. Before anything is done one ought to assess the situation:
how is the organization perceived by the individuals who make up the organiza-
tion?

If indeed the communication of a "mission" and the establishment of a certain
organizational culture is important, then one does well to exercise concern by
assessing just what that culture and mission are perceived to be.

A diagnosis/assessment approach to the analysis of the character and operation of an organization and its units is desirable—and increasingly possible (see, for example, Braskamp & Maehr, 1985; Maehr & Braskamp, 1986). Thus, even at this early stage of organizational evaluation and assessment, there is good reason to believe in the ultimate worth of a data-based approach in building the organization into a smoothly functioning organism in which the separate parts are truly invested in the overall functions and goals. Data very seldom tell a manager specifically what to do, but they are very often the first step and a necessary step in the process (Braskamp & Brown, 1980). As managers consider production figures and ledger sheets, they also do well to view the health of the organizational culture. With increasing evidence that work motivation might be significantly determined by organizational culture, the necessity to systematically identify, assess, and evaluate this variable, rightly becomes a significant concern at the highest levels of the organization.

Assessment lays a basis for action and for the evaluation of such actions. But what action might be taken?

Evaluation. There are few better ways of expressing what is expected than through the evaluation process and the *reward* and *recognition* that accompany this process. In attempting to foster organizational change of almost any type it is this domain that must be extensively considered. Of course, top-level managers personally evaluate the performance of only a few and certainly do not administer or actualize the evaluation process in a specific or direct way in many cases. But they do play a major role in establishing *what* is valued. They also set the tone for *how* evaluation is to be accomplished. In these two respects they can communicate the broad goals and mission of the organization.

To be a bit more concrete about this: Managers can choose to concern themselves with setting up systematic evaluation procedures and stress certain criteria. The mere fact that he/she establishes a group to do this and gives it some visibility may itself be sufficient to make it clear that there is concern and interest not only in evaluation but in certain performance criteria. Most important of all, doubtless, is that the manager must be seen to act in terms of the evaluation information. They must take it seriously and be recognized for so doing. In one form of the evaluation process, performance appraisal, it is clear that one can communicate what is expected through indicating an association between performance and reward (see, for example, Lawler, 1971; 1977).

Evaluation and assessment are integral parts of the management style I am proposing. Evaluation implies a caring and an interest in what is being accomplished. Not to evaluate is to imply indifference. Evaluation, although at times painful and difficult to do has several important consequences. It provides an occasion for articulating the goals and mission of the organization for specific programs, persons, and units. The mere fact that evaluation occurs, indicates that the organization cares about what is done. Properly done, evaluation can also reflect a concern for the growth of the individual worker as a contributor to the organization and suggest a stance that is generally growth oriented rather than static. It is through a concern with evaluation that leaders affect the organizational culture. It is one of the buttons they can press for action in this regard.

The exercise of power.   It is in the exercise of power over the organization's resources that the manager can make an important contribution to the establishment and communication of the organizational mission and to its work climate, to its culture. As one makes decisions, one communicates the purposes, goals, and *modus operandi* of the organization. In this regard a major issue is how the power will be shared. How are decisions made? To what degree is the decision-making process delegated to others?

There is, of course, considerable literature on the decision-making process in general and on the matter of decision sharing (or the delegation of authority) in particular. For the most part that literature relates to how worker participation in the decision-making process affects productivity. A review of the research literature shows a somewhat mixed conclusion about the consequences of participatory management (see, for example, Wexley & Yukl, 1984; Yukl, 1981). The point to make at this juncture is, however, somewhat broader in nature. That point relates to how sharing of authority is likely to affect perceptions of the situation or the work context and personal investment as a result. Here, one general principle must be kept firmly in mind: as one is given responsibility for actions, one is more likely to take initiative in performing them. In other words, the delegation of decisionmaking or the encouragement of broad participation in decisionmaking may serve to create a task and/or excellence personal incentive orientation. It might also serve to enhance the feeling in those to whom authority has been delegated that they are important, thus enhancing their sense of competence.

But focusing as we are on the organizational level, the point is that if one desires an organization in which initiative and personal responsibility are encouraged and exercised at all levels of management, one has to be clear about sharing and/or delegating authority. In some fashion this point has often been made in the management literature. Recently, however, there has arisen a new perspective on this question that promises to revise how we view work organizations. Richard Hackman (1985) has argued persuasively for the development of self-management systems across the organization as a way to promote the overall effectiveness of the organization. Increasingly, it is possible within work organizations for various persons and units to operate somewhat autonomously. That is, leaders can delegate considerable authority to those who actually do the work, authority to decide how they will organize and manage that work to reach certain objectives—objectives, of course, that are determined by the larger demands of the organization. In such cases, upper-level management may define those objectives and articulate goals, but leave the means of attaining these largely to the work unit. Such systems enhance the importance for upper-level management to be concerned with overall goals and mission and to communicate these to others. But, sponsoring "self-managed systems" also enhances the importance of individual work units and workers in determining what must and can be done in their particular work domain.

It is in the sharing of authority that leaders perhaps best reflect the manager's respect for others in the organization. Delegation of responsibility in a systematic and explicit fashion communicates trust. The autonomy that is given to others will encourage not only loyalty but special commitment to exert one's every effort. Of course, delegation can only be practiced to the extent that the delegatee can indeed handle the responsibility. This implies not only that the delegatee has the requisite ability but also requisite information. As Hackman (1985) emphasizes, self-managed systems most importantly demand a sharing of information—and not only information directly related to the specific jobs to be done, but also information on the overall activities, needs, and objectives of the organization as a whole.

But to return to the central point: it is only as workers are given an optimal level of autonomy that one can expect optimal personal investment (cf. Maehr & Braskamp, 1986). The "Art of Management" lies in knowing the limits of this principle in any given case.

Symbolizing the Mission

Throughout the organizational culture literature, considerable attention is given to the existence of symbols, rituals, and myths (Bolman & Deal, 1984; Deal & Kennedy, 1982). However, there is little hard evidence on the role that those play in the development or articulation of an organization's culture. There is even less evidence on whether or not leaders and managers can initiate culture change through slogans, the initiation of ritual, or though the creation and promotion of myth. This would seem to be an area where new research might take us beyond our current level of understanding. Ethnography and case study methods have outlined the possible importance of these facets of organizational culture (Frost et al., 1985; Kilmann et al., 1985; Sergiovanni & Corbally, 1984). Now is the time to begin exploring their effects in a more controlled and systematic fashion.

There is a related course of action that is more straightforward and perhaps better understood: that course of action concerns the establishment of persons which embody goals as values and expectations of the organization. In formal and informal observations of organizational behavior it is regularly found that managers do single out certain individuals as examples. Thus, in stating what they want in the organization, particularly the kind of personal investment they desire, they are most likely to identify a specific person. If this person is not already a public figure, they will make him or her one to make their point. It may be suggested that in doing this they can have a most important influence on the climate, culture, and overall personal investment in the organization. To put it boldly: leaders and managers establish expectations and purpose in the organization as they identify, describe, and refer to those who, in their opinion, excel. They identify or create heroes who represent concrete embodiments of what is worth striving for and what is of value. By identifying or creating such heroes, leaders and managers represent in a tangible way, viable and valued options for the people who compose the organization. In short, heroes serve as models of desired behavior. Moreover, one may conjecture that heroes are really human exemplars of values. It is through pointing to such exemplars that leaders can convey what is expected and what is valued. And, it is for this reason that heroes are important within an organization.

Throughout the organizational culture literature, it is repeatedly emphasized that well-established, successful organizations typically have their heroes. The effective manager, the true leader, if you will, is skillful in referring to the characterics of these heroes as they reflect what is desired in the organization. Not every organization has a George Steinmetz or a Thomas Watson. But they do have employees who actualize what is desired in the organization. Managers and supervisors have it in their power to identify significant performance of employees in the organization, to interpret their performance in terms of organizational values and goals—and to make the performance widely visible in the organizational community. This is an opportunity for influencing the organizational culture that managers should take seriously and handle skillfully—it is not something to be left to chance. The manager does well to identify publicly with these contemporary "heroes" and use such an identification as an opportunity to express the salient and valued goals of the corporation.

Thus, management's use of reward and recognition of particular individuals not only reinforces the behavior of the employees rewarded and recognized but can symbolize what is desired throughout the organization. It may be noted further that examples of excellence can be taken from all ranks of the organization. Even in the common practice of singling out an "employee of the month" one can infer a great deal about the goals of the organization as a whole.

Summary.   In summary, there are several main points that must be considered by the leader of any organization or work unit within an organization as he attempts to affect personal investment. Of special importance, is the conscious establishment of a coherent set of goals and organizational mission. Leaders should be conscious of what they are trying to accomplish. They should establish the overall purposes of the organization and specify for workers the opportunities that exist for participating in this mission and for fulfilling their own personal incentives. Only as they establish a direction for the organization or work unit and relate this to the individual worker will they be successful. Indeed, I would argue that it is this expression of a direction for the organization that is a most important activity for any leader (cf. Bass, 1985; Bennis, 1983; 1984).

A final point relates to the issue of power and particularly to the creation of self-management units within the organization. The creation of a strong task orientation in an organization is important to the effectiveness of the organization. Such a task orientation is significantly dependent on the degree to which the employee is given some degree of responsibility over what is to be done and wishes to have such responsibility. One of the more important tasks of leadership is to identify where and under what conditions self-managed systems can be created. More broadly, leaders do well to create a climate in which self-management can become a part of the organizational culture. Evaluation plays a major role here also. One cannot supervise too closely if one wants self-management. If one wants self-management to be effective, one must also be clear about evaluation criteria. Moreover, self-management interlocks with the importance of establishing an organizational mission. As Hackman (1985) points out, the establishment of and the communication of purposes are doubly important as authority is delegated.

CONCLUSION

In this chapter I have endeavored to organize particles of research into a useful understanding of organizational culture. I have attempted to define organizational culture in such a way that it can be employed as a manipulable variable which affects motivation, the *personal investment* of individuals. The driving hypothesis of this chapter is that one can affect organizational culture in such a fashion that one can elicit the participation and the commitment of the membership. The culminating hypothesis is that by concentrating on the definition and communication of organizational purposes, goals, and values one is most likely to have the kind of pervasive effort that is hoped for. I use the word "hypothesis" advisedly. A "cookbook" for action has not been, and, at this point, cannot be provided. At best, a road marker or two has been placed which might help those in leadership positions to find their way toward establishing policies and procedures which encourage personal investment at a particular time and place. If I have at least suggested an idea worth exploring, this chapter has fulfilled its mission.

NOTES

1. This chapter draws heavily on research reported in greater detail in a recently published volume (Maehr & Braskamp, 1986). The tables and figures have all been adapted from that volume with the permission of the publisher (Lexington Press, Lexington, MA). The author is also indebted to many colleagues, particularly Carole Ames, Larry Braskamp, and Douglas Kleiber.

REFERENCES

Ames, C. (1984). Competitive, cooperative and individualistic goal structures: A cognitive-instructional analysis. In R. Ames & C. Ames (Eds.), *Research on motivation in education, Vol. 1: Student motivation* (pp. 177–207). New York: Academic Press.

318 MARTIN L. MAEHR

Ames, R., & Ames, C. (Eds.) (1984). *Research on motivation in education, Vol. 1: Student motivation.* New York: Academic Press.
Bass, B. M. (1981). *Stoodill's handbook of leadership.* New York: Free Press.
Bass, B. M. (1985). Leadership: Good, better, best. *Organizational Dynamics, 13,* 26–40.
Bennis, W. (1983). *The chief.* New York: William Morrow.
Bennis, W. (1984). Transformative power and leadership. In T. J. Sergiovanni & J. E. Corbally (Eds.), *Leadership and organizational culture.* Urbana: University of Illinois Press.
Boje, D. M., Fedor, D. B., & Rowland, K. M. (1982). Myth making: A qualitative step in OD interventions. *Journal of Applied Behavioral Science, 18,* 17–28.
Bolman, L. G., & Deal, T. E. (1984). *Modern approaches to understanding and managing organizations.* San Francisco, CA: Jossey-Bass.
Braskamp, L. A., & Brown, R. D. (Eds.) (1980). *Utilization of evaluation information.* San Francisco: Jossey-Bass.
Braskamp, L. A., & Maehr, M. L. (1985). *Spectrum: An organizational development tool.* Champaign, IL: Metritech, Inc.
Brousseau, K. R. (1983). Toward a dynamic model of job-person relationships: Findings, research questions and implications for work system design. *Academy of Management Review, 8,* 33–45.
Campbell, J. P., Dunnette, M. D., Lawler, E. E., & Weick, K. E. (1970). *Managerial behavior, performances, and effectiveness.* New York: McGraw-Hill.
Cook, J. D., Hepworth, S. J., Wall, T. D., & Warr, P. D. (1981). *The experience of work.* New York: Academic Press.
Covington, M. V. (1984). The motive for self-worth. In R. Ames & C. Ames (Eds.), *Research on motivation in education, Vol. 1: Student motivation* (pp. 77–112). New York: Academic.
Deal, T. E., & Kennedy, A. A. (1982). *Corporate cultures: The rites and rituals of corporate life.* Reading, MA: Addison-Wesley.
Deci, E. L., & Ryan, R. M. (1985). *Intrinsic motivation and self-determination.* New York: Plenum.
Denison, D. R. (1984). Bringing corporate culture to the bottom line. *Organizational Dynamics, 13,* 5–22.
Denison, D. R. (1985). *Corporate culture and organizational effectiveness: A behavioral approach to financial performance.* New York: Wiley.
Dweck, C. S. (1984). Motivation. In R. Glaser & A. Lesgold (Eds.), *The handbook of psychology and education* (Vol. 1). Hillsdale, NJ: Erlbaum.
Dweck, C. S., & Elliott, E. S. (1983). Achievement motivation. In P. Mussen & E. M. Hetherington (Eds.), *Handbook of child psychology* (Vol. 4, pp. 643–691). New York: Wiley.
Endler, N. S. (1981). Persons, situations, and their interactions. In A. I. Rabin, J. Arnoff, A. M. Barclay, & R. A. Zucker (Eds.), *Further explorations in personality.* New York: Wiley.
Frost, P. J., Moore, L. F., Louis, M. R., Lundborg, C. C., & Martin, J. (Eds.) (1985). *Organizational culture.* Beverley Hills, CA: Sage.
Goodenough, W. H. (1963). *Cooperation in change.* New York: Russell Sage Foundation.
Goodenough, W. H. (1971). *Culture, language, and society.* Reading, MA: Addison-Wesley.
Hackman, J. R. (1985, August). The psychology of self-management in organizations. APA Master Lecture Series: Psychology and work. American Psychological Association Convention, Los Angeles, CA.
Hackman, J. R., & Oldham, G. R. (1980). *Work redesign.* Reading, MA: Addison-Wesley.
James, L. R., & Jones, A. P. (1974). Organizational climate: A review of theory and research. *Psychological Bulletin, 81,* 1096–1112.
Kellerman, B. (1984). *Leadership: Multidisciplinary perspectives.* Englewood Cliffs, NJ: Prentice-Hall.
Kleiber, D. A., & Maehr, M. L. (Eds.) (1985). *Advances in Motivation and Achievement, Vol. 4: Motivation and adulthood.* Greenwich, CT: JAI Press.
Kilman, R. H. (1985, April). Corporate culture. *Psychology Today,* 62–68.

Kilman et al. (1985). *Gaining control of the corporate culture.* San Francisco: Jossey-Bass.

Lawler, E. E., III (1971). *Pay and organization development.* Reading, MA: Addison-Wesley.

Lawler, E. E., III (1977). Reward systems. In J. R. Hackman & J. L. Suttle (Eds.), *Improving life at work.* Pacific Palisades, CA: Goodyear.

Lawler, E. E., III, Hall, D. T., & Oldham, G. R. (1974). Organizational climate: Relationship to organizational structure, process, and performance. *Organizational Behavior and Human Performance, 11,* 139–155.

Maehr, M. L. (1974a). Culture and achievement motivation. *American Psychologist, 29,* 887–896.

Maehr, M. L. (1974b). *Sociocultural origins of achievement.* Monterey, CA: Brooks/Cole.

Maehr, M. L. (1976). Continuing motivation. *Review of Educational Research, 46,* 443–462.

Maehr, M. L. (1983). On doing well in science: Why Johnny no longer excels; why Sarah never did. In S. Paris, G. Olson, & H. Stevenson (Eds.), *Learning and motivation in the classroom.* Hillsdale, N.J.: Lawrence Erlbaum.

Maehr, M. L. (1984a). Meaning and motivation. In R. Ames & C. Ames (Eds.), *Research on motivation in education, Volume 1: Student motivation.* New York: Academic Press.

Maehr, M. L. (1984b). Maintaining faculty motivation and morale in an era of decline. *Proceedings: 10th Annual International Conference on Improving University Teaching.* College Park: University of Maryland.

Maehr, M. L., & Braskamp, L. (1986). *The motivation factor: A theory of personal investment.* Lexington, MA: Lexington Books.

Maehr, M. L., & Kleiber, D. A. (Eds.) (1987). *Advances in motivation and achievement, Vol 5: Enhancing motivation.* Greenwich, CT: JAI Press.

Mayberry, P. (1985). Congruencies among organizational components and their relationship to work attitudes. Unpublished doctoral dissertation. Urbana: University of Illinois.

McClelland, D. C. (1978). Managing motivation to expand human freedom. *American Psychologist, 33,* 201–210.

McClelland, D. C. (1985a). *Human motivation.* Glenview, IL: Scott Foresman.

McClelland, D. C. (1985b). How motives, skills, and values determine what people do. *American Psychologist, 40,* 812–825.

McClelland, D. C., & Winter, D. G. (1971). *Motivating economic achievement.* New York: Free Press.

Miller, A. (1981). Conceptual matching models and interactional research in education. *Review of Educational Research, 51,* 33–84.

Mintzberg, H. (1973). *The nature of managerial work.* New York: Harper & Row.

Nadler, D. A., Hackman, J. R., & Lawler, E. E., III (1979). *Managing organizational behavior.* Boston: Little, Brown.

Nicholls, J. G. (1983). Concepts of ability and achievement motivation: A theory and its implications for education. In S. G. Paris, G. M. Olson, & H. W. Stevenson (Eds.), *Learning and motivation in the classroom.* Hillsdale, N.J.: Erlbaum.

Nicholls, J. G., & Miller, A. T. (1984). Development and its discontents: The differentiation of the concept of ability. In J. G. Nicholls (Ed.), *The development of achievement motivation.* Greenwich, CT: JAI Press.

Ouchi, W. (1981). *Theory Z corporations: How American business can meet the Japanese challenge.* Reading, MA: Addison-Wesley.

Peters, T., & Austin, N. (1985). *A passion for excellence.* New York: Random House.

Peters, T. J., & Waterman, R. H., Jr. (1982). *In search of excellence: Lessons from America's best-run companies.* New York: Harper & Row.

Schein, E. H. (1978). *Career dynamics: Matching individual and organizational needs.* Reading, MA: Addison-Wesley.

Schein, E. H. (1984). Coming to a new awareness of organizational culture. *Sloan Management Review, 25,* 3–16.

Schein, E. H. (1985). *Organizational culture and leadership*. San Francisco: Jossey-Bass.

Schneider, B., & Snyder, R. A. (1975). Some relationships between job satisfaction and organizational climate. *Journal of Applied Psychology, 60*, 318–328.

Sergiovanni, T. J., & Corbally, J. E. (Eds.) (1984). *Leadership and organizational culture*. Urbana: University of Illinois Press.

Stern, G. (1970). *People in context: Measuring person-environment congruence in education and industry*. New York: Wiley.

Triandis, H. C., et al. (1972). *The analysis of subjective culture*. New York: Wiley.

Wexley, K. N., & Yukl, G. A. (1984). *Organizational behavior and personnel psychology* (Rev. Ed.). Homewood, IL: Richard D. Irwin.

Whetten, D. A. (1984). Effective administration: Good management on the college campus. *Change, 16*, 38–43.

Yukl, G. A. (1981). *Leadership in organizations*. Englewood Cliffs, N.J.: Prentice-Hall.

AUTHOR INDEX

SUBJECT INDEX

Research Annuals and Monographs in Series in the
BEHAVIORAL SCIENCES

Research Annuals

Advances in Adolescent Mental Health
Edited by Ronald, A. Feldman and Arlene R. Stiffman, *Center for Adolescent Mental Health, Washington University*

Advances in Behavioral Assessment of Children and Families
Edited by Ron Prinz, *Department of Psychology, University of South Carolina*

Advances in Behavioral Medicine
Edited by Edward S. Katkin, *Department of Psychology, State University of New York at Buffalo* and Stephen B. Manuck, *Department of Psychology, University of Pittsburgh*

Advances in Business Marketing
Edited by Arch G. Woodside, *College of Business Administration, University of South Carolina*

Advances in Descriptive Psychology
Edited by Keith E. Davis, *Department of Psychology, University of South Carolina* and Thomas O. Mitchell, *Department of Psychology, Southern Illinois University*

Advances in Developmental and Behavioral Pediatrics
Edited by Mark Wolraich, *Department of Pediatrics, University of Iowa* and Donald K. Routh, *Department of Psychology, University of Iowa*

Advances in Early Education and Day Care
Edited by Sally J. Kilmer, *Department of Home Economics, Bowling Green State University*

Advances in Family Intervention, Assessment and Theory
Edited by John P. Vincent, *Department of Psychology, University of Houston*

Advances in Health Education and Promotion
Edited by William B. Ward, *School of Public Health, University of South Carolina*

Advances in Human Psychopharmacology
Edited by Graham D. Burrows, *Department of Psychiatry, University of Melbourne* and John S. Werry, *Department of Psychiatry, University of Auckland*

Advances in Law and Child Development
Edited by Robert L. Sprague, *Institute for Child Behavior and Development, University of Illinois*

Advances in Learning and Behavioral Disabilities
Edited by Kenneth D. Gadow, *Office of Special Education, State University of New York, Stony Brook*

Advances in Marketing and Public Policy
Edited by Paul N. Bloom, *Department of Marketing, University of Maryland*

Advances in Mental Retardation and Developmental Disabilities
Edited by Stephen E. Breuning, Director of Psychological Services and Behavioral Treatment Polk Center, Johnny L. Matson, *Department of Learning and Development, Northern Illinois University*, and Rowland P. Barrett, *Section on Psychiatry and Human Behavior, Brown University Program in Medicine*

Advances in Motivation and Achievement
Edited by Martin L. Maehr, *Institute for Child Behavior and Development, University of Illinois*

Advances in Nonprofit Marketing
Edited by Russell W. Belk, *Department of Marketing, University of Utah*

Advances in Psychophysiology
Edited by Patrick K. Ackles, *Institute for the Study of Developmental Disabilities, University of Illinois at Chicago*, Richard Jennings, *Western Psychiatric Institute and Clinic, University of Pittsburgh School of Medicine* and Michael G.H. Coles, *Department of Psychology, University of Illinois*

SM 39932
48.50
N/D
IEH
(ANV)

This book is to be returned on or before
the last date stamped below.

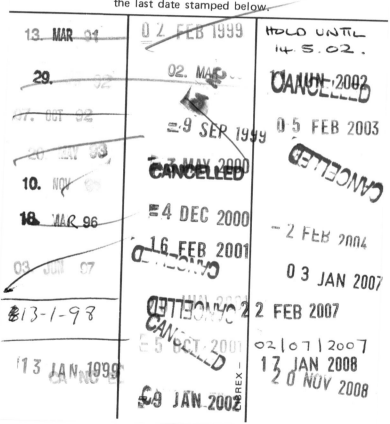

		HOLD UNTIL
13. MAR 91	02 FEB 1999	14.5.02.
29. 92	02. MAR	CANCELLED 2002
07. OCT 92	-9 SEP 1999	05 FEB 2003
20 MAY 93	-7 MAY 2000 CANCELLED	CANCELLED
10. NOV	-4 DEC 2000	-2 FEB 2004
18 MAR 96	16 FEB 2001	03 JAN 2007
03 JUN 07	CANCELLED	22 FEB 2007
13-1-98	CANCELLED 5 OCT 2001	02/07/2007 17 JAN 2008
13 JAN 1999	9 JAN 2002	20 NOV 2008

LIBREX —

B12891